Personal Mathematics and Computing:
Tools for the Liberal Arts

New Liberal Arts Series

Light, Wind, and Structure: The Mystery of the Master Builders
by Robert Mark, 1990

The Age of Electronic Messages
by John G. Truxal, 1990

Medical Technology and Society: An Interdisciplinary Perspective
by Joseph D. Bronzino, Vincent H. Smith, and Maurice L. Wade, 1990

Understanding Quantitative History
by Loren Haskins and Kirk Jeffrey, 1990

Personal Mathematics and Computing: Tools for the Liberal Arts
by Frank Wattenberg, 1990

This book is published as part of an Alfred P. Sloan Foundation program.

New
Liberal
Arts
Series

Personal Mathematics and Computing: Tools for the Liberal Arts

Frank Wattenberg

The MIT Press
Cambridge, Massachusetts
London, England

The programs and data used in this book are available in a diskette in either Macintosh or IBM and compatible format. If you write to the author at the Department of Mathematics, University of Massachusetts, Amherst, MA 01003 enclosing $10 to cover costs, he will send you a copy. He also expects to write Mathematica notebooks to be used with this course. Please write to him for further information about Mathematica and this course.

This book was printed and bound by The MIT Press in the United States of America.

Library of Congress Cataloging-in-Publication Data

Wattenberg, Frank, 1943–
    Personal mathematics and computing : tools for the liberal arts / Frank Wattenberg.
        p.   cm.—(The New liberal arts series)
    Includes index.
    ISBN 0–262–23157–3 (hc)
    1. Mathematics.   2. Programming (Electronic computers)
I. Series.
QA39.2.W378   1990
510′.285′562–dc20   90–6390
                                                          CIP

Contents

Series Foreword

The Alfred P. Sloan Foundation's New Liberal Arts (NLA) Program stems from the belief that a liberal education for our time should involve undergraduates in meaningful experiences with technology and with quantitative approaches to problem solving in a wide range of subjects and fields. Students should understand not only the fundamental concepts of technology and how structures and machines function, but also the scientific and cultural settings within which engineers work, and the impacts (positive and negative) of technology on individuals and society. They should be much more comfortable than they are with making calculations, reasoning with numbers and symbols, and applying mathematical and physical models. These methods of learning about nature are increasingly important in more and more fields. They also underlie the process by which engineers create the technologies that exercise such vast influence over all our lives.

The program is closely associated with the names of Stephen White and James D. Koerner, both vice-presidents (retired) of the foundation. Mr. White wrote an internal memorandum in 1980 that led to the launching of the program two years later. In it he argued for quantitative reasoning and technology as "new" liberal arts, not as replacements for the liberal arts as customarily identified, but as liberating modes of thought needed for understanding the technological world in which we now live. Mr. Koerner administered the program for the foundation, successfully leading it through its crucial first four years.

The foundation's grants to 36 undergraduate colleges and 12 universities have supported a large number of seminars, workshops, and symposia on topics in technology and applied mathematics. Many new courses have been developed and existing courses modified at these colleges. Some minors or concentrations in technology studies have been organized. A Resource Center for the NLA Program, located at the State University of New York at Stony Brook, publishes and distributes a monthly newsletter, collects and disseminates syllabi, teaching modules, and other materials prepared at the colleges and universities taking part in the program, and serves in a variety of ways to bring news of NLA activities to all who express interest and request information.

As the program progressed, faculty members who had developed successful new liberal arts courses began to prepare textbooks. Also, a number of the foundation's grants to universities were used to support

writing projects of professors—often from engineering departments—
who had taught well-attended courses in technology and applied mathematics that had been designed to be accessible to liberal arts undergraduates. It seemed appropriate not only to encourage the preparation
of books for such courses, but also to find a way to publish and thereby
make available to the widest possible audience the best products of these
teaching experiences and writing projects. This is the background with
which the foundation approached The MIT Press and the McGraw-Hill
Publishing Company about publishing a series of books on the new liberal arts. Their enthusiastic response led to the launching of the New
Liberal Arts Series.

The publishers and the Alfred P. Sloan Foundation express their ap-
preciation to the members of the Editorial Advisory Board for the New
Liberal Arts Series: John G. Truxal, Distinguished Teaching Professor,
Department of Technology and Society, State University of New York,
Stony Brook, Chairman; Joseph Bordogna, Alfred Fitler Moore Professor and Dean, School of Engineering and Applied Science, University of
Pennsylvania; Robert W. Mann, Whitaker Professor of Biomedical Engineering, Massachusetts Institute of Technology; Merritt Roe Smith,
Professor of the History of Technology, Massachusetts Institute of Technology; J. Ronald Spencer, Associate Academic Dean and Lecturer in
History, Trinity College; and Allen B. Tucker, Jr., Professor of Computer Science, Bowdoin College. In developing this new publication
program, The MIT Press has been represented by Frank P. Satlow and
the McGraw-Hill Publishing Company by Eric M. Munson.

Samuel Goldberg
Program Officer
Alfred P. Sloan Foundation

Acknowledgments

I would like to thank many people for their help with this book. First, last, and always I thank my family. It is traditional to thank one's family for their patience and understanding during a long enterprise, and mine certainly deserves these traditional thanks, but, in addition, they were very much part of the creation of this book. My son, Marty, is an accomplished programmer and mathematician, and he has helped me in innumerable ways with the book itself. He is a valuable colleague. My wife, Julie, has been a great help both with my prose and by giving me a perspective on how a nonmathematician might read things. Both my son, Marty, and my daughter, Alina, were students while most of this book was written, first in high school and later in college. Their interest and enthusiasm for learning was a constant source of motivation. In a very real way I wrote this book for them.

I also thank the students who worked with early drafts of this book. Teaching and learning are a partnership and this book is the product of that partnership. My students have helped improve it in many ways and deserve a good deal of the credit for the final version. More important, however, the ultimate reason for teaching and for writing a textbook is the students. I have been fortunate to have had many excellent students, and it has been a great joy to me to teach and to learn with them.

Very special thanks go to the members of the Massachusetts Special Commission on Local Aid and to its advisory committee. Working with the commission was a real eye opener. I met many public officials who are extraordinarily talented, hard-working and dedicated men and women. They deserve our admiration and our thanks. I would like to thank particularly Senator Richard Kraus and Representative Patricia Fiero, cochairs of the commission, and Mark Perrault, who has worked on local aid in various capacities for many years. Massachusetts is fortunate to have public officials with their combination of ability and commitment to the common good. My own life has been enriched by working with them.

I would like to thank Frank Satlow, Lorrie LeJeune, and the staff at The MIT Press for all their help.

The excerpt from *Consumers Report* in chapter 2 is Copyright 1978 by Consumers Union of the United States, Inc., Mount Vernon, NY 10553. Reprinted by permission from CONSUMER REPORTS, April 1978. I would like to express my thanks to Consumers Union for permission to reprint this excerpt.

The map of the 351 cities and towns of Massachusetts in chapter 5 was drawn from data supplied by University Computing Services at the University of Massachusetts, Amherst MA 01003. I give thanks for these data.

Introduction

In recent years there has been a great deal of discussion about the need for universal computer literacy. For a number of reasons the educated man or woman of today must know something about computers and how they are used. First, more and more frequently public policy decisions hinge on data that have been analyzed by computers. For example, much of the evidence available to us about carcinogens and other environmental health hazards is statistical evidence. Interpreting this evidence requires computer-based quantitative analysis.

Second, with personal computers individual private citizens now have access to the computing power and often the data needed to understand and, in some cases, even challenge conclusions that have been reached by others. People who are unable to exploit the power of personal computers deprive themselves not only of an effective tool for personal understanding but also cede a part of their citizenship to the "experts."

And third, computers and the mathematical analysis of problems that goes hand in hand with computer use together form a powerful set of strategies for formulating and thinking about problems. Writing a computer program to accomplish a particular task forces one to think about the task precisely and completely. All of the factors must be considered explicitly, and the ways in which they interact must be carefully analyzed. Thus, the exercise of writing such a computer program often leads to a much better understanding of the problem.

The final reason is that the use of computers is one of the most interesting, important, and pervasive activities of our time. Perhaps the most important characteristic of intellectually alive people is their curiosity and their urge to participate in and to understand fully the world in which they live. An educated person living today cannot be a mere bystander while others enjoy the power and excitement of computer-based mathematical reasoning.

This book is called *Personal Mathematics and Computing* instead of just *Personal Computing* because its purpose is not simply to teach you how to use computers. You can use computers in various ways—to play games, for word processing, and so forth. This book has a more ambitious purpose: to teach you how to use mathematics to reason about a variety of real, important problems. I will teach mathematics as a tool to use rather than as a concept to be studied in the abstract.

Courses designed to meet the demand for a first-year computer or computer literacy course usually fall into one of two categories. Some concentrate on the philosophical and political issues posed by computers (for instance, the threat to privacy raised by computerized databases and networks). Such courses usually involve only extremely elementary programming or, worse, rely completely on the use of canned programs. Other courses concentrate on teaching programming; however, in these courses programming often becomes synonymous with coding. Students spend an entire semester on the details of a programming language and an editor. The actual coding of a computer program in a language like Pascal or True BASIC is the easiest and least interesting part of programming. The hardest and most interesting part is formulating the problem in a way that is appropriate for computer analysis.

This is a very demanding course. It is designed for students who are interested in their world; in politics, economics, and taxes; in the environment, public health, and ecology; in probability, statistics, and gambling. It is designed for students who want to learn how to use personal computing power to understand more. The emphasis in this course is on applications rather than mathematics and programming. However, students will need to be comfortable with high school, college preparatory mathematics, including algebra and geometry but not trigonometry or calculus.

This course and this book are divided into two parts. The first part of the course (roughly five weeks) covers coding. Modern programming languages and operating systems, especially those widely available on personal computers, make it entirely possible to learn the basics of computer programming in a month. Indeed it is common for bright junior high school students to learn programming on their own in a few days on a personal computer. This aspect of the course will be less extensive than existing standard first-semester computer programming courses.

This book is designed to be used with True BASIC; however, it can be used with any other modern programming language. Part I contains a brief introduction to programming in True BASIC. Students using True BASIC will not need to buy an additional book on programming. Students who wish to use a different language will need to have access to a book on programming in that language. In addition, students who wish to go beyond the basics of True BASIC programming may eventually want to buy one of the many excellent books available on programming in True BASIC.

The first part of the course contains eight programming projects that aim to teach by example True BASIC programming. Each project introduces several elements of True BASIC and several programming techniques. Together these projects provide a basic introduction to True BASIC programming and illustrate a variety of interesting applications and methods of computer-based quantitative reasoning.

The second part of the course is its heart. In this part we will work on a small number of applications of mathematics and computing to real problems. The emphasis is on the problems themselves and on real programming, the art of expressing problems in ways that are amenable to computer analysis. Students will write a number of computer programs during this part of the course.

This book contains much more material than can possibly be covered in one semester; it presents a wide variety of possible applications so that an individual course can be tailored to the interests of a particular instructor and particular students. It is my hope that this course will whet the student's appetite for computers and their applications and that he or she will want to continue using the computer. The extra material not covered in a course can be used for independent study or even for a follow-up course.

This book is intended to be nearly self-contained. However, it is impossible for one book to contain all the information needed for all of the existing personal computers. You will need to know some additional basic information about your particular computer facilities—how to turn the computer on and off, how to use the printer, how to use a disk drive to store programs and data, and how to edit programs. This book contains two appendixes with this information for standard configurations of Macintosh computers, IBM PCs, and IBM clones. Students using True BASIC with other facilities will be able to find this information in the books that came with True BASIC or the computer. For some classes the instructor will provide handouts with the necessary information.

I close this introduction with an extremely important note to the student: the best way to learn mathematics and computer programming is by doing. You should read this book with pencil and paper and a calculator or a personal computer at hand. Work out the exercises as you read the text. Exercises marked with an asterisk have answers in appendix E at the end of the book. Try things out with your calculator and your computer. Above all, if you have questions, experiment and try out alternatives.

I   LEARNING TO PROGRAM

This first part of the book and the course consists of eight programming projects that aim to teach by example the art of programming. Learning anything—programming, writing, dancing, or windsurfing—is best done by watching and doing. Ultimately the only way to learn something is by doing it. There is no substutute for getting up on a windsurfer if one wants to learn to windsurf. But one can also learn a great deal by watching other windsurfers—seeing what they do and then copying the techniques of the better windsurfers. We will use the same strategy in this course. The eight programming projects include a large number of examples, well-written programs, that you can study and from which you can learn. They also include many programming assignments that ask you to write your own programs. Sometimes you will be able to write these programs by making simple changes to the sample programs; sometimes you will need to write completely new programs. However, you will find that bits and pieces from the sample programs will be helpful even when you are writing completely new programs.

Many of the details of coding in True BASIC are summarized in appendix A. Appendix A and this first part of the book complement each other. Here I am attempting to teach programming by example. I introduce new elements of True BASIC one at a time with a lot of discussion about how they are used. Appendix A summarizes briefly all the elements of True BASIC used in this book. Appendix A is intended as a reference section; this part of the book is intended for learning.

1 Eight Programming Projects

1.1 Turning On and PRINTing

Begin this first project by reading this section. After you have read it completely, take this book with you to the computer lab, and go through this section again doing all the exercises at the computer as you come to them.

This first project actually has two purposes. The first is to familiarize yourself with the procedure for using True BASIC on your computer. The procedures vary depending on the computer you are using and whether it is part of a network or is freestanding. If you are reading this book as part of a course, then your teacher will provide information about using True BASIC on whatever computers are available. If you are using your own computer, you will find the necessary information in your computer manuals and in the books that came with True BASIC. Before starting this project, you should know how to turn on and turn off the computer and how to access True BASIC. You will also need to know how to enter a computer program and how to edit it. You will eventually want to know how to use a printer and how to store programs on a disk. However, neither of these skills is necessary for this first project. The appendixes contain all the necessary information for using True BASIC on standard configurations of Macintosh computers, IBM PCs, and IBM clones.

The second purpose of this project is to write and to run your first computer programs. The first programs will print out a few words and a few numbers. The programs in this project may not seem exciting—all they do is some simple printing. However, they are enormously important. You could have the fastest computer in the world, but if it wasn't able to output its results, it would be completely useless. One of the arts of programming is designing output that is pleasant to read and conveys a lot of information in a form that is easy to grasp. Part of the power of modern personal computers is their ability to display information using pictures as well as columns of gray numbers. Well-designed output, like good writing, can grab people's attention and convey information clearly and effectively. Experienced programmers often spend more time designing the appearance of the output than figuring out the actual computations.

I need to clarify the terms *output*, *printing*, and *drawing*. Personal computers often use a monitor very much like a television set for their output. Results, both pictures and text, are displayed on the video screen. This method is good for trees since it saves paper; however, it has a disadvantage; information displayed on a video screen leads a precarious existence, ready to disappear whenever the power is turned off or even when it is crowded off the screen by new information. Use a notebook while working at the computer so that you can write down important information before it disappears. Many computers have a printer attached that uses paper and records information, pictures, and text, in a more permanent way. Computer types call this "hardcopy." You will frequently want to use the printer to obtain a permanent record of some of your work. You will rapidly discover that old computer output is a marvelous source of scratch paper. Save a tree and recycle it.

We are now ready for our first computer program:

```
!    My First Program
!
!    Written October 8, 1989
!
PRINT "This is my first computer program."
END
```

This program has a very simple purpose: to print the sentence "This is my first computer program." on the screen. The True BASIC instruction that prints text is very simple. It consists of the word "PRINT" followed by the text that is to be printed enclosed in quotation marks. In our first program the statement

```
PRINT "This is my first computer program."
```

does all the work. The rest of the program is window dressing. The last statement

```
END
```

marks the end of the program so that True BASIC knows the program is complete. Every True BASIC program must end with this same line.

The first four lines are comments. They have no effect at all on what the computer does. They are there for human beings who read programs. But although they have nothing to do with the functioning of the program, comments are enormously important. They are notes written in English that record information about the program. Experienced programmers include lots of comments because they can make a program much easier to read and because they provide an important record of information about the program. It is good practice to begin every program with comments describing the program and the date when it was written. Comments begin with an exclamation point. The exclamation point tells True BASIC to ignore the rest of the information on that line. Some comments will have an entire line to themselves, like the comments in our first program. It is also possible for a line to have part of the program itself followed by an exclamation point and a comment. For example, the line

```
PRINT "This is my first computer program." ! Print sentence
```

accomplishes exactly the same thing as the line

```
PRINT "This is my first computer program."
```

except that it includes a brief comment. This comment, like any other comment, has absolutely no effect on what the program does.

Do the following exercises before continuing.

Exercises

Exercise 1.1.1 Write and run a program that prints the sentence, "This is my own first program."

Exercise 1.1.2 Write and run a program that prints two sentences, "This program prints two sentences." and "This is the second sentence." as shown below:

```
This program prints two sentences.
This is the second sentence.
```

The next program illustrates how numbers can be printed using True BASIC:

```
!      Printing Numbers
!
!      Written October 8, 1989
!
PRINT USING "##": 12
PRINT USING "###": 12
PRINT USING "####": 12
PRINT USING "#####": 12
PRINT USING "##.###": 4/3
PRINT USING "##.####": 4/3
PRINT USING "##.#####": 4/3
PRINT USING "##.######": 4/3
PRINT USING "##.#######": 4/3
PRINT USING "##.##############": 4/3
PRINT USING "##.###############": 4/3
PRINT USING "##.################": 4/3
PRINT USING "##.#################": 4/3
END
```

True BASIC uses a particularly good method of printing numbers. The True BASIC statement for printing numbers begins with the words "PRINT USING" followed by a "map" or "template" that describes the appearance of the printed number. For example, the template "##" tells True BASIC to print a number using two columns. The template "###" tells True BASIC to print a number using three columns. Either of these templates will print a whole number. The printed number will appear with no decimal point. If the number does not fill up the space allowed, then the number will appear "right justified"—that is, it will appear at the right side of the space allowed. The output from the preceding program is shown below:

```
12
 12
  12
   12
  1.333
  1.3333
```

```
1.33333
1.333333
1.3333333
1.3333333333333330
1.33333333333333300
1.333333333333333000
1.3333333333333330000
```

The first four lines of this output were produced by the first four lines of the program. Notice both the number printed (12) and its appearance. For example, the third line of the program

```
PRINT USING "####": 12
```

produced the output

```
  12
```

in which the number 12 occupies four columns. Since it does not completely fill the four columns, the first two columns are blank.

To print a number with a decimal point, one uses a template like "###.####". This template specifies that the number should occupy eight columns. The first three columns are used for the digits to the left of the decimal point. The fourth column is used for the decimal point. The last four columns are used for four digits to the right of the decimal point. Compare each of the lines of the program with its output. Notice that there is a surprise. The number 4/3 written as a decimal is 1.33333... with the digit 3 repeating forever. However, the last four lines of the output end with zeros where one would expect 3s. The reason is that a computer has only a finite amount of space for working with numbers. It does not work with the entire decimal 1.3333... since that would require an infinite amount of space. If you ask the computer to print out more digits than it has available, you will get odd results like the results above. True BASIC allocates enough space for each number so that, except in unusual circumstances, this problem does not occur.

There are many variations of the PRINT USING statement. For example,

```
PRINT USING "###.###  ##.####":1/3, 7/5
```

will print two numbers (1/3 and 7/5) side by side. The template

```
"###.###  ##.####"
```

specifies that the first number should appear in a space seven columns wide with three digits followed by the decimal point and then three digits after the decimal point. This will be followed by two spaces because there are two spaces between "###.###" and "##.####". The second number will occupy seven columns with two digits before the decimal point, then the decimal point, and then four more digits. The output produced by this statement is

.333   1.4000

In general a PRINT USING statement consists of the following elements in the indicated order

- The words PRINT USING.
- A template or map enclosed in quotation marks.
- A colon (:).
- A list of the numbers to be printed separated by commas.

The template tells True BASIC exactly how each number should be printed. So far we have seen templates with three symbols:

1. The symbol "#". Basically each of these symbols is replaced by one digit of the number to be printed. This is done in an intelligent way. For example, if the number "123" is printed out using the template "######" then the first three "#"s will be replaced by blanks so that the output is "   123" rather than "000123".

2. The symbol ".". This indicates the position of the decimal point when the number is printed.

3. The symbol " " (a blank). Each blank in the template will produce a blank in the output. These blanks are very important. They can be used to introduce space into the output, making it easier to read.

The template can be very fancy. For example, to print a number like 43,112,345.67, one can use a template like "##,###,###.##" that includes the commas used to make the number easier to read. One can even add a dollar sign for printing dollar amounts. For example, the template "$#,###.##" would print the number 123456 as "$1,234.56". The PRINT USING statement is extremely powerful. Try various experiments to find out what it can do. Start with the following exercises, and then try additional experiments of your own.

Exercises

Exercise 1.1.3 Write and run a program that will produce the following output:

```
1    12.34    56,789
2     2.34     1,342
3      .12        12
4     1.23        34
```

Exercise 1.1.4 What happens when you print a negative number using PRINT USING? Try the statement:

```
PRINT USING "##,###": -34
```

Exercise 1.1.5 What happens when you try to print a number and the template does not allow enough space? Try the statement:

```
PRINT USING "##": 123
```

Exercise 1.1.6 What does the PRINT USING statement do when you ask it to print a number like 12.3456 with only three digits following the decimal point? Does it round off, or does it simply forget the last digit?

You can mix text and numbers using the PRINT USING statement. For example, the statement

```
PRINT USING "Deposit $##,###.##": 12345.678
```

produces the output

```
Deposit $12,345.68
```

Notice that at the end of this statement, we have "12345.678" with no comma. If we had used a comma, that is, if we had written

```
PRINT USING "Deposit $##,###.##": 12,345.67
```

then True BASIC would not have interpreted this statement in the way in which it was intended. Commas are used within templates to indicate that we want a comma to appear in the output. However, True BASIC usually uses commas to separate items that appear in lists. Thus, in the

PRINT statement above, 12,345.67 would be interpreted by True BASIC as the number 12 followed by the number 345.67. For this reason you must be very careful with commas. We conclude with one last exercise. You should also experiment on your own trying more variations on the PRINT USING statement. Often the easiest and best way to find out more about True BASIC or to answer a particular question is to try things out. The more you experiment, the more you will learn.

Exercise

Exercise 1.1.7 Write and run a program to produce the output

Name	Age
Joe Smith	12
Tom Jones	6
Mary Wilson	10
Alice Dayle	8

1.2   Free Lunches and Time Travel

We all want schools, roads, fire and police protection, water, sewers, and many other public services, but we all complain about the taxes that we must pay to purchase these public services. Our desires are contradictory. We all know and accept the fact that we must pay for groceries at the supermarket. Yet somehow, collectively, we don't accept the fact that we must pay for public services with taxes. This puts public officials in a bind. On the one hand we, the voters, demand good public services. On the other hand, we complain about taxes. In some states, voters have even enacted by referendum laws that place strict limits on taxes. Recently governors and state legislators have discovered a magic money tree that produces money to pay for public services without taxing the voters: the lottery.

Lotteries are voluntary. Nobody is forced to buy tickets. Yet, lured by flashy advertising and the chance of big prizes, people voluntarily give money to the state, money the state can use to support much-needed public services. Lotteries create the illusion of a free lunch. We get needed public services without the bill.

Of course there is a catch: there is no such thing as a free lunch. Some voters choose to buy lottery tickets. They do get something for their money: a chance to win various prizes. However, they pay considerably more than that chance is actually worth. The difference between the price they pay and the fair value of the chance they buy is used (minus the overhead for advertising and running the lottery) to pay for public services for everyone in the state, even people who don't buy lottery tickets. This means that the gamblers are subsidizing those who don't buy lottery tickets. Whether you think this is fair is a good question for philosophical debate. I have some doubts.

A modest lottery might be reasonable. Proponents argue that people would gamble in any case and a modest lottery derives some public benefit from that gambling instinct. This argument may originally have had some validity. Now, however, there are many very slick advertisements for state lotteries. A heavily advertised lottery is not merely tapping existing gambling; it is stimulating new gambling.

If you are trying to decide whether to buy a lottery ticket, there are two key numbers you should analyze. The first number is the *payoff*. It is the total amount of prize money paid out in a lottery. The second number is the *handle*. This is the total amount of money wagered in a lottery. The payoff/handle ratio gives some idea of whether the lottery is a good bet. If this ratio is 1, then collectively the gamblers win back all the money that they wager; however, the ratio is always less than 1. The state (or anyone else running a lottery) always keeps some money for itself. If the ratio is close to 1, then *mathematically* the lottery is a reasonable bet, but if it is much less than one, then it is (still mathematically) a rather poor bet. However, there are other relevant factors. People who buy lottery tickets purchase more than just a chance to win. For example, a buyer of a chance at becoming a millionaire can spend many happy hours deciding how to spend a million dollars. The value of such daydreams is not included in our mathematical analysis.

We will examine the payoff in some detail. The way to determine the payoff is to add up the total amount of prize money. For example, suppose that a lottery had one hundred $10 prizes, ten $200 prizes, and one $10,000 prize. The total payoff would be:

Prize	Number of Prizes	Total Value
$10	100	$1,000
$200	10	$2,000
$10,000	1	$10,000
Total		$13,000

This seems simple enough, but there is a catch. The biggest prizes often are a little misleading. For example, one common prize is the million dollar grand prize, but sometimes there is fine print. The fine print says the prize is $50,000 per year for twenty years. Which would you rather have: $1 million right now or $50,000 per year for twenty years? In order to compare these two prizes, we need to study time travel, particularly time travel for money.

Time travel for people is hard, but time travel for money is easy. We have two very common vehicles available for such time travel. If you want to send money into the future, you put the money into a bank now and withdraw it in the future when you need it. There is even a bonus—interest. For example, suppose that you want to send $2,000 one year into the future. You might put that money into a bank account that earns 6% interest per year.* When you withdraw it after one year, you've earned $120 interest. Thus, your $2,000 now is equivalent to $2,120 next year. We call $2,000 the *present value* and $2,120 the *future value* of this particular investment. Notice that the relationship between the future value and the present value depends on the interest rate your money is earning.

To bring money from the future to the present, you can take out a loan, but there is a catch: you must pay interest on the loan. For example, if you were to borrow $2,000 today at 12% interest for one year, you would have to pay back $2,240 next year, so $2,240 is the future value of $2,000 next year at 12% interest.

Of course, banks don't really have time travel machines for money. A bank is a broker between people who have money today and want to

---

*There are some technicalities in computing interest, technicalities that make a lot of difference in real dollars and cents. We will compute interest year by year. At the end of each year, the interest due on a bank account is paid by the bank into the account. That interest (along with the original deposit) earns interest in subsequent years. The technical name for this procedure is *compounding*. Since the interest is paid each year, we say it is compounded yearly.

send it into the future and those who need money today and would like to bring some money back from the future. If the two examples were arranged by a bank, then it would receive \$2,000 from the depositor now and immediately give it to the borrower. Next year the borrower would pay the bank \$2,240 and the bank would return \$2,120 to the depositor, making a profit of \$120 on the two deals.

Our first computer program will compute the future value of a particular investment. In order to understand this program, let's work out an example of a typical future value calculation.

Example

Suppose that you deposit \$3,000 in a certificate of deposit earning 9% interest for three years. What is the future value of this deposit when you cash it in at the end of three years? The following table shows the history of the value of this certificate of deposit:

Item	Amount	Value of Certificate
Initial deposit	\$3,000.00	\$3,000.00
First year's interest	270.00	3,270.00
Second year's interest	294.30	3,564.30
Third year's interest	320.79	3,885.09

The following BASIC program carries out this calculation:

```
!   This program computes the future value of $3,000
!   invested at 9% interest for three years.
!
LET value = 3000                    ! Initial deposit
FOR year = 1 TO 3                   ! Do calcs for 3 years
LET value = value + 0.09 * value    ! Add 9% interest
NEXT year                           ! End of FOR...NEXT
PRINT USING "Future value $##,###.##":value    ! Print ans
END
```

This program introduces two new elements of True BASIC. The first element is called a *variable*. A variable is like a piece of paper on which one can write down a piece of information for later use. The line

```
LET value = 3000
```

instructs True BASIC to write the number 3000 on a piece of paper. It also gives that piece of paper a name. In this case the name of the piece of paper is "value." The piece of paper is just a metaphor. The number is really stored in a part of the computer called RAM. We will use the word *variable* rather than piece of paper. A True BASIC statement that begins with the word "LET" tells True BASIC to put some information into a variable. Such a statement has four elements:

1. The word "LET".

2. A name for the variable. In the example, the name is "value." Usually the programmer chooses a name that describes the significance of the variable.

3. An equal sign (=).

4. The information that should be written into the variable. In this example, the information is the number 3000. However, a variable can also store alphabetic information. For example, the statement

```
LET name$ = "Quasimodo"
```

will write the word "Quasimodo" into the variable called name$. The name of a variable that stores alphabetic information must always end with a dollar sign.

After a piece of information has been written into a variable, it may be read any number of times. The same variable may also be used over again to store a different piece of information. Metaphorically, one can read the information on a piece of paper any number of times. Still metaphorically, one can erase the old piece of information and write a new piece of information onto the same piece of paper at any time. When a variable is reused in this way, the old information is lost. The new information can be read any number of times. A variable may be reused in this way many times. Notice that each time a new piece of information is put into a variable, any old information previously put into that variable is lost. However, a piece of information in a variable may be read any number of times without being lost. *Reading information from a variable leaves the information untouched, but writing new information into a variable erases any old information.*

There is a second LET statement in the future value program:

```
LET value = value + 0.09 * value   ! Add 9% interest
```

This statement does the same calculations that the bank would do each year. Each year the bank looks into the bank account and computes the interest due—9% of the amount in the account. Then this interest is added to the amount in the account, and the total is put into the account. The True BASIC statement reads the amount of money in the account. This amount was written earlier in the variable called value. The statement adds 9% to this amount and then writes the new total into the variable called value. This example illustrates a typical use of the LET statement. It does some calculations, usually using information found in some of the variables, and then it writes the result of these calculations into a variable.

True BASIC uses, as much as possible, the usual symbols to describe arithmetic operations: "+" for addition, "–" for subtraction, and "/" for division. One exception is multiplication. True BASIC uses the asterisk "*" for multiplication. True BASIC uses the symbol "^" for exponentiation. For example, the computation

$$\frac{x}{y} + a(1 + y^3)$$

would be written

```
x/y + a * (1 + y^3)
```

in True BASIC.

Notice that we compute interest at 9% by multiplying by 0.09. This is because 9% is really 9/100, or 0.09.

The two lines described so far tell True BASIC how to simulate our investor's initial deposit

```
LET value = 3000
```

and how to simulate the bank's calculations each year

```
LET value = value + 0.09 * value
```

We want to tell True BASIC to repeat these calculations three times. This is accomplished by two lines:

```
FOR year = 1 TO 3
NEXT year
```

These lines tell True BASIC to repeat all the lines included between
the first line (`FOR year = 1 TO 3`) and the last line (`NEXT year`) three
times. In this program the line

```
LET value = value + 0.09 * value   ! Add 9% interest
```

which simulates the way that the bank pays interest into the account is
repeated three times. A piece of a program like

```
FOR year = 1 TO 3
LET value = value + 0.09 * value   ! Add 9% interest
NEXT year
```

is sometimes called a *loop* or a *FOR ... NEXT loop* because True BASIC
will "run around the loop" in a figurative circle, repeating the enclosed
statements as many times as specified by the `FOR` statement.

Exercises

*__Exercise 1.2.8__ Type the future value program into your computer and
run it.

*__Exercise 1.2.9__ Change the program to compute the future value of
$3,000 invested for three years at 8% interest.

*__Exercise 1.2.10__ Change the program to compute the future value of
$3,000 invested for four years at 8% interest.

__Exercise 1.2.11__ Change the program to compute the future value of
$4,000 invested for four years at 8% interest.

Our last program was fairly useful but it has one major flaw. Every
time one wants to solve a new future value problem, one must change the
program itself. Our next program is designed to be used to solve future
value problems *interactively*; that is, a user will sit at the keyboard of a
computer running this program. The program will ask the user for input
describing a future value problem and then will print out the solution
to the problem. This program will ask the user for three pieces of data,
called *input*, that describe the user's future value problem:

1. The present value of the investment, that is, the amount of money the depositor will invest. For example, this might be the amount of money that an investor deposits in a bank account.

2. The interest rate paid by the bank. This will be entered as a percentage. For example, if the account pays $5\frac{1}{2}\%$ interest, the user would type "5.5".

3. The duration of the investment. For example, this might be the number of years that the investor leaves the money in the bank account before withdrawing it.

The output of the program will be a single number, the future value of the investment—for example, the amount of money that the investor will receive when he or she closes out the bank account after the specified number of years.

```
!                       *** Compute Future Value ***
!
!                   INPUT       Present Value
!                               Interest Rate
!                               Number of Years
!
!                   OUTPUT      Future Value
!
PRINT "Enter Present Value."      ! Ask for present value
INPUT value                        ! Input present value
PRINT "Enter Interest Rate (as a percent)." ! Ask int.
INPUT percent                      ! Input int.
LET rate = percent/100             ! Convert pct
PRINT "Enter Number of Years."     ! Ask for time
INPUT NumberYears                  ! Input time
FOR year=1 TO NumberYears          ! Repeat calcs
LET value = value + rate * value   ! Add interest
NEXT year                          ! End of loop
PRINT USING "Future value $###,###.##":value ! Print result
END
```

This program uses one new True BASIC statement, the INPUT statement, to achieve a dialogue between the user and the computer. The dialogue might go something like this:

Computer:	Enter present value.
User:	3000
Computer:	Enter Interest Rate (as a percent).
User:	9
Computer:	Enter Number of Years.
User:	5
Computer:	Future value $4,615.87

The computer's side of this dialogue consists of three requests for information about the problem, followed by the answer to the problem. After each request for information, there is an INPUT instruction. This instruction does two things. First, it tells True BASIC to pause and wait for the user to type in some information. When this statement is executed by True BASIC, it displays a question mark and a blinking cursor as a signal that the user should type in some information. After the user types in the information, the input statement puts that information into a variable. The INPUT statement has two elements:

1. The word "INPUT"

2. A variable or a list of variables separated by commas

The statement pauses and waits for the user to type in a piece of datum or a list of several pieces of data separated by commas. There must be the same number of pieces of data as there are variables in the INPUT statement. True BASIC prints a question mark ("?") and displays a flashing cursor while it waits for the user to type in the data. The user types in the data followed by a "carriage return" or "enter." If you were to run this program you would see the following:

```
Enter Present Value.
? 3000
Enter Interest Rate (as a percent).
? 9
Enter Number of Years.
? 5
Future value $  4,615.87
```

Notice the question marks printed by True BASIC while it was waiting for the user to type in the requested data.

Exercises

Type in and run the program above. Use it to answer the following questions.

*Exercise 1.2.12 Suppose that you invest $20,000 at 10% interest. How much will you have after 10 years?

*Exercise 1.2.13 Suppose that you borrow $20,000 at 14% interest. If you repay this loan in one lump sum after 10 years, how much will you have to pay?

*Exercise 1.2.14 If a bank were to broker the two transactions described above, how much profit would it make?

Exercise 1.2.15 Suppose that you need to borrow $5,000 to buy a new car. The automobile manufacturer is running a special promotion. You have two choices:

1. Get a rebate of $500 now. Borrow the remaining $4,500 at an interest rate of 12%, paying it back in one lump sum in three years.
2. No rebate but you can borrow the $5,000 at a special rate of 5%, paying it back in one lump sum after three years.

Which is the better deal? Why?

We have looked at the problem of computing future value if we know present value. Now we want to consider the reverse problem: we know future value and want to compute present value. As before we will begin with an example.

Example

Suppose that your rich aunt has promised to give you $10,000 on your twenty-first birthday. Today is your eighteenth birthday. You wish that you had the money today instead of having to wait three years. You can take out a loan at 12%. How much money can you borrow today if you will pay back the loan in three years in one lump sum of $10,000 using your aunt's gift?

A very naive guess might be to borrow $10,000, but that would get you into trouble, as you can see by computing the future value (the amount you would have to pay back) of $10,000 borrowed at 12% interest for three years:

Item	Amount	Value of Loan
Initial deposit	$10,000.00	$10,000.00
First year's interest	1,200.00	11,200.00
Second year's interest	1,344.00	12,544.00
Third year's interest	1,505.28	14,049.28

If you were to borrow the entire $10,000, then you would have to pay back $14,049.28 after three years. Your aunt's gift would leave you short by $4,049.28.

In order to find out how much money you can borrow now, we need to reverse the procedure, starting with a future value of $10,000 and working backward to compute its present value. Before reversing the procedure, we will simplify it a bit. Notice that we compute the interest (at 12%) on a deposit of V dollars by multiplying V by 0.12:

$$\text{Interest} = 0.12V$$

The new value after adding interest is

$$V + 0.12V = 1.12V$$

Thus, for each of the three years we can summarize the two steps—compute interest, add interest to value—in one step:

Explanation	Amount
Initial deposit	$10,000.00
Total after one year	11,200.00
Total after two years	12,544.00
Total after three years	$14,049.28

In this calculation each line was obtained from the preceding line in one step by multiplying by 1.12. Now you can see how to reverse the calculation to find the initial deposit corresponding to a final debt of $10,000. Start with a bottom line of $10,000 and work your way up the table line by line by dividing by 1.12. The beginning of this calculation is shown in the following table. Complete this table by filling in the blanks.

Explanation	Amount
Initial deposit	
Total after one year	
Total after two years	8,928.57
Total after three years	$10,000.00

After looking at these numbers, you might want to reconsider the idea of borrowing the money. $10,000 loses a lot when it travels backward three years in a time machine.

Now we are ready for your first major programming assignment. You may want to review this section if you have difficulty writing the program. In the next section we will return to the question that started us thinking about time travel for money, the true value of $50,000 per year for 20 years.

Exercises

Exercise 1.2.16   Write a computer program whose input will be

- Future value
- Interest rate
- Number of years

and whose output will be

- Present value

Make sure that this program works by comparing the results that you obtained in the example above with the answer you obtain by using your program.

Use this program to answer the following questions.

Exercise 1.2.17   Under the terms of your rich uncle's will, you will receive $25,000 in five years. You would like to spend the money now. If

you borrow money at 14% interest and pay it back in one lump sum in five years with your uncle's bequest, how much money can you borrow?

Exercise 1.2.18   Under the terms of your rich uncle's will, you will receive $25,000 in five years. You would like to spend the money now. If you borrow money at 12% interest and pay it back in one lump sum in five years with your uncle's bequest, how much money can you borrow?

Exercise 1.2.19   Under the terms of your rich uncle's will, you will receive $25,000 in five years. You would like to spend the money now. If you borrow money at 8% interest and pay it back in one lump sum in five years with your uncle's bequest, how much money can you borrow?

Exercise 1.2.20   Under the terms of your rich uncle's will, you will receive $25,000 in five years. You would like to spend the money now. If you borrow money at 6% interest and pay it back in one lump sum in five years with your uncle's bequest, how much money can you borrow?

1.3   When Is $1,000,000 a Million Dollars?

Now we are ready to answer the question that started us thinking about time travel for money. We are interested in the real present value of a typical million-dollar lottery prize. We want to compare $1 million right now with $50,000 per year for 20 years. In order to do this we need to assume a particular interest rate—and the interest rate makes a huge difference. We will work out an example with an interest rate of 10%.

Example

The first step is to compute the present value of each of the 20 $50,000 payments. The first payment is immediate. Its present value is $50,000. The second payment is made after one year. Its present value is

$$\frac{\$50,000}{1.10} = \$45,454.55.$$

You can compute the present value of each of the remaining payments by using the program you wrote in the previous section. The results are shown in Table 1.1. The final total was obtained by adding up the 20

Table 1.1
Present Value of Prize Payments

Payment	Present Value
1	$50,000.00
2	45,454.55
3	41,322.32
4	37,565.75
5	34,150.68
6	31,046.08
7	28,223.71
8	25,657.92
9	23,325.39
11	19,277.18
12	17,524.71
13	15,931.56
14	14,483.24
15	13,166.58
16	11,969.62
17	10,881.47
18	9,892.25
19	8,992.95
20	8,175.41
Total	$468,246.27

present values. Notice that the total present value of the million dollar prize is actually less than half that of a real present-day million dollars.

Now we would like to write a computer program that will do the calculations shown in Table 1.1. This is a fairly large problem. We will make use of the most important trick of programming:

When confronted with a large problem, break it down into several smaller, more manageable problems.

In this case we will break the large problem into two smaller problems:

1. Find the present value of each of the 20 payments.

2. Add up the 20 present values.

You solved the first of these two problems in an exercise in the last section that asked you to write a program to compute present value given future value. Here is one example of a program that solves this problem:

```
!       Compute present value given future value
!
!       Input:  Future value
!               Number of years
!               Interest rate (as a percent)
!
!       Output: Present value
!
PRINT "Enter future value"
INPUT value
PRINT "Enter number of years"
INPUT years
PRINT "Enter interest rate (as a percent)"
INPUT rate
LET multiplier = 1 + (rate/100)
FOR i = 1 TO years
    LET value = value / multiplier
NEXT i
PRINT USING "$###,###.##": value
END
```

This program solves the first of our two subproblems. We want to
use this program as *part* of the program we will write in this section—
a common situation. We have a program that by itself can solve part
of a larger problem and want to use it as part of the solution for the
larger problem. True BASIC has a number of elements designed to help
in exactly this situation. We will use a True BASIC element called a
function.

The present value program shown above is designed to be used interactively by a human being. If this program is rewritten as a *function*,
it can be used interactively by another program. This same program
rewritten as a function looks like this:

```
!       Function:
!       Compute present value given future value
!
```

```
!        Input:   Future value
!                 Number of years
!                 Interest rate (as a percent)
!
!        Output: Present value
!
DEF PresentValue (FutureValue, NumberYears, InterestRate)
LET multiplier = 1 + (InterestRate/100)
LET value = FutureValue
FOR i = 1 TO NumberYears
    LET value = value / multiplier
NEXT i
LET PresentValue = value
END DEF
```

A function has the following elements:

- The first line of every function (except possibly for comments) must always begin with **DEF** followed by the name of the function and a list of the function's input in parentheses separated by commas. This particular function is named "PresentValue" and has three items of input: FutureValue, NumberYears, and InterestRate.

- The **DEF** statement is followed by the main part of the function. This part performs the necessary computations using the input. It is almost identical to the original program written for human use except that it simply refers to the input items listed in the **DEF** statement by name rather than INPUTing them from the keyboard.

- The main part of the function always includes at least one statement of the form:

  ```
  LET FunctionName = ...
  ```

  In our example this line is:

  ```
  LET PresentValue = value
  ```

  This statement is the equivalent of a **PRINT** statement for a human user. It passes the output to the program using the function.

- The final statement of a function (END DEF) tells True BASIC that the function is complete. Every function must end with this same line.

To use a function within another program, write a phrase like:

```
PresentValue(50000, 8, 10)
```

This phrase gets the output of the PresentValue function with input 50000, 8, 10—the present value of a payment of $50,000 received eight years from now assuming an interest rate of 10%.

More generally, a phrase using a function has the name of the function and the input to the function enclosed in parentheses, with the items separated by commas.

The following program computes the present value of $50,000 per year for several years. The input to this program is the interest rate as a percentage and the number of payments. Its output is the total present value of all the payments:

```
!       Compute present value of $50,000 per year
!       for twenty years
!
!       Input: Interest rate
!              Number of payments
!
!       Function:
!       Compute present value given future value
!
!       Input:  Future value
!               Number of years
!               Interest rate (as a percent)
!
!       Output: Present value
!
DEF PresentValue (FutureValue, NumberYears, InterestRate)
LET multiplier = 1 + (InterestRate/100)
LET value = FutureValue
FOR i = 1 TO NumberYears
    LET value = value / multiplier
NEXT i
```

```
LET PresentValue = value
END DEF
!
PRINT "Enter Interest Rate"
INPUT rate
PRINT "Enter number of payments"
INPUT payments
LET total = 50000
FOR year = 1 TO (payments - 1)
    LET total = total + PresentValue(50000, year, rate)
NEXT year
PRINT USING "Total present value $###,###": total
END
```

Notice the way that it uses the PresentValue function to find the present value of each of the 19 future payments.

Exercises

*Exercise 1.3.21   Use the preceding program to compute the present value of $50,000 per year for 20 years assuming an interest rate of 12%.

Exercise 1.3.22   Use the same program to compute the present value of $50,000 per year for 20 years assuming an interest rate of 8%.

Exercise 1.3.23   Use the same program to find the present value of $50,000 per year for 30 years assuming an interest rate of 8%.

Exercise 1.3.24   Use the same program to find the present value of $50,000 per year for 40 years assuming an interest rate of 8%.

Exercise 1.3.25   Use the same program to find the present value of $50,000 per year for 50 years assuming an interest rate of 8%.

Exercise 1.3.26   Use the same program to find the present value of $50,000 per year for 100 years assuming an interest rate of 8%.

Exercise 1.3.27   What do you think would be the present value of $50,000 per year forever assuming an interest rate of 8%?

*Exercise 1.3.28   This is a major programming assignment and draws together elements from all our programming work to date. The next project will not involve any programming in order to give you time to complete this assignment.

Suppose that you would like to save up some money for a college education for your child. You can afford to save $2,000 per year. You make your first deposit on the day the child is born. Then you deposit $2,000 each year on your child's birthday until she reaches the age of 19. On her nineteenth birthday how much money is in the account immediately after you make the last deposit? Assume an interest rate of 6%. You may want to read the following comments on the program development cycle before starting this exercise.

Exercise 1.3.29   Repeat the preceding exercise assuming an interest rate of 4%.

Exercise 1.3.30   Repeat the preceding exercise assuming an interest rate of 8%.

Program Development Cycle

The program development cycle is a procedure for writing computer programs that will save you time and increase the probability that your programs work correctly.

Step 1: Write a clear explanation of the purpose of the program that includes descriptions of the input, the output, and the methods used to compute the output.

Step 2: Work out a simple example. For example, if you were writing a program to compute the total present value of $50,000 per year for 20 years at 12% interest, you might work out an example with only three yearly payments.

The importance of this step cannot be overemphasized. It is essential for two reasons. First, working out an example helps you to understand exactly what the program is to do and how it is to do it. Second, the example will be used in Step 4 to check that the program is working correctly. For complicated programs, it may be necessary to work out several examples.

Step 3: Write the program.

Step 4: Check that the program is working by using it to recalculate the example from Step 2. You may have wondered why the lottery prize program was written to allow the user to input the number of payments. The reason was to make it easier to check out the program to make sure that it worked. It was relatively easy to do the calculations by hand for a small number of payments.

Step 5: Finally, and only after the program has been thoroughly checked out, use it.

Notice that the actual writing of the program is the third step, *not the first step*.

This section concludes with a major optional assignment.

Exercise

Exercise 1.3.31 If your state has a lottery, find out the total handle and the total payoff last year (or for the most recent year for which such figures are available). Find out whether the information you have obtained uses the present value of any prizes that are paid out in installments. If not, correct this oversight. If so, find out the interest rate used in this calculation. If you disagree with the interest rate used, recalculate the present value using a more reasonable interest rate. Explain why you chose a particular interest rate. After you are satisfied that you know the present value of the payoff, compute the ratio payoff/handle. Find out how much of the "profit" from the lottery is used to pay for the costs of running the lottery and how much is used to pay for public services. Based on all these calculations, what is your opinion of the lottery? Would you buy lottery tickets?

A Warning

Frequently a programmer uses the same variable name in a function and in a program using the function. This might happen in two very different circumstances:

- The programmer made a mistake. The programmer wrote the function and then wrote the rest of the program later using the same name, forgetting that it had been used before.

- The programmer deliberately wanted to use the same variable in both the function and the program that used the function.

True BASIC is a powerful language with many options. One is how it interprets this situation. When a function is written and used the way we have in this chapter, True BASIC will assume that the use of the same variable name in both the program and the function was deliberate—that the programmer intended both the function and the program to use the same piece of paper. There are some circumstances in which this is good, but there are some circumstances in which this is very bad. It can lead to errors that are extremely difficult to detect. For example, the following program is almost identical to our earlier program except that I have used the same variable name i twice—once in the function and once in the program. As a result this program won't work:

```
!       **** Warning!  Don't use this program. ****
!       **** It contains an error.              ****
!
!       Compute present value of $50,000 per year
!       for twenty years
!
!       Input: Interest rate
!              Number of payments
!
DEF PresentValue (FutureValue, NumberYears, InterestRate)
LET multiplier = 1 + (InterestRate/100)
LET value = FutureValue
FOR i = 1 TO NumberYears
    LET value = value / multiplier
```

```
NEXT i
LET PresentValue = value
END DEF
!
PRINT "Enter Interest Rate"
INPUT rate
PRINT "Enter number of payments"
INPUT payments
LET total = 50000
FOR i = 1 TO (payments - 1)
    LET total = total + PresentValue(50000, i, rate)
NEXT i
PRINT USING "Total present value $###,###": total
END
```

1.4   Tall Buildings and Linear Functions

The last project involved lots of programming. This project has none at all. It has two purposes. First, we will be looking at a practical problem: finding the height of a tall building, a tree, or a mountain. Second, we have a mathematical purpose: learning about linear functions and how they can be used. Linear functions are extremely useful and easy to use—a perfect combination. We will be using linear functions in this project as a means for finding the height of a tall building, but this is only one of many uses to which they can be put. We will use linear functions frequently thoughout this book. We are studying them now in part to give you time to finish the programming exercises from Project 3.

For this project you will need a simple surveyor's tool, a *theodolite*, to help determine the height of a tall building. You can construct a homemade theodolite from a few cheap components:

- A protractor.
- One sheet of paper.
- A piece of string. This should be thin string, about 2 feet long.
- A few pieces of tape.

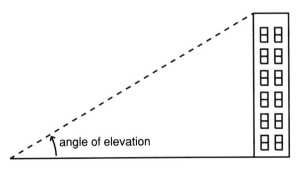

Figure 1.1
Angle of elevation

- A small weight. A fishing weight or sinker is ideal.

- A 30 foot length of cord. This should be somewhat thicker and stronger than the other string, but it does not have to be too strong since it will not be used to support anything. The length of this piece of cord should be measured carefully. You will eventually use it to measure the distance between two points. A long measuring tape would be even better.

A theodolite is a device for measuring the *angle of elevation* made by a person's line of sight when that person is looking at an object. Figure 1.1 shows a tall building. Think of an observer on the ground with his or her eye at the point of the triangle. The observer is looking at the top of the building. The dashed line is the observer's line of sight. The angle that this line makes with the ground is the angle of elevation.

The first step in making a theodolite is to roll the piece of paper into a tight tube that you will use as a sight to look at the top of the building. A tube with a diameter between 1/4 and 1/2 inch seems to work well, but you can experiment to find the size that works best for you.

The second step is to attach the tube to the protractor as shown in Figure 1.2. The tube must line up exactly with the flat edge of the protractor.

The third step is to attach the piece of string at the exact center of the protractor. When a protractor is used to measure angles, the "point" or "vertex" of the angle is placed at the center of the protractor. This center should be clearly marked on your protractor. Frequently there will be a small hole at the exact center. If there isn't a small hole, you should make one. Then attach one end of the piece of string to this hole

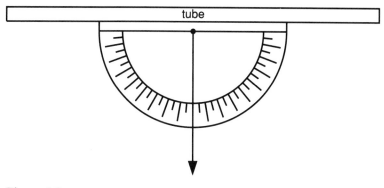

Figure 1.2
Homemade theodolite

in such a way that the string is free to swing from the hole. (If you are a bicyclist and have some spare spokes around, you can make an excellent theodolite by using a spare spoke instead of a string and weight. The hub end of the spoke goes through the hole in the protractor.)

The final step is to attach the weight to the other end of the string. Figure 1.2 shows the completed theodolite.

Now we are ready to use the theodolite to measure the height of a building, tree, or other tall object. First find a convenient place to work—one that is level with the bottom of the object to be measured and where there is enough space so that you can find *two* spots from which to make measurements of the angle of elevation as shown in Figure 1.3. The two spots must be on a direct line with the object whose height you want to determine, and they must be far enough apart so that the two angles of elevation are quite different. You must also be able to measure the distance between the two spots. You can use the 30-foot length of cord from the components list to measure this distance.

Measure the angle of elevation at each of these two spots in exactly the same way. Standing at the first spot, sight through the tube at the top of the object. The weight at the end of the piece of string will pull the string so that it is hanging straight downward. Have a friend read the angle on the protractor opposite the hanging string. We will call this angle T. For example, if the building were exactly the same height as the observer, then T would be 90 degrees. The angle of elevation is

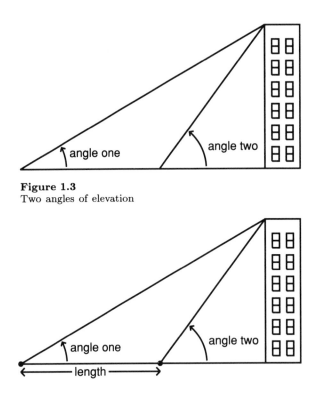

Figure 1.3
Two angles of elevation

Figure 1.4
Measurements

90 degrees minus T. Repeat this procedure standing at the second spot
to obtain the second angle of elevation.

In summary, you need to make the following three measurements:

1. The distance between the two spots from which you measure the angle
   of elevation.

2. The angle of elevation from spot number 1.

3. The angle of elevation from spot number 2.

These measurements are shown in Figure 1.4. When you have made
the measurements indicated in Figure 1.4, you have completed the field
work for this project. It is time to come back inside for some refreshment
and mathematical analysis of these measurements. The mathematical
tool we will need is *linear functions*.

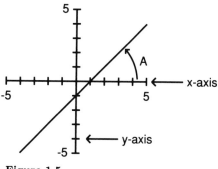

Figure 1.5
The slope via the angle

Linear Functions

A linear function is a function whose graph is a straight line. An equation describing a linear function is of the form

$$y = mx + b$$

where m is a number called the *slope* and b is a number called the *y-intercept*. The slope determines the steepness of the line. If the slope is positive, the line is rising from left to right. If the slope is negative, the line is falling from left to right. Lines with a large slope are steeper than lines with smaller slopes. (The words *larger* and *smaller* here refer to the size of the absolute value of the slope. For example, -4 is "larger" than 2.)

   The y-intercept indicates the point at which the line intersects the y-axis since on the y-axis $x = 0$. So

$$y = m(0) + b = b.$$

   We will need to be able to determine the slope of a straight line. There are two methods of doing this. The first method is to measure the angle between the x-axis and the line. This angle will be called A. You can measure it with a protractor. See Figure 1.5.

   If you have taken a trigonometry course, you may recall that the slope of the line is just $\tan(A)$ (read "tangent of A"). Even if you haven't taken a trigonometry course, it seems intuitively clear that the angle A can be used to determine the slope of the line. Table 1.2 gives the slope of a line from the angle A, which is measured in degrees.

Table 1.2
Angle and Slope Table

Angle	Slope	Angle	Slope	Angle	Slope
0	.00000	30	.5774	60	1.7321
1	.01746	31	.6009	61	1.8040
2	.03492	32	.6249	62	1.8807
3	.05241	33	.6494	63	1.9626
4	.06993	34	.6745	64	2.0503
5	.08749	35	.7002	65	2.1445
6	.10510	36	.7265	66	2.2460
7	.12278	37	.7536	67	2.3559
8	.14054	38	.7813	68	2.4751
9	.15838	39	.8098	69	2.6051
10	.17633	40	.8391	70	2.7475
11	.19438	41	.8693	71	2.9042
12	.21256	42	.9004	72	3.0777
13	.23087	43	.9325	73	3.2709
14	.24933	44	.9657	74	3.4874
15	.26795	45	1.0000	75	3.7321
16	.28675	46	1.0355	76	4.0108
17	.30573	47	1.0724	77	4.3315
18	.32492	48	1.1106	78	4.7046
19	.34433	49	1.1504	79	5.1446
20	.36397	50	1.1918	80	5.6713
21	.38386	51	1.2349	81	6.3138
22	.40403	52	1.2799	82	7.1154
23	.42447	53	1.3270	83	8.1443
24	.44523	54	1.3764	84	9.5144
25	.46631	55	1.4281	85	11.4301
26	.48773	56	1.4826	86	14.3007
27	.50953	57	1.5399	87	19.0811
28	.53171	58	1.6003	88	28.6363
29	.55431	59	1.6643	89	57.2900
				90	infinity

As an example, consider the slope of the line shown in Figure 1.5. The angle that this line makes with the x-axis is 45 degrees. You can measure this angle with a protractor. Looking up 45 degrees in Table 1.2 we see that the slope of the line is 1.

Notice that if the angle is 90 degrees, then the slope in the table is listed as infinity. An angle of 90 degrees corresponds to a vertical line. We say that the slope of a vertical line is infinite. This will make a little more sense later in this section when we discuss the slope of a line from another point of view.

If you have a "scientific" calculator, you don't need this table. You can find the slope of a line with angle A by typing in A and then pressing the

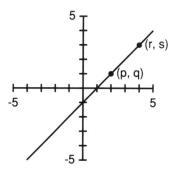

Figure 1.6
Finding the slope from two points

"tan" key. (**Warning:** There are several different units for measuring angles. Mathematicians, scientists, and engineers use a unit called the *radian*; however, for nontechnical work, one usually uses the *degree* as a unit for measuring angles. Your calculator probably can handle either degrees or radians. In fact, calculators frequently offer an additional option, the *gradian*. There may be a switch or some other method of setting your calculator for degrees or radians. Be sure that your calculator is set for degrees before you use it.)

In your fieldwork you were looking at two straight lines. The first was the line from your first observing point to the top of the building. The second was the line from your second observing point to the top of the building (Figure 1.4). These lines are called the "lines of sight" from your observing points to the top of the building. You have already measured the angle each of these lines makes with the horizontal using your homemade theodolite. Now you can use Table 1.2 to determine the slope of each of these two lines.

We need a few more techniques for working with straight lines. The first technique we will discuss is not actually used to find the building's height. We will use it in the exercises and later in Section 1.6. This technique can also give you some intuition about what the slope of a line actually is. It enables us to find the slope of a line if we know any two points on the line. Consider the line $y = mx + b$. Suppose we are given two points on the line as shown in Figure 1.6.

The slope of a line measures how fast the line is rising. To determine the slope of a line from two points, we measure the difference between the y-coordinates of the two points. This difference is called the *change in y*:

change in $y = s - q$.

Next we measure the difference between the two x-coordinates. This difference is called the *change in x*:

change in $x = r - p$.

The slope of the line is the quotient

$$\text{slope} = \frac{\text{change in } y}{\text{change in } x} = \frac{s - q}{r - p}.$$

Notice that the slope describes how fast the y-coordinate changes as compared to the x-coordinate as one moves along the line. For example, if the slope is 2, then the line rises two units for every one unit that one moves to the right. If the slope were -3, then the line would fall three units for every one unit that one moved to the right.

Earlier in this section I used the word *slope* for the constant m in the equation of a line $y = mx + b$. The following argument shows that the calculations above agree with this use of the word *slope*.

Since the two points are on the line $y = mx + b$,

$$s = mr + b$$

and

$$q = mp + b.$$

Subtracting, we get

$$\begin{aligned}
s - q &= mr + b - (mp + b) \\
&= mr + b - mp - b \\
&= mr - mp \\
&= m(r - p).
\end{aligned}$$

Dividing both sides by $(r - p)$ we get

$$m = \frac{s - q}{r - p} = \frac{\text{change in } y}{\text{change in } x}.$$

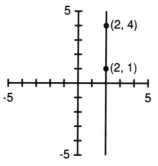

Figure 1.7
The slope of a vertical line

This shows that the earlier use of the term *slope* for the number m agrees with this new way of determining the slope of a linear function.

Finally, consider a straight line that is vertical (the angle it makes with the x-axis is 90 degrees). See Figure 1.7, for example.

For this particular line we see

$$\text{slope} = \frac{\text{change in } y}{\text{change in } x} = \frac{3}{0},$$

which doesn't make any sense since one cannot divide by zero. The same will happen for any vertical line.

This is the reason that we say that a vertical line has an infinite slope. If we look at two points on a vertical line, then the change in x is zero, so compared to x, which isn't changing at all, y is changing infinitely fast.

The next technique we need is a technique for finding the equation of a line if we know two things: the slope of the line and any point on the line. We begin by working out an example.

Example

This example is shown in Figure 1.8. In this example we know that the slope of the line is 3 and that it goes through the point $(2,4)$.

Since the line has slope 3, we know that its equation is of the form $y = 3x + b$. We must figure out what b is. Since the point $(2,4)$, is on this line we know that

$$4 = (3)(2) + b;$$

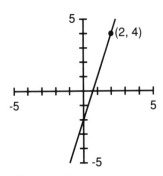

Figure 1.8
Line with slope 3 through (2, 4)

therefore,

$4 = 6 + b$

and

$-2 = b$.

So the equation of this line is $y = 3x - 2$.

This same method allows us to determine the equation of any line if we know its slope and any point (p, q) on the line. Since we know the slope, the only problem is determining the y-intercept b.

Since the point (p, q) is on the line

$q = mp + b$,

$b = q - mp$.

The equation of the line is $y = mx + (q - mp)$.

Now look at the measurements you made out in the field. We are interested in the two lines of sight, one from each of the two observing points to the top of the building. A drawing of this situation together with the measurements I made is shown in Figure 1.9. Compare this with Figure 1.4. Figure 1.9 is drawn on graph paper. This drawing was made with the first observing point at the origin. The x-axis is the ground, and the second observing point is at the point (40, 0) because when I made these measurements in the field, the two observing points were 40 feet apart. The two angles of elevation for my observations were 34 degrees and 47 degrees, as marked on Figure 1.9.

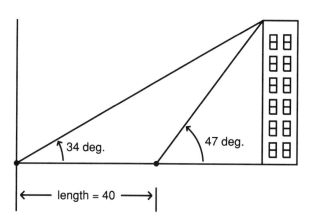

Figure 1.9
Measurements

Using these measurements and this drawing, we can determine the slope of each of the two lines of sight using Table 1.2:

Slope of first line $= \tan 34 = 0.675$.

Slope of second line $= \tan 47 = 1.072$.

The first line goes through the origin, so its equation is

$$y = 0.675x.$$

The second line goes through the point $(40, 0)$, so its equation is determined as follows:

$$0 = (1.072)(40) + b$$
$$= 42.88 + b$$
$$b = -42.88$$

and, therefore, the equation of the second line is

$$y = 1.072x - 42.88.$$

In order to determine the height of the building, we need to know the point at which these two lines intersect. That point is the top of the building. We determine this point of intersection by solving the two equations

$$y = 1.072x - 42.88 \quad \text{and} \quad y = 0.675x$$

simultaneously.

Subtracting the second equation from the first, we get

$$0 = 0.397x - 42.88$$
$$0.397x = 42.88$$
$$x = 42.88/0.397$$
$$= 108.01.$$

We determine the corresponding value of y by using either of our two equations:

$$y = 1.072x - 42.88 = (1.072)(108.01) - 42.88 = 72.91$$

or

$$y = 0.675x = (0.675)(108.01) = 72.91.$$

Thus, we have determined that the height of the building is 72.91 feet. (Actually we have determined the height of the building above the observer's eye. My eye is 5.8 feet above ground level. Therefore, the height of the building above ground level is 72.91 feet + 5.8 feet = 78.71 feet.)

As a bonus, we also have found out how far the building is from the first observing point: 108.01 feet. Our measurements were all somewhat rough—the homemade theodolite is not a precision scientific instrument or even a precision surveying instrument—but they do give us an idea of the height of the building. It would be much better to report our results by saying that the height of the building is *roughly* 80 feet.

This method is called the method of *triangulation*.

Exercises

*Exercise 1.4.32** Determine the point at which the two lines shown in Figure 1.10 intersect.

Exercise 1.4.33 Determine the height of several interesting buildings and trees.

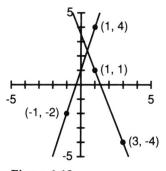

Figure 1.10
Find the point of intersection

1.5   The Property Tax, I

This book is about mathematics and computing and how they may be
used; however, it has a subtext. I believe strongly that in a democracy
individual citizens must participate fully and *knowledgeably* in their government. Too often we allow self-proclaimed "experts" to make important decisions on our behalf. Too often we allow ourselves to be swayed
by simplistic appeals. We vote on the basis of "sound bites" rather than
reasoned arguments. As I write, the clarion call "no new taxes" is ring-
ing throughout the land. Of course, we would prefer not to have new
taxes or, even better, to have taxes lowered, but it makes no sense at
all to say "no new taxes" without considering what, if anything, we will
have to give up. Taxes pay for important and necessary public services.
We must evaluate the trade-offs. Are we willing to have poorer schools,
less police and fire protection, and more potholes in exchange for lower
taxes?

It is not enough simply to talk about raising or lowering taxes. We
must talk about who pays taxes and how much. Today the average
citizen has the power to participate fully as an equal in the debate about
taxes. We do not need to place our trust in the "experts," who may very
well have different ideas about what is best than we do. This project is
an example of one way in which one might act as a citizen.

Sometimes it seems that we pay a numbing number of taxes—income
taxes, sales taxes, property taxes, excise taxes—to at least three different
levels of government: the federal government, our state government, and
our town or city government. Painful as these taxes are, we pay them for

a good reason: to purchase for our individual and common good schools, fire and police protection, public parks, and, perhaps most important, programs aimed at the goal of a fair and just society.

The projects in this section and the following one are about the property tax. We look in detail at a particular case, the property tax in the Commonwealth of Massachusetts. This choice was motivated by two considerations. First, I live, read the newspapers, and pay property taxes in Massachusetts, so it is the state with which I am most familiar. Second, this state is similar to many others, and the discussion of taxes in Massachusetts will apply generally to many other states. In Massachusetts the property tax is the main source of tax revenue for cities and towns. It is an extremely controversial tax. In fact, in November 1980 voters in Massachusetts passed a referendum known as Proposition $2\frac{1}{2}$ that placed severe restrictions on the property tax rate. Voters in many other states have also passed property tax restrictions.

I believe that the property tax is essentially a sound element of the overall system of taxation, although there is some criticism of it. Some of the criticism of the *current* property tax is justified. I will suggest variations in response to this criticism. The main purpose of this section is to investigate some of these variations and to compare them to the present property tax.

The basic principle behind any system of taxation should be that each of us pays taxes according to our ability. This idea is embodied in the U.S. income tax, where higher tax rates apply to higher income brackets. The intent is that citizens with higher incomes should pay a larger percentage of their income than citizens with smaller incomes. In practice loopholes frequently frustrate this intent.

One important factor in a person's ability to pay is his or her wealth. Income refers to the money a person is earning from a job, from interest, or other sources. Wealth refers to the amount of money and property that a person owns. For example, a person's wealth might include the following items:

- a house valued at $125,000.
- a car valued at $15,000.
- stock in the ABC Company valued at $115,000.
- a savings account containing $5,000.

His or her income might include the following items:

- $50,000 annual salary
- $7,000 annual dividends from the ABC Company.
- $250 annual interest from the savings account.

The federal government, 45 states, and many local governments base a large part of their taxes on income taxes. The property tax is one of the very few taxes based on wealth. Because wealth is an important ingredient in a person's ability to pay, this is an appropriate tax. Nevertheless, some valid objections have been raised to the current property tax, including the following

1. The property tax is a tax on a necessity. For the vast majority of people, the property tax is a tax on their home. Shelter, food, and clothing are the basic necessities of life. Such necessities should be taxed at a minimal rate, if at all. In Massachusetts, for example, food is exempt from the sales tax for this reason.

2. The property tax is regressive. The adjectives *progressive* and *regressive* are used to make an important distinction about taxes. Poorer people must spend almost all of their money on basic necessities. They have little left over for discretionary spending. In contrast, richer people have a larger fraction of their income available for discretionary spending. Thus, if everyone is taxed at the same rate, the burden on poor people is much larger than that on richer people. A *progressive* tax taxes richer people at a higher rate than poorer people. The federal income tax includes several features intended to make it more progressive, for example; the system of tax brackets. A tax that is not progressive is called *regressive*.

3. The property tax can place a particularly heavy burden on retired people who often have low incomes. Although they may own their own homes and appear to be wealthy in that sense, this is quite misleading. Their homes are their shelter. They have few sources of income, and this income often has not kept up with inflation. Property taxes must be paid from current income and may be an unfair percentage of that income.

I will propose a variation on the property tax that attempts to meet the first two objections, but first we look at the third objection. This last objection has a great deal of validity and is one of the most effective arguments given by proponents of property tax–limiting measures like Proposition $2\frac{1}{2}$. However, the best way to correct this problem is with legislation aimed specifically at this problem. One example of such legislation is Chapter 59, Section 5, Clause 41A of the General Laws of Massachusetts. This measure allows persons over the age of 65 with an annual income under $20,000 to defer all or part of the property tax on their residence. This is a good response to the dilemma of retired people who are property rich and income poor. The unpaid portion of their property tax becomes a lien on their property. The actual payment of the tax is deferred until the property is sold or the owner (and his/her spouse) dies.

This is only one example of the kinds of legislation that are appropriate for alleviating the plight of retired home owners with limited incomes. By targeting remedies specifically at such people, it is possible to give them much more relief from property taxes than could possibly be gained from any general limitation on property taxes.

Now we want to look at a proposal that responds to the first two objections. The current property tax is a fixed percentage of the value of the property. Our modification is based on an idea that is an integral part of the federal income tax. The federal income tax allows each taxpayer a personal exemption of $2,000 (as of tax year 1989) for himself or herself and for each dependent. I suggest applying the same idea to property taxes.

Example

The First Plan

This plan applies only to residential property. A home owner's taxes would be determined as follows. The basic tax rate would be $3\frac{1}{2}\%$, but the first $20,000 of the value of the home owner's residence would be deducted before taxes were computed. For example, a home owner whose house was valued at $50,000 would pay taxes on $30,000 ($50,000 − $20,000), so the tax would be $3\frac{1}{2}\%$ of $30,000, or $1,050.

Now we would like to look at a short True BASIC program that computes a home owner's tax bill under this proposed First Plan. This program computes the tax according the following recipe.

- If the value of the house is less than \$20,000, then the tax is zero.
- Otherwise the tax is $3\frac{1}{2}\%$ of the value of the house minus \$20,000.

We can describe this formula symbolically as follows:

$$\text{Tax} = \begin{cases} 0, & \text{if } v \leq \$20,000; \\ .035(v - \$20,000), & \text{otherwise.} \end{cases}$$

where v denotes the full value of the house.

The instructions for computing the tax bill contain two different formulas. One formula ($\text{Tax} = 0$) is used when the full value of the house is below \$20,000. The other ($\text{Tax} = .035(v - \$20,000)$) is used when the value of the house is above \$20,000. True BASIC contains a method for handling this situation. In the middle of the following program, you will see several lines that implement this formula:

```
!   Compute the tax bill for a house under the "First Plan"
!
PRINT "Please enter the full value of your house"
INPUT value
IF value <= 20000 THEN
     LET tax = 0
   ELSE
     LET tax = .035 * (value - 20000)
END IF
PRINT USING "Your tax bill will be $##,###.##":tax
END
```

The key lines are the lines

```
IF value <= 20000 THEN
     LET tax = 0
   ELSE
     LET tax = .035 * (value - 20000)
END IF
```

This set of lines is called an IF ... THEN ... ELSE statement. Such a statement always has the following elements:

- The word IF. This word signals the start of an IF ... THEN ... ELSE statement.

- A condition. In this example the condition is value <= 20000. The condition may use the usual symbols "<", ">", and "=" to mean "less than," "greater than," or "equal to." In addition the symbols "<=" and ">=" are used for "less than or equal to" and "greater than or equal to."

- The word THEN.

- The first possible action. In this example, the first possible action is LET tax = 0. This is the action to be taken if the condition is met.

- The word ELSE.

- The second possible action. In this example, the second possible action is LET tax = .035 * (value - 20000). This is the action to be taken if the condition is not met.

- The words END IF. These words signal the end of the IF ... THEN ... ELSE statement.

Exercises

Exercise 1.5.34 Type the program into the computer, and use it to find the tax bill on a residence whose full value is $100,000.

Exercise 1.5.35 Modify this program to compute the tax for the following modification of the First Plan.

$$\text{New Tax} = \begin{cases} 0, & \text{if } v \le \$30,000; \\ .035(v - \$30,000), & \text{otherwise.} \end{cases}$$

IF ... THEN ... ELSE statements are very powerful. They can be used to implement detailed instructions for computation. For example, one variation on the property tax might provide a larger exemption for people whose age was over 65. In words we could describe such a variation by the following:

- If the home owner's age is less than or equal to 65 and the value of the house is less than $20,000, then the tax is 0.

- If the home owner's age is less than or equal to 65 and the value of the house is above \$20,000, then the tax is $3\frac{1}{2}\%$ of (value - \$20,000).

- If the home owner's age is greater than 65 and the value of the house is less than \$40,000, then the tax is 0.

- If the home owner's age is greater than 65 and the value of the house is above \$40,000, then the tax is $3\frac{1}{2}\%$ of (value - \$40,000).

Symbolically we would write this same rule as

$$\text{Tax} = \begin{cases} 0, & \text{if } a \le 65 \text{ and } v \le \$20,000; \\ .035(v - \$20,000), & \text{if } a \le 65 \text{ and } v > \$20,000; \\ 0, & \text{if } a > 65 \text{ and } v \le \$40,000; \\ .035(v - \$40,000) & \text{if } a > 65 \text{ and } v > \$40,000. \end{cases}$$

where a denotes the home owner's age.

In True BASIC this formula could be expressed as follows:

```
!       Compute Property Tax with Special Exemption
!                 for Home owners over 65
!
PRINT "Enter home owner's age"
INPUT age
PRINT "Enter value of house"
INPUT value
IF (age <= 65) AND (value <= 20000) THEN
    LET tax = 0
  ELSEIF (age <= 65) AND (value > 20000) THEN
    LET tax = .035 * (value - 20000)
  ELSEIF (age > 65)  AND (value < 40000) THEN
    LET tax = 0
  ELSE
    LET tax = .035 * (value - 40000)
END IF
PRINT USING "Tax $##,###.##":tax
END
```

The IF ... THEN ... ELSE lines in this program illustrate two new possibilities. First, one may use the words AND and OR with their usual meanings. Second, it is possible to have many different options. It

is even possible to use IF ... THEN ... ELSE statements within IF ...
THEN ... ELSE statements. For example, the same formula might be
implemented with the following program:

```
!       Compute Property Tax with Special Exemption
!                 for Home owners over 65
!
PRINT "Enter home owner's age"
INPUT age
PRINT "Enter value of house"
INPUT value
IF age <= 65 THEN
     IF value < 20000 THEN
        LET tax = 0
     ELSE
        LET tax = .035 * (value - 20000)
     END IF
   ELSE
     IF value < 40000 THEN
        LET tax = 0
     ELSE
        LET tax = .035 * (value - 40000)
     END IF
END IF
PRINT USING "Tax $##,###.##":tax
END
```

Another possible variation on the property tax would be a system of tax
brackets aimed at taxing less valuable property at a low rate and more
valuable property at a higher rate. For example, one might compute the
tax as follows:

- If the value were less than $20,000, then the tax would be 0.

- If the value were between $20,000 and $100,000, then the tax would
  be 3% of (value - $20,000).

- If the value were over $100,000, then the tax would be 3% of $80,000
  plus 4% of (value - $100,000).

In other words the home owner would pay 3% tax on the value of the
house between $20,000 and $100,000 plus 4% of any value over $100,000.
This formula could be expressed symbolically as:

$$\text{Tax} = \begin{cases} 0, & \text{if } v \leq \$20,000; \\ .03(v - \$20,000), & \text{if } \$20,000 < v \leq \$100,000; \\ \$2,400 + .04(v - \$100,000), & \text{otherwise.} \end{cases}$$

We will call this formula the Second Plan.

Exercises

Exercise 1.5.36   Write a program that will compute the property tax
based on the "Second Plan."

Now we would like to compare the First Plan with the current property
tax. The current property tax is a flat rate of $2\frac{1}{2}$% on the full value of
a house. (Actually by 1990 the rate was much lower for most cities and
towns of Massachusetts.) We will use the rate $2\frac{1}{2}$% since that is the cap
mandated by Proposition $2\frac{1}{2}$. Figure 1.11 compares the tax bill under
the First Plan to the current tax bill for houses whose full value is up

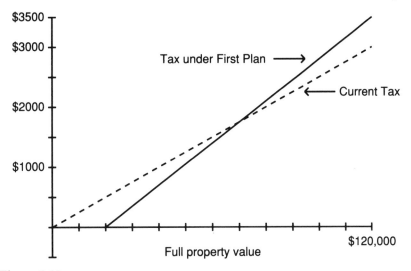

Figure 1.11
Comparison of the First Plan with current tax

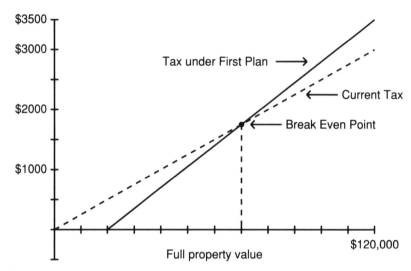

Figure 1.12
The break-even point for First Plan and the current tax

to \$120,000. Notice that for less expensive houses, the tax bill would be lower under the First Plan, while for more expensive houses it would be higher. Thus, the First Plan shifts some of the tax burden from poorer to wealthier individuals.

We note in Figure 1.11 that home owners with inexpensive houses pay lower taxes under the First Plan than under the current property tax. Home owners with expensive homes pay higher taxes under the First Plan than under the current property tax. We can compute the break-even point using the methods of Section 3. The break-even point is the point at which the two tax plans are the same, the value of a house whose tax bill would be exactly the same under the two different plans being considered. This point is indicated in Figure 1.12.

If we let v denote the value of a home owner's residence, then the current property tax is given by the formula

Current Tax $= .025v$

and the tax under the First Plan is given by the formula

$$\text{New Tax} = \begin{cases} 0, & \text{if } v \le \$20,000; \\ .035(v - \$20,000), & \text{otherwise.} \end{cases}$$

The break-even point is found by solving the equation:

$$\text{New Tax} = \text{Current Tax}$$
$$.035(v - \$20,000) = .025v$$
$$.035v - \$700 = .025v$$
$$.01v = \$700$$
$$v = \$70,000.$$

Thus, a home owner whose residence has a valuation under $70,000 will save money under this new proposal, and one whose home is valued over $70,000 will pay higher taxes.

This proposed tax accomplishes its objectives: it lowers taxes on basic shelter, a modest residence, and raises taxes on expensive houses, which should quite properly be considered in part as an investment, as wealth.

Exercises

Exercise 1.5.37 Draw a graph comparing the current property tax (a flat rate of $2\frac{1}{2}\%$), the First Plan and the Second Plan.

*Exercise 1.5.38** What is the break-even point when one compares the current tax with the Second Plan?

Exercise 1.5.39 What is the break-even point when one compares the Second Plan and the First Plan?

At this point it is appropriate to consider the plight of renters. We think of the property tax as a tax on home owners; however, property taxes have an indirect but no less real impact on renters because landlords usually pass on their costs to renters. Any increase in taxes will result in an increase in rents. It is important to bear this in mind during any discussion of property taxes. The property tax is intended as a tax on wealth. Renters generally do not own homes. If they did, they wouldn't be likely to rent. Thus, it is generally not appropriate for renters to pay a property tax.

If a program like the First Plan were adopted, it would be essential to alleviate any adverse consequences for renters. There are various mechanisms for doing this. For example, one could enact an offsetting income tax credit for renters. I will not go into any further details here except to emphasize the importance of this aspect of any plan that changes the current property tax.

The First Plan is just one example of the property tax variations that we wish to investigate. All of these variations are built around the same ideas:

- A personal residence exemption, an amount that each home owner deducts from the value of his or her residence before computing the tax.

- A higher tax rate than is currently assessed is applied to the remaining portion of the residence's value.

For the First Plan, the personal residence exemption was \$20,000, and the tax rate was $3\frac{1}{2}\%$.

We will denote the personal residence exemption by the letter E and the tax rate by the letter R. Thus, the tax can be described by the formula

$$\text{New Tax} = \begin{cases} 0, & \text{if } v \leq E; \\ R(v - E), & \text{otherwise.} \end{cases}$$

where, as before, v denotes the full value of the residence.

We are now studying a whole range of possible property taxes. By choosing different levels for the personal tax exemption and different levels for the tax rate, we get different property taxes. We want to compare them.

Our first point of comparison will be the break-even point. We calculated the break-even point for the First Plan earlier in this section and found that it was \$70,000. This figure gives us a good idea of who will benefit and who will pay more under a new tax system. We can determine the break-even point for one of these new taxes as follows:

$$\text{Tax} = \text{Current Tax}$$
$$R(v - E) = .025v$$
$$Rv - RE = .025v$$
$$Rv - .025v = RE$$
$$v(R - .025) = RE$$
$$v = \frac{RE}{R - .025}.$$

Exercises

*__Exercise 1.5.40__   Find the break-even point if the personal residence exemption is $20,000 and the tax rate is 3.0%.

*__Exercise 1.5.41__   Find the break-even point if the personal residence exemption is $30,000 and the tax rate is 3.0%.

__Exercise 1.5.42__   Find the break-even point if the personal residence exemption is $40,000 and the tax rate is 3.0%.

__Exercise 1.5.43__   Find the break-even point if the personal residence exemption is $40,000 and the tax rate is 3.5%.

__Exercise 1.5.44__   Write a program whose input is the tax rate R and the personal residence exemption E and whose output is the break-even point.

In the next section we will compare these various possible property taxes more systematically.

1.6   The Property Tax, II

The purpose of this project is twofold: to compute two tables that will be helpful in considering the various possible alternatives proposed to the current property tax and to introduce an extremely powerful programming concept. Our first goal is to produce Table 1.3. This table shows the break-even point for a whole family of variations of the First Plan.

Each of the entries in Table 1.3 was calculated using the formula for the break-even point that we found at the end of the last section:

$$\text{Break-even point} = \frac{RE}{R - .025}. \tag{1.1}$$

For example, the entry in the row labeled 3.3 in the column labeled $15,000 was calculated by

$$\frac{(.033)(\$15,000)}{.033 - .025} = \frac{\$495}{.008} = \$61,875.$$

Table 1.3
Break Even Point Table

Tax Rate(%)	Personal Residence Exemption				
	$10,000	$15,000	$20,000	$25,000	$30,000
2.6	$260,000	$390,000	$520,000	$650,000	$780,000
2.7	135,000	202,500	270,000	337,500	405,000
2.8	93,333	140,000	186,667	233,333	280,000
2.9	72,500	108,750	145,000	181,250	217,500
3.0	60,000	90,000	120,000	150,000	180,000
3.1	51,667	77,500	103,333	129,167	155,000
3.2	45,714	68,571	91,429	114,286	137,143
3.3	41,250	61,875	82,500	103,125	123,750
3.4	37,778	56,667	75,556	94,444	113,333
3.5	35,000	52,500	70,000	87,500	105,000
3.6	32,727	49,091	65,455	81,818	98,182
3.7	30,833	46,250	61,667	77,083	92,500
3.8	29,231	43,846	58,462	73,077	87,692
3.9	27,857	41,786	55,714	69,643	83,571
4.0	26,667	40,000	53,333	66,667	80,000

Table 1.3 was produced with the aid of a new programming technique. I will begin by showing how this table was produced. In the exercises at the end of this section, you will be asked to produce a similar table with additional information that will be helpful in considering these various property tax alternatives.

As we saw in Section 1.3, one of the most important tricks for writing complicated programs is breaking up the original problem into smaller, more manageable subproblems. We can break this particular problem into two pieces:

1. Compute each individual entry of Table 1.3.

2. Arrange the entries into Table 1.3.

The first problem is simple. We can write the procedure for computing the break-even point as a simple function:

```
!       Compute break even point
!
```

```
DEF break (r, e)
   LET break = (1 * e) / (r - .025)
END DEF
```

In fact, this step is so easy that it hardly seems worthwhile to split it off from the original problem as a separate step. The original rationale for breaking a large problem into several smaller subproblems or modules was that the subproblems would be shorter and easier to solve. However, there is another, sometimes even more valuable, advantage to this style of programming. Often the individual modules will be useful in other contexts. We will put a lot of effort into producing Table 1.3. Later we will want to produce another table similar to Table 1.3 but with different information. Because our program will be written with modules, it will be an easy matter to produce this second table simply by substituting another module for the break-even module in the original program.

Organized Information

We have already used variables to work with single pieces of information. The data in Table 1.3 are organized into 15 rows and five columns. We could use 15 individual variables to hold the 15 different tax rates represented in this table. However, by using 15 individual variables, we would miss the organization of the data. True BASIC uses a new kind of variable, called an *array*, to hold organized information. The True BASIC statement

```
DIM rate(15)
```

creates an array that can be thought of as a list of 15 individual but related pieces of information. Visualize an array as a filing cabinet with a number of drawers, each one of which can hold one piece of information. Each drawer is exactly like an ordinary variable. The True BASIC DIM statement tells True BASIC to set up a filing cabinet. Following the word DIM is the name of the filing cabinet (in this example, the name is "rate") and, in parentheses, the number of drawers in the filing cabinet. The word "DIM" is an abbreviation for "dimension" or the size of the filing cabinet. Once you have set up an array using a DIM statement, you can use each drawer in the filing cabinet exactly like any other variable.

A drawer is referred to by the name of the filing cabinet followed by the drawer number in parentheses. For example, the statement

```
LET rate(5) = .03
```

puts the number .03 (3%) into the fifth drawer of the filing cabinet named "rate."

Now we can see some of the power of an array. If we were to fill up these 15 variables in the most obvious way we would need 15 statements:

```
LET rate(1) = .026
LET rate(2) = .027
LET rate(3) = .028
   ⋮
LET rate (15) = .040
```

However, we can make use of the fact that an array is organized storage to put the same numbers in the same variables with just three lines:

```
FOR i = 1 TO 15
LET rate(i) = .025 + .001 * i
NEXT i
```

We can organize the five different exemptions being considered in Table 1.3 in a similar way:

```
DIM exemption(5)
FOR i = 1 TO 5
LET exemption(i) = 5000 + i * 5000
NEXT i
```

Sometimes, as in Table 1.3, it is convenient to organize data in a table with both rows and columns. The True BASIC statement DIM can be used to do this. For example, the statement

```
DIM breakeven(15, 5)
```

creates a table of variables with 15 rows and five columns. This table is organized exactly like Table 1.3. One can refer to individual variables within this table as, for example, breakeven(2, 3), which refers to the variable in row 2 and column 3. Using organized data in this way together with the subroutine we wrote earlier, we can compute all of the entries in Table 1.3 by

```
!        Create Break Even Point Table
!
DEF break (r, e)           ! Compute break even point.
    LET break = (r * e) / (r - .025)
END DEF
!
DIM rate(15)               ! 15 rows -- rates.
DIM exemption(5)           ! 5 columns -- exemptions.
DIM breakeven (15, 5)      ! Table 15 rows 5 columns.
!
FOR i = 1 TO 15            ! Put rates into rate array.
LET rate(i) = .025 + .001 * i
NEXT i
!
FOR j = 1 TO 5            ! Put exemptions into exemption array.
LET exemption(j) = 5000 + 5000 * j
NEXT j
!
FOR i = 1 TO 15           ! Compute table entries.
    FOR j = 1 TO 5
        LET breakeven (i, j) = break(rate(i), exemption(j))
    NEXT j
NEXT i
END
```

We have already discussed each part of this program except for the section

```
FOR i = 1 TO 15           ! Compute table entries.
    FOR j = 1 TO 5
        LET breakeven (i, j) = break(rate(i), exemption(j))
    NEXT j
NEXT i
END
```

This section computes the entries for each place in the table. The first and last lines

```
FOR i = 1 TO 15
NEXT i
```

enclose a section of code that will be repeated 15 times—once for each row of the table.

Just inside these lines we have

```
FOR j = 1 TO 5
NEXT j
```

This section of code encloses a line that for each row will be repeated five times—once for each column. That is, the innermost line

```
LET breakeven = break(rate(i), exemption(j))
```

will be repeated 75 times (five times for each of the 15 rows). It computes the entry in each column of each row. It does this using the subroutine **break(rate, exemption)** that we wrote earlier. Notice it gives this subroutine the appropriate input, **rate(i)** and **exemption(j)**, for each entry. That is, for each row and each column it uses the function **break** to compute the break-even point for the tax rate corresponding to the given row and the exemption corresponding to the given column. For example, for row 3 and column 2 it will use **break** to compute the break-even point for the tax rate 2.8% (**rate(3)**) and the exemption $15,000 (**exemption(2)**).

We have now done all the computing necessary to produce Table 1.3. It remains only to print the results of these computations. The following code accomplishes this task:

```
FOR i = 1 TO 15              !  Print 15 rows
   PRINT USING "##.#": 100 * rate(i);     ! Print tax rate
   FOR j = 1 TO 5            !  Print five columns
      PRINT USING "  $###,###": breakeven(i, j);
   NEXT j
   PRINT                     !  End of line
NEXT i
```

The outermost two lines of this code

```
FOR i = 1 TO 15              !  Print 15 rows
NEXT i
```

tell True BASIC to repeat the enclosed code 15 times (once for each row). The second line of this code

```
PRINT USING "##.#": 100 * rate(i);     ! Print tax rate
```

prints the label for each row of the table at the far left. Notice that we have multiplied the rate by 100 to convert it to a percentage. All the PRINT statements we have used so far automatically send a "carriage return" signal to the printer. That is why normally each PRINT statement has an output line all to itself. However, in this case we want to print some more information on the same line. In order to tell True BASIC *not to send a carriage return* signal to the printer, this PRINT statement ends with a semicolon.

- If a PRINT statement ends with a semicolon, then it will not send a carriage return signal to the printer.

- If a PRINT statement does not end with a semicolon, then it will send a carriage return signal to the printer, and the next PRINT statement will start printing at the beginning of a new line.

The next three lines

```
FOR j = 1 TO 5          !  Print five columns
    PRINT USING "  $###,###": breakeven(i, j);
NEXT j
```

cause True BASIC to print the entries in the five columns in the body of the table for each row. Notice that the PRINT statement for each entry

```
PRINT USING "  $###,###": breakeven(i, j);
```

ends with a semicolon because we do not want a carriage return until the entire row has been printed.

Finally, the statement

```
PRINT
```

prints nothing. However, because this statement does not end with a semicolon, it does cause a carriage return, so the next row will begin on a new line.

The entire program to compute Table 1.3 follows:

```
!       Create Break Even Point Table
!
```

```
DEF break (r, e)              ! Compute break even point.
    LET break = (r * e) / (r - .025)
END DEF
!
DIM rate(15)                  !  15 rows -- rates.
DIM exemption(5)              !  5 columns -- exemptions.
DIM breakeven (15, 5)         !  Table 15 rows 5 columns.
!
FOR i = 1 TO 15               ! Put rates into rate array.
LET rate(i) = .025 + .001 * i
NEXT i
!
FOR j = 1 TO 5                ! Put exemptions into exemption array.
LET exemption(j) = 5000 + 5000 * j
NEXT j
!
FOR i = 1 TO 15               ! Compute table entries.
    FOR j = 1 TO 5
        LET breakeven (i, j) = break(rate(i), exemption(j))
    NEXT j
NEXT i
!
FOR i = 1 TO 15               !  Print 15 rows
   PRINT USING "##.#": 100 * rate(i);    ! Print tax rate
   FOR j = 1 TO 5             !  Print five columns
      PRINT USING "  $###,###": breakeven(i, j);
   NEXT j
   PRINT                      !  End of line
NEXT i
END
```

Exercises

Exercise 1.6.45 Type in this program and run it.

Exercise 1.6.46   Modify the program so that it produces a table with 15 rows and four columns for the personal exemptions $10,000, $20,000, $30,000, and $40,000

Exercise 1.6.47   Modify the program so that it produces a table with 11 rows for the tax rates 3.0%, 3.2%, 3.4%, . . . , 5.0%.

Balancing the Budget

Table 1.3 gives quite a bit of the information that we need to understand these new variations on the property tax. We can see from this table that they can be used to redistribute the burden of the property tax so that it is more in keeping with the philosophical objectives of minimizing taxes on basic necessities and placing more of the burden of taxation on those whose ability to pay is greater. By choosing different amounts for the tax rate and for the personal residence exemption we can adjust the distribution of the burden of the property tax in accordance with these objectives.

There is an additional important consideration: the actual amount of money raised by taxation. We need to raise enough money to pay for essential public services. Thus, if we advocate changing the property tax, we need to be mindful of how any changes will affect the total amount of money raised by the property tax. The next step in our analysis of these variations is this consideration.

In order to see how much money is actually raised by these variations on the property tax, we need to know something about the values of the homes being taxed. I collected some rough data by choosing a sample of 500 houses in Amherst, Massachusetts. I chose only houses that were apparently occupied by their owners. I omitted those that were not owner occupied because I was concerned about the impact of these variations of the property tax on renters. Landlords usually raise rents to compensate for any increased taxes on their rental property. Thus, any increased tax on rental housing might have to be offset in some way by tax credits for renters. I will not go into this aspect of these taxes any further here except to say that it is an important consideration and that the discussion here is compatible with offsetting tax credits to renters.

Table 1.4
Housing Data

Assessed Value	Number of Homes	Assessed Value	Number of Homes
$32,500 – 37,499	1	$107,500 – 112,499	12
37,500 – 42,499	1	112,500 – 117,499	11
42,500 – 47,499	11	117,500 – 122,499	8
47,500 – 52,499	28	122,500 – 127,499	3
52,500 – 57,499	48	127,500 – 132,499	1
57,500 – 62,499	47	132,500 – 137,499	2
62,500 – 67,499	54	137,500 – 142,499	4
67,500 – 72,499	38	142,500 – 147,499	1
72,500 – 77,499	60	147,500 – 152,499	1
77,500 – 82,499	32	152,500 – 157,499	1
82,500 – 87,499	26	157,500 – 162,499	2
87,500 – 92,499	33	162,500 – 167,499	2
92,500 – 97,499	32	167,500 – 172,499	1
97,500 – 102,499	21	172,500 – 177,499	0
102,500 – 107,499	16	177,500 – 182,499	1
		182,500 – 187,499	1
		187,500 – 192,499	1

Table 1.4 summarizes the data from the 500 houses in my sample. The data are very rough but give a general idea of how these variations will work.

The bar graph shown in Figure 1.13 gives a visual impression of the distribution of home values in Amherst. We can see at a glance from the graph that most of the houses in Amherst have values between $45,000 and $120,000. There are a few houses with values slightly below $45,000 and a scattering of houses with values well above $120,000. Bar graphs are an effective way of presenting data. Notice how much easier it is to grasp the overall pattern of the data in Figure 1.13 than it is in Table 1.4.

Now we are ready to begin writing a computer program to compute the effect of the property tax variations on the revenue collected. We will simplify Table 1.4 by assuming that all the houses in each group have the same value. This results in Table 1.5.

Table 1.6 illustrates how this information is used to compute the total revenues produced by the First Plan. The first column of Table 1.6 shows a value of a home. The second column lists the tax bill for that

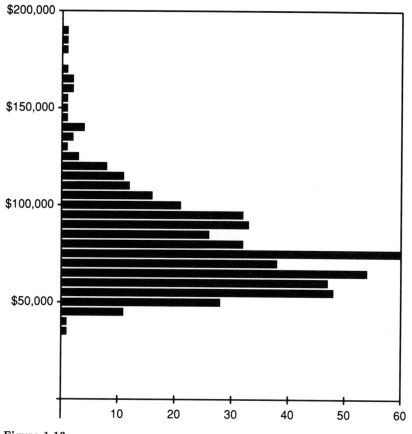

Figure 1.13
Number of houses at various prices

value. The third column shows the number of homes with that value. The fourth column shows the total tax produced by those homes; it is the product of columns 2 and 3. The total revenue produced is the total of the entries in the last column.

We want to write a computer program that will do these calculations for us for different variations of the property tax—a rather big job. As usual we begin by breaking the big job into several smaller pieces or modules:

- Enter the data from Table 1.5 into the computer.

Table 1.5
Housing Data Simplified

Assessed Value	Number of Homes	Assessed Value	Number of Homes
$35,000	1	$110,000	12
40,000	1	115,000	11
45,000	11	120,000	8
50,000	28	125,000	3
55,000	48	130,000	1
60,000	47	135,000	2
65,000	54	140,000	4
70,000	38	145,000	1
75,000	60	150,000	1
80,000	32	155,000	1
85,000	26	160,000	2
90,000	33	165,000	2
95,000	32	170,000	1
100,000	21	175,000	0
105,000	16	180,000	1
		185,000	1
		190,000	1

- Find out from the user what variation of the First Plan he or she wants to study—that is, ask the user for the tax rate and exemption.
- Find the tax for one house having a particular value.
- Add up the total tax collected on all the houses.

The first task is the hardest. We need to enter a large amount of data into the computer. This information is necessary for our computations. The information will be organized within the computer using two arrays. Each array will have 31 entries—one for each line of Table 1.5. We create these two arrays by the True BASIC lines

```
DIM value(31)
DIM number(31)
```

The information in Table 1.5 is in a disk file called **HouseData**. Your instructor will give you a copy of this disk file.* A listing of this file is

---

*If you are using this book on your own, you can create your own data file. First, open True BASIC as if you were going to write a new program. Then type the information in the listing of **HouseData** exactly as it is shown. Finally, save this as if it were a program with the name **HouseData**.

Table 1.6
Total Revenue Calculations

Value	Tax on One Home	Number of Homes	Total Tax
$35,000	$525	1	$525
40,000	700	1	700
45,000	875	11	9,625
50,000	1,050	28	29,400
55,000	1,225	48	58,800
60,000	1,400	47	65,800
65,000	1,575	54	85,050
70,000	1,750	38	66,500
75,000	1,925	60	115,500
80,000	2,100	32	67,200
85,000	2,275	26	59,150
90,000	2,450	33	80,850
95,000	2,625	32	84,000
100,000	2,800	21	58,800
105,000	2,975	16	47,600
110,000	3,150	12	37,800
115,000	3,325	11	36,575
120,000	3,500	8	28,000
125,000	3,675	3	11,025
130,000	3,850	1	3,850
135,000	4,025	2	8,050
140,000	4,200	4	16,800
145,000	4,375	1	4,375
150,000	4,550	1	4,550
155,000	4,725	1	4,725
160,000	4,900	2	9,800
165,000	5,075	2	10,150
170,000	5,250	1	5,250
175,000	—	0	—
180,000	5,600	1	5,600
185,000	5,775	1	5,775
190,000	5,950	1	5,950
Total			$1,027,775

shown below. The file has 31 lines corresponding to the 31 nonzero lines of Table 1.5. Each line has two pieces of data corresponding to the two columns of Table 1.5:

```
35000, 1
40000, 1
45000, 11
50000, 28
55000, 48
60000, 47
65000, 54
70000, 38
75000, 60
80000, 32
85000, 26
90000, 33
95000, 32
100000, 21
105000, 16
110000, 12
115000, 11
120000, 8
125000, 3
130000, 1
135000, 2
140000, 4
145000, 1
150000, 1
155000, 1
160000, 2
165000, 2
170000, 1
180000, 1
185000, 1
190000, 1
```

We want to place the contents of this disk file into the two arrays value and number. True BASIC can input data from a disk file in exactly the same way that it inputs data from the keyboard. It uses a slight variation of the INPUT statement. The statement we will use is

```
INPUT #1: value(i), number(i)
```

This statement is exactly like the ordinary input statement. It will input two pieces of data and put them into the variables **value(i)** and **number(i)** except that instead of inputting these pieces of data from the keyboard, it will input them from a disk file. We need another statement

```
OPEN #1: NAME "HouseData"   ! Data file
```

to specify which input file is to be used. This statement is called an **OPEN** statement. It has the following elements:

- The word "**OPEN**".

- The symbol "**#**" followed by an integer. The same symbol followed by the same integer and a colon (**:**) must be used in the **INPUT** statement that will read data from this disk file.

- The word "**NAME**".

- The name of the disk file enclosed in quotation marks.

The following statements will read in the information from the disk file **HouseData**.

```
OPEN #1: NAME "HouseData"        ! Data file
FOR i = 1 TO 31                  ! Input data
    INPUT #1: value(i), number(i)
NEXT i
```

Now we are ready to present a program designed to compute the total revenue produced by various variations of the First Plan. Study this program carefully. Notice how each of the modules or subproblems that we identified earlier is handled. For example, the first few lines define a function that computes the tax on a single house. The input to this function is the value of the house. However, the function also makes use of the information in the variables **rate** and **exemption**. This is an example of the way that a program and a function can share information by using the same variables. Study this program carefully and make sure that you understand how it works.

```
!    Compute Total Tax Collections
!
```

```
!      Amherst Housing Data
!
DEF tax (value)      ! Compute tax bill for one house
    IF value < exemption THEN
       LET tax = 0
    ELSE
       LET tax = rate * (value - exemption)
    END IF
END DEF
!
DIM value(31)
DIM number(31)
OPEN #1: NAME "HouseData"      ! Data file
FOR i = 1 TO 31                     ! Input data
    INPUT #1: value(i), number(i)
NEXT i
!
PRINT "Enter tax rate (percent)"
INPUT percent
LET rate = percent/100
PRINT "Enter exemption"
INPUT exemption
LET TOTAL = 0
FOR i = 1 TO 31                     ! Find total tax raised
    LET TOTAL = TOTAL + number(i) * tax(value(i))
NEXT i
PRINT USING "$###,###,###": total
END
```

We can use this program to compare the current tax program (a tax rate of $2\frac{1}{2}\%$ with no personal residence exemption) with the First Plan. The current tax program yields \$984,125; the First Plan yields \$1,027,775. Thus, these two programs yield approximately the same total revenue.

Exercises

Exercise 1.6.48 Your basic assignment for this project is to write, check out, and run a program to produce a table somewhat like Table 1.3. Table 1.3 gives the break-even point for each of several possible variations of the property tax. The new table will examine the same variations; however, instead of the break-even point for each variation, it should show the revenue produced by each variation. The entries in this table will be computed by the methods of the program above.

You can answer this exercise by modifying the break-even table program, taking advantage of its modular construction. Once you have produced the new table, use it to decide which of the property tax variations we have been discussing are feasible in the sense that they collect roughly the same total amount of revenue as the current tax.

In addition to this basic assignment, you may want to use the techniques that we have developed in this project to explore these and other property tax variations in other ways.

Exercise 1.6.49 Produce a table similar to Table 1.3 that gives the number of home owners whose tax bill would go down (compared to their current bill) if each of these variations were adopted.

Exercise 1.6.50 Experiment with a system of property tax brackets— for example:

- The first $20,000 of the value would be exempt from taxes.
- The second $40,000 would be taxed at $2\frac{1}{2}\%$.
- Anything over $60,000 would be taxed at $3\frac{1}{2}\%$

One of the most important results of the personal computer revolution is that individual citizens now have the ability to participate fully in debates about public policy matters like taxation. All the data used in this project were public information, readily available. For example, I assembled Table 1.4 in a single afternoon by comparing the property tax rolls (public information available from the assessor's office) with the telephone book. I assumed that if the home owner was listed in

the telephone book with the same address as shown on the property tax
rolls, then that address was the home owner's residence. These data are
somewhat rough, but quite sufficient for this kind of discussion.

1.7   Experimenting with the Laws of Chance

This section and Section 1.8 are about the laws of chance. Our lives
are influenced in many important ways by random events. In these two
projects we will use the computer as an experimental tool, flipping a
coins thousands of times in order to build up experimental evidence we
can use to gain insight into the ways of chance. Chapter 2 will investigate
the laws of chance in much greater depth.

The idea behind this use of the computer can be illustrated by a simple
example. Suppose that you flip a coin 10 times. How likely are you to
get exactly five heads? In Chapter 2 we will discuss a theoretical method
for answering this question, but now we are going to try to answer it in
a much more elementary way: running some experiments.

Even without a computer you could run such experiments. For example, you could flip a coin 10 times and count the number of heads. Then
you could repeat this 1,000 times and keep track of how often you got
exactly five heads. I just flipped a coin 10 times. It took me 35 seconds.
Thus, it should be possible to do this experiment in 35,000 seconds or
about 10 hours. After 10 hours and probably several blisters on your
coin-flipping finger, you would have a rough idea of how likely it is to
get exactly five heads in 10 throws.

The activity in which we are interested is flipping a coin 10 times.
This is called a *trial*. The total experiment consists of 1,000 trials (or
10,000 coin flips.)

We can use a computer to do exactly the same thing and the computer
will do it much faster, without getting blisters and without getting bored.
The main tool for doing experiments like this one is called a random
number generator. To use the random number generator in True BASIC
write a line like:

```
LET a = RND
```

A random number generator works much like the spinners that come
with some games. It is a tool that picks a number at random. One
might visualize a random number generator as a spinner whose dial is

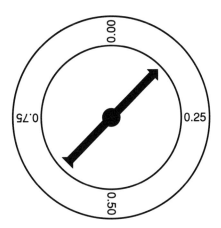

Figure 1.14
Game spinner

marked with the numbers from 0 to 1. When one spins such a spinner, it spins around for a while and then comes to rest pointing at the dial at a number between 0 and 1 (Figure 1.14).

When the statement

```
LET a  = RND
```

is executed, it "spins a spinner," produces a random number between 0 and 1, and puts that number in the variable **a**. Each time this statement is executed, it "spins the spinner" again and produces another random number. Here is a very short True BASIC program that produces and prints 10 random numbers:

```
!      Generate and print ten random numbers
!
FOR i = 1 TO 10
LET a = RND
PRINT USING "##.######": a
NEXT i
END
```

Table 1.7 is the output from a run of this program. Notice that it produced a list of 10 apparently random numbers.

We can use the random number generator to simulate flipping a coin 10 times. We will think of the spinner as being divided into two parts.

Table 1.7
Ten Random Numbers

Random Numbers
.548508
.078269
.687876
.335258
.951922
.823726
.540729
.084583
.391326
.582497

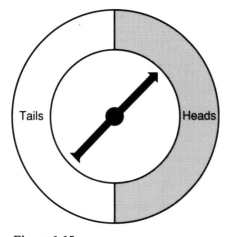

Figure 1.15
A game spinner for flipping coins

One part, corresponding to the numbers 0–0.50 we will call "heads" and the other part corresponding to the numbers between 0.50–1 we will call "tails" (Figure 1.15).

The following True BASIC program uses this idea to "flip a coin" 10 times and print out the results:

```
!      "Flip a coin" ten times
!
FOR i = 1 TO 10
LET a = RND
IF a < 0.5 THEN
```

```
      PRINT "Heads"
   ELSE
      PRINT "Tails"
END IF
NEXT i
END
```

Table 1.8
Ten Coin Flips

Face of Coin
Tails
Heads
Tails
Heads
Tails
Tails
Tails
Heads
Heads
Tails

The output from this program is shown in Table 1.8. You should compare this output with that in Table 1.7. Both True BASIC programs generated the same sequence of random numbers. The difference is that the second program did not print out the random numbers. Instead it printed either "Heads" if the random number was less than 0.5 or "Tails" if the random number was greater than or equal to 0.5.

Before continuing, note one fine point. The random number generator in True BASIC produces random numbers that are greater than or equal to 0 and are less than 1. That is, $0 \leq \text{RND} < 1$. In other words, the random numbers generated can sometimes be 0 but are never 1.

Using this random number generator it is simple to write a program that will simulate the experiment discussed earlier. Try to do so now. Write a program that will do 1,000 trials. Each trial will involve flipping a coin 10 times. Your program should keep track of how often exactly five heads occur. After you have tried to write your own program, look at the following True BASIC program:

```
!      Do 1000 coin-flipping experiments
!
!      This function does one trial.
!
DEF flip
LET count = 0
FOR i = 1 TO 10    ! Flip a coin ten times
IF RND < 0.5 THEN LET count = count + 1
NEXT i
IF count = 5 THEN
    LET flip = 1
  ELSE
    LET flip = 0
  END IF
END DEF
!
LET fives = 0              ! Number of five head trials
FOR trial = 1 TO 1000     ! Do 1,000 trials
LET fives = fives + flip
NEXT trial
PRINT USING "Number of fives ####": fives
END
```

When I ran this program, exactly five heads occurred 259 times. Your result will probably be fairly close to this one. These results do not tell us exactly how often exactly five heads will occur; they are just experiments. But these experiments do give us a good idea of how likely one is to get exactly five heads in 10 flips. We would expect exactly five heads roughly one-quarter of the time.

Next we want to look at two of the finer points of random number generators:

1. Experiments like this do not give exact results. If different people run the same experiment, they may very well obtain different results. One question you might have is how accurate these experimental results are. How widely are experimental results likely to differ from theoretically perfect results? One way to get some idea about how

much experimental results can vary is to run many different experiments and compare their results. It is thus important to be able to run different experiments. In order to do this we need to be able to produce a different sequence of random numbers for each experiment. The True BASIC statement RANDOMIZE causes RND to generate a new sequence of random numbers. Using this statement, you can perform many different experiments.

2. It is important to be able to repeat a program and get exactly the same sequence as the last time it was run. This is an essential capability when you are checking out a program. True BASIC always gives the same sequence unless the RANDOMIZE statement is used.

Compare the following True BASIC program with our original program. Each time you run the original program, you will obtain exactly the same results. However, the program below will usually yield different results each time it is run because of the RANDOMIZE statement.

```
!       Do 1000 coin-flipping experiments
!
!       This function does one trial.
!
DEF flip
LET count = 0
FOR i = 1 TO 10    ! Flip a coin ten times
IF RND < 0.5 THEN LET count = count + 1
NEXT i
IF count = 5 THEN
    LET flip = 1
  ELSE
    LET flip = 0
  END IF
END DEF
!
RANDOMIZE
LET fives = 0            ! Number of five head trials
FOR trial = 1 TO 1000    ! Do 1,000 trials
LET fives = fives + flip
```

```
NEXT trial
PRINT USING "Number of fives ####": fives
END
```

The remainder of this project consists of three examples followed by some exercises. Read all of the examples carefully since they illustrate a number of important techniques. Then do the exercises.

Example

We would like to know how likely the number 7 is to occur when two dice are thrown. Each die has six numbers—1, 2, 3, 4, 5, 6—which are equally likely to occur. In order to simulate the throw of one die, we need to be able to choose randomly an element from the set: $\{1, 2, 3, 4, 5, 6\}$. The random number generator RND produces random real numbers between 0 and 1 (possibly 0 but never 1). Suppose we multiply such a number by 6. Notice:

$$0 \leq \text{RND} < 1$$

So,

$$0 \leq 6 * \text{RND} < 6$$

and adding 1 we get:

$$1 \leq 1 + 6 * \text{AND} < 7.$$

In other words $1 + 6 * \text{RND}$ is a number like:
1.5463 or 6.395 or 3.9782 or 6.8224 or 2.8300 or 4.1194 or ...
We will convert this into an integer by the True BASIC statement:

```
LET a = INT (1 + 6*RND)
```

The INT function takes a nonnegative real number and removes everything to the right of the decimal point. Thus, for example:

$$\text{INT}(2.8574) = 2$$

and INT (1 + 6*RND) will be either 1, 2, 3, 4, 5, or 6. The following short True BASIC program illustrates this technique:

```
!    Simulate ten throws of a die
!
FOR i = 1 TO 10
LET a = INT(1 + 6 * RND)
PRINT a
NEXT i
END
```

The output from this program is shown in Table 1.9. Compare Tables 1.7, 1.8, and 1.9. They use the same 10 random numbers in different ways.

When a person rolls a pair of dice, he or she adds together the numbers that come up. For example, if one die stops with the number 3 on top and the other stops with the number 5 on top, we say that $3 + 5 = 8$ was rolled. This can be simulated by a statement like:

```
LET r = INT (1 + 6 * RND) + INT (1 + 6 * RND)
```

Notice that this is quite different from:

```
Let s = 2 * INT (1 + 6 * RND)
```

The first statement simulates rolling two dice and adding the results. The second statement simulates rolling just one die and doubling the result.

Now we can write a program to do an experiment that simulates 1,000 trials. In each trial we simulate rolling a pair of dice and record which number was rolled. We keep track of how many times the number 2 is rolled in the variable count(2), of how many times the number 3

Table 1.9
Ten Rolls of a Die

Face
4
1
5
3
6
5
4
1
3
4

was rolled in the variable count(3), and so forth. The lowest possible result of rolling two dice is 2 (two 1s, sometimes called snake eyes). The highest possible result is 12 (two 6s, sometimes called box cars).

```
!       Experiment rolling a pair of dice 1,000 times
!
!       This function does one trial
!
DEF trial
    LET trial = INT(1 + 6 * RND) + INT(1 + 6 * RND)
END DEF
DIM count(2 to 12)
FOR i = 1 TO 1000
LET result = trial
LET count(result) = count(result) + 1
NEXT i
FOR i = 2 TO 12
PRINT USING "## ###":i,count(i)
NEXT i
END
```

The results from one run of this program are shown in Table 1.10. Of course, your results may be somewhat different. This program also demonstrates one of the fine points of the DIM statement. Notice that the only possible results of throwing a pair of dice are 2, 3, 4, ..., 12. Thus, we only need 11 drawers in the file cabinet created by the DIM statement labeled 2, 3, 4, ..., 12. We can create a file cabinet of this sort by the statement

```
DIM count (2 to 12)
```

We have saved a very small amount of memory by using this statement instead of

```
DIM count(12)
```

However, this new kind of DIM statement often is very powerful. Later we will frequently use statements like

```
DIM a(0 to 100)
```

because it is useful to have a drawer labeled "drawer 0."

Table 1.10
Results of Rolling a Pair of Dice

Result	Number of Times
2	24
3	42
4	79
5	130
6	147
7	165
8	143
9	101
10	81
11	68
12	20

Example

In this example we will study an interesting situation involving examinations in a college course. You may have had the experience of preparing for an examination and feeling that you were well prepared, only to find out when the examination was passed out that the teacher "asked all the wrong questions." This example will explore this phenomenon.

Suppose that the examination in question will be graded according to the curve shown in Table 1.11. Suppose further that you know roughly 85% of the material in the course very well—or, more precisely, that of all the possible questions the teacher might ask, you would be able to answer 85% correctly. Thus, you would expect to get a solid B.

But the exam has only a certain number of questions. For this example we will suppose that the exam has 25 questions. The probability that you will be able to answer the first question correctly is 85%, or 0.85.

Table 1.11
Examination "Curve"

Result	Grade
90 – 100%	A
80 – 89%	B
70 – 79%	C
60 – 69%	D
0 – 59%	E

The probability that you will be able to answer the second question correctly is also 0.85, and so on.

Our model for this situation is that for each of the 25 questions, the teacher reaches into a bag containing all the possible questions she might ask. She chooses each question randomly, so there is an 85% likelihood that each choice will be a question that you can answer. We will simulate each choice by using the random number generator to choose a random number between 0 and 1. If the number is less than 0.85 then she has chosen a question that you can answer. If the number is greater than or equal to 0.85, then she has chosen a question that you cannot answer. Each trial consists of choosing 25 random numbers and counting the total number of answerable questions. Our experiment will consist of 1,000 trials, and we will keep track of how many trials result in a grade of A, B, C, D, and F. The following program carries out this experiment. You might try to write such a program yourself before looking at the program here which uses a new element of True BASIC: a *subroutine*. A subroutine is very much like a function. The difference is that a subroutine does not return a single piece of output the way that a function does. A subroutine does some computations and performs various tasks. The result may be no output, lots of output, graphics, or even sound. A subroutine begins with a line like SUB NameofSubroutine and ends with the line END SUB. Another program or another subroutine or function uses a subroutine with a line like CALL NameofSubroutine.

```
!    Simulate 25 examinations
!
!    Subroutine to simulate one exam
!
SUB OneExam
    LET score = 0
    FOR question = 1 TO 25
    IF RND < .85 THEN
        LET score = score + 1
    END IF
    NEXT question
    IF score/25 < 0.60 THEN
        LET f = f + 1
```

```
    ELSE IF score/25 < 0.70 THEN
       LET d = d + 1
    ELSE IF score/25 < 0.80 THEN
       LET c = c + 1
    ELSE IF score/25 < 0.90 THEN
       LET b = b + 1
    ELSE
       LET a = a + 1
    END IF
END SUB
!
LET a = 0    ! Number of a's
LET b = 0    ! Number of b's
LET c = 0    ! Number of c's
LET d = 0    ! Number of d's
LET f = 0    ! Number of f's
!
FOR trial = 1 to 1000
CALL OneExam
NEXT trial
!
PRINT USING "Number of As ###":a
PRINT USING "Number of Bs ###":b
PRINT USING "Number of Cs ###":c
PRINT USING "Number of Ds ###":d
PRINT USING "Number of Fs ###":f
END
```

The output from this program, shown in Table 1.12, is rather startling. In 58% of the trials, the test score agreed with the expected grade, B. But 42% of the time it did not. Notice that 16.5% of the time the exam grade was lower than the expected grade. In fact, for 28 trials (2.8% of the time) the exam grade was a D.

Before panicking, notice that this experiment is only a small beginning in studying the vicissitudes of course examinations. We used an extremely simple model. Our model assumed that the possible questions

Table 1.12
Examination "Curve"

Result	Number of Times
A	252
B	583
C	137
D	28
E	0

on the exam were all independent of each other. By this we mean that each choice the teacher made had nothing to do with any of the other choices. In fact, when a teacher writes an exam, she is usually very careful to choose questions that evenly represent the topics covered in the class. She is careful not to omit any topic or to choose too many questions on any single topic. Thus, her choices are not independent of each other.

Many other factors are important in an actual exam. For example, a student who happens to have three exams on the same day will be unable to spend as much time the day before the exam studying for each one as if they were on different days, or a student might have a terrible cold, or might have been awake very late the night before, or.... A large part of the intelligent use of computers to answer real questions is designing models that are good representations of the actual situation.

Example

Two baseball teams are about to play in the World Series. Team A is considerably better than team B. In fact, on any given day Team A has a 55% chance of beating Team B. In the World Series the teams play up to seven games. The first team to accumulate four victories wins the series.

The purpose of this experiment is to estimate experimentally how likely Team A is to win the World Series. Each trial in our experiment will consist of simulating seven games. The experiment will have 1,000 trials and will count how many times Team A wins the series. The following program carries out this experiment. Attempt to write such a program yourself before looking at this program.

```
!   World Series Simulation
!
!   Subroutine to Play One World Series
!
SUB OneSeries
LET WonGames = 0
FOR game = 1 TO 7
IF RND < .55 THEN
   LET WonGames = WonGames + 1
END IF
NEXT game
IF WonGames >= 4 THEN
   LET wins = wins + 1
END IF
END SUB
!
LET wins = 0   ! Number of won World Series.
FOR series = 1 TO 1000
CALL OneSeries
NEXT series
PRINT USING "Team A won ### times.":wins
END
```

A World Series simulation using this program resulted in 617 wins for Team A and 383 wins for Team B. Despite the fact that Team A is significantly better than Team B, Team A appears to have a substantial chance of losing the World Series.

Once again, our model is simple. For example, it assumes that each game is independent of the others when in fact the games are actually closely related. For example, suppose one team has a spectacular starting pitcher. If he is used in a game, he cannot start again for at least three or four days.

Think of the following exercises as a starting point for your explorations with the laws of chance. You may want to try other experiments involving questions of particular interest to you.

Exercises

As you may have already discovered, some of these programs can take a long time to run. Depending on your time, computer, and patience, you may want to do fewer trials than are asked for in the exercises. This is particularly true during checkout. Your results will be much more reliable if you use a large number of trials. However, to conserve time, you may want to use fewer trials until you are certain that your program is working.

Exercise 1.7.51 One way in which teachers try to make their exams fair is to use longer exams. Repeat the second example, but use an exam with 50 questions.

Exercise 1.7.52 Repeat the World Series example but try a series with the best of nine games.

Exercise 1.7.53 In the next election 53% of the voters will vote for Hiram Winner, and 47% will vote for Joe Loser. Barbara Poler is doing a survey for a national news magazine and interviews 500 voters chosen at random. She asks each voter for whom he or she will vote. On the basis of these 500 interviews she will predict the winner. Her predictions are based on the following: If at least 52% of her interviewees will vote for a particular candidate, then she predicts that candidate will win. If neither candidate has a 52% majority, then she reports that the race is too close to call.

How likely is she to predict correctly that Hiram Winner will win?

How likely is she to predict incorrectly that Joe Loser will win?

How likely is she to conclude that the race is too close to call?

1.8   Some Investigations into Jury Selection

This project was inspired by Hans Zeisel's extremely interesting article, "Dr. Spock and the Case of the Vanishing Women Jurors," *University of Chicago Law Review*, volume 37 (1969-1970), pages 1-18.

During the Vietnam War, Dr. Benjamin Spock was one of the most well-known antiwar activists. He and several associates were tried for

Table 1.13
Do you describe yourself as a "hawk" or a "dove?"

Gender	Hawk	Dove	No opinion
Men	50%	33%	17%
Women	32%	49%	19%

conspiring to violate the Military Service Act of 1967. The case was argued on January 7, 1969, before a jury of 12—none of them women. This fact was cause for some concern on the defense side and might well have been heartening to the prosecution. Dr. Spock is a well-known pediatrician and the author of a best-selling book on child care. He is a particularly respectable and respected figure, especially to millions of mothers. Moreover, a Gallup Poll taken in April 1968 showed that women were more likely than men to be doves. Table 1.13 reports the answers in the Gallup Poll to the question:

"People are called 'hawks' if they want to step up our military effort in Vietnam. They are called 'doves' if they want to reduce our military effort in Vietnam. How would you describe yourself—as a 'hawk' or a 'dove'?"

The trial was held in the U.S. District Court for the District of Massachusetts. The selection of the jury began with a list of all residents aged 21 and older; 56% of the people on this list were women. From this list a "venire" of potential jurors was selected. The actual jury is chosen in court by the judge and lawyers from this venire. In the Spock trial the venire contained only 9% women. The article on which this section is based contains a detailed description of the process by which the original list containing 56% women was reduced to a venire with only 9% women. In this project we want to examine the next stage of the process, the one that finally resulted in no women at all being on the jury.

The final stage in the selection of a jury occurs in the courtroom. Prospective jurors from the venire are interviewed one by one. Lawyers from both sides can ask questions and can ask the judge to disqualify a prospective juror *for cause*. For example, if a prospective juror personally knows one of the people on trial, he or she would be disqualified for cause. In addition, each side has a certain number of *peremptory challenges* which allow the disqualification of a juror without requiring any justification. This final stage in the selection of the jury continues until enough people (usually 12 plus several alternates) have been chosen. The choice of a jury is a crucial part of the trial. Both sides try to obtain a jury that is most likely to favor their own side. The peremptory challenges provide an important weapon for lawyers trying to shape the jury in their favor. In the Dr. Spock case the prosecution used one peremptory challenge to eliminate the only woman from the final jury.

This case raises a large number of questions. One set of questions deals with the system that allowed a venire with only 9% women in the first place. Some of these questions are discussed in the article. Since the Dr. Spock trial, a number of changes have been made in the process by which venires are selected. The other set of questions involves the idea and use of peremptory challenges. There are some sound reasons for allowing the use of peremptory challenges; however, this use can have serious consequences. The purpose of this project is to study these consequences so that if we do accept the use of peremptory challenges, at least we are aware of the consequences.

Often one lawyer or another might want to eliminate members of a minority from a jury. For example, the prosecution in a case against a physician might want to eliminate physicians from the jury. In a case involving an elderly victim the defense might want to eliminate elderly jurors. Although women are a majority of the general population, they were a small minority of the venire from which the Dr. Spock jury was chosen.

We want to examine how and to what extent the system of peremptory challenges makes it possible to eliminate members of a minority from a jury. The laws governing jury selection vary from jurisdiction to jurisdiction and from one time to another. We will work with the system prevailing for the Dr. Spock jury. In this system the jury was composed of 12 people, and each side had three peremptory challenges. We will also assume that one side is using its peremptory challenges solely to eliminate members of a particular minority, and the other side is using its peremptory challenges solely in order to increase the number of that same minority on the eventual jury by eliminating as many members of the majority as possible. These assumptions are, of course, simplifications; nonetheless, this model will enable us to get some insight into the potential consequences of the system of peremptory challenges.

The sample program below is a first attempt to understand how the system of peremptory challenges can influence the number of minority members on a jury. This program runs an experiment consisting of 1000 trials (*trials* used in the statistical sense). Each trial consists of the selection of one jury of 12 people with one side using its peremptory challenges to eliminate members of the minority and the other side using its peremptory challenges to eliminate members of the majority. The program will keep track of the minority membership of the resulting juries. As in the Dr. Spock trial this program assumes that 9% of people in the venire are members of the minority.

It would be worthwhile to try to write this program yourself. If necessary you may look at the True BASIC program below. After you have attempted to write this program and have looked at the program below, read the notes following the program to be sure that you understand it.

```
!     Investigate Jury Selection
!
!     Simulate the choice of a Jury for a Trial
!
DEF OneTrial
   LET MinorityChallenges = 0
   LET MajorityChallenges = 0
   LET Jury = 0
   LET NumberMinority = 0
   DO WHILE (Jury < 12)
      IF RND < .09 THEN
         IF MinorityChallenges < 3 THEN
            LET MinorityChallenges = MinorityChallenges + 1
         ELSE
            LET Jury = Jury + 1
            LET NumberMinority = NumberMinority + 1
         END IF
      ELSE
         IF MajorityChallenges < 3 THEN
            LET MajorityChallenges = MajorityChallenges + 1
```

```
          ELSE
              LET Jury = Jury + 1
          END IF
      END IF
   LOOP
   LET OneTrial = NumberMinority
END DEF
!
DIM count (13)
FOR trial = 1 TO 1000
LET i = OneTrial + 1
LET count(i) = count(i) + 1
NEXT trial
FOR i = 0 TO 12
PRINT USING "Minority members ## count ###":i,count(i+1)
NEXT i
END
```

This program uses a new True BASIC element: the DO WHILE ...
LOOP statements. These statements, like the FOR ... NEXT statements,
are used to repeat a part of the program several times. A DO WHILE ...
LOOP section of code requires three parts.

A statement marking the start of the loop. This statement has the
following parts:

- The words DO WHILE.

- A condition enclosed in parentheses. True BASIC will keep repeating the statements enclosed between the DO WHILE statement and
  the LOOP statement as long as this condition is true. In the program
  above, the condition is Jury < 12 and the appropriate statements
  will be repeated until there are 12 people on the jury.

1. The statements that are to be repeated.

2. The statement LOOP. This statement marks the end of the loop.

This program uses a function OneTrial to simulate the selection of a
jury for one trial. This function uses four variables to keep track of the
current status of jury selection:

1. The variable `MinorityChallenges` keeps track of how many peremptory challenges have been used so far in this jury selection by one side to exclude minority members from the jury. At the beginning of the trial, the value of this variable is set to 0.

2. The variable `MajorityChallenges` keeps track of how many peremptory challenges have been used so far in this jury selection by the other side to exclude majority members from the jury. At the beginning of the trial, this variable is set equal to 0.

3. The variable `Jury` keeps track of how many jurors have already been selected. At the beginning of the trial, this variable is set equal to 0.

4. The variable `NumberMinority` keeps track of the number of minority members on the jury.

The statements repeated by the `DO WHILE ... LOOP` simulate the consideration of a single prospective juror. These statements are repeated until the jury is complete (12 jurors have been seated). The first statement of this loop

```
IF RND < PercentMinority/100 THEN
```

checks whether the next prospective juror is a member of the minority. If so, the next statements

```
        IF MinorityChallenges < 3 THEN
            LET MinorityChallenges = MinorityChallenges + 1
        ELSE
            LET Jury = Jury + 1
            LET NumberMinority = NumberMinority + 1
        END IF
```

check whether the side trying to exclude minority members has any peremptory challenges left (`IF MinorityChallenges < 3`). If so, 1 is added to the count of challenges used to exclude minority members and the prospective juror is excluded by a peremptory challenge. If not, the prospective juror is seated on the jury; 1 is added to the count of jurors (`Jury`), and 1 is added to the count of minority members on the jury (`NumberMinority`).

If the prospective juror is not a member of the minority, then the following statements are executed:

```
IF MajorityChallenges < 3 THEN
    LET MajorityChallenges = MajorityChallenges + 1
ELSE
    LET Jury = Jury + 1
END IF
```

The first statement in this group checks to see whether the side trying to exclude majority members (in order to include minority members) has any peremptory challenges left. If so, 1 is added to the count of peremptory challenges used to exclude majority members and the prospective juror is excluded by a peremptory challenge. If not, the prospective juror is seated on the jury, and 1 is added to the count of jurors.

This process continues until the jury has been filled (12 jurors have been chosen). The function **OneTrial** then returns the number of minority members on the resulting jury to the main part of the program.

The main part of the program has no new elements.

You can now use this program to get a rough idea of how effectively peremptory challenges can eliminate minority members from juries. My results are shown in Table 1.14. Notice that 928 juries of 1,000 included no women at all and another 51 juries included only one woman. You can see that the system of peremptory challenges, in effect, gives each side the power to eliminate a 9% minority from the jury. This is not a 100% certainty, but it is close—roughly 93% sure. If you run this same program, your results may be somewhat different because it uses a random simulation.

Your programming assignment for this project is to write a program that will use the following input:

- The percentage of a given minority in the venire.
- The number of peremptory challenges each side has.

The program will perform 1000 trials. Each trial will simulate the selection of a jury of 12 people, with one side using its challenges to eliminate members of the minority and the other side using its challenges to eliminate members of the majority. The output of the program will be a list showing how many juries have no minority members, how many have one minority member, how many have two minority members, and so on.

Table 1.14
Jury Results for a Minority of 9%

Minority Members	Number of Trials
0	928
1	51
2	18
3	3
4	0
5	0
6	0
7	0
8	0
9	0
10	0
11	0
12	0

Exercises

Exercise 1.8.54 Run your program with a minority that is 10% of the venire and with each side having three peremptory challenges. Make a bar graph showing the results of this run.

Exercise 1.8.55 Run your program with the same minority percentage but with each side having only two peremptory challenges. Make a bar graph showing the results of this run.

Exercise 1.8.56 Do the same for one peremptory challenge.

Exercise 1.8.57 Do the thing for zero peremptory challenges.
   Finally, compare the four bar graphs.

II USING PERSONAL MATHEMATICS

This part is the heart of this book and course. Now that you know some basic programming in True BASIC, we will use mathematics and computers to investigate real problems of real importance in the real world.

2 Probability and Statistics

In Sections 1.7 and 1.8 we used the computer to investigate some phenomena involving the laws of chance. In this chapter we will study probability, the science of chance and its extremely useful offspring, statistics. The experimental techniques we studied in the last two sections will be very useful in this chapter as well. In addition, we will learn about some theoretical techniques for studying probability and statistics.

Statistical evidence has become extremely important in our society. For example, it is often the first evidence warning about a particular public health problem. In fact, statistical evidence is often the most important evidence involved in studying public health problems. Used intelligently, this evidence can be an extremely powerful and useful tool.

Every four years we are bombarded with statistical evidence in the form of public opinion polls telling us which candidate is ahead in the race for president. Candidates often use public opinion polls to determine what the voters think about particular issues. Sometimes they even modify their own opinions or at least their rhetoric in response to the polls. These public opinion polls make interesting reading, but they are quite dangerous. Slight changes in the way questions are worded or how they are asked can produce large changes in how people answer. There is a fundamental difference between answering a question for a poll taker and actually voting for president. Thus, even the best election eve polls can be misleading. Poll takers interviewing voters as they exited the polls in the elections of fall 1989 found out that voters sometimes even lie. In those exit polls voters were asked for whom they had just voted. The responses were off by as much as 10% when they were compared later with the actual vote tally.

Even more worrisome is the specter of candidates' tailoring their speeches to the results of public opinion polls. We need leaders with a clear sense of direction for the country, not technicians who are adept at adding up the figures on computer printouts and putting together a speech with the right catch phrases to assemble a majority.

This is primarily a course in computer-based quantitative reasoning. We will concentrate on the mathematical aspects of probability and statistics. These mathematical aspects are fundamental to understanding statistics, but they are only one part of the study and use of statistics.

2.1   Some Basic Probability Theory

We begin this chapter by considering carefully exactly what we mean by the likelihood or probability of a particular event. We will always measure probability using a number between 0 and 1. When we say that the probability of a particular event is 0, we mean that this event will not occur. When we say that the probability of a particular event is 1, we mean that it will occur without any doubt. In everyday English we usually say we are "100% sure" of something rather than saying that it has "probability 1." However, these two phrases express exactly the same thought. When we say that an event has probability 1/2, we mean that it has a 50% chance of occurring. In other words it is equally likely to occur or not to occur.

The easiest situation in which to study probability is when there are only a finite number of possibilities. For example, suppose that we are interested in studying what happens when we throw a pair of dice. There are exactly 36 possible outcomes. In order to keep the two dice straight, we will use one that is white and one that is gray. We will use the notation (a, b) to mean that the white die lands with face a up and the gray die lands with face b up. For example, $(2, 4)$ means that the white die lands with face 2 up, and the gray die lands with face 4 up. Using this notation, we can list the 36 possible outcomes:

(1, 1)(1, 2)(1, 3)(1, 4)(1, 5)(1, 6)
(2, 1)(2, 2)(2, 3)(2, 4)(2, 5)(2, 6)
(3, 1)(3, 2)(3, 3)(3, 4)(3, 5)(3, 6)
(4, 1)(4, 2)(4, 3)(4, 4)(4, 5)(4, 6)
(5, 1)(5, 2)(5, 3)(5, 4)(5, 5)(5, 6)
(6, 1)(6, 2)(6, 3)(6, 4)(6, 5)(6, 6)

The set of all possible outcomes is called the *probability space*. For this example the probability space is the set shown in Figure 2.1. We will denote this set by the letter W. If we are rolling fair dice, then each of the 36 outcomes in the set W is equally likely. Thus, each outcome has probability 1/36. We are often interested in the probability of a particular subset of the probability space. For example, suppose we want to know how likely we are to roll a 7. That is, we are interested in

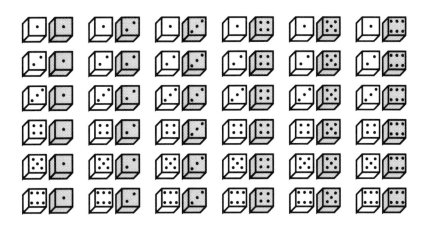

Figure 2.1
Possible outcomes of throwing two dice

Figure 2.2
The event of rolling 7

the set E of outcomes shown in Figure 2.2. Symbolically we denote the set E by

$$E = \{(1, 6), (2, 5), (3, 4), (4, 3), (5, 2), (6, 1)\}.$$

The set E is called the event of "rolling a 7." We will use the following terms for discussing probability:

- The set of possibilities is called the *probability space*.

- Each possibility is called an *outcome*.

- A subset of the probability space is called an *event*.

We are usually interested in the probability of a particular event, E. Consider the following events:

- The event, D, of rolling "doubles." That is, the two dice have the same face up:

$$D = \{(1,1),(2,2),(3,3),(4,4),(5,5),(6,6)\}.$$

- The event, T, of rolling at least 11:

$$T = \{(5,6),(6,5),(6,6)\}.$$

If the probability space, W, is finite and each of the outcomes is equally likely, then the probability of an event, E, is

$$\text{Probability of } E = \frac{\text{Number of elements in } E}{\text{Number of elements in } W}.$$

We will use the notation $P(E)$ for the probability of an event E and $\overline{\overline{E}}$ for the number of elements in the set E. Thus,

$$P(E) = \overline{\overline{E}}/\overline{\overline{W}}.$$

In our first example E was the event of rolling a 7 and

$$P(E) = \frac{6}{36} = \frac{1}{6}.$$

For the next two examples,

$$P(D) = \frac{6}{36} = \frac{1}{6}$$

and

$$P(T) = \frac{3}{36} = \frac{1}{12}.$$

Sometimes the outcomes are not all equally likely. Perhaps some nefarious character has skillfully shaved some of the edges or weighted some of the faces of a pair of dice. If so, certain faces would be more likely to come up than other faces. Such dice are called "loaded" dice and make the probabilist's job more difficult. If the outcomes are not equally likely, then we need to know the probability of each outcome.

Table 2.1
Probability of Each Face

Face	Probability
1	0.1
2	0.1
3	0.1
4	0.2
5	0.2
6	0.3

For example, suppose one die has been modified so that the probability of each face is as given in Table 2.1.

Notice that the probabilities in Table 2.1 add up to 1 because it is certain that one of these six faces will come up. Our probability space is $W = \{1, 2, 3, 4, 5, 6\}$, and the probability of each outcome is given by Table 2.1. For example, $P(2) = 0.1$ and $P(5) = 0.2$. Now suppose that we are interested in the probability of rolling an odd number. In other words, we are interested in the event $E = \{1, 3, 5\}$. We can calculate the probability of this event by adding up the probabilities of each of the outcomes in E:

$$P(E) = P(1) + P(3) + P(5) = 0.1 + 0.1 + 0.2 = 0.4.$$

More generally, if E is any event in a finite probability space, then

$$P(E) = \text{The sum of the probabilities of the outcomes in } E.$$

Exercises

The following exercises all have to do with flipping a coin four times. The possible outcomes of this experiment are listed in Table 2.2. We are interested in the following probability space:

$$W = \{HHHH, HHHT, HHTH, HHTT, HTHH, HTHT, HTTH,$$
$$HTTT, THHH, THHT, THTH, THTT, TTHH, TTHT,$$
$$TTTH, TTTT\}.$$

Notice that there are 16 possible outcomes. If the coin is a fair one, flipped in a fair way, then these 16 outcomes are all equally likely. Find the probability of each of the following events.

Table 2.2
Possible Outcomes of Four Coin Flips

Flip 1	Flip 2	Flip 3	Flip 4	Abbreviation
Heads	Heads	Heads	Heads	HHHH
Heads	Heads	Heads	Tails	HHHT
Heads	Heads	Tails	Heads	HHTH
Heads	Heads	Tails	Tails	HHTT
Heads	Tails	Heads	Heads	HTHH
Heads	Tails	Heads	Tails	HTHT
Heads	Tails	Tails	Heads	HTTH
Heads	Tails	Tails	Tails	HTTT
Tails	Heads	Heads	Heads	THHH
Tails	Heads	Heads	Tails	THHT
Tails	Heads	Tails	Heads	THTH
Tails	Heads	Tails	Tails	THTT
Tails	Tails	Heads	Heads	TTHH
Tails	Tails	Heads	Tails	TTHT
Tails	Tails	Tails	Heads	TTTH
Tails	Tails	Tails	Tails	TTTT

*Exercise 2.1.1** Flipping a total of two heads and two tails.

*Exercise 2.1.2** Flipping a total of three heads and one tail.

*Exercise 2.1.3** Flipping a total of one head and three tails.

*Exercise 2.1.4** Flipping either all heads or all tails.

For the next four exercises, we will assume that we are flipping a loaded coin. This coin has been weighted so that on each flip, the probability of getting heads is 0.6 and the probability of getting tails is 0.4. Table 2.3 gives the probability of each of the 16 outcomes using this loaded coin. Notice that these probabilities add up to 1.

Later in this section, we will discuss the way in which the probability of each of these individual outcomes was calculated. Find the probability of each of the following events:

*Exercise 2.1.5** Flipping a total of two heads and two tails.

Exercise 2.1.6 Flipping a total of three heads and one tail.

Exercise 2.1.7 Flipping a total of three tails and one head.

Exercise 2.1.8 Flipping either all heads or all tails.

Table 2.3
Possible Outcomes of Four Coin Flips

Flip 1	Flip 2	Flip 3	Flip 4	Abbreviation	Probability
Heads	Heads	Heads	Heads	HHHH	.1296
Heads	Heads	Heads	Tails	HHHT	.0864
Heads	Heads	Tails	Heads	HHTH	.0864
Heads	Heads	Tails	Tails	HHTT	.0576
Heads	Tails	Heads	Heads	HTHH	.0864
Heads	Tails	Heads	Tails	HTHT	.0576
Heads	Tails	Tails	Heads	HTTH	.0576
Heads	Tails	Tails	Tails	HTTT	.0384
Tails	Heads	Heads	Heads	THHH	.0864
Tails	Heads	Heads	Tails	THHT	.0576
Tails	Heads	Tails	Heads	THTH	.0576
Tails	Heads	Tails	Tails	THTT	.0384
Tails	Tails	Heads	Heads	TTHH	.0576
Tails	Tails	Heads	Tails	TTHT	.0384
Tails	Tails	Tails	Heads	TTTH	.0384
Tails	Tails	Tails	Tails	TTTT	.0256

One of the most important notions in probability is that of independence. This is a precise mathematical notion that is intended to capture the intuitive idea that two different events have nothing to do with each other. The opposite side of this idea is that two events have something to do with each other. In this case we say they are dependent. We will discuss these ideas in the context of our example: rolling two fair dice. This is a good mathematical context in which to study this idea because it exhibits the mathematical ideas involved without any complicating factors. There are lots of potential complicating factors. For example, one might be interested in a particular public health problem like the effect of a particular beverage on, say, heart disease. Often the first evidence that there might be a problem is a study showing a difference in the rate of heart disease between two groups of individuals: one group that regularly drinks a certain beverage and another group that rarely drinks the beverage. A careful scientist would note that regular consumption of this beverage is *associated* with an increased probability of heart disease. A statistician would say that the two events—regular consumption of the beverage and heart disease—are dependent. Notice that neither the scientist nor the statistician would say that consumption of the beverage *causes* heart disease on the basis of this evidence alone. In fact, there are many possible explanations for the observed fact that

regular consumption of the beverage is associated with an increased risk
of heart disease. For example, people who drink the beverage regularly
might frequently accompany it with a doughnut, or people who drink
the beverage regularly might be drinking it to help them stay awake. As
a group they might be eating more snack food or getting less sleep than
the nondrinkers. Other factors associated with regular consumption of
the beverage might be involved rather than the beverage itself. Scientists working on these questions must and do design careful experiments
to answer questions about the causal relationships between potential
health hazards and their possible effects.

It is important to understand two facts about statistical evidence.
First, by itself statistical evidence can be misleading. One must take
into account factors that can make its interpretation difficult. Second,
however, statistical evidence can be very good and reliable. Many people
have learned the first fact. One hears statements like: "there are three
kinds of lies: lies, damn lies, and statistics." There are books with
titles like *How to Lie with Statistics*. However, responsible scientists
and statisticians are quite good at designing experiments that can yield
reliable statistical evidence. Moreover, frequently statistical evidence
can be augmented by more direct evidence. The cigarette industry has
a long and dreadful history of denying that cigarettes kill people. The
statistical evidence is absolutely overwhelming. There is abundant medical evidence showing observable physical damage caused by cigarette
smoking. The case against cigarette smoking has been proved a thousand times over beyond any reasonable doubt. The fact that statistics
can be misused must not be used as an excuse to ignore the information
that careful, intelligent use of statistics can give us.

One must be careful and thoughtful about statistical evidence; however, statistical evidence is extraordinarily important and extremely useful. We will now examine the ideas of dependence and independence in
a simpler context. We will return to our dice.

Suppose we are told that a person rolled a pair of dice and that he
rolled a 7 (the two dice added up to 7). Now we are asked how likely
it is that at least one of the dice showed a 3. We are interested in two
events:

$$A = \{(3,1),(3,2),(3,3),(3,4),(3,5),(3,6),$$
$$(1,3),(2,3),(4,3),(5,3),(6,3)\}$$

and

$$B = \{(1,6),(2,5),(3,4),(4,3),(5,2),(6,1)\}.$$

Event A is the event that the person rolled at least one 3. Notice that this set has 11 elements. Event B is the event that the person rolled a 7. This set has six elements. Event A is pictured in Figure 2.3, and Event B is pictured in Figure 2.4.

We want to know the probability of Event A given the information that the outcome is in Event B. There is a special notation for this: $P(A|B)$. The probability of A given the information that the outcome is in B is called the *conditional probability* of A given B.

We know that one of the following outcomes occurred:

$$(1,6),(2,5),(3,4),(4,3),(5,2),(6,1).$$

Of these six outcomes, two are in the set A, $(3,4)$ and $(4,3)$. Since the outcomes are all equally likely, the probability we seek, $P(A|B)$, is 2/6 = 1/3.

Before we were told that the person rolled a 7, we knew that the probability of A was 11/36 (since A has 11 elements). After being told that the person rolled a 7, we knew that the probability of A was 1/3.

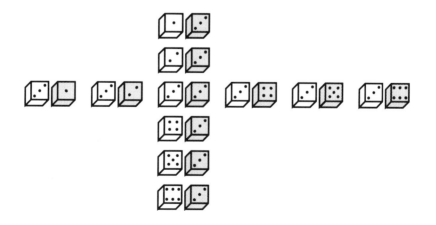

Figure 2.3
Event A: Rolling at least one 3

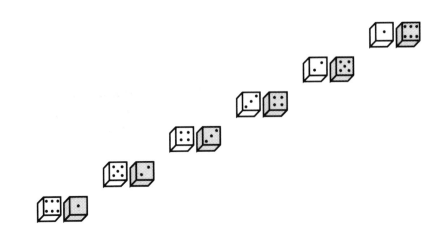

Figure 2.4
Event B: Rolling 7

Notice that these two probabilities are different. The information that the person rolled a 7 enabled us to change our evaluation of the probability that one of the two dice showed a 3. This is an example of two events that are *dependent*.

Now consider a second example. Suppose we are told that a person rolled the dice and the white die was a 1. Now we are asked how likely it is that both dice were the same. We are interested in two events:

$$C = \{(1,1), (2,2), (3,3), (4,4), (5,5), (6,6)\}$$

and

$$D = \{(1,1), (1,2), (1,3), (1,4), (1,5), (1,6)\}.$$

Event C is the event that both dice were the same. Notice that this set has six members so that the probability of this event with no further information is $6/36 = 1/6$. Event C is shown in Figure 2.5.

Event D is the event that the white die was a 1. This set has six elements. Event D is shown in Figure 2.6.

We want to know the probability of C given the information that the outcome is in D, $P(C|D)$. We know that one of the following outcomes occurred:

$$(1,1), (1,2), (1,3), (1,4), (1,5), (1,6).$$

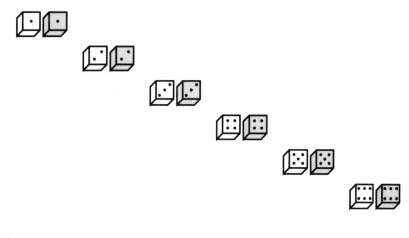

Figure 2.5
Event C: Both dice are the same

Figure 2.6
Event D: The white die is a 1

Of these six outcomes, only one $(1, 1)$ is in the set C. Since the outcomes are equally likely, the probability we seek, $P(C|D)$, is 1/6.

Before we were told that the white die was a 1, we knew that the probability of C was 1/6. After we were told that the white die was a 1, we knew that the probability of C was 1/6. Therefore, the information that the white die was a 1 did not enable us to change our evaluation of the probability of C. This is an example of two events that are *independent*.

Now we want to develop a formula for calculating conditional probabilities. Suppose we are interested in a probability space W and two events A and B. We want to calculate the conditional probability of A given B, $P(A|B)$.

The information that the outcome is in B means that we can eliminate some of the possible outcomes from consideration. This means that the remaining outcomes become more likely. We can think of B as a new

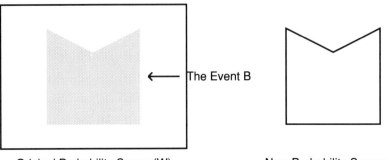

Original Probability Space (W)   New Probability Space (B)

Figure 2.7
Two probability spaces

probability space (Figure 2.7). We need to figure out the probability of each outcome in B. We are looking at two probability spaces:

Original probability space $W = \{a, b, c, ...\}$.

New probability space $B = \{a, c, ...\}$.

(The sets shown above are just examples. I have named a few of the elements in W for convenience: a, b, and c and also have shown some of the elements in B: a, and c.)

Suppose that the probability of a in the space W is $P(a)$ and that the probability of c in the space W is $P(c)$. We will denote the probabilities of a and c in the new probability space B by $P'(a)$ and $P'(c)$. Since some of the possible outcomes in W have been eliminated to get B, the remaining possible outcomes will be more likely. That is, we would expect that, for example, $P'(a) > P(a)$.

We obtained B by eliminating some of the possible outcomes from W. This information does not change our evaluation of the relative likelihood of a and c. For example, if we knew originally that c was twice as likely as a, then the information that the outcome is in B does not alter that fact. Thus, if $P(c)/P(a)$ was 2 in the old probability space, W, then in the new probability space, B, $P'(c)/P'(a)$ would also be equal to 2. This is a general rule; eliminating some outcomes from W to get B doesn't alter the relative probabilities of the remaining outcomes in B. Therefore, $P'(c)/P'(a) = P(c)/P(a)$ for any two elements a and c in B.

Let a be one particular element of W, and let k denote the number $P'(a)/P(a)$. If c is any other element of B, then

$$\frac{P'(c)}{P'(a)} = \frac{P(c)}{P(a)}.$$

So,

$$P'(c)P(a) = P(c)P'(a)$$

and

$$\frac{P'(c)}{P(c)} = \frac{P'(a)}{P(a)} = k.$$

Thus,

$$P'(c) = kP(c).$$

This argument shows that the ratio of the new probability $P'(c)$ to the old probability $P(c)$ is the same number k for any element c. We need to find out what the number k is.

Since we are considering B as a probability space, the sum of the probabilities $P'(a)$ for all the elements in B must be 1. But this sum is just the sum of $kP(a)$ for all the elements a in B. Therefore,

$$k \times (\text{sum of } P(a) \text{ for all the elements } a \text{ in } B) = 1$$

and

$$k = \frac{1}{(\text{sum of } P(a) \text{ for all the elements } a \text{ in } B)} = \frac{1}{P(B)}.$$

Finally, the conditional probability $P(A|B)$ is:

sum of $P'(a)$ for all the elements a of A that are in B

$$= k \times \text{sum } P(a) \text{ for all the elements } a \text{ of } A \cap B$$

$$= \left(\frac{1}{P(B)}\right) \times (\text{sum of } P(a) \text{ for all the elements } a \text{ of } A \cap B)$$

$$= \frac{P(A \cap B)}{P(B)}.$$

This is the formula we have been looking for:

$$P(A|B) = \frac{P(A \cap B)}{P(B)}.$$

Using this formula, we can prove an interesting theorem.

THEOREM 1   If knowledge that the outcome is in Event A doesn't tell us anything about Event B, then knowledge that the outcome is in Event B doesn't tell us anything about Event A.

Proof   Since knowledge that the outcome is in Event A doesn't tell us anything about Event B:

$$P(B|A) = P(B).$$

Therefore,

$$\frac{P(A \cap B)}{P(A)} = P(B).$$

So,

$$P(A \cap B) = P(A)P(B)$$

and

$$\frac{P(A \cap B)}{P(B)} = P(A).$$

That is,

$$P(A|B) = P(A),$$

and knowledge that the outcome is in Event B doesn't tell us anything about Event A.   ∎

Using our formula for conditional probability, we can make our definition of independence precise:

Definition:
    Two events, A and B, are *independent* if $P(A \cap B) = P(A)P(B)$. Note that this is equivalent to saying that $P(A|B) = P(A)$ and also that $P(B|A) = P(B)$.

This precise mathematical notion corresponds to our intuitive idea that A and B have nothing to do with each other.

Exercises

Determine by calculating $P(A), P(B)$, and $P(A \cap B)$ whether each of the following pairs of events is independent. Do your answers match your intuition? The first four exercises refer to the probability space described in Table 2.2 (p. 202). The coin is a fair coin, so each outcome is equally probable.

*Exercise 2.1.9

A = Flip 1 is heads.
B = Flip 3 is heads.

*Exercise 2.1.10

A = There is a total of two heads and two tails.
B = Flip 1 is heads.

*Exercise 2.1.11

A = There is a total of three heads and one tail.
B = Flip 2 is heads.

*Exercise 2.1.12

A = The first three flips are heads.
B = Flip 4 is tails.

The next four exercises refer to the probability space described in Table 2.3 (p. 103) with a loaded coin.

*Exercise 2.1.13

A = Flip 1 is heads.
B = Flip 3 is heads.

Exercise 2.1.14

A = There is a total of two heads and two tails.
B = Flip 1 is heads.

Exercise 2.1.15

A = There is a total of three heads and one tail.
B = Flip 2 is heads.

Exercise 2.1.16

A = The first three flips are heads.

B = Flip 4 is tails.

Exercises 2.1.12 and 2.1.16 are particularly interesting. In everyday conversation one frequently hears statements like:

"He's about due for a hit. He usually bats about .300, and he's gone 10 times at bat without a hit."

"The roulette wheel has landed on red five times in a row. Black is about due to come up."

"I've lost the last 10 times we've played chess. I'm about due for a win."

"The last three flips of the coin have been heads. It's about time for a tail."

The speaker often justifies such a statement by an appeal to the law of averages. The law of averages says, for example, that if a fair coin is flipped many, many times, then on the average the fraction of times that heads comes up will be approximately 1/2. It doesn't tell us anything about any individual flip of the coin. The last statement above is based on the intuitive idea that after three heads in a row, a tail is needed "to compensate" for all those heads. This statement is untrue. After many, many flips, the fraction of heads will be approximately 1/2, not exactly 1/2. This tells us nothing about any individual flip. When you do Exercises 2.1.12 and 2.1.16 you will see in two specific examples that knowledge about the first three flips doesn't give any new information about the fourth flip.

So far we have worked with finite probability spaces in which we know the probability of each individual outcome. In practice we are usually interested not in individual outcomes but in events. We have been able to develop some rules for working with probabilities of events. Now we want to summarize these rules:

Rule 1. For each event E, $P(E)$ is a number between 0 and 1; that is,

$$0 \leq P(E) \leq 1.$$

Rule 2.   The probability of the whole probability space W is 1; that is,

$$P(W) = 1.$$

Rule 3.   The probability of the empty event, $\emptyset$, is 0.

$$P(\emptyset) = 0.$$

Rule 4.   If A and B are two disjoint events (i.e., $A \cap B = \emptyset$), then

$$P(A \cup B) = P(A) + P(B).$$

Rule 5.   If A and B are two independent events, then

$$P(A \cap B) = P(A)P(B).$$

The only rules that weren't discussed earlier are Rules 3 and 4. They are intuitively clear and require no further discussion.

In practice we usually compute probabilities using these five rules rather than going back and adding up probabilities of outcomes. By working with these rules directly, we can work with very large probability spaces and even with infinite probability spaces. The following examples show how to compute probabilities by using these rules.

Example

A gambler bets \$1 on each of two spins of a roulette wheel. The probability that he wins his first bet is 18/38. The probability that he wins his second bet is 18/38. The two spins of the wheel are independent.

a. What is the probability that he wins both bets?

b. What is the probability that he loses his first bet?

c. What is the probability that he loses his second bet?

d. What is the probability that he loses both bets?

To solve these problems, we will use the following notation:

W = the probability space.

A = event that he wins his first bet.

B = event that he wins his second bet.

C = event that he loses his first bet.

D = event that he loses his second bet.

Question a asks for the probability of $A \cap B$. Since A and B are independent, $P(A \cap B) = P(A)P(B) = (18/38)(18/38) = 0.2244$.

Question b asks for the probability of C. Since A and C are disjoint events, $P(A) + P(C) = P(A \cup C) = P(W) = 1$. Therefore $P(C) = 1 - P(A) = 1 - 18/38 = 20/38$.

Question c asks for the probability of D. A similar calculation to the one above shows $P(D) = 20/38$.

Question d asks for the probability of $C \cap D$. Since C and D are independent, $P(C \cap D) = P(C)P(D) = (20/38)(20/38) = 0.2770$.

Example

Another gambler has a weighted coin. When this coin is flipped heads will occur with probability 0.6, and tails will occur with probability 0.4. The gambler flips the coin twice. The two flips are independent of each other. What is the probability that she gets two heads?

We will let A be the event that she gets heads on the first flip and B be the event that she gets heads on the second flip. The coin is weighted so that $P(A) = 0.6$ and $P(B) = 0.6$.

The event that she gets heads on both flips is $A \cap B$, and since A and B are independent, $P(A \cap B) = P(A)P(B) = (0.6)(0.6) = 0.36$.

So far we have talked only about independence in the context of two events. Frequently, however, we are interested in many events. For example, a gambler might flip a coin 100 times, and each one of these flips would be completely independent of the others. It turns out that the same rule works for computing probabilities of more than two independent events. For example, if A, B, C, and D are independent events, then $P(A \cap B \cap C \cap D) = P(A)P(B)P(C)P(D)$. This is the rule we used to compute the probabilities in Table 2.3.

Exercise

Exercise 2.1.17   Verify a few of the probabilities given in Table 2.3 using the rule above. Hint: To verify the first probability, $P(HHHH) = 0.1296$, let

A = event that heads occurs on the first flip.
B = event that heads occurs on the second flip.
C = event that heads occurs on the third flip.
D = event that heads occurs on the fourth flip.

and notice that $\{HHHH\} = A \cap B \cap C \cap D$ and that A, B, C and D are independent events.

2.2   A Matter of Taste

The following is reprinted in part from the "Once Over" section of the April 1978 issue of *Consumer Reports*.

LET IT BE LOWENBRAU—AMERICAN STYLE

What do you get when you pay a premium for a beer with a grand old European name? We put that question to a test when we got wind of the controversy involving *Lowenbrau*, a beer that originated in Germany but is now also brewed in the United States under license by Miller Brewing Co.

One element of the controversy surfaced when Anheuser-Busch Inc.—brewers of an admittedly domestic premium beer, *Michelob*—asked the Federal Trade Commission to investigate Miller for possible "consumer deception." Anheuser-Busch claims, among other things, that the *Lowenbrau* made by Miller in the U.S. is brewed with different ingredients and under a different process than the German beer.

Whether that's true or not, there's another interesting comparison to be made. Miller also brews *Miller High Life* beer. An evident difference between Miller's *Lowenbrau* and *Miller High Life* is price. Miller beer with the German name sells for $2.50 a six-pack; Miller beer with the Miller name sells for \$1.80. Miller must believe there's a difference between the two to merit the big price difference.

To determine whether there is a difference between domestic *Lowenbrau* and *Miller High Life* that would be discernible to the average beer drinker, we assembled a taste-test panel of 24 staffers. Panelists were given three glasses of beer to taste, two of which were from the same bottle, and asked to identify which glass contained the beer that was different.

Only 11 of the total of 24 judgements were correct. If the panelists were only guessing which of the three glasses of beer was the correct one, they would be expected to get the right answer about one-third of the time, or 8 of the 24. Although the 11 correct choices were an improvement over pure guesswork, we don't consider that to be statistically significant evidence that a beer drinker can tell domestic *Lowenbrau* from *Miller High Life*.

This article appears to be suggesting that there might be no tastable difference between Miller's Lowenbrau beer and Miller High Life beer. Of course, one could do a chemical analysis to determine precisely the chemical differences between the two beers, but the beer drinker is more concerned with taste than chemical analyses. The most direct way to find out about taste is by tasting as *Consumer Reports* did.

This leads us to one of the most important problems studied by statisticians: *Consumer Reports* is considering a particular hypothesis and has accumulated some statistical evidence that it believes is relevent to this hypothesis. *Does this evidence confirm or refute the hypothesis?* The reason that this question is difficult to answer is that the hypothesis involves an element of chance. Let us consider two examples that illustrate this point. Suppose a scientist is studying a particular coin and forms the hypothesis that the coin weighs 0.15 gram. This hypothesis is easy to check by weighing the coin. Now let us consider a different hypothesis about the coin: the hypothesis that the coin is fair, that is, if it were flipped a very large number of times, 50% of the time it would come up heads and 50% of the time it would come up tails. It is easy to see how to gain some evidence about this hypothesis. One might, for example, flip the coin 100 times and count the number of times it came up heads. But it is difficult to see how to interpret the results. Even a perfectly fair coin might not come up heads exactly 50 times. The problem is that this hypothesis involves an element of chance. Therefore the hypothesis does not predict a particular number; it really says that *usually* one would expect the number of heads to be *close* to 50*.

In the *Consumer Reports* case the hypothesis under consideration is, "There is no tastable difference between Miller's Lowenbrau and Miller High Life beer." This hypothesis implies that each taster will choose one of the three glasses in a completely random fashion. Since each taster must choose one of three glasses and each glass is equally likely to be chosen, the chances of his or her choosing the right glass are 1/3. We have just completed the most important step of our analysis: a clear statement of the hypothesis. This hypothesis has a special name. It is called the *null hypothesis:*

The null hypothesis: *Each taster will choose one of the three glasses in a completely random fashion.*

If this null hypothesis is true, then since *Consumer Reports* used a panel of 24 tasters, we would expect 1/3 of 24, or eight right choices. The actual result of the taste test was 11 correct choices. The question we want to examine is whether this result confirms or refutes the null hypothesis. The actual result is different from the result predicted by the null hypothesis. However, it is really unrealistic to predict that there will be exactly eight correct choices. Chance variation will enter into an experiment of this kind even if the null hypothesis is correct.

To get a rough idea of what such chance variation looks like, I wrote a short computer program to simulate the *Consumer Reports* experiment assuming the null hypothesis was correct. This program simulated 1,000 trials. Each trial simulated 24 random tasters by choosing 24 random numbers. A random number less than 1/3 corresponded to a correct choice, and a random number greater than 1/3 corresponded to an incorrect choice. For each trial the program counted the number of correct choices. Table 2.4 shows the results of these 1,000 trials. It indicates the percentage of trials resulting in 0, 1, 2, . . . , or 24 correct choices.

---

*In spirit these two examples are very good ones. In practice the line between the two is not so clear-cut. Frequently when one measures a physical quantity like the weight of a coin, there are some elements of chance involved. For example, the scale used to measure the weight of the coin might perform differently at different temperatures. Thus, the measured "weight" might depend on the temperature when the coin was weighed.

Table 2.4
Simulated Results of Random Beer Tasting

Number of Correct Choices	Percentage of Trials	Number of Correct Choices	Percentage of Trials
0	0.0%	13	1.6%
1	0.1%	14	0.4%
2	0.4%	15	0.4%
3	1.6%	16	0.1%
4	3.5%	17	0.0%
5	8.1%	18	0.0%
6	11.3%	19	0.0%
7	16.7%	20	0.0%
8	17.3%	21	0.0%
9	15.5%	22	0.0%
10	12.2%	23	0.0%
11	7.2%	24	0.0%
12	3.6%		

Notice that exactly eight correct choices occurred only 17.3% of the time. Thus, we cannot conclude that the null hypothesis was wrong just because the *Consumer Reports* panel did not report exactly eight correct choices. It is unreasonable to expect exactly eight correct choices. But it is reasonable to expect the number of correct choices to be close to eight. For example, the sum of the percentages for seven, eight and nine correct choices $(16.7 + 17.3 + 15.5)$ is 49.5%. Thus, almost half of the time, the number of correct choices was within one of the theoretically predicted number.

In Table 2.5 I computed some other probabilities based on Table 2.4. For each number n, I computed the probability that the experimental

Table 2.5
Probability of Being Close to Theoretical Prediction

n	Probability of within n	not within n
0	17.3%	82.7%
1	49.5%	50.5%
2	73.0%	27.0%
3	88.3%	11.7%
4	95.4%	4.6%
5	98.6%	1.4%

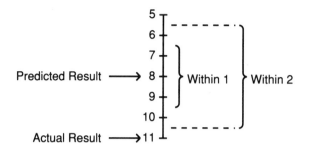

Figure 2.8
Distance between theoretical and actual result

result was within n of the predicted result, eight, and also the probability that the experimental result was not within n of the predicted result. For example, the second line of Table 2.5 shows that the probability of being within 1 of the predicted result is 49.5% and the probability of being not within 1 of the predicted result is 50.5%. The first figure is just the calculation we made above. The second figure is just 1 minus the first figure.

Table 2.5 together with Figure 2.8 provides the key to interpreting the *Consumer Reports* experimental result. Looking at Figure 2.8 we see that the actual result that *Consumer Reports* obtained just missed being within 2 of the theoretical result. Now looking at Table 2.5 we see that one would expect that 73% of the time the experimental result to be within 2, and 27% of the time the experimental result would be outside this range. Thus, the fact that the *Consumer Reports* result was 3 away from the predicted result is not at all startling even *if the null hypothesis is true* since if the null hypothesis is true, the actual result will be at least 3 correct choices away from the predicted results 27% of the time.

This computer experiment helps us to understand the last sentence quoted from the *Consumer Reports* article: "Although the 11 correct choices were an improvement over pure guesswork, we don't consider that to be statistically significant evidence that a beer drinker can tell domestic Lowenbrau from Miller High Life." This is an example of the concept of statistical significance, one of the most important concepts in the use and interpretation of statistical evidence. Let us summarize step by step exactly what we did:

1. We formulated a null hypothesis. This hypothesis describes a possible model for an observed phenomenon. In this example the model was that the 24 tasters were choosing randomly among the three glasses of beer. This is the most important part of the discussion.

2. We calculated the exact result predicted by the null hypothesis. In this example the predicted result was eight correct choices.

3. We calculated the probability of each possible result. In this example these probabilities were roughly calculated using a computer simulation. These probabilities were given in Table 2.4.

4. We made a chart (Table 2.5) showing for each number, n, how likely the result is to be within n of the predicted result and also the probability of not being within n of the predicted result.

5. We considered the actual result. In our example (Figure 2.8), the actual result was three choices away from the predicted result, so we looked at the line $n = 2$ since the actual result was greater than two away from the predicted result. This line tells us how likely the actual result or worse would be if the null hypothesis is correct. For our example, we saw that the actual result or worse would happen purely by chance with a probability of 27%. (Actually it is a little more professional to say with a probability of .27 rather than 27%.)

If this final probability is very low, then it is unlikely that we would have gotten the results we did if the null hypothesis was right. This would be strong evidence that the null hypothesis is wrong. The lower this final probability is, the stronger the evidence would be that the null hypothesis is wrong. Statisticians usually consider the evidence statistically signficant if this final probability is less than 5% (0.05). They are even happier if the final probability is less than 1% (0.01). Most statisticians will not use the phrase "statistically significant" all by itself. They will say something like, "These results are statistically significant at the .05 level," or "These results are statistically significant at the .01 level."

This analysis has to be interpreted carefully. It talks about only the null hypothesis. And even talking about the null hypothesis, it is very one-sided. This analysis can result in conclusions that refute the null hypothesis but it cannot result in conclusions that support the null hypothesis. The reason is that our discussion considered only the null hypothesis itself. There may well be other alternative models that make the same predictions as the null hypothesis. For example, perhaps the first taste of beer always tastes different from subsequent tastes. Thus, a taster might always choose the first taste regardless of anything else.

Our analysis relied on Table 2.4. The figures in this table are only rough estimates of the actual probabilities. They were obtained by a computer simulation using the random number generator. In the next section I will show how to compute these figures exactly. For the exercises below, you will need to compute tables similar to Tables 2.4 and 2.5. Use computer simulations for your computations. Because you will be using computer simulations, your answers may not be exactly right, and different members of the class may get somewhat different answers.

Exercises

Exercise 2.2.18   Suppose that a taste panel of 48 beer tasters performed a taste testing similar to the *Consumer Reports* taste testing and that the result was that 22 of 48 panelists correctly identified the different beer. Notice that this is the same proportion as in the *Consumer Reports* test. Would this new result be statistically significant at the .05 level? at the .01 level?

Exercise 2.2.19   Suppose that a taste panel of 96 beer tasters performed a taste testing similar to the *Consumer Reports* taste testing and that the result was that 44 of 96 panelists correctly identified the different beer. Notice that this is the same proportion as in the *Consumer Reports* test. Would this new result be statistically significant at the .05 level? at the .01 level?

Exercise 2.2.20   A parapsychologist has been doing an experiment to test whether a particular subject has extrasensory perception. He randomly selects one of four cards. One of the four cards has a red dot on one side, one has a green dot, one has a blue dot, and the last has a yellow dot. The other side of each card is completely blank. He chooses one of these cards randomly. He concentrates very hard on the color he has chosen and then asks the subject to identify that color. He repeats this 60 times and counts the number of correct choices his subject makes. One of his subject chooses the correct color 22 times. Is this statistically

significant at the .05 level? at the .01 level? Remember to formulate
your null hypothesis very carefully.

2.3   A Better Method

In Section 2.2 we used computer-based simulation to get a rough idea
of certain probabilities. Computer-based simulation is a powerful and
useful method, but it does have some drawbacks. Because it is based on
random simulation, it gives only a rough estimate of the actual probabilities. By simulating a large number of trials, one can get a fairly
good estimate, but there are practical limits to how many trials one can
simulate in a reasonable amount of time.

In this section we will develop a method that will enable us to calculate
exact probabilities for problems like the one we looked at in Section 2.2.
In addition, the ideas we develop in this section will be powerful and
flexible, so they will be useful for a surprising number and variety of
problems.

Many very different sounding problems turn out to be mathematically
similar. We will begin this section by describing a number of problems
that are mathematically identical to the problem of Section 2.2.

Example

Suppose you have a spinner divided into two sections like the one
shown in Figure 2.9. One section comprises one-third of the spinner and
is gray, the other comprises the remaining two-thirds of the spinner and
is white. Thus, each time the spinner is spun, there is a probability
of 1/3 that it will stop in the gray section and a probability of 2/3
that it will stop in the white section. We will assume that the spins
are independent of each other. That is, the result of each spin has no
influence on the result of any other spin.

Suppose you spin the spinner 24 times and win $1 for each time the
spinner stops in the gray. How likely are you to win $0? to win $1? to
win $2? ... to win $24?

This situation is mathematically analogous to the *Consumer Reports*
experiment of Section 2.2. Assuming the null hypothesis in Section 2.2,
each choice made by a taste tester is equivalent to spinning a spinner

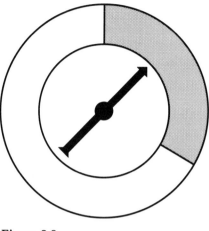

Figure 2.9
Spinner

randomly. The probability of choosing the correct glass is equal to 1/3 (= the probability of spinning gray). The 24 taste testers correspond to 24 spins of the spinner. The probability of, for example, 11 correct choices is equal to the probability of winning $11 (spinning gray 11 times).

Example

Senator Longtime is being challenged by Congressman Upstart in the next election. Senator Longtime asks one of his staffers to do a quick poll to find out how the voters are likely to vote in the election. Suppose that one-third of the voters are planning to vote for Congressman Upstart. The staffer interviews 24 voters and reports the number of voters who say that they plan to vote for the senator. How likely is he to report that 11 voters plan to vote for the congressman?

This situation is analogous to our first example and to the *Consumer Reports* experiment. The action of choosing a voter to interview is analogous to spinning the spinner. With probability 1/3, the staffer will choose a voter who plans to vote for the congressman. This is analogous to spinning the spinner and landing in gray. Choosing 24 voters is analogous to spinning the spinner 24 times.

Because this mathematical situation is so common, I will introduce some special notation. Suppose we have a spinner in which a fraction p is gray and $(1 - p)$ is white. Suppose that we spin this spinner n times and that we want to know the probability that exactly k of the spins land in the gray. This probability will be denoted $\mu(k, n, p)$. The symbol μ is the Greek letter mu. You should read this notation as "$\mu(k, n, p)$ is the probability of hitting gray k out of n times when the probability of hitting gray each time is p."

In our examples we were interested in $\mu(11, 24, 1/3)$ since the probability of hitting gray each time was $1/3$, the spinner was spun 24 times, and we wanted to know the probability of landing in the gray section exactly 11 times.

The purpose of this section is to develop an algorithm (an algorithm is a precise step-by-step method for computing something) for computing these probabilities. Some of these numbers are very easy to compute. See Table 2.6.

We will build a table like Table 2.7 with the numbers $\mu(k, n, p)$. Notice that this table has a triangular shape. It gets half of its name from its shape and the other half from the mathematician Blaise Pascal. It is called *Pascal's Triangle*.

The first column of Pascal's Triangle gives the probability of each possible result when the spinner is spun once. The second column of Pascal's Triangle gives the probability of each possible result when the spinner is spun twice. The third column gives the probability of each possible result when the spinner is spun three times, and so on. We already know how to compute the first column of this table, $\mu(0, 1, p) = (1 - p)$ and $\mu(1, 1, p) = p$. We also know how to compute the second column of the table (Table 2.6). Table 2.8 shows the first two columns filled in.

The heart of our algorithm for computing this table is a method that will enable us to compute each column once we have computed the preceding column. I will illustrate this method by computing the third column of Table 2.7.

The top entry, $\mu(0, 3, p)$, is easy to compute. This is the probability of spinning white on all three spins of the spinner. For each spin of the spinner, the probability of white is $(1 - p)$. Since the three spins of the spinner are independent of each other, the probability of spinning white all three times is $(1 - p)(1 - p)(1 - p) = (1 - p)^3$.

Table 2.6
Some Easy Values of $\mu(k, n, p)$

Probability	Value
$\mu(1,1,p)$	This is the probability of spinning gray once in one spin of the spinner. We already know the answer. The probability of spinning gray in one spin of the wheel is p.
$\mu(0,1,p)$	This is the probability of spinning gray zero times in one spin of the spinner. It is the same as the probability of spinning white once in one spin of the spinner. Since the probability of spinning gray is p, the probability of spinning white is $(1-p)$.
$\mu(2,2,p)$	This is the probability of spinning gray twice out of two spins. The probability of spinning gray on the first spin is p. The probability of spinning gray on the second spin is also p. Let A be the event that the first spin is gray and let B be the event that the second spin is gray. Notice that $P(A) = p$ and $P(B) = p$. We are interested in the event $A \cap B =$ the event that both spins are gray. Since these events are independent, this probability is $P(A)P(B) = pp = p^2$.
$\mu(0,2,p)$	This is the probability of spinning white twice out of two spins. The probability of spinning white on the first spin is $(1-p)$. The probability of spinning white on the second spin is also $(1-p)$. Since these are independent events, the probability of spinning white on both the first and second spins is $(1-p)(1-p) = (1-p)^2$.
$\mu(1,2,p)$	This is the probability of spinning gray exactly once in two spins of the spinner. Let C denote this event. In order to compute $P(C)$, we will break this event up into two disjoint events. Let D be the event: the first spin is gray and the second spin is white. Let E be the event: the first spin is white and the second spin is gray. Thus, $P(C) = P(D) + P(E)$. To compute $P(D)$ we notice that the probability of the first spin's being gray is p and the probability of the second spin's being white is $(1-p)$. These are independent events, so the probability of D is $p(1-p)$. Similarly, the probability of E is $(1-p)p = p(1-p)$. Thus, $P(C) = P(D) + P(E) = p(1-p) + p(1-p) = 2p(1-p)$.

The bottom entry, $\mu(3,3,p)$, is also easy to compute. This is the probability of spinning gray all three times. For each spin of the spinner, the probability of spinning gray is p. Since the three spins of the spinner are independent of each other, the probability of spinning gray all three times is $ppp = p^3$. When we add these entries to Table 2.8, we get Table 2.9.

Table 2.7
Pascal's Triangle

Number of Grays	Number of Spins			
	1	2	3	4
0	$\mu(0,1,p)$	$\mu(0,2,p)$	$\mu(0,3,p)$	$\mu(0,4,p)$
1	$\mu(1,1,p)$	$\mu(1,2,p)$	$\mu(1,3,p)$	$\mu(1,4,p)$
2		$\mu(2,2,p)$	$\mu(2,3,p)$	$\mu(2,4,p)$
3			$\mu(3,3,p)$	$\mu(3,4,p)$
4				$\mu(4,4,p)$
⋮				

Table 2.8
Pascal's Triangle

Number of Grays	Number of Spins			
	1	2	3	4
0	$(1-p)$	$(1-p)^2$	$\mu(0,3,p)$	$\mu(0,4,p)$
1	p	$2p(1-p)$	$\mu(1,3,p)$	$\mu(1,4,p)$
2		p^2	$\mu(2,3,p)$	$\mu(2,4,p)$
3			$\mu(3,3,p)$	$\mu(3,4,p)$
4				$\mu(4,4,p)$
⋮				

Table 2.9
Pascal's Triangle

Number of Grays	Number of Spins			
	1	2	3	4
0	$(1-p)$	$(1-p)^2$	$(1-p)^3$	$\mu(0,4,p)$
1	p	$2p(1-p)$	$\mu(1,3,p)$	$\mu(1,4,p)$
2		p^2	$\mu(2,3,p)$	$\mu(2,4,p)$
3			p^3	$\mu(3,4,p)$
4				$\mu(4,4,p)$
⋮				

Now we come to the key part of this algorithm. Suppose we want to compute $\mu(1,3,p)$. We are interested in the event of spinning gray exactly once in three spins. Call this Event E. We will compute $P(E)$ by breaking E into two disjoint events. Let A be the event of spinning gray once in the first two spins and then spinning white on the third spin. Let B be the event of spinning gray zero times in the first two

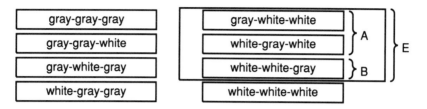

Figure 2.10
Three spins

spins and then spinning gray on the third spin. Notice that $E = A \cup B$ and that A and B are disjoint. See Figure 2.10.

We have been using the language of set theory to say something very simple: there are two ways to spin gray exactly once in three spins—by spinning gray once in the first two spins and then spinning white on the last spin, or by spinning gray zero times in the first two spins and then spinning gray on the last spin.

But now $P(A)$ is easy to compute. Event A is the intersection of two independent events: spinning gray once in the first two spins and spinning white on the third spin. The probability of spinning gray once in the first two spins is $\mu(1, 2, p)$, which we already know is $2p(1-p)$. The probability of spinning white on the third spin is just $(1-p)$. Therefore, $P(A) = \mu(1, 2, p)(1 - p) = 2p(1 - p)(1 - p) = 2p(1 - p)^2$.

It is equally easy to compute $P(B)$. The event B is the intersection of two independent events: spinning gray zero times in the first two spins and spinning gray on the third spin. The probability of spinning gray zero times on the first two spins is $\mu(0, 2, p)$, which we already know is $(1 - p)^2$. The probability of spinning gray on the third spin is just p. Therefore, $P(B) = \mu(0, 2, p)p = (1 - p)^2 p$.

Finally,

$$
\begin{aligned}
P(E) &= P(A) + P(B) \\
&= \mu(1, 2, p)(1 - p) + \mu(0, 2, p)p \\
&= 2p(1 - p)^2 + (1 - p)^2 p \\
&= 3p(1 - p)^2.
\end{aligned}
$$

Before continuing, try to do the following exercises.

Exercises

These exercises all refer to a spinner with $p = 0.4$. That is, on each spin, the probability of stopping on gray is 0.4, and the probability of stopping on white is 0.6.

*Exercise 2.3.21 Compute the first three columns of Pascal's Triangle for this spinner. That is, fill in numbers for each entry in the table below.

Number of Grays	Number of Spins		
	1	2	3
0	$\mu(0,1,0.4)$	$\mu(0,2,0.4)$	$\mu(0,3,0.4)$
1	$\mu(1,1,0.4)$	$\mu(1,2,0.4)$	$\mu(1,3,0.4)$
2		$\mu(2,2,0.4)$	$\mu(2,3,0.4)$
3			$\mu(3,3,0.4)$

Exercise 2.3.22 Compute $\mu(0,4,0.4)$.

*Exercise 2.3.23 Find a general formula for $\mu(0,n,p)$.

Exercise 2.3.24 Compute $\mu(4,4,0.4)$.

*Exercise 2.3.25 Find a general formula for $\mu(n,n,p)$.

Our algorithm for computing Pascal's Triangle has two parts:

1. The computation of the first column of the table. I have already done this. The top entry, $\mu(0,1,p)$, is $(1-p)$ and the bottom entry, $\mu(1,1,p)$, is p.

2. A method for computing the nth column of the table once we have computed the preceding (the $(n-1)$st) column of the table. Since we have computed the first column in part 1, we can use this method to compute the second column. Then having computed the second column, we can use this method again to compute the third column. Then, having computed the third column, this method can be used again to compute the fourth column, and so forth.

This method has three parts.

a. First we compute $\mu(0, n, p)$. This is the probability of spinning white on all n spins. The probability of spinning white on the first spin is $(1 - p)$, the probability of spinning white on the second spin is also $(1 - p)$, the probability of spinning white on the third spin is again $(1 - p)$, ... and the probability of spinning white on the last spin is $(1 - p)$. These are all independent events, so the probability of spinning white on all n spins is

$$\mu(0, n, p) = \underbrace{(1 - p)(1 - p)(1 - p) \cdots (1 - p)}_{n \text{ factors}} = (1 - p)^n.$$

b. Next we compute $\mu(n, n, p)$. This is the probability of spinning gray on all n spins. We can use the same reasoning as above to see that

$$\mu(n, n, p) = p^n.$$

c. The next step is computing the middle entries of the nth column. We want to compute $\mu(k, n, p)$ for $k = 1, 2, \ldots, (n-1)$. The method is analogous to the computation of $\mu(1, 3, p)$ above. You may want to review that computation before reading on.

Let E be the event of spinning gray exactly k times in n spins. In order to compute $\mu(k, n, p) = P(E)$, we will break E up into two disjoint events. Let A be the event of spinning gray exactly k times in the first $(n - 1)$ spins and then spinning white on the last spin. Let B be the event of spinning gray exactly $(k - 1)$ times in the first $(n - 1)$ spins and then spinning gray on the last spin. Notice that $E = A \cup B$ and that A and B are disjoint. Therefore, $P(E) = P(A) + P(B)$.

But now $P(A)$ is easy to compute. Event A is the intersection of two independent events: spinning gray exactly k times in the first $(n - 1)$ spins and spinning white on the last spin. The probability of spinning gray exactly k times on the first $(n - 1)$ spins is just $\mu(k, n - 1, p)$, which we have already computed. The probability of spinning white on the last spin is $(1 - p)$. Therefore, $P(A) = \mu(k, n - 1, p)(1 - p)$.

It is equally easy to compute $P(B)$. Event B is the intersection of two independent events: spinning gray exactly $(k - 1)$ times in the first $(n-1)$ spins and spinning gray on the last spin. The probability of spinning gray exactly $(k-1)$ times in the first $(n-1)$ spins is $\mu(k-1, n-1, p)$, which we have already computed. The probability of spinning gray on the last spin is p. Therefore, $P(B) = \mu(k-1, n-1, p)p$.

Finally,

$$\mu(k, n, p) = P(E)$$
$$= P(A) + P(B)$$
$$= \mu(k, n-1, p)(1-p) + \mu(k-1, n-1, p)p.$$

We summarize this algorithm as follows:

1. Compute the first column of the table:

$$\mu(0, 1, p) = 1 - p$$
$$\mu(1, 1, p) = p$$

2. Having computed the $(n-1)$st column of the table, compute the nth column as follows:

$$\mu(0, n, p) = (1-p)^n$$
$$\mu(n, n, p) = p^n$$

For each of the middle entries $(k = 1, 2, \ldots, n-1)$:

$$\mu(k, n, p) = \mu(k, n-1, p)(1-p) + \mu(k-1, n-1, p)p.$$

Start by using part 1 to compute the first column. Then use part 2 to compute the second column. Then use part 2 to compute the third column. Continue applying part 2 to compute as many columns as needed.

In Section 2.2 we needed to know

$$\mu(0, 24, 1/3), \ \mu(1, 24, 1/3), \ \ldots \mu(24, 24, 1/3).$$

That is, we needed the 24th column of Pascal's Triangle for $p = 1/3$. Now try to write a program to do this computation before looking at the program below. This program is included below only because we will discuss one fine point later. You have two pieces of information that you can use to check your program. First, you can compare your results for the first three columns with the earlier computations. Second, you can compare your results with the experimental results (Table 2.4) from Section 2.2. They should be fairly close but probably will not be exactly the same.

```
!     Compute The 24th Column of Pascal's Triangle
!
!     Written January 3, 1990
!
DIM mu(0 to 24, 1 to 24)
LET p = 1/3
LET mu(0,1) = 1 - p                ! First column
LET mu(1,1) = p
FOR n = 2 TO 24
LET mu(0, n) = (1 - p)^n           ! Compute nth column
LET mu(n, n) = p^n                 ! from (n-1)st column
FOR k = 1 TO n-1
LET mu(k,n) = mu(k, n-1)*(1 - p) + mu(k-1, n-1)*p
NEXT k
NEXT n
PRINT "Number of "                 ! Print out results
PRINT "gray spins  Probability"
FOR i = 0 TO 24
PRINT USING "        ##        #.####":i,mu(i, 24)
NEXT i
END
```

Exercises

Exercise 2.3.26 Recalculate Table 2.5 using the exact probabilities computed by your program instead of the rough estimates (Table 2.4) we used in Section 2.2.

Exercise 2.3.27 Try to do the last three exercises of Section 2.2 using
the exact methods of this section. You may run into some difficulty
and get messages like "Out of memory". If so, you will have to read on
before doing this exercise.

The previous program uses a two-dimensional array, mu, to keep track
of all the entries in the table. I wrote the program in this way because it is the easiest way to think about this algorithm. However,
this program has a problem. Suppose that you wanted to compute
the 100th column of the table. You would need the much larger array mu(1 to 100, 0 to 100), which would require the computer to
set aside space for over 10,000 variables. Depending on your particular computer, you may or may not have that much memory (RAM)
available.

We can make do with much less memory by making one observation
and then doing a little extra work. The observation is that we never need
the whole table at once. All we ever need at one time is two columns.
We begin by computing the first column and then use it to compute the
second column. Once the second column has been computed, the first
column is no longer needed. Next we use the second column to compute
the third column. Once the third column has been computed, the second
column is no longer needed. Each column is used to compute the next
column and then may be discarded.

Thus, we can modify our program to use only two columns: the current
column and the next one. The program below shows how this can be
done:

```
!     Compute The 24th Column of Pascal's Triangle
!
!     Written January 3, 1990
!
DIM oldcol(0 to 24), newcol(0 to 24)
LET p = 1/3
LET oldcol(0) = 1 - p                    ! First column
LET oldcol(1) = p
FOR n = 2 TO 24
LET newcol(0) = (1 - p)^n                 ! Compute nth column
```

```
LET newcol(n) = p^n                      ! from (n-1)st column
FOR k = 1 TO n-1
LET newcol(k) = oldcol(k)*(1 - p) + oldcol(k-1)*p
NEXT k
FOR i = 0 to 24
LET oldcol(i) = newcol(i)
NEXT i
NEXT n
PRINT "Number of "                       ! Print out results
PRINT "gray spins  Probability"
FOR i = 0 TO 24
PRINT USING "         ##        #.####":i,oldcol(i)
NEXT i
END
```

2.4   A Winning Strategy in Roulette

In this section we will be studying the game of roulette. Unless you are an uncommonly sophisticated gambler you will probably be surprised by the results of this study. Figure 2.11 shows a roulette wheel.

A roulette wheel has 38 slots numbered: 1, 2, 3, ..., 36, 0, and 00. The slots numbered 1, 2, 3, ..., 36 are colored red and black. In our black and white picture, the slots are colored gray and white. Half of these slots are gray, and half are white. The other two slots, numbered 0 and 00, are colored green. In our black and white picture, the green slots are colored dark gray. We are interested in two possible bets. A gambler can bet either GRAY or WHITE. Roulette is a more complicated game, and other bets are possible; however, we will discuss only these two bets. After the gambler places his bet, the wheel is spun, and a metal ball is thrown onto the spinning wheel. The ball bounces around quite a bit from slot to slot. But as the wheel slows and comes to a stop, the ball eventually comes to rest in one slot. There are two possible outcomes:

1. The ball comes to rest in a slot of the color on which the gambler bet—for example, if he bets GRAY and the ball comes to rest in a GRAY slot. In this case the gambler wins. He gets back his original

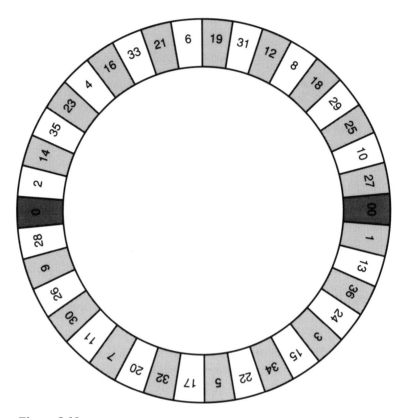

Figure 2.11
Roulette wheel

bet plus the amount that he bet. For example, if the gambler bet $4 he will get back $8 (the original $4 plus "winnings" of $4).

2. The ball comes to rest in a slot of a different color—for example, if he bets GRAY and the ball comes to rest in a WHITE or DARK GRAY slot. In this case the gambler loses whatever amount he bet.

Since there are 38 slots and 18 of them match the color on which the gambler bet, his chances of winning on each spin of the wheel are 18/38. Notice that because of the two DARK GRAY slots, he is more likely to lose than to win. (This fact ought not to be surprising. Casinos are in business to make money. Since they choose the games, it is to be expected that they choose games that are biased in their favor.)

Now suppose George Gambler has $10. He needs $20 to buy a new calculator and decides to play roulette in order to win enough money to buy it. George is contemplating two possible playing strategies.

Strategy 1: George will be a flamboyant gambler. He will stride purposefully up to the roulette wheel and with a carefree look will bet his entire $10 on one spin of the wheel. He will either win $10 on that one spin, giving him the $20 he needs, or he will go broke. We will call this the *go-for-broke* strategy.

Strategy 2: George will walk timidly up to the roulette wheel and glance nervously around at the big-time gamblers. He will hesitantly bet $1 on each spin of the wheel. On each spin, he will either win $1 or lose $1. He will keep playing this way and biting his nails until he either loses all his money or reaches the $20 he needs. This is called the *conservative* strategy.

Our problem is to advise George which strategy will give him the better chance of winning the money he needs to buy the calculator. Before reading on, you might pause and make a guess as to which strategy you think is the better one.

Exercise

Exercise 2.4.28   Think about the two playing strategies. Which do you think is better? Or are they equivalent? Why? Write down your intuitive ideas.

The go-for-broke strategy is easy to analyze. Only one spin of the wheel is involved, and the probability of winning on one spin of the wheel is $18/38 = 0.473684$. Thus, with this strategy, his chance of winning enough money to buy the calculator is 0.473684, or slightly less than $1/2$.

The conservative strategy is harder to analyze; however, one can write a computer program to simulate it. Your next assignment in this section is to write a program that will simulate 1,000 trials to see roughly how likely George is to win with the conservative strategy.

The following careful description of the conservative strategy may help you write your program (it is often useful to write a careful description like this one before trying to write a computer program):

1. Enter the casino with $10 in your wallet.

2. Bet $1 and spin the wheel.

3. If you win this spin of the wheel add $1 to your wallet.

   If you lose this spin of the wheel subtract $1 from your wallet.

4. Check how much money is in your wallet.

   If you have $20 quit and go buy a calculator.

   If you have nothing, quit and go home. Put on some good music.

   Otherwise, go back to step 2 and bet again.

Exercise

Exercise 2.4.29   Write a program to simulate 1,000 trials using the conservative strategy. Based on the results of running this program, what advice do you have for George?

The simulation in the previous exercise will give you a rough idea of which is the better strategy. Now we want to do a more exact calculation of the probability of winning using the conservative strategy.

The conservative strategy involves a gambler who starts with $10 and bets $1 on each spin of the wheel until he goes broke or reaches $20. At any time the gambler has a certain amount of money. He starts out with $10 and will quit when he has either nothing or $20. Since he bets $1 at a time, the possible amounts of money he can have at any given time are: $0, $1, $2, $3, ..., or $20. These possibilities are called *states*.

The gambler starts out with $10—in other words, in the $10 state. Thus, the probability that he is in the $10 state is 1.00, and the probability that he is in any other state is 0.00.

After one spin of the wheel, he will either have $9 (if he loses the first spin) or $11 (if he wins the first spin). Thus, the probability that he is in the $9 state is $20/38 = 0.5263$; the probability that he is in the $11

Table 2.10
State and Probability table

State	Probability of this state	
	In the beginning	After one spin
$0	0.000	0.000
$1	0.000	0.000
$2	0.000	0.000
$3	0.000	0.000
$4	0.000	0.000
$5	0.000	0.000
$6	0.000	0.000
$7	0.000	0.000
$8	0.000	0.000
$9	0.000	$20/38 = 0.526$
$10	1.000	0.000
$11	0.000	$18/38 = 0.474$
$12	0.000	0.000
$13	0.000	0.000
$14	0.000	0.000
$15	0.000	0.000
$16	0.000	0.000
$17	0.000	0.000
$18	0.000	0.000
$19	0.000	0.000
$20	0.000	0.000

state is $18/38 = 0.4737$; and the probability that he is in any other state is 0.00. (Table 2.10.)

Our basic strategy is to extend Table 2.10. Table 2.10 tells us that in the beginning the probability that our gambler has $10 is 1.00 and that after one spin of the roulette wheel the probability that he has $9 is 0.5263 and the probability that he has $11 is 0.4737. Table 2.11 gives us similar information after zero, one, two, three, four, five, six and seven spins of the wheel.

The first two columns of Table 2.11 are identical with Table 2.10; however, the rest of this table is new. This table tells us how likely our gambler is to be in each state after a certain number of spins of the wheel. For example, after four spins of the wheel the gambler will have $6 with probability 0.077, $8 with probability 0.276, $10 with probability 0.373, $12 with probability 0.224, and $14 with probability 0.050.

We want to compute the entries in Table 2.11. In order to compute the columns of a table like this, we need to know two things:

Table 2.11
State and Probability Table

State	Probability of each state after x spins							
	0	**1**	**2**	**3**	**4**	**5**	**6**	**7**
$0	0.000	0.000	0.000	0.000	0.000	0.000	0.000	0.000
$1	0.000	0.000	0.000	0.000	0.000	0.000	0.000	0.000
$2	0.000	0.000	0.000	0.000	0.000	0.000	0.000	0.000
$3	0.000	0.000	0.000	0.000	0.000	0.000	0.000	0.011
$4	0.000	0.000	0.000	0.000	0.000	0.000	0.021	0.000
$5	0.000	0.000	0.000	0.000	0.000	0.040	0.000	0.071
$6	0.000	0.000	0.000	0.000	0.077	0.000	0.115	0.000
$7	0.000	0.000	0.000	0.146	0.000	0.182	0.000	0.190
$8	0.000	0.000	0.277	0.000	0.276	0.000	0.258	0.000
$9	0.000	0.526	0.000	0.394	0.000	0.327	0.000	0.285
$10	1.000	0.000	0.499	0.000	0.373	0.000	0.310	0.000
$11	0.000	0.474	0.000	0.354	0.000	0.294	0.000	0.257
$12	0.000	0.000	0.224	0.000	0.224	0.000	0.209	0.000
$13	0.000	0.000	0.000	0.106	0.000	0.133	0.000	0.139
$14	0.000	0.000	0.000	0.000	0.050	0.000	0.075	0.000
$15	0.000	0.000	0.000	0.000	0.000	0.024	0.000	0.042
$16	0.000	0.000	0.000	0.000	0.000	0.000	0.011	0.000
$17	0.000	0.000	0.000	0.000	0.000	0.000	0.000	0.005
$18	0.000	0.000	0.000	0.000	0.000	0.000	0.000	0.000
$19	0.000	0.000	0.000	0.000	0.000	0.000	0.000	0.000
$20	0.000	0.000	0.000	0.000	0.000	0.000	0.000	0.000

1. The first column.

2. A method for computing each column using the information in the preceding column. This method is determined by the game's rules. These rules are sometimes called the *transition rules*.

For this example the transition rules are as follows:

- If the gambler is in state $0 (broke), he stays there.

- If the gambler is in state $20 (he has won enough to buy the calculator), he stays there.

- If he is in any other state (he has i dollars and $1 \leq i \leq 19$), then with probability 18/38 he wins \$1 and now has $(i + 1)$ dollars; with probability 20/38 he loses \$1 and now has $(i-1)$ dollars. For example, if a gambler has \$2, then with probability 18/38 after the next spin of the wheel he will have \$3, and with probability 20/38 he will have \$1.

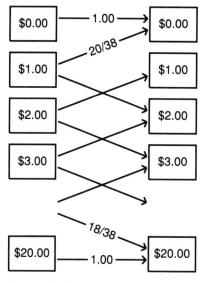

Figure 2.12
Transition rules

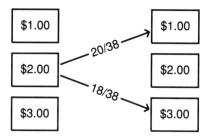

Figure 2.13
Transition rules

Figures 2.12, 2.13, and 2.14 describe these transition rules pictorially. As you read these rules, look at Figures 2.12, 2.13, and 2.14 to observe that the rules describe what is happening. We will compute the columns of Table 2.11 by looking at these transition rules backward.

As we compute the columns of Table 2.11, we will use the following notation. The entries of the column that we have just finished computing will be col(0), col(1), ..., col(20). The entries of the column that we are now computing will be newcol(0), newcol(1), ..., newcol(20).

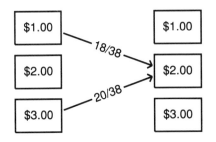

Figure 2.14
Transition rules

For example, the old probability of having $7 is `col(7)`, and after this spin, the new probability of having $7 will be `newcol(7)`. We compute the entries in each new column on the basis of the entries in the preceding column as follows:

- `newcol(0) = col(0) + (20/38) * col(1)`

  The first term on the right says that if the gambler was broke, then he stays that way. The second term on the right says that if the gambler had $1, then with probability 20/38 he will lose that dollar and become broke.

- `newcol(1) = (20/38) * col(2)`

  The only way to reach $1 is by having $2 and losing on the next spin of the wheel. The gambler can't reach $1 from $0, since he would have quit if he went broke.

- If $2 \le i \le 18$ then

  `newcol(i) = (18/38) * col(i-1) + (20/38) * col(i+1)`

  The first term on the right corresponds to the fact that with probability 18/38, a gambler with $(i-1)$ dollars will win on the next spin of the wheel and move up to i dollars. The second term on the right corresponds to the fact that with probability 20/38 a gambler with $(i+1)$ dollars will lose on the next spin of the wheel and move down to i dollars.

- `newcol(19) = (18/38) * col(18)`

  The only way to reach $19 is by having $18 and winning the next spin of the wheel. The gambler can't reach $19 from $20 since if he had accumulated $20, he would have quit and left to buy a calculator.

- `newcol(20) = col(20) + (18/38) * col(19)`

The first term on the right says that when the gambler reaches $20 he stays there. The second term on the right says that a gambler with $19 has a probability of 18/38 of winning the next spin of the wheel and reaching $20.

The best way to understand these rules is by looking at Figures 2.12, 2.13, and 2.14. Now you have all the information you need to write a computer program to compute the columns of Table 2.11. You should write such a program. It will be best to print out only one column. You will be using this program to print out the results after a large number of spins. Design your program to ask the user for the number of spins and then print out the final result after the requested number of spins. As a first step in checking out your program, use it to recompute the results in Table 2.11. Then use it to compute the probability of each state after 50 spins of the wheel. You can check this result against the output in Table 2.12.

Table 2.12
States After 50 Spins

State	Probability after 50 Spins
$0	0.260185
$1	0.000000
$2	0.046589
$3	0.000000
$4	0.080225
$5	0.000000
$6	0.100097
$7	0.000000
$8	0.106519
$9	0.000000
$10	0.101023
$11	0.000000
$12	0.086280
$13	0.000000
$14	0.065673
$15	0.000000
$16	0.042635
$17	0.000000
$18	0.020055
$19	0.000000
$20	0.090721

Now we can use this output to give us lots of information. Looking at the $0 state, we see that after 50 spins of the wheel, the probability is about 26% that our gambler has lost all his money. Looking at the $20 state, we see that the probability that he has won is about 9%. After 50 spins of the wheel, he is most likely to be still playing. In fact, the probability is about 10% that he is right back where he started, with $10 in his wallet. Use your program to compute the probability of each state after 100, 200, 300, and 400 spins of the wheel. Answer the following questions using your program.

Exercises

Exercise 2.4.30   What is the probability that the gambler will win playing the conservative strategy? Compare your answer with the answer you obtained earlier using simulation.

Exercise 2.4.31   What is the probability that the gambler is still playing after 100 spins of the wheel? after 200 spins of the wheel?

Exercise 2.4.32   Suppose that you have a friend who is planning to play roulettte. Of course, he likes to win, but he would also like to play for a while. What can the results of this section tell your friend?

2.5   Polls

Senator Smith has just received the results of a preelection poll in his home state. The pollsters interviewed 100 voters with the results shown in Table 2.13.

Table 2.13
Results from a Small Poll

	"If the election were held today for whom would you vote?"
Senator Smith	54
Opponent	46
Total	100

Suppose that the poll was done carefully and that the pollsters really did pick a random sample of voters. Suppose also that none of the voters will change their minds between the time of the poll and election day. Based on the information in Table 2.13, what is the chance that Senator Smith will win? The purpose of this section is to attempt to answer this question.

Interpreting data like those in Table 2.13 involves two main steps. The first step is to set up a null hypothesis. This must be done in a very precise way. For example, intuitively the null hypothesis that the senator would like to reject is, "I am going to lose." This may sound like a perfectly reasonable null hypothesis, but for our purposes we have to be more precise. The second step is to determine to what extent the data collected are consistent or inconsistent with the null hypothesis.

Typically the null hypothesis makes a prediction about what the data should look like. Even if the null hypothesis is correct, the actual data usually are not exactly as predicted. For example, when you flip a fair coin 100 times, it is unrealistic to expect exactly 50 heads and 50 tails. We want to know how likely the actual data are *assuming that the null hypothesis is true*.

For the senator's poll, our null hypothesis will be: "50% of the voters plan to vote for the senator." Our intuitive null hypothesis was "Senator Smith will lose." When we make this null hypothesis more precise, we have a number of possibilities—for example, "Senator Smith will only get 40% of the vote," "Senator Smith will only get 45% of the vote," or "Senator Smith will only get 49.9999% of the vote." Any one of these results would imply that Senator Smith would lose. In fact, if Senator Smith received exactly 50% of the vote, the election would be a tie. We chose the null hypothesis "Senator Smith will receive 50% of the vote" because from Senator Smith's perspective, it makes little difference whether he fails to be elected by a landslide or just the thinnest of margins—losing is losing. Hence, we choose this null hypothesis out of all the possible null hypotheses because this is the one that would be most likely to mislead us.

We are interested in rejecting this null hypothesis. The actual data reported 54 voters for the senator. The prediction of the null hypothesis is 50 voters for the senator, a difference of four voters. Following the procedure of Section 2.3 the next step would be to compute the probability (assuming that the null hypothesis were true) of obtaining actual data with a difference of at least 4 from the predicted 50 votes for the senator. In other words we would sum the probabilities of 54, 55, 56, ..., 100 and 46, 45, 44, ..., 0 voters saying that they planned to vote for the senator. In this situation, however, there is a twist: the senator is interested in not just rejecting the null hypothesis but in rejecting it in favor of his winning. In other words Senator Smith would not be happy if he only learned that the null hypothesis misstated the proportion of voters who will vote for him. He really is hoping that the null hypothesis *underestimates* the number of voters who will vote for him.

If you want to reject the null hypothesis, then a report of 46 voters voting for the senator is equally good evidence against the null hypothesis as a report of 54 voters voting for the senator. But if you want to reject the null hypothesis in favor of the senator's winning, then a report of 46 voters voting for the senator is not good at all.

This is a very common situation. We are often interested not merely in rejecting the null hypothesis but in rejecting it in a certain direction. Here are some other examples.

Example

The CEO (chief executive officer) of a large corporation has heard rumors that the workers in one of the company's assembly plants have been doing sloppy work. She wants to find out whether this plant's production is of lower quality than the other assembly plants. The company's records show that 1% of the units produced by the whole company are returned for repairs within the first year. She wants to compare the return rate for the suspect plant with this overall rate. Only if the return rate is significantly *higher* than 1% will she have evidence *in support of the rumor*.

Example

A small company has been accused of discriminatory hiring practices and, in particular, of discriminating against Hispanics. The labor pool from which this company draws its employees contains 15% Hispanics. An enterprising reporter finds out the percentage of the company's workers who are Hispanic. Only if this percentage is significantly *under* 15% will he have evidence suggesting that the company may be discriminating *against* Hispanics.

Table 2.14
Probabilities Assuming the Null Hypothesis

Number of Votes for Senator Smith	Probability
35	0.001
36	0.002
37	0.003
38	0.004
39	0.007
40	0.011
41	0.016
42	0.022
43	0.030
44	0.039
45	0.048
46	0.058
47	0.067
48	0.074
49	0.078
50	0.080
51	0.078
52	0.074
53	0.067
54	0.058←
55	0.048←
56	0.039←
57	0.030←
58	0.022←
59	0.016←
60	0.011←
61	0.007←
62	0.004←
63	0.003←
64	0.002←
65	0.001←

Now we return to our poll. Table 2.14 shows the probability for each possible result of the poll assuming the null hypothesis. I have omitted entries that are less than 0.001. The arrows in Table 2.14 indicate those rows corresponding to results that are at least as favorable (from the senator's point of view) as the results of the actual poll. We sum the indicated rows to find out the probability of getting results at least as favorable as the actual results assuming the null hypothesis. The sum is 0.241. Thus, we can conclude that the data reported in Table 2.14 suggest that the senator will win with a confidence of about 76%. More

Table 2.15
Probabilities Assuming the Null Hypothesis

Number of Votes for Senator Smith	Probability	New Column
35	0.001	0.999
36	0.002	0.998
37	0.003	0.997
38	0.004	0.994
39	0.007	0.990
40	0.011	0.982
41	0.016	0.972
42	0.022	0.956
43	0.030	0.933
44	0.039	0.903
45	0.048	0.864
46	0.058	0.816
47	0.067	0.758
48	0.074	0.691
49	0.078	0.618
50	0.080	0.540
51	0.078	0.460
52	0.074	0.382
53	0.067	0.309
54	0.058	0.242←
55	0.048	0.184
56	0.039	0.136
57	0.030	0.097
58	0.022	0.067
59	0.016	0.044
60	0.011	0.028
61	0.007	0.018
62	0.004	0.010
63	0.003	0.006
64	0.002	0.003
65	0.001	0.002

precisely, if the senator were going to lose, then we would expect results at least as misleading as those of Table 2.13 24% of the time.

We can save some work by having the computer add another column to Table 2.14. The entries in it will show for each row the sum of the probabilities for that row and all the following rows. For example, the entry in Table 2.15 indicated by the arrow gives the probability of 54 or more votes for the senator. This is the same probability we calculated earlier. (The number is slightly different because in our earlier calculation we ignored all the rows with entries less than 0.001. The computer calculation did not ignore these rows).

Exercises

*Exercise 2.5.33 Suppose the senator's pollster had reported that 58 of the 100 voters interviewed planned to vote for him. How confident could you be that the senator would win?

Exercise 2.5.34 The senator is not very happy with the results of our analysis. He is mulling over the possibility of spending an additional $1 million on television advertising but before committing this amount of money wants to see if it is really necessary, so he sends his pollster out to do a much larger poll. This time the pollster interviews 300 voters and reports the results shown in Table 2.16. Based on these results, how confident could you be that the senator would win? (Notice that the percentage voting for the senator is the same in this poll as in the earlier poll.)

Exercise 2.5.35 In some elections a two-thirds majority is necessary to pass a particular proposition. Given the results shown in Table 2.17, how confident could you be that the measure would pass?

Table 2.16
Probabilities Assuming the Null Hypothesis

	"If the election were held today, for whom would you vote?"
Senator Smith	162
Opponent	138
Total	300

Table 2.17
Another Poll

	"If the election were held today, would you vote for or against Proposition 8?"
For	86
Against	34
Total	120

Table 2.18
Yet Another Poll

	"If the election were held today, how would you vote on Proposition 8?"
For	90
Against	30
Total	120

Exercise 2.5.36   Consider the same proposition as in the preceding exercise. Given the results shown in Table 2.18 how confident could you be that the measure would pass by a two-thirds majority?

In this chapter I have talked about two different ways of rejecting the null hypothesis. In Section 2.3 we were interested in simply rejecting it. In this section we were interested in rejecting it in a certain direction. The null hypothesis predicted that with a poll of 100 voters, 50 should be planning to vote for the senator. The actual data showed 54 voters planning to vote for him. If we were simply interested in rejecting the null hypothesis, then we would have summed the probabilities for all of the following results: 54, 55, 56, ..., 100, 46, 45, 44, ..., 0. But the senator wanted to reject the null hypothesis in one direction—the direction of his victory. Thus we summed the probabilities for only the following results: 54, 55, ..., 100. We use the following technical terms to make this distinction. In the first case, we needed to compute the probability of the *two-sided tail*: 54, 55, ..., 100, 46, 45, ..., 0. In the second case, we needed to compute the probability of the *one-sided tail*: 54, 55, ..., 100.

We can never answer exactly the intuitive question the senator wants answered: how likely is he to win? or to lose? Instead we have answered a different question. The data collected provide some evidence that he will win. We ask, If he were going to lose, how likely is it that such misleading data would have been collected? This gives us a "confidence" for his winning. It is not really the answer he wants, but it is the best that can be done with the information available. (Of course, there are many other factors involved that could have an impact on his chances of winning. For example, his ne'er-do-well sibling might be arrested on election eve for espionage.)

2.6   The Bell-Shaped Curve

The polls discussed in Section 2.5 were relatively small ones involving one hundred or two hundred interviews. With these polls it is difficult to detect with much confidence small differences between candidates. In order to make accurate predictions, pollsters frequently interview a thousand or more voters before an important election. The ideas involved in analyzing results from such large polls are exactly the same as those for smaller ones. We do, however, run afoul of a rather significant practical problem: the programs we have been running are sometimes painfully slow. Depending on what kind of computer you have been using, you may already have found yourself twiddling your thumbs while waiting impatiently for the program to finish. If we were to use the same programs for polls involving large numbers of interviews, we would find them far too slow.

Fortunately there is a much faster way to compute the necessary probabilities for polls involving large numbers. In fact, it will turn out that polls with large numbers of interviews can actually be analyzed faster than polls with smaller numbers.

The *bell-shaped curve*, sometimes called the *normal curve*, can be used to estimate the probabilities we need. The discovery and use of this formula for statistical problems is one of the most important accomplishments of probabilists. Its name comes from its shape (Figure 2.15). (A discussion of why this particular curve works is beyond the scope of the present book. You can find out about more about it in almost any book about probability or statistics.)

The Normal Curve

The formula below (written in True BASIC) estimates $\mu(k, n, 0.5)$, the probability of hitting GRAY k times out of n spins of a spinner in which the probability of hitting GRAY each time is 0.5. To use this formula for working with polling data, notice that if 50% of the voters will vote for a particular candidate, then if n voters are interviewed at random, the probability of k of them voting for that candidate is $\mu(k, n, 0.5)$:

$$\mu(k, n, 0.5) \simeq$$

```
EXP(-((2*k-n)^2)/(2*n))/SQR(1.570796327*n)
```

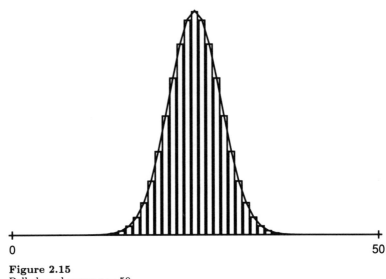

Figure 2.15
Bell-shaped curve $n = 50$

(The symbol "$\simeq$" expresses the fact that the True BASIC formula on
the right side *estimates* $\mu(k, n, 0.5)$.)

In order to see how good this estimate is, we will work out some examples comparing estimates obtained using this formula with the exact
probabilities obtained by the methods of the preceding sections. The
program below makes the necessary calculations:

```
!        Compare mu(k, n 0.5) with estimates by normal curve
!
!        Written January 6, 1991
!
!        Part I:   Compute exact values
!
PRINT "Enter n:";
INPUT n
DIM oldcol(0 to 100), newcol(0 to 100)
LET newcol(0) = 0.5
LET newcol(1) = 0.5
FOR m = 2 TO n
FOR k = 0 TO m - 1
```

```
LET oldcol(k) = newcol(k)
NEXT k
LET newcol(0) = 0.5^m
LET newcol(m) = 0.5^m
FOR k = 1 TO m-1
LET newcol(k) = 0.5*oldcol(k-1) + 0.5*oldcol(k)
NEXT k
NEXT m
!
!     Part II: Compute estimated values
!
DIM bell(0 to 100)
FOR k = 0 TO n
LET bell(k) = EXP(-((2*k-n)^2)/(2*n))/SQR(1.570796327*n)
NEXT k
!
!     Part III: Print comparison
!
PRINT "   k     Exact   Estimate"
PRINT
FOR k = 0 TO n
PRINT USING " ###    #.#####    #.#####":k,newcol(k),bell(k)
NEXT k
END
```

Following is the output from this program for N = 10:

k	Exact	Estimate
0	.00098	.00170
1	.00977	.01028
2	.04395	.04171
3	.11719	.11337
4	.20508	.20658
5	.24609	.25231
6	.20508	.20658
7	.11719	.11337

8	.04395	.04171
9	.00977	.01028
10	.00098	.00170

The three figures in this section make the same comparisons graphically. Figure 2.16 compares the bell-shaped curve with the exact probabilities for $n = 10$. The bar chart in this figure is the output from the exact calculations, and the line graph is the normal curve. Figure 2.15 and Figure 2.17 show output for $n = 50$ and $n = 100$, respectively. As you can see from these figures and from the computer output, for large values of n, the normal curve is a very close approximation to the exact answers—a happy situation. If n is small, then the normal curve is not a good approximation, but it is easy to compute the exact answers using our earlier methods. If n is large, then the computation of the exact answers is time-consuming, but the normal curve is a good approximation. Thus, we can get good results in either case. If n is small, we use the earlier methods for finding exact answers. If n is large, we use the normal curve approximation.

This new method using the normal curve allows us to compute tables like Table 2.14 and Table 2.15 for large numbers of interviews. Thus,

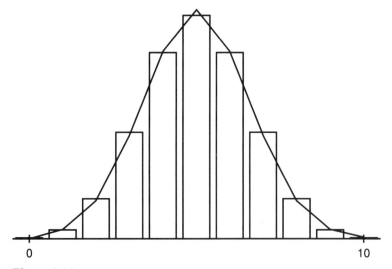

Figure 2.16
Bell-shaped curve $n = 10$

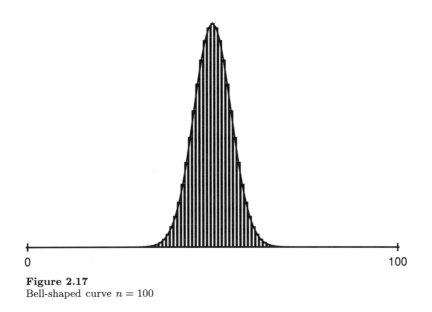

Figure 2.17
Bell-shaped curve $n = 100$

we can now answer questions like those we discussed in Section 2.5 for polls involving larger numbers of voters.

Exercises

Exercise 2.6.37   Use the normal curve to redo the four exercises at the end of Section 2.5.

*__Exercise 2.6.38__   A newspaper polls 1,000 voters and reports the results shown in the table below. Based on the results of this poll, at what confidence level can you reject the null hypothesis that the Democratic candidate will lose?

Choice	Votes
Democratic	515
Republican	485
Total	1000

*__Exercise 2.6.39__   A gambler has just lost $1,500 playing a game that involves flipping a coin. He suspects that he has been cheated and that his opponent used a weighted coin. He surreptitiously pockets the coin.

When he gets home, he does an experiment flipping the coin 500 times, with the results shown in the table below. Based on this experiment, at what confidence level can you reject the null hypothesis that the coin is fair?

Face	Number
Heads	270
Tails	230

2.7   The Baltimore LIFE Experiment

When a prisoner is discharged after completing his term in a state prison, he is usually given a small amount of "gate money."* In 1975 this was most often in the range of $50–$200. Typically the newly released ex-prisoner comes from a poor background. He is ineligible for welfare and unemployment insurance. He has no job. He faces all the expenses—food, shelter, clothes—that everybody else faces. In short, he has an immediate need for money and few resources immediately available. Some ex-prisoners have families and friends who can help tide them over until they can find a job and start earning money of their own, but these families and friends are usually themselves financially strapped. The pressure on ex-prisoners to raise some money, and soon, is enormous.

It seems reasonable to speculate that this combination of circumstances might play a significant role in the number of ex-prisoners who turn to crime, and particularly to theft. We might even suggest that a modest program of initial "unemployment insurance" for released ex-prisoners might significantly lower the recidivism rate. The cost of theft to society in both dollars and fear is very high. The cost of incarceration to society in both dollars and the loss of potentially productive people is also very high. If we can lower the amount of theft by instituting an unemployment insurance program that would give ex-prisoners some time to find jobs, then we should do so.

_____

* This section was inspired by the book *Money, Work, and Crime: Experimental Evidence* by Peter H. Rossi, Richard A. Berk, and Kenneth J. Lenihan, (New York: Academic Press 1980.)

Table 2.19
Baltimore LIFE Weekly Payments

Weekly Gross Earning	Weekly Financial Aid
$ 0–39	$60
40–49	55
50–59	50
60–69	45
70–79	40
80–89	35
90–99	30
100–109	25
110–119	20
120–150	15
151–	0

The Baltimore LIFE (Living Insurance for Ex-Prisoners) project begun in 1971, was designed to test the impact of such financial aid on newly released ex-prisoners. It was an important experiment, and illustrates very nicely some key statistical concepts.

It involved 432 individuals. Half of these were enrolled in a modest program of "unemployment insurance." Each of these 216 ex-prisoners was eligible to receive $60.00 per week for up to 13 weeks. This payment was reduced if the individual was employed according to Table 2.19.

This schedule of payments was designed to give ex-prisoners a base of support while at the same time encouraging them to work. The level of support is quite modest. As you can see from Table 2.19, those ex-prisoners who did find work lost part of their benefits but there was still a significant incentive to work. They could earn up to $39.99 with no loss of benefits and even with earnings above $40.00, they lost only about $0.50 in benefits for each $1.00 earned.

The group of 216 prisoners who were eligible for this financial aid was called *Group A*. The remaining 216 individuals were not given any financial aid as part of this project. This was the control group and was called *Group B*. The idea of the experiment was to compare these two groups to see if there was any signficant difference in the number of crimes they committed.

There is no direct way to count the number of crimes committed by an individual. You can, of course, ask people how many crimes they have committed, but their answers are not necessarily reliable. The Baltimore LIFE project worked with arrest records. This is not perfect—often

Table 2.20
Arrest Records from Baltimore LIFE Project

Arrest Charge	Group A (Received Aid)	Group B (Control Group)	Total
Theft crimes	48	66	114
Other serious crimes	42	35	77

crimes are committed that do not lead to an arrest, or an individual is arrested for a crime that he did not commit—but arrest records were the best data available. Some of the data collected by the Baltimore LIFE project are summarized in Table 2.20.

The category "theft crimes" includes robbery, burglary, and larceny. The category "other serious crimes" includes murder, rape, and assault. Notice that the number of persons arrested for theft crimes is 27% lower for Group A than for the control group. This certainly appears to be strong evidence supporting the concept of giving such financial aid to newly released ex-prisoners. But wait! The number of persons arrested for other serious crimes is 20% *higher* for Group A than for the control group—a rather unexpected and apparently discouraging result. These data prompt a number of interesting questions. First, are these data statistically significant? This is essentially the same question we have been considering throughout this chapter. There will always be some random variation in data of this kind. The question we need to ask is whether the variation we see could reasonably have occurred because of mere chance.

As usual we begin by carefully formulating a null hypothesis. In this case the null hypothesis is:

Receiving financial aid and being arrested are independent events.

We wish to see to what extent the data in Table 2.20 refute this hypothesis. We will work with each line of Table 2.20 individually. First let us examine the theft data.

A total of 114 arrests were made with a charge of theft. Thus, the probability of being arrested for theft is $114/432 = 0.2639$. Exactly half the ex-prisoners were in Group A. Thus, the probability of being in Group A is 0.5. If these two events were independent (if the null hypothesis is true), then the probability of being in Group A and being arrested for theft would be $(0.5)(0.2639) = 0.1319$. Thus, we would

Table 2.21
Arrest Records from Baltimore LIFE Project

Arrest Charge	Group A (Received Aid)	Group B (Control Group)	Total
Theft crimes	57	57	114

expect $(0.1319)(432) = 57$ ex-prisoners to be in group A and arrested for theft crimes. Similarly, we would expect $(0.1319)(432) = 57$ ex-prisoners to be in Group B and arrested for theft crimes. In other words, assuming the null hypothesis, we would expect the first row of Table 2.20 to look like Table 2.21.

Of course, it is unreasonable to expect to get exactly these figures because of the chance involved in this experiment. So although the results should be reasonably close to Table 2.21, it is unrealistic to expect them to agree exactly. We begin by setting up a computer simulation of the null hypothesis to get a rough idea of whether the data of Table 2.20 are convincing evidence refuting the null hypothesis.

Our simulation is based on the following model. We will choose 114 thieves randomly by using a spinner (on the computer, a random number generator) divided into two sections: one corresponding to ex-prisoners from group A and the other corresponding to ex-prisoners from the control group. We will spin the spinner 114 times to simulate choosing 114 thieves. This simulation will be somewhat different from that in Section 2.2, where we were able to use the same spinner for each choice. This will not work for this problem. To see why, consider the following examples.

In the beginning there are 216 prisoners in Group A and 216 prisoners in the control group. Therefore, the spinner should be divided into two equal sections (Figure 2.18) because a randomly chosen ex-prisoner is equally likely to be from Group A or from the control group. Suppose after 30 spins, 30 thieves have been chosen, all from Group A. Now there are 186 ex-prisoners left in Group A and 216 ex-prisoners left in the control group. Therefore, we need a different spinner with the probability of landing in the Group A section $186/402$ and the probability of landing in the control group section $216/402$ (Figure 2.19).

This is very easy to do in a computer program. The True BASIC program below carries out this simulation and runs 1,000 trials. The results are given in Table 2.22. Look at this program and try to under-

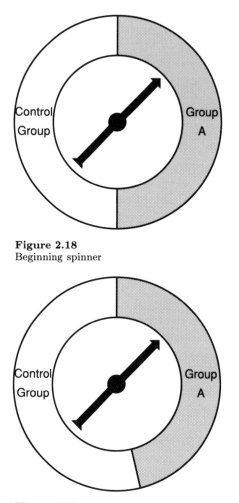

Figure 2.18
Beginning spinner

Figure 2.19
Possible later spinner

stand how it works, but you need not try to write and run it yourself.
This program takes a fairly long time to run. We will write a better and
quicker program later using the ideas from Section 2.3.

```
!    Baltimore LIFE Simulation
!
```

```
!    Written January 6, 1990
!
!    Do one trial
!
DEF trial
LET groupa = 0          ! At start no one from group a
!                         has been arrested
FOR i = 1 TO 114        ! Simulate 114 arrests.
IF RND < (216-groupa)/(433-i) THEN LET groupa = groupa+1  <===
NEXT i
LET trial = groupa
END DEF
!
!    End of trial
!
DIM count(0 to 114)     ! count(i) counts the number
!                         of times i ex-prisoners from
!                         Group A were arrested.
FOR k = 1 TO 1000       ! Do 1000 trials.
LET arrest = trial
LET count(arrest) = count(arrest) + 1
NEXT k
FOR i = 0 TO 114
IF count(i) > 0 THEN PRINT USING "## ###":i, count(i)     ****
NEXT i
END
```

We want to look at one particular line of this program. The subroutine in the beginning does the actual work of simulating one trial. In this trial 114 ex-prisoners are chosen randomly as thieves. The variable i counts the number of choices made. Notice that i goes from 1 to 114. The variable **groupa** counts the number of choices made that happen to be from Group A. We want to look at the statement indicated by an arrow (<===). This is the statement that does the actual choosing (that spins the spinner). Each time this statement is executed, it is choosing the ith thief. Thus, $(i-1)$ thieves have already been chosen. This means

Table 2.22
Baltimore LIFE Simulation

Group A	Number	Group A	Number
39	1	58	84
41	1	59	85
44	2	60	68
46	5	61	55
47	6	62	46
48	18	63	39
49	20	64	27
50	21	65	21
51	47	66	15
52	45	67	9
53	57	68	7
54	59	69	2
55	82	72	1
56	93	75	1
57	83		

that the pool of unarrested ex-prisoners is $432 - (i-1) = 433 - i$. At this point in the simulation, *groupa* thieves have been chosen from Group A. Thus, the remaining pool of unarrested ex-prisoners from Group A is $(216 - groupa)$. Thus, the probability of choosing a thief from Group A is $(216 - groupa)/(433 - i)$. The statement indicated by the arrow simulates a spinner in which the fraction $(216 - group)/(433 - i)$ is marked "Group A."

Now look at the statement marked by four stars (****). If we were to print out all the results from this simulation, we would get a lot of output. There are 115 possibilities for the number of ex-prisoners from Group A who are arrested for theft. Most of the possibilities are extremely unlikely. In fact, in the simulation shown in Table 2.22, none of the trials resulted in fewer than 39 ex-prisoners' from Group A being arrested for theft. If one line of output was printed for each of the 115 possibilities, it would waste a lot of paper with lots of zeros. The starred statement skips printing any line with zero.

By eyeballing this output, you can get a rough idea of how much variation might occur in the Baltimore LIFE experiment by pure chance. We will analyze this question more carefully after computing more exact results using the methods of Section 2.3.

Now we want to use the ideas from Section 2.3 to write a program that will give us more exact results than the rough results obtained from

Table 2.23
Some Baltimore LIFE Probabilities

Number of thieves from Group A	Number of Thieves Chosen So Far				
	1	2	3	4	5
0	0.5000	0.2494	0.1241	0.0616	0.0305
1	0.5000	0.5012	0.3759	0.2500	0.1555
2		0.2494	0.3759	0.3767	0.3140
3			0.1241	0.2500	0.3140
4				0.0616	0.1555
5					0.0305

the simulation above. As we discuss this new program, think in terms of the previous simulation using a spinner or a random number generator.

We will be computing a table of probabilities somewhat like Pascal's Triangle. The beginning of this table will be like Table 2.23. The entries in Table 2.23 are probabilities. The first column gives the probabilities for the results of the first choice of a thief. When the first thief is chosen, it is equally likely that he will be in Group A or in the control group. Thus, after one choice, the probability of no thieves from Group A is 0.5000, and the probability of one thief from Group A is also 0.5000.

For this computation, it is helpful to think of probabilities in the following way. Think of doing a great many trials like those simulated by our earlier program. The entries in the first column tell what fraction of those trials had zero thieves from Group A after one thief had been chosen and what fraction of those trials had one thief from Group A after one thief had been chosen. The entries in the second column will tell us what fraction of the trials had zero, one, or two thieves from Group A after two thieves have been chosen. The entries in this column were computed as follows.

We begin by considering those trials in which the first choice was an ex-prisoner from the control group. Look at Figure 2.20. We are now looking at those trials in the top box on the left, the 50% of the trials that have zero thieves from Group A after one thief has been chosen. The pool of remaining ex-prisoners has 431 members, of whom 215 are from the control group and 216 are from Group A. Thus the probability of choosing the next thief from the control group is 215/431, and the probability of choosing the next thief from Group A is 216/431. This is indicated by the arrows going to the right from the top box on the left to the top two boxes on the right. The fraction 215/431 on the top arrow

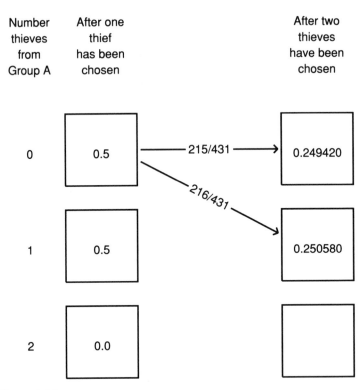

Figure 2.20
Choosing the second thief

indicates the probability of going from the top entry in column 1 to the top entry in column 2 (choosing another ex-prisoner from the control group). The 216/431 on the bottom arrow indicates the probability of going from the top entry in column 1 to the second entry in column 2 (choosing an ex-prisoner from Group A). This results in .249420 = (.5)(215/431) of the trials being in the top entry in column 2. This also puts .250580 = (.5)(216/431) of the trials into the second entry in the second column.

Next we want to look at those trials that start out by choosing an ex-prisoner from Group A. These trials correspond to the second entry in the left-hand column. Look at Figure 2.21. After the first choice has been made from Group A, the pool of remaining ex-prisoners contains 431 ex-prisoners: 215 from Group A and 216 from the control group.

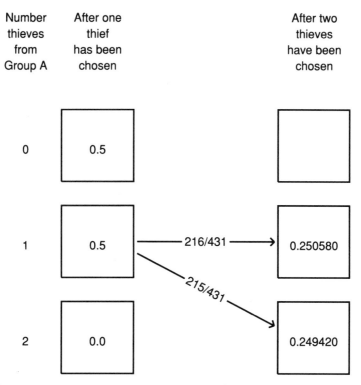

Figure 2.21
Choosing the second thief

On the next choice, the probability of choosing an ex-prisoner from the control group is 216/431, and the probability of choosing an ex-prisoner from Group A is 215/431 (indicated by the numbers on the arrows in Figure 2.21). Notice that with probability 216/431, an ex-prisoner from the control group is chosen, and the total number of thieves from Group A is still one. With probability 215/431, an ex-prisoner from Group A is chosen, and now two thieves from Group A have been chosen. Looking at these trials, we see $0.250580 = (0.5)(215/431)$ of the trials going into the second entry in the second column and $0.249420 = (0.5)(215/431)$ going into the third entry of the second column.

Now we look at Figure 2.22, which puts all of the information from Figures 2.20 and 2.21 together in one place. Notice that there is only one way after making two choices to be in the top entry of the right-hand

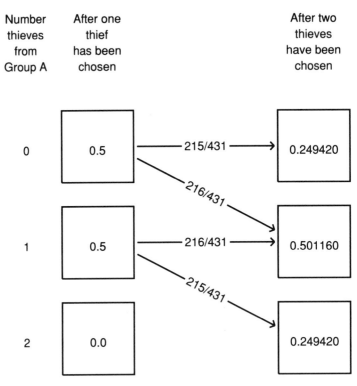

Figure 2.22
Choosing the second thief

column (to have chosen two ex-prisoners from the control group): to have chosen a control group ex-prisoner on the first "spin" and another control group ex-prisoner on the second "spin." Thus, the fraction of trials with no prisoners from Group A after two choices is 0.249420 (from Figure 2.20).

There are two ways to have chosen one ex-prisoner from Group A and one from the control group: by choosing first an ex-prisoner from the control group and then an ex-prisoner from Group A (shown in Figure 2.20) or by choosing first an ex-prisoner from Group A and then an ex-prisoner from the control group (shown in Figure 2.21). In Figure 2.22 we see two arrows leading into the second box on the right. Thus, the fraction of trials with exactly one ex-prisoner from Group A after two choices is $0.501160 = 0.250580$ (from Figure 2.20) + 0.250580 (from Figure 2.21).

There is only one way after making two choices to be in the bottom box on the right (to have chosen two ex-prisoners from Group A): to have chosen an ex-prisoner from Group A on the first choice and also on the second choice. Thus, the fraction of trials with two ex-prisoners from Group A after two choices is 0.249420 (from Figure 2.21).

Before continuing, try to compute the entries in the third column of Table 2.23. It will be easier to understand the following discussion if you have worked out these computations yourself.

Exercise

Exercise 2.7.40   Compute the entries in the third column of Table 2.23.

Now we are ready to work out a general method for computing each column having already computed the preceding column. Suppose that we are working on computing column i. In other words we are about to choose the ith thief. We have the results in column $(i - 1)$ for the probabilities after the choice of $(i - 1)$ thieves. The total pool of ex-prisoners is now $432 - (i - 1) = 433 - i$.

Our first step is to compute the first row of column i. That is, we want to know the probability of choosing no thieves from Group A after i choices. Look at Figure 2.23. We are looking at the top box in column i. In order to be in this box, we must have chosen no thieves from Group A in the first $(i - 1)$ choices, and we must choose a thief from the control group on the ith choice as well. You can see this in Figure 2.23 since the top box on the right has only one arrow coming in from the left. The top box on the left corresponds to choosing no thieves from Group A in the first $(i - 1)$ choices. Thus, $(i - 1)$ thieves have been chosen from the control group. This means that the remaining pool of prisoners from the control group is $216 - (i - 1) = 217 - i$. Therefore, the probability of choosing an ex-prisoner from the control group is:

$$\frac{217 - i}{433 - i}.$$

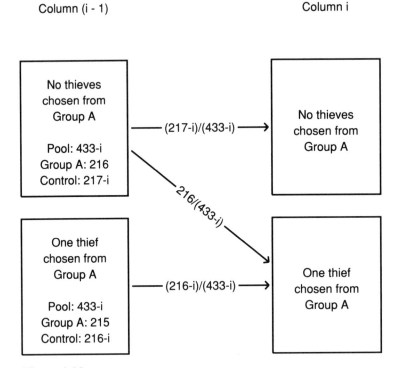

Figure 2.23
Computing probabilities for the next column

If we let `thiscol(0)` contain the probability of being in box 0 in the $(i-1)$st column and `nextcol(0)` contain the probability of being in box 0 in the ith column, then we can compute `nextcol(0)` by:

`LET nextcol(0) = thiscol(0) * (217 - i)/(433 - i)`

Now we want to compute the remaining rows of column i. Refer to Figure 2.24. Suppose that we want to compute row j, that is, the probability of choosing j thieves from Group A after i choices. As you can see from Figure 2.24, there are two ways to choose j thieves in i choices: choose $(j-1)$ thieves from Group A in the first $(i-1)$ choices and then another thief from Group A on the ith choice, or choose j thieves from Group A in the first $(i-1)$ choices and then a thief from the control group on the ith choice. This is indicated in Figure 2.24 by two arrows coming into the jth box on the right from the left.

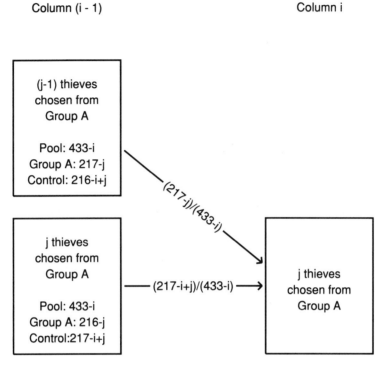

Figure 2.24
Computing probabilities for the next column

We noted above that after $(i-1)$ choices, there is a pool of $432 - (i-1) = 433 - i$ ex-prisoners remaining from which to choose.

Suppose that after $(i-1)$ choices, we are in the top box of Figure 2.24; in other words, $(j-1)$ of the thieves were chosen from Group A. Then the remaining Group A pool contains $216 - (j-1) = 217 - j$ people. Thus, the probability of choosing a Group A person on the next choice is

$$\frac{217 - j}{433 - i}.$$

If `thiscol(j - 1)` is the probability of being in the top box on the left in Figure 2.24, then this box contributes:

`thiscol(j-1) * (217-j)/(433-i)`

to `nextcol(j)`, the probability of being in the box on the right in Figure 2.24.

Now look at the bottom box on the left. In this box we have chosen j thieves from Group A out of $(i-1)$ choices. Therefore, we have chosen $(i-1-j)$ thieves from the control group. Thus, the remaining control group pool is $216 - (i-1-j) = 217 - i + j$. Therefore the probability of choosing an ex-prisoner from the control group on the ith choice is

$$\frac{217 - i + j}{433 - i}.$$

If `thiscol(j)` is the probability of being in the bottom box on the left in Figure 2.24, then this box contributes:

```
thiscol(j) * (217 - i + j)/(433 - i)
```

to `nextcol(j)`, the probability of being in the box on the right in Figure 2.24.

Putting everything together we see that:

```
nextcol(j) = thiscol(j-1)*(217-j)/(433-i) +
             thiscol(j)*(217-i+j)/(433-i)
```

We are now ready to write a True BASIC program to compute the 114th column of Table 2.23. This program is printed below, and its output is shown in Table 2.24. Although writing this program is not an assignment, it would make good practice. In any case, be sure that you understand this program before continuing.

```
!     Probabilities of Possible Results Assuming
!     `the Null Hyopthesis for the Baltimore LIFE
!     Theft Data
!
DIM thiscol(0 to 114), nextcol(0 to 114)
LET thiscol(0) = 0.5       ! Probabilities after
LET thiscol(1) = 0.5       ! first choice
FOR i = 2 TO 114           ! Make choices 2 - 114
LET nextcol(0) = thiscol(0)*(217-i)/(433-i)
FOR j = 1 TO i
LET a = thiscol(j-1)*(217-j)/(433-i)
LET b = thiscol(j)*(217-i+j)/(433-i)
LET nextcol(j) = a + b
NEXT j
```

```
FOR j = 0 to i
LET thiscol(j) = nextcol(j)
NEXT j
NEXT i
FOR j = 0 TO 114
IF thiscol(j)>0.0001 THEN PRINT USING "### #.####":j,thiscol(j)
NEXT j
END
```

(Notice that to conserve paper we have omitted printing all the entries
in which the probability is less than 0.0001.)

We now have all the information needed to find out whether the reduction in the number of thefts among prisoners from Group A is statistically significant. The output in Table 2.24 gives the probability of
each possible result assuming that being arrested for theft is independent of being in Group A (assuming the null hypothesis). In this case
the expected number of thieves from Group A is 57.

In the Baltimore LIFE data, the actual number of thieves from Group
A was 48, or nine fewer than the expected number.   We are interested

Table 2.24
Probabilities of Results Assuming the Null Hypothesis

Thieves from Group A	Probability	Thieves from Group A	Probability
41	.0002	59	.0790
42	.0004	60	.0702
43	.0008	61	.0595
44	.0016	62	.0481
45	.0028	63	.0370
46	.0049	64	.0272
47	.0081	65	.0190
48	.0127	66	.0127
49	.0190	67	.0081
50	.0272	68	.0049
51	.0370	69	.0028
52	.0481	70	.0016
53	.0595	71	.0008
54	.0702	72	.0004
55	.0790	73	.0002
56	.0849	74	.0001
57	.0869		

Table 2.25
Probabilities of Results Assuming the Null Hypothesis

Thieves from Group A	Probability	Thieves from Group A	Probability
41	.0002←	59	.0790
42	.0004←	60	.0702
43	.0008←	61	.0595
44	.0016←	62	.0481
45	.0028←	63	.0370
46	.0049←	64	.0272
47	.0081←	65	.0190
48	.0127←	66	.0127
49	.0190	67	.0081
50	.0272	68	.0049
51	.0370	69	.0028
52	.0481	70	.0016
53	.0595	71	.0008
54	.0702	72	.0004
55	.0790	73	.0002
56	.0849	74	.0001
57	.0869		

in rejecting the null hypothesis that being arrested for a theft crime is independent of being in Group A or Group B. In fact, we are interested in not merely rejecting this null hypothesis but in rejecting it in the direction that this unemployment insurance scheme reduces the likelihood of recidivism. Therefore, we are interested in the one-sided tail of choosing: 0, 1, 2, ..., 48 thieves from Group A. Table 2.25 is a copy of Table 2.24 with arrows marking the probabilities that we must add.

Adding up these entries we get 0.0315 (I have omitted the probabilities less than 0.0001 which were omitted from Table 2.25. This omission does not make a significant difference). With a study involving this number of ex-prisoners, we see that this result is significant at a little better than the .03 level. This result is certainly encouraging enough by itself to warrant further study. If there is even a 10% drop in the arrest rate for theft for released ex-prisoners as a result of this kind of unemployment insurance program, then the program will be worthwhile. Our data show a 27% drop, and we have been able to reject the null hypothesis that the arrest rate for theft crimes is independent of the unemployment insurance program at the .03 level.

"Wait!" the skeptics justifiably interject, "What about the other results of the Baltimore LIFE experiment? It may very well be that the theft arrest rate was lowered by this program, but it appears that the other serious crime arrest rate went up!" The next exercise asks you to look at the results for other serious crimes and determine whether there is statistically significant evidence for this claim.

Exercises

Exercise 2.7.41   Are the results in Table 2.20 for other serious crimes statistically significant?

Exercise 2.7.42   Suppose that the Baltimore LIFE experiment had been carried out with twice as many prisoners (864) with all the results doubled, that is, with the results shown in Table 2.26. Would these results have been statistically significant?

Table 2.26
Arrest Records from Baltimore LIFE Project

Arrest Charge	Group A (Received Aid)	Group B (Control Group)	Total
Theft crimes	96	132	114
Other serious crimes	84	70	77

3 Economic Models

All of us need food and shelter, but very few of us raise our own crops or build our own houses. We live in a world of individuals but rely on each other in very complex ways. We trade our own work for the products of other people's work. This chapter is about economics and economic models. The first half of this chapter is about the law of supply and demand, one of the theoretical mechanisms that economists have used to help explain prices. Prices are an extremely important part of our lives. They determine how much of our own work we must trade for food, shelter, transportation, and so on.

As individuals we must make many decisions—some easy, others more difficult. Some decisions involve elements of chance and some competition. The second part of this chapter is about decision theory.

This is intended as a teaser—to give you a peek at some of the possibilities of economic modeling. I hope that you will pursue this subject by reading more about it, by taking courses, or by experimenting on your own.

3.1 The Law of Supply and Demand

I teach mathematics and write books. I eat food and heat my house with oil. How do I exchange a book like the one you're reading now for a dozen ears of corn or a barrel of oil? The answer, of course, is money. How many copies of this book must be sold to heat a house for one winter? Who decides, and how? What determines the relative price of books and oil?

There is no one answer to these questions. For some commodities and services, prices are regulated by government action. The supply of some products is controlled by a few suppliers who are able to control the price. For example, OPEC was able for a number of years to control the price of oil. For some other commodities prices are determined in the rough and tumble of the marketplace.

Most of us encounter prices every day. We rarely stop to think about them, but they perform an extremely important function. Money is the medium of exchange that enables a farmer in Illinois to trade wheat for a book written by an author in Massachusetts. Prices determine the

relative value of a bushel of wheat, a book, a house, and a ticket to a
concert.

In the next few sections we will study some models of how prices might
be determined in the marketplace. The marketplace we will study is
a very idealized shadow of the real marketplace (for example, we will
ignore advertising). It is the dream of free market economists. They
believe that it is impossible for any group of people to determine how
many bushels of wheat should be traded for how many books. They
believe that price controls and price regulation are based on a false
premise—that it is possible for people, even people assisted by banks of
computers and reams of data, to determine rationally the relative values
of different commodities.

They believe that the price of a book should be determined in the
marketplace. A bookseller should put a price tag on the book. If the
price is too high, the book will sit on the shelf gathering dust until the
price is lowered. If the price is too low, then all copies will be sold, and
the bookseller will be able to raise the price when the next shipment
arrives.

This is a very attractive theory. It allows the actions of millions of
consumers, manufacturers, and store owners to determine prices, but it
relies on a number of assumptions. First, it assumes that the product in
question is not a necessity. Housing, for example, is a necessity. People
cannot go without housing because the price is too high. Second, it
assumes a large number of consumers and a large number of producers
and sellers all acting independently. Otherwise it would be possible
for a single producer or group of producers acting in collusion to control
prices. Sometimes it is even possible for a few large consumers to control
prices. Third, it ignores advertising. Consumers' willingness to pay a
particular price for a commodity depends on their perception of its value.
Advertising can alter that perception.

We will discuss a simple model in order to illustrate the basic principles
of a free market economy. In our model only one commodity or product
is bought and sold. We will call this product Byties. Byties are a
particularly delicious breakfast roll. There is nothing quite so good as
a cup of coffee and a warm, fresh Bytie for breakfast. There is nothing
quite so disappointing as a stale Bytie, and there is no good way to store
Byties.

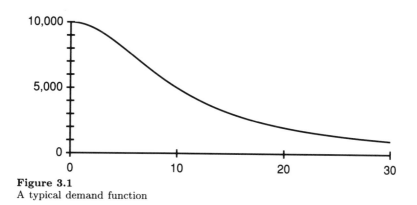

Figure 3.1
A typical demand function

Byties are baked by lots of cottage bakers. Before dawn each morning each baker bakes a batch of Byties, and at about 6:00 a.m. they bring them to the market. Each morning lots of potential customers come down to the marketplace and buy Byties to eat on the spot.

We are interested in the price of Byties, which depends completely on two factors. These two factors, in turn, depend on the price of Byties. The first factor is consumer demand for Byties. The number of Byties that the consumers will buy depends on the price. If the price is low, consumers will buy lots of Byties. If the price is high, they will buy fewer Byties. This consumer behavior is described by a function, $D(p)$, that gives the number of Byties consumers will buy at a given price, p. This function is called the *demand function*. Figure 3.1 shows the graph of a typical demand function. Notice that when the price is zero, the demand is very high. Everybody will "buy" enough free Byties to stuff themselves. As the price rises, however, the demand for Byties drops.

The second factor is the number of Byties baked. The number is determined by the current price of Byties. If the price is too low, the bakers won't bake any Byties at all. The price must be at least high enough to pay for the ingredients. In fact, the bakers will bake very few Byties unless the price is high enough to make up for having to get up early and work over a hot oven. As the price rises, more people will decide to bake Byties, and those who are already baking Byties will get up earlier and work even harder. This baker behavior is described by a function, $S(p)$, that gives the number of Byties that will be baked at a given price, p. This function is called the *supply function*. Figure 3.2 shows the graph of a typical supply function. Notice that there is a

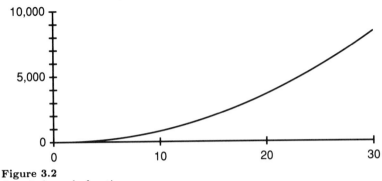

Figure 3.2
A typical supply function

minimum price below which the supply, $S(p)$, is zero. As the price rises
beyond this price, the supply rises due to more and more industrious
bakers.

This is a very simple model that does not take many factors into
account. For example, we have assumed that demand goes down as
prices go up. This seems sensible and is what one would expect with
rational consumers; however, this is not always true. Sometimes a high
price can create an impression of quality. In this case a higher price can
actually increase demand. Similarly, we have assumed that as the price
goes down, the supply will also go down. Again this is not always true.
If we were discussing a very poor community in which baking Byties
were the only possible source of income for the bakers, then a drop in
price might increase the supply because each individual baker would try
his best to make up in volume for the lost profit due to the falling price.

The idea of a free market economy is that the price will be determined
by these two factors: the demand and the supply. Figure 3.3 shows a
graph with both the supply function and the demand function appearing
on the same graph. If the price is low, the demand is higher than the
price. This means that each morning lots of hungry customers will be
milling around the marketplace looking for warm, fresh Byties. There
won't be enough Byties to satisfy all the customers. So after all the
Byties are sold, there will be hungry, unsatisfied customers wandering
around. In this situation, the bakers will be able to raise their prices,
and they will.

But also notice that if the price is very high, then the supply will
be greater than the demand. This means that each morning after all

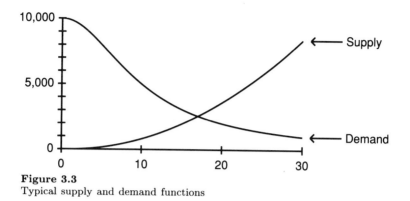

Figure 3.3
Typical supply and demand functions

the customers are gone, some bakers will be staring at unbought Byties starting their certain descent into staleness. There is no way to store Byties. In this situation, with more Byties than customers, the customers will be able to haggle and search for bargains. This will drive the price down. Figure 3.4 shows the same two functions as Figure 3.3 except that I have marked the areas in which the price is too low, creating excess demand and driving prices up, or the price is too high, creating excess supply and driving prices down. There is one price at which the supply and the demand are exactly equal. This is the price at which the graph of the supply function intersects the graph of the demand function. It is called the *equilibrium price*. According to the theory of a free market economy, a commodity will be priced at its equilibrium price. The following examples illustrate how for some simple functions one can find the equilibrium price.

Example

Suppose that the demand function for Byties is

$$D(p) = 1000 - 500p$$

and that the supply function for Byties is

$$S(p) = 100(p - 1).$$

What is the equilibrium price?

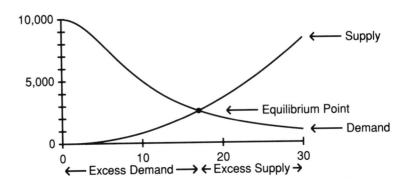

Figure 3.4
Equilibrium price

The equilibrium price is the price at which supply and demand are equal. Thus, we must solve the equation:

$$S(p) = D(p)$$
$$100(p - 1) = 1000 - 500p$$
$$100p - 100 = 1000 - 500p$$
$$600p = 1100$$
$$p = \frac{1100}{600}$$
$$p = \frac{11}{6}$$
$$p = 1.8333.$$

Example

Suppose that the demand function for Byties is

$$S(p) = \begin{cases} 0 & \text{if } p \le 2.50; \\ 100p^2 - 500p + 625, & \text{if } 2.50 \le p. \end{cases}$$

and that the demand function for Byties is

$$D(p) = \begin{cases} 10,000 - 200p^2 & \text{if } p \le 7.0711, \\ 0 & \text{if } 7.0711 \le p. \end{cases}$$

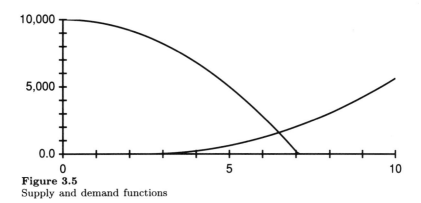

Figure 3.5
Supply and demand functions

These two functions are shown in Figure 3.5. In this graph we can see
that the equilibrium price is between 2.50 and 7.0711. Thus, we can find
the equilibrium price by solving the equation

$$100p^2 - 500p + 625 = 10,000 - 200p^2$$
$$300p^2 - 500p - 9,375 = 0$$

by the quadratic formula to get

$$p = \frac{500 \pm \sqrt{(500)^2 - 4(300)(-9,375)}}{600}$$

$$= \frac{500 \pm \sqrt{250,000 + 11,250,000}}{600}$$

$$= \frac{500 \pm 3,391.165}{600}$$

$$= 6.4858 \text{ or } -4.8186.$$

The second of these two solutions is irrelevant for this problem since we
are looking for a solution between $p = 2.50$ and $p = 7.0711$. Thus the
equilibrium price is 6.4858.

Exercises

***Exercise 3.1.1** Find the equilibrium price for the following supply and demand functions:

$S(p) = 2000(p - 1)$

$D(p) = 1000 - 200p$

Exercise 3.1.2 Find the equilibrium price for the following supply and demand functions:

$S(p) = 2000(p - 1)$

$D(p) = 1000 - 100p$

Exercise 3.1.3 Find the equilibrium price for the following supply and demand functions:

$S(p) = 2000(p - 1.50)$

$D(p) = 1000 - 200p$

Exercise 3.1.4 Find the equilibrium price for the following supply and demand functions:

$S(p) = 2000(p - 1.50)$

$D(p) = 1000 - 100p$

***Exercise 3.1.5** Find the equilibrium price for the following supply and demand functions:

$$S(p) = \begin{cases} 2000(p - 1)^2, & \text{if } p \geq 1; \\ 0, & \text{otherwise.} \end{cases}$$

$D(p) = 1000 - 200p$

***Exercise 3.1.6** Find the equilibrium price for the following supply and demand functions:

$$S(p) = \begin{cases} 2000(p - 1)^2, & \text{if } p \geq 1; \\ 0, & \text{otherwise.} \end{cases}$$

$D(p) = 1000 - 100p$

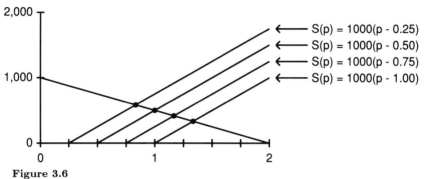

Figure 3.6
One demand function with four supply functions

The Cost of Ingredients

In practice the supply function doesn't depend on the price of Byties alone; it actually depends on the *profit* that bakers make for each Bytie sold. The profit is the difference between the price at which Byties are sold and the cost of the ingredients for each Bytie. If the cost of ingredients is denoted by d, then the supply function is a function of $(p - d)$. The next few exercises ask you to look at some models that consider both price p and the cost of ingredients d.

Example

Consider the following demand function

$$D(p) = 1000 - 500p$$

and the following supply function

$$S(p) = 1000(p - d)$$

where d denotes the cost of ingredients. Figure 3.6 shows this demand function with several different supply functions (corresponding to $d = 0.25$, 0.50, 0.75, and 1.00). Notice that as the cost of ingredients goes up, the equilibrium price also goes up. The following exercises ask you to explore this idea.

Exercises

Exercise 3.1.7 One of the most interesting practical problems in economics is what happens when one price someplace goes up. For example, when the price of oil rises, that affects college tuition because colleges must buy oil to heat their buildings. The purpose of this exercise is to investigate this idea in the context of our simple model.

We will be working with a basic model with the following demand and supply functions:

$$D(p) = 10,000 - 1,000p$$
$$S(p) = 1,000(p - d)$$

where d is the cost of ingredients for one Bytie.

Suppose that the price of the ingredients for Byties rises from \$0.30 to \$0.50. Thus, before the price rise, the supply function is

$$S(p) = 1,000p - 300,$$

and after the price rise, the supply function is

$$S(p) = 1,000p - 500.$$

What happens to the equilibrium price for Byties when the cost of ingredients rises from \$0.30 to \$0.50? Who pays for the rise in the cost of ingredients? How many Byties will be baked and sold at the equilibrium price for Byties before the price rise? How many Byties will be baked and sold at the equilibrium price for Byties after the price rise? What can you say about the job market for Bytie bakers as a result of the rise in the cost of ingredients? What happens if the cost of ingredients rises again to \$0.70?

*Exercise 3.1.8 This exercise looks at the same kinds of questions as the preceding exercise. We will be working with a basic model with the following demand and supply functions:

$$D(p) = 10,000 - 800p$$
$$S(p) = 1,000(p - d)$$

where d is the cost of ingredients for one Bytie.

Suppose that the price of the ingredients for Byties rises from \$0.30 to \$0.50. Thus, before the price rise, the supply function is

$$S(p) = 1,000p - 300,$$

and after the price rise, the supply function is

$$S(p) = 1,000p - 500.$$

What happens to the equilibrium price for Byties when the cost of ingredients rises from \$0.30 to \$0.50? Who pays for the rise in the cost of ingredients? How many Byties will be baked and sold at the equilibrium price for Byties before the price rise? How many Byties will be baked and sold at the equilibrium price for Byties after the price rise? What can you say about the job market for Bytie bakers as a result of the rise in the cost of ingredients? What happens if the cost of ingredients rises again to \$0.70?

Exercise 3.1.9 This exercise looks at the same kinds of questions as the preceding exercise. We will be working with a basic model with the following demand and supply functions:

$$D(p) = 10,000 - 100p$$
$$S(p) = 1,000(p - d)$$

where d is the cost of ingredients for one Bytie.

Suppose that the price of the ingredients for Byties rises from \$0.30 to \$0.50. Thus, before the price rise, the supply function is

$$S(p) = 1,000p - 300,$$

and after the price rise, the supply function is

$$S(p) = 1,000p - 500.$$

What happens to the equilibrium price for Byties when the cost of ingredients rises from \$0.30 to \$0.50? Who pays for the rise in the cost of ingredients? How many Byties will be baked and sold at the equilibrium price for Byties before the price rise? How many Byties will be baked and sold at the equilibrium price for Byties after the price rise? What can you say about the job market for Bytie bakers as a result of the rise in the cost of ingredients? What happens if the cost of ingredients rises again to \$0.70?

Exercise 3.1.10 This exercise looks at the same kinds of questions as the preceding exercise. We will be working with a basic model with the following demand and supply functions:

$$D(p) = 10,000 - 100p$$

$$S(p) = \begin{cases} 1,000(p-d)^2, & \text{if } p \geq d; \\ 0, & \text{otherwise.} \end{cases}$$

where d is the cost of ingredients for one Bytie.

Suppose that the price of the ingredients for Byties rises from \$0.30 to \$0.50. Thus, before the price rise, the supply function is

$$S(p) = 1,000(p - 0.30)^2,$$

and after the price rise, the supply function is

$$S(p) = 1,000(p - 0.50)^2.$$

What happens to the equilibrium price for Byties when the cost of ingredients rises from \$0.30 to \$0.50? Who pays for the rise in the cost of ingredients? How many Byties will be baked and sold at the equilibrium price for Byties before the price rise? How many Byties will be baked and sold at the equilibrium price for Byties after the price rise? What can you say about the job market for Bytie bakers as a result of the rise in the cost of ingredients? What happens if the cost of ingredients rises again to \$0.70?

3.2   Changing Prices

We will now begin our study of *dynamic* or changing economic models. When we buy things, we notice that prices change. We want to understand some of the factors that might be involved in such change. As an example, we will continue studying the same kinds of supply and demand models as in the previous section.

Our model will still deal with one commodity, Byties. Byties are traded in an ideal marketplace. Each morning at about 6:00 a.m. bakers bring their predawn production to the town square. They arrange their wares on trays and post the day's price for Byties. The bakers look around at each other and generally post the same price. If one baker was tempted to charge more than the others, he would notice his neighbors' prices and realize that he wouldn't get any business. If another baker posted a lower price than his neighbors, he would realize that he was making less profit per Bytie than his neighbors. Thus, we will assume that all the bakers are charging the same price.

Soon hungry townspeople start arriving. As the morning progresses, fresh, warm Byties make their way from the bakers' trays to the customers' stomachs. Toward the end of the morning one of three things will happen depending on the current price of Byties:

1. The current price of Byties is equal to the equilibrium price. At the end of the day, all the Byties will have been sold, and all the customers are satisfied.

2. The current price of Byties is above the equilibrium price. Now the supply will be greater than the demand. As the sun rises higher, the bakers' trays will still have some Byties despite the fact that only a few customers and eventually no customers remain in the marketplace. As the last customers wander off, the Byties will start their certain descent into staleness. We say that there is an *excess supply*. Fresh Byties are wonderful, but day-old Byties are not very good at all. Toward the end of the morning both bakers and customers will notice that there are lots of Byties left and very few customers. They will begin to bargain. One baker will start offering 13 Byties for the price of 12. Another will drop his prices. Customers will begin to haggle. The price of Byties will begin to fall.

3. The current price of Byties is below the equilibrium price, and the demand will be greater than the supply. As the Byties begin to disappear from the bakers' trays, there will still be lots of hungry customers milling around. We say that there is an *excess demand*. Both bakers and customers will notice that there are more customers than Byties. Some customers, in pursuit of the last few Byties, may start to bid against each other. The few bakers with remaining Byties will raise their prices.

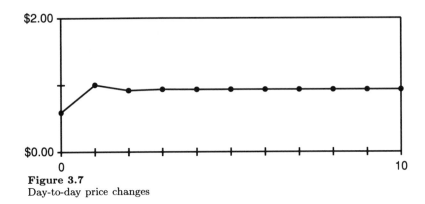

Figure 3.7
Day-to-day price changes

We will illustrate these ideas by looking at a model with the following supply and demand functions:

$$S(p) = 1000p - 400$$
$$D(p) = 1000 - 500p.$$

We will be looking at the price of Byties and how that price changes from day to day. We will name the days day 0, day 1, and so on. The price of Byties on day 0 will be denoted $p(0)$, the price of Byties on day 1 will be denoted $p(1)$, and so forth. We will be drawing graphs like Figure 3.7 showing how the prices change from day to day.

The most important factor for explaining the way that prices fluctuate is excess demand. At a given price p, we can compute the demand for Byties, $D(p)$, and the supply of Byties, $S(p)$. The difference, $D(p) - S(p)$ is the excess demand:

Excess Demand = $D(p) - S(p)$.

For example, if the price is 0.80 we compute:

$$D(0.80) = 1000 - 500(0.80)$$
$$= 600$$

and

$$S(0.80) = 1000(0.80) - 400$$
$$= 400.$$

So,

Excess demand $= 600 - 400 = 200$.

This means that there will be hungry customers for 200 Byties prowl-ing around the marketplace looking for Byties at the end of the morning and no Byties left to be purchased. Notice that:

- If the demand is bigger than supply, the excess demand $D(p) - S(p)$ will be positive.
- If the demand is lower than the supply, the excess demand $D(p) - S(p)$ will be negative.
- If the demand and the supply are equal, the excess demand $D(p) - S(p)$ will be zero.

Now let $p(n)$ denote the price of Byties on day n. For this day, we can compute the demand, the supply and the excess demand for Byties:

$$D(p(n)) = 1000 - 500p(n)$$
$$S(p(n)) = 1000p(n) - 400$$
$$\text{Excess demand} = D(p(n)) - S(p(n))$$
$$= 1000 - 500p(n) - [1000p(n) - 400]$$
$$= 1400 - 1500p(n).$$

The next day's price will respond to the facts of the marketplace as follows:

- If excess demand is zero, everyone goes away happy, and the price will not change.
- If excess demand is positive, the bakers ran out of Byties before they ran out of customers. The price of Byties will rise. How much it will rise depends on how many customers remain at the end of the morning. If there is just a small excess demand, one would expect only a small rise in the price of Byties, but if there is a large excess demand, the price will rise by quite a bit.
- If the excess demand is negative, the bakers ran out of customers before they ran out of Byties. The price of Byties will fall. How much it will fall depends on how many Byties they have left over.

One possible way to model this behavior is by the formula:

$$p(n + 1) = p(n) + k[\text{Excess demand}]$$
$$= p(n) + k[1400 - 1500p(n)].$$

This formula requires some explanation. First, notice that $p(n)$ denotes the price of Byties on day n. Then notice that $p(n + 1)$ denotes the price of Byties on the next day, day $n + 1$. For example, if the current day is day 14, then $p(n) = p(14)$, the price of Byties on day 14, and $p(n + 1) = p(15)$, the price of Byties on the next day, day 15.

The letter k represents a positive constant. It regulates how strongly the marketplace reacts to excess supply and demand. If k is a relatively large number, then the marketplace reacts quickly and strongly to market conditions. Prices will change rapidly. If k is a relatively small number, then the marketplace reacts more sluggishly. In a real marketplace, one would determine the value of k by observation. It depends on such factors as the personalities of bakers and customers.

Notice that since k is positive, the price will rise if the excess demand is positive (if there is an excess demand) and will fall if the excess demand is negative (if there is an excess supply).

This is a good place for some experimentation. We will work out some examples trying different values of k to see what happens. After looking at these examples, we will try to develop a theory to explain our observations.

The first step is to find the equilibrium price for this particular model. As usual we must solve the equation

$$S(p) = D(p)$$
$$1000p - 400 = 1000 - 500p$$
$$1500p = 1400$$
$$p = 1400/1500$$
$$= 0.8333.$$

Now we will work out three examples of the dynamics of this model all starting on day 0 with a current price of \$1.50, considerably above the equilibrium price. Our three examples will have $k = .0002$, $k = .0004$, and $k = .0008$.

For $k = .0002$ we have

$$p(1) = p(0) + .0002[1400 - 1500p(0)]$$
$$= 1.50 + .0002[1400 - (1500)(1.50)]$$
$$= 1.50 + .0002(-850)$$
$$= 1.50 - 0.17$$
$$= 1.33$$

$$p(2) = p(1) + .0002[1400 - 1500(p(1)]$$
$$= 1.33 + .0002[1400 - (1500)(1.33)]$$
$$= 1.21.$$

Continuing these calculations we obtain the results shown in Table 3.1. Figure 3.8 shows these same results graphically.

Table 3.1
Prices for Ten Days, $k = .0002$

Day Number	Price
0	1.5000
1	1.3300
2	1.2110
3	1.1277
4	1.0694
5	1.0286
6	1.0000
7	0.9800
8	0.9660
9	0.9562
10	0.9493

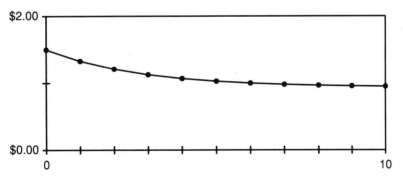

Figure 3.8
Prices for 10 days, $k = .0002$

Table 3.2
Prices for Ten Days, $k = .0004$

Day Number	Price
0	1.5000
1	1.1600
2	1.0240
3	0.9696
4	0.9478
5	0.9391
6	0.9357
7	0.9343
8	0.9337
9	0.9335
10	0.9334

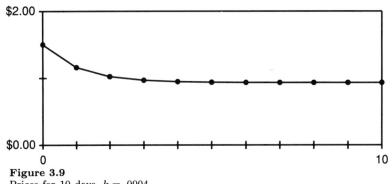

Figure 3.9
Prices for 10 days, $k = .0004$

For $k = .0004$ we obtain the results shown in Table 3.2. Figure 3.9 shows these same results graphically.

For $k = .0008$ we obtain the results shown in Table 3.3. Figure 3.10 shows these same results graphically.

Look over all three of these examples. Notice that for k relatively small ($k = .0002$), prices change relatively slowly, but they do drop steadily toward the equilibrium price $p = 0.9333$. For k somewhat larger ($k = .0004$), prices drop more rapidly toward the equilibrium price. For k even larger ($k = .0008$), prices change so rapidly that they actually drop below the equilibrium price, then rise above it, then drop below it, and eventually reach the equilibrium price only after oscillating around it for a bit.

We will see that this behavior is fairly typical, but before continuing, you should work out some examples of your own.

Table 3.3
Prices for Ten Days, $k = .0008$

Day Number	Price
0	1.5000
1	0.8200
2	0.9560
3	0.9288
4	0.9342
5	0.9332
6	0.9334
7	0.9333
8	0.9333
9	0.9333
10	0.9333

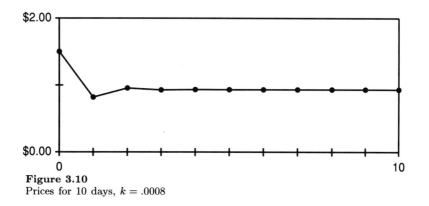

Figure 3.10
Prices for 10 days, $k = .0008$

Exercises

*Exercise 3.2.11 Do calculations and draw a graph similar to the ones above with $k = .0002$ and an original price on day 0 of $p(0) = 0.30$.

Exercise 3.2.12 Do calculations and draw a graph similar to the ones above with $k = .0004$ and an original price on day 0 of $p(0) = 0.30$.

Exercise 3.2.13 Do calculations and draw a graph similar to the ones above with $k = .0008$ and an original price on day 0 of $p(0) = 0.30$.

Exercise 3.2.14 Try $p(0) = 1.50$ and $k = .0010$.

Exercise 3.2.15 Try $p(0) = 0.30$ and $k = .0010$.

*Exercise 3.2.16 Try $p(0) = 1.20$ and $k = .0020$.

Exercise 3.2.17 Try $p(0) = 0.80$ and $k = .0020$.

You may get some surprising results. Try to explain them. You may want to write a computer program to do your calculations for this set of exercises.

Now we want to examine the change equation

$$p(n + 1) = p(n) + k[1400 - 1500p(n)]$$

more carefully. Notice that $p(n + 1)$ will equal $p(n)$ if

$$1400 - 1500p(n) = 0,$$

that is, if

$$p(n) = 1400/1500 = 0.9333,$$

the equilibrium price.

This is our first observation: the current price will not change if and only if it is the equilibrium price. If we rewrite the change equation as follows,

$$\begin{aligned} p(n + 1) &= p(n) + k[1400 - 1500p(n)] \\ &= p(n) + 1500k[0.9333 - p(n)], \end{aligned}$$

we see that the price will drop if it is above the equilibrium price, 0.9333, and it will rise if it is below the equilibrium price. This is exactly what we would expect since there will be an excess demand if the price is below the equilibrium price and an excess supply if the price is above the equilibrium price.

The next question we might ask is how much the price will rise or fall from day to day. If, by chance, $1500k$ happened to be exactly 1, then the previous equation would become

$$\begin{aligned} p(n + 1) &= p(n) + (1)[0.9333 - p(n)] \\ &= .9333 \end{aligned}$$

and $p(n + 1)$ would be exactly equal to the equilibrium price.

Table 3.4
Prices for Ten Days, $k = .0020$

Day Number	Price
0	1.2000
1	0.4000
2	2.0000
3	-1.2000
4	5.2000
5	-7.6000
6	18.0000
7	-33.2000
8	69.1999
9	-135.5990
10	273.9990

If $1500k$ is less than 1, then the price won't rise or fall all the way to the equilibrium price. If $1500k$ is greater than 1, then the price will rise or fall too far and go past the equilibrium price. In our three examples we looked at $k = .0002$, $k = .0004$, and $k = .0008$. In these three cases we see

for $k = .0002$ $1500k = 0.3 < 1$

for $k = .0004$ $1500k = 0.6 < 1$

for $k = .0008$ $1500k = 1.2 > 1$

which explains our observation that in the first two cases, the price went directly toward the equilibrium price without overshooting it, but in the third case the price overshot the equilibrium price, fluctuating around it.

Exercises 3.2.14 and 3.2.15 were more of the same, only worse: the price overshot the equilibrium price by a wider margin. The fluctuations were larger, but the price did eventually tend toward the equilibrium price. These kinds of examples are typical of the free market economy at its theoretical best. The law of supply and demand brings the price to the equilibrium price.

Exercises 3.2.16 and 3.2.17, however, produced much worse results—for example, Exercise 3.2.16 yields the results shown in Table 3.4 and Figure 3.11. In this case k is so big, the market is so volatile, that the price overshoots the equilibrium price by so much that it keeps getting further away from the equilibrium price. In fact, it soon becomes negative. Of course, this is impossible: it would mean that bakers were

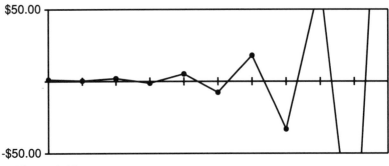

Figure 3.11
Prices for 10 days, $k = .0020$

paying customers to eat their Byties. This example indicates that markets can't react too strongly or too quickly to excess suppy or demand without causing very serious problems. Unfortunately one can sometimes observe this kind of behavior in the real world.

The unfettered law of supply and demand can work disastrously in some circumstances—for example, with farm prices. Farmers have to contend with a number of difficult problems. The vagaries of the weather, not only on their own farm but in the rest of the world, can have a huge impact on the supply of a particular commodity reaching the market and, hence, on the price they receive for that commodity. Farmers must decide on their production far in advance of market day—at least one year ahead. Typically they borrow money to finance each year's planting and hope to be able to repay it after the harvest. An oversupply of their produce can cause prices to drop below their production costs. They may be forced to sell at a price too low to repay their loans. In the short term this is good news for consumers but bad news for farmers. But in the longer term it is also bad news for consumers. When farmers are forced out of business, the next year's supply may be very low, bringing prices back up—way up.

We have worked with variations of one particular example in this whole section. The exercises ask you to apply these techniques to another example.

Exercises

All of these exercises involve a commodity very much like Byties. The supply and demand functions for this commodity are:

$$S(p) = 1500p - 500$$
$$D(p) = 2000 - 1000p$$

*Exercise 3.2.18 Find the equilibrium price for this commodity.

Now consider the change equation:

$$p(n+1) = p(n) + k(D(p(n)) - S(p(n))).$$

*Exercise 3.2.19 Let $p(0) = 0.50$ and $k = .0003$ and make a table and graph similar to the ones in this section showing the price on days 0, 1, 2, ..., 10.

Exercise 3.2.20 Repeat the previous exercise with $p(0) = 1.50$ and $k = .0003$.

Exercise 3.2.21 Repeat the previous exercise with $p(0) = 0.50$ and $k = .0005$.

Exercise 3.2.22 Repeat the previous exercise with $p(0) = 1.50$ and $k = .0005$.

Exercise 3.2.23 Repeat the previous exercise with $p(0) = 1.50$ and $k = .0010$.

*Exercise 3.2.24 Determine for which values of k:

- The price will go directly toward the equilibrium price without overshooting.
- The price will overshoot the equilibrium price, but still tend toward the equilibrium price.
- The price will overshoot and fluctuate wildly around the equilibrium price and eventually crash by becoming negative.

3.3   Variations on a Theme

We have been talking about the marketplace for Byties as if it were completely self-contained, but it is not. Events outside the town square can have a big impact on what happens to the market for Byties. For example, the bakers must obtain the ingredients for Byties someplace. The price of those ingredients might rise or fall. In Section 3.1 we investigated the dependence of the equilibrium price of Byties on the cost of ingredients. As an example, we looked at a supply function,

$$S(p) = 1000(p - d),$$

that depended on both the price, p, of Byties and the cost, d, of the ingredients for Byties. Now we want to investigate how a sudden change in the cost of the ingredients for Byties will affect the marketplace. As an example, we will work with the supply function above and the demand function

$$D(p) = 1000 - 500p.$$

Suppose that the price of ingredients, d, has been \$0.30 for some time and then jumps suddenly to \$0.50. We want to study the marketplace for five days before the change and 10 days after the change. We will name the days day 0, day 1, ..., day 15 and assume that d changes on day 5. Figure 3.12 shows a graph of d.

On days number 0, 1, 2, 3, and 4 the supply function is

$$S(p) = 1000(p - 0.30)$$
$$= 1000p - 300.$$

and on days number 5, 6, 7, ..., 15 the supply function is

$$S(p) = 1000(p - 0.50)$$
$$= 1000p - 500.$$

We will continue to use the same demand function:

$$D(p) = 1000 - 500p.$$

Figure 3.13 shows this demand function and the two different supply functions.

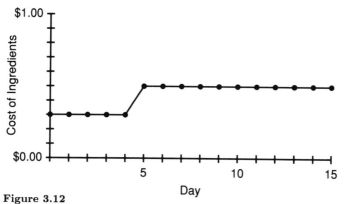

Figure 3.12
The cost of ingredients for Byties

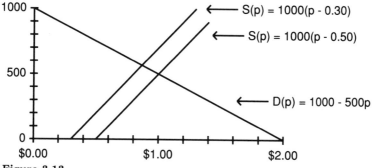

Figure 3.13
Demand function with two different supply functions

Next we want to find the equilibrium price on day 0–day 4 when $d = 0.30$ and $S(p) = 1000p - 300$. As usual we find the equilibrium price by solving the equation

$$S(p) = D(p)$$
$$1000p - 300 = 1000 - 500p$$
$$1500p = 1300$$
$$p = 1300/1500$$
$$= 0.8667.$$

Similarly, we can find the equilibrium price on day 5–day 15

$$S(P) = D(p)$$
$$1000p - 500 = 1000 - 500p$$
$$1500p = 1500$$
$$p = 1500/1500$$
$$= 1.0000.$$

Now we want to combine this work with our dynamic model from Section 3.2 to see how the price of Byties might change when the cost of ingredients goes from \$0.30 to \$0.50. We will assume that the price of Byties on day 0 is the equilibrium price 0.8667 and that the price changes from day to day according to the change equation

$$p(n + 1) = p(n) + k(\text{Excess demand})$$
$$= p(n) + k[D(p(n)) - S(P(n))].$$

Notice that for $n = 0, 1, 2, 3, 4,$

$$D(p(n)) - S(p(n)) = 1000 - 500p(n) - [1000p(n) - 300]$$
$$= 1300 - 1500p(n)$$

and that for $n = 5, 6, 7, \ldots, 15,$

$$D(p(n)) - S(p(n)) = 1000 - 500p(n) - [1000p(n) - 500]$$
$$= 1500 - 1500p(n).$$

For $n = 0, 1, 2, 3, 4,$

$$p(n + 1) = p(n) + k[1300 - 1500p(n)]$$

and for $n = 5, 6, 7, \ldots, 15,$

$$p(n + 1) = p(n) + k[1500 - 1500p(n)].$$

We will use $k = .00115$ as an example. Using the above equations, we compute the day-to-day prices for Byties as follows:

$$p(0) = 0.8667 \quad (\text{Our assumption})$$

$$p(1) = p(0) + (.00115)[1300 - 1500p(0)]$$
$$= 0.8667 + (.00115)[1300 - (1500)(0.8667)]$$
$$= 0.8667$$

$$\vdots$$

$$p(5) = p(4) + (.00115)[1300 - 1500p(4)]$$
$$= 0.8667 + (.00115)[1300 - (1500)(0.8667)]$$
$$= 0.8667$$

$$p(6) = p(5) + (.00115)[1500 - 1500p(5)] \qquad \leftarrow \text{ NOTE!!}$$
$$= 0.8667 + (.00115)[1500 - (1500)(0.8667)]$$
$$= 1.0967$$

$$p(7) = p(6) + (.00115)[1500 - 1500p(6)]$$
$$= 1.0967 + (.00115)[1500 - (1500)(1.0967)]$$
$$= 0.9299$$

$$\vdots$$

Continue the calculations for the next few days. Figure 3.14 shows the results of this model graphically.

On days 0–4 nothing interesting happens. The price is already at the equilibrium. Each day the bakers and buyers leave the marketplace happy. There are no Byties left over and no unsatisfied customers remaining. On day 5, the cost of ingredients rises to $0.50. The supply function changes: fewer bakers are willing to make Byties because their profit has gone down. As a result on day 5 there are not enough Byties for all the customers. This shortage causes the price of Byties to jump

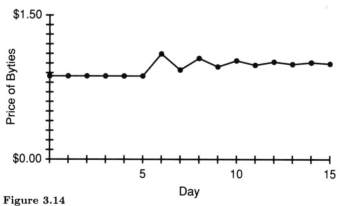

Figure 3.14
Prices after rise in cost of ingredients

way up on day 6. The higher price draws more bakers into business, and, in fact, on day 6 there is an oversupply of Byties. The price falls on day 7. In our example, the price jumps around a bit but appears to be settling down to the new equilibrium price of 1.00. The marketplace has worked very well. After some initial wandering around, the price changed from the old equilibrium price to the new equilibrium price.

Notice that the old equilibrium price was 0.8667 and the new equilibrium price is 1.00. The difference is 0.1333, so the buyers have absorbed 0.1333 of the 0.2000 increase in the cost of ingredients, and the bakers have absorbed the remaining 0.0667. In this example, the bakers are unable to pass all of their increased costs on to consumers.

We have worked out one particular example—a small start in studying economic models. You should try to carry on from here. The models have been very simple, and you can probably see lots of ways to change them more in line with your own ideas about how the marketplace might work. The following exercises ask you to do some simulations. After you finish them, try to think up some models of your own. You may be able to use some of the methods of this chapter and your programming skills to explore your own models. As a start on expanding these ideas, in Section 3.4 I will discuss some possible models that incorporate consumer reaction to inflation.

Exercises

Most of the exercises in this section can be done with a calculator or by writing short computer programs.

***Exercise 3.3.25** Do the calculations and draw a graph showing the change in the price of Byties for an example exactly like the example above except that $k = .0004$.

Exercise 3.3.26 Do the calculations and draw a graph showing the change in the price of Byties for an example exactly like the example above except that $k = .0006$.

Exercise 3.3.27 Do the calculations and draw a graph showing the change in the price of Byties for an example similar to the example above except that the cost of the ingredients for Byties drops from $0.30 to $0.20 instead of rising from $0.30 to $0.50. Use $k = .00115$.

Exercise 3.3.28 Repeat the previous exercise with $k = .0006$.

Exercise 3.3.29 The number k reflects the speed with which the price responds to any excess demand or supply. If k is relatively small, the price changes relatively slowly. If k is relatively large, the price changes more rapidly. Explore the effect of k on how quickly the price reaches the new equilibrium level following the change in the cost of ingredients. Repeat the calculations of the original example with the following values of k: $k = 0.0001, 0.0002, 0.0003, \ldots, 0.0015$ (this exercise requires a computer).

Make a table showing how many days it takes the price to reach the new equilibrium price (within .001) after the change in the cost of ingredients rises for each value of k. Describe any other interesting aspects of your results.

In all of our examples so far, we assumed that when the price of ingredients rose, the bakers did not directly raise their prices. Instead the supply went down because some bakers quit or baked fewer Byties. The bakers in a real life situation might very well react this way; however, there are other possibilities. One is that the bakers might immediately try to pass all of the increased cost of ingredients on to the consumers. When they found about about the rise in the cost of their ingredients, the bakers might talk informally among themselves, complaining about the sudden jump in their cost of doing business. A consensus might develop that they should raise their prices 0.20 to maintain their "profit margin."

In this situation the prices would be determined as follows:

days 0-4:	$p = 0.8667$	exactly the same as before.
day 5:	$p(5) = 1.0667$	price rises 0.20 by consensus.
days 6-15:	$p(n+1) = p(n) + k[1500 - 1500p(n)]$.	

The last formula (for $n = 5, 6, 7, \ldots$) is exactly the same as before. The usual laws of supply and demand take over after the bakers' initial agreement.

Exercise

Exercise 3.3.30 Explore the model above. Work out examples with $k = .0008$ and $k = .0010$. Discuss your results comparing them to our earlier results.

We have explored only a few of many possible models. Economic modeling is an art. The idea behind a mathematical model is to capture the most important parts of a complicated situation. Modeling requires a sense of what is important. Building a mathematical model can help you clarify your own thinking about the way in which an economy works. It can help you explore the consequences of your ideas. Try out some of your own ideas about economic models in addition to looking at the ideas presented here.

3.4   Inflation

One of the most important methods by which we reach an understanding of how the world works is modeling. We build mental images or models of the phenomena we wish to study. Some of the most useful models are mathematical. Mathematical models can be quite complicated and require a tremendous amount of calculation. Computers can be extremely useful for studying such models. In fact, computers can be useful in two different ways: they enable us to simulate complicated models with relative ease, and their languages are powerful for expressing models.

The purpose of this chapter is to illustrate some of the ideas and techniques involved in computer-based mathematical modeling of economic systems. With these basic techniques, you will be able to construct models of your own and to understand models suggested by others. Building a mathematical model requires an interplay between one's intuitive ideas about how things work in the real world and the mathematical representation of these ideas. The goals of this interaction usually include a sharpened understanding of the real world and a useful model.

To illustrate these ideas we will study inflation and, especially, the way that consumers react to it and how that reaction might affect prices. When we go to the market to purchase any commodity, for example, fish, we decide what to buy partly on the basis of price. We don't just look at the day's price: we compare it with the previous day's price. For example, when the price of bluefish drops from $2.29 to $1.99 per pound, $1.99 seems like a wonderful deal. But if the price of bluefish rises from $1.79 to $1.99 per pound, then the same $1.99 doesn't seem so wonderful.

Consumers might react to inflation in several different ways:

- They might ignore it, considering only the current price each day.

- They might buy more when prices are falling than one would expect on the basis of the current price alone because the actual price on a given day seems lower by comparison with the previous day's price. Similarly, they might buy less than one would otherwise expect when prices are rising because the actual price on a given day seems higher by comparison with the previous day's price.

- They might buy less when prices are going down than one would expect on the basis of the current price alone because they might expect prices to drop even further so they could get a better deal by postponing a purchase. Similarly, they might buy more than one would otherwise expect when prices are rising because they expect prices to continue rising and this might be their last chance to buy before prices rise even higher. The most dramatic form of this behavior is the hoarding of goods that sometimes occurs during periods of inflation. Of course, hoarding applies only to goods that can be saved for future use.

We would like to build a model that can be used to simulate the various kinds of consumer behavior. We will work with one example and one of the many possible ways in which such behavior might be modeled.

We will continue to study the ups and downs of the price of Byties. Each day—day 0, day 1, and so forth—we will consider the price $p(n)$ on that particular day and also the following *fractional change*:

$$\text{Fractional Change} = \frac{p(n) - p(n-1)}{p(n-1)}.$$

The numerator, $p(n)-p(n-1)$, of this fraction is the change in price from the previous day, day $(n-1)$, to the current day, day n. We divide this

Table 3.5
Computation of Fractional Change

Previous Price	Current Price	Fractional Change
$1.00	$1.25	0.25
$2.00	$2.40	0.20
$1.00	$0.80	-0.20
$3.00	$2.40	-0.20

change by the previous day's price, $p(n-1)$, to determine how much the price has changed as a fraction of its previous price. See, for example, Table 3.5. Notice that the fractional change is positive when prices are rising and negative when prices are falling.

In the last few sections we have been using the demand function

$$D(p) = 1000 - 500p,$$

so that on day n, the demand for Byties is

$$\text{Demand} = 1000 - 500p(n).$$

We want to modify this demand function in view of the change in price between the previous day and the current day. One possible way is to use the following demand function:

$$\text{Modified demand} = m(1000 - 500p(n)).$$

In this modified formula the original demand is multiplied by some number m depending on the consumers' reaction to changing prices. The number m will be called the *inflation multiplier*.

If consumers ignore inflation, the inflation multiplier, m, will be 1 and the modified demand will be the same as the original demand. Otherwise m will depend on the fractional change

$$\frac{p(n) - p(n-1)}{p(n-1)}.$$

We will use the following formula for m,

$$m = 1 + q\left(\frac{p(n) - p(n-1)}{p(n-1)}\right),$$

where q is a constant. The actual value of q will depend on the way that consumers react to inflation:

- If $q = 0$ then $m = 1$, and this model will represent demand for consumers who ignore inflation and make their decisions solely on the basis of the current price. In other words, if $q = 0$, the modified demand function is exactly the same as the original unmodified demand function.

- If $q < 0$ then when prices are rising, m will be less than 1 and consumers will buy fewer Byties than they would be expected to buy on the basis of the current price alone. Conversely, when the price of Byties is falling, m will be greater than 1 and consumers will buy more Byties than they would be expected to buy on the basis of the current price alone. This is the most intuitive kind of behavior. Consumers are more likely to buy when prices are falling since each day's price seems like a good deal in the light of recent memory. Consumers are less likely to buy when prices are rising because each day's price seems high in the light of recent memory.

- If $q > 0$ then when prices are rising, m will be larger than 1, and consumers will buy more Byties than they would be expected to buy on the basis of the current price alone. Conversely, if prices are falling, m will be less than 1, and consumers will buy fewer Byties than they would be expected to buy on the basis of the current price alone. This kind of behavior, while less immediately intuitive, is nonetheless quite plausible. Customers observing falling prices might expect prices to continue falling and hence might buy less in the expectation that they could buy the same goods for even less the following day. Similarly, customers observing rising prices might expect them to continue rising and hasten to buy Byties now before the price rises even further.

This model enables us to model three different kinds of consumer behavior simply by changing the value of the constant q. It's worthwhile to work out an example to illustrate this idea.

Example

The current day's price is $1.20, and the previous day's price was $1.00. That is,

$$p(n) = 1.20$$

$p(n-1) = 1.00.$

Prices are rising. Using our original demand formula the demand would be:

$$\text{Original demand} = 1000 - (500)(1.20)$$
$$= 1000 - 600$$
$$= 400.$$

Now we consider our new formula with three different possibilities:

1. Consumers ignore changing prices (i.e., $q = 0$):

   $$\text{Modified demand} = m[1000 - 500p(n)].$$

   First we calculate the inflation multiplier, m

   $$m = 1 + q\left(\frac{p(n) - p(n-1)}{p(n-1)}\right)$$
   $$= 1 + 0\left(\frac{p(n) - p(n-1)}{p(n-1)}\right)$$
   $$= 1.$$

   So,

   $$\text{Modified demand} = 1[1000 - 500(1.20)]$$
   $$= 400,$$

   exactly the same as the original unmodified demand.

2. Consumers react to inflation by buying less when prices are rising and more when prices are falling ($q < 0$). For this example, we will let $q = -0.5$. First we calculate the inflation multiplier, m:

   $$m = 1 + q\left(\frac{p(n) - p(n-1)}{p(n-1)}\right)$$
   $$= 1 - 0.5\left(\frac{1.20 - 1.00}{1.00}\right)$$
   $$= 1 - 0.10$$
   $$= 0.90.$$

So,

$$\text{Modified demand} = 0.90[1000 - 500(1.20)]$$
$$= (0.90)(400)$$
$$= 360,$$

which is less than the original unmodified demand.

3. Consumers react to inflation by buying more when prices are rising and less when prices are falling ($q > 0$). For this example, we will let $q = 0.5$. First we calculate the inflation multiplier, m:

$$m = 1 + q\left(\frac{p(n) - p(n-1)}{p(n-1)}\right)$$
$$= 1 + 0.5\left(\frac{1.20 - 1.00}{1.00}\right)$$
$$= 1 + 0.10$$
$$= 1.10.$$

So,

$$\text{Modified demand} = 1.10[1000 - 500(1.20)]$$
$$= (1.10)(400)$$
$$= 440,$$

which is more than the original unmodified demand.

Before continuing, make sure that you understand how this model works—why the constant q reflects consumer behavior as described. It would be helpful to work out the following exercises.

Exercises

*__Exercise 3.4.31__ Work out an example similar to the example. Use the same values of q, but use $p(n) = 1.20$ and $p(n-1) = 1.50$. This exercise will illustrate what happens to demand when prices are falling.

__Exercise 3.4.32__ Repeat the preceding exercise with $q = -1.0$, $q = 0$, and $q = 1.0$.

We want to investigate how these different possible consumer reactions to changing prices might affect the marketplace. We will build on the last of our models from Section 3.3. The model starts out with everything in equilibrium on days 0, 1, 2, 3, and 4. The price is the equilibrium price. Actually the use of the term *equilibrium price* requires some elaboration now that inflation has reared its ugly head.

In our model from Section 3.3, prices change according to the equation

$$p(n + 1) = k(\text{Excess demand})$$
$$= p(n) + k[\text{Demand} - \text{supply}].$$

If demand = supply, then $p(n+1) = p(n)$. Hence, once the price reaches the equilibrium price, it stays there.

With our new model we have prices changing according to the equation

$$p(n + 1) = k(\text{Excess demand})$$
$$= p(n) + k[\text{Modified demand} - \text{supply}].$$

Now the modified demand depends on two prices: the current day's price, $p(n)$, and the previous day's price, $p(n - 1)$. It is quite possible for the modified demand to be different from the supply even if the price is the equilibrium price. Here are some examples.

Examples

In all these examples the current price $p(n)$ is the equilibrium price and $q = 0.5$. The unmodified demand function is

$$D(p) = 1000 - 500p,$$

and the supply function is

$$S(p) = 1000p - 300.$$

We determined the equilibrium price for this supply and demand function in Section 3.3:

Equilibrium price $= 1300/1500 = 0.8667$.

At this price, the supply and the unmodified demand are equal:

$$S(0.8667) = 566.6667$$

$D(0.8667) = 566.6667$

and, thus, excess demand $= 0$.

Now we want to examine what happens when the modified demand function is used.

Example 1

Prices have been falling, and consumers react by buying less than they would normally at the current price ($q > 0$). This is the way they might behave if they were anticipating further price drops. The current price is the equilibrium price:

$$p(n - 1) = 1.0000$$
$$p(n) = 0.8667$$
$$q = 0.5.$$

We compute the inflation multiplier m as follows:

$$m = 1 + q \left(\frac{p(n) - p(n - 1)}{p(n - 1)} \right)$$
$$= 1 + 0.5 \left(\frac{0.8667 - 1.0000)}{1.0000} \right)$$
$$= 1 + (0.5)(-0.1333)$$
$$= 0.9333.$$

The modified demand is

$$\text{Modified demand} = 0.9333[1000 - (500)(0.8667)]$$
$$= (0.9333)(566.6667)$$
$$= 528.87.$$

This is considerably less than the original unmodified demand and the supply. Thus, there will be a negative excess demand—an excess supply. This will cause the price of Byties to fall although it is currently at the equilibrium price.

Example 2

Prices have been rising, and consumers react by buying more than they would normally at the current price ($q > 0$). This is the way that they might behave if they were anticipating further price increases. The current price is the equilibrium price:

$$p(n-1) = 0.8000$$

$$p(n) = 0.8667$$

$$q = 0.5.$$

We compute the inflation multiplier m as follows:

$$m = 1 + q \left(\frac{p(n) - p(n-1)}{p(n-1)} \right)$$

$$= 1 + 0.5 \left(\frac{0.8667 - 0.8000)}{0.8000} \right)$$

$$= 1 + (0.5)(0.0834)$$

$$= 1.0417.$$

The modified demand is

$$\text{Modified demand} = 1.0417[1000 - (500)(0.8667)]$$

$$= (1.0417)(566.6667)$$

$$= 590.29,$$

considerably more than the original unmodified demand and the supply. Thus, although the current price is the equilibrium price, there will be an excess demand. This will cause the price of Byties to rise although it is at the equilibrium price.

Example 3

Both the current price and the previous price are the same: the equilibrium price $p = 0.8667$. Consumers react in the same way to rising and falling prices as in the previous two examples:

$$p(n-1) = 0.8667$$

$$p(n) = 0.8667$$

$$q = 0.5.$$

We compute the inflation multiplier m as follows:

$$m = 1 + q \left(\frac{p(n) - p(n-1)}{p(n-1)} \right)$$

$$= 1 + 0.5 \left(\frac{0.8667 - 0.8667)}{0.8667} \right)$$

$$= 1 + (0.5)(0.0)$$

$$= 1.0,$$

so the modified demand is

$$
\begin{aligned}
\text{Modified demand} &= 1.0[1000 - (500)(0.8667)] \\
&= (1.0)(566.6667) \\
&= 566.6667.
\end{aligned}
$$

This is the same as the original unmodified demand and the supply. Thus, excess demand will still be zero, and the price will remain at the equilibrium price.

Looking at these three examples, we see that if the price is at the equilibrium level *for two consecutive days*, it will remain there. However, if the price is rising or falling, then it is quite possible to have either excess demand or excess supply even if the current price is temporarily at the equilibrium level.

Now we are ready to examine how consumer reaction to inflation might affect the rise and fall of prices. We will build on the model we examined at the end of Section 3.3. In Section 3.3 we looked at the change equation

$$
\begin{aligned}
p(n + 1) &= p(n) + k(\text{Excess Demand}) \\
&= p(n) + k(\text{Unmodified Demand} - \text{Supply}).
\end{aligned}
$$

We will use $k = .0008$ and the same supply and unmodified demand functions as we did at the end of Section 3.3:

$$
S(p) = \begin{cases} 1000p - 300, & \text{for days } 0, 1, 2, 3, 4; \\ 1000p - 500, & \text{for days } 5, 6, 7, \ldots \end{cases}
$$

$$
D(p) = 1000 - 500p
$$

so that the change equation becomes

$$
p(n + 1) = \begin{cases} p(n) + .0008[1300 - 1500p(n)], & \text{for } n = 0, 1, \ldots, 4; \\ p(n) + .0008[1500 - 1500p(n)], & \text{for } n = 5, 6, 7, \ldots \end{cases}
$$

Recall that this model represents a situation in which the marketplace for Byties has been in equilibrium for some time and then the price of the ingredients suddenly rises from $0.30 to $0.50. We will start out with the price of Byties at the equilibrium price on day 0 and watch what happens. The results are shown in Table 3.6 and graphically in Figure 3.15.

Table 3.6
Simulation in which Consumers Ignore Inflation ($q = 0.00$)

Day Number	Price
0	0.8667
1	0.8667
2	0.8667
3	0.8667
4	0.8667
5	0.8667
6	1.0267
7	0.9947
8	1.0011
9	0.9998
10	1.0000

Figure 3.15
Simulation in which consumers ignore inflation

When the cost of the ingredients is \$0.30, the equilibrium price for Byties is 0.8667. After the cost of the ingredients rises to \$0.50, the equilibrium price becomes \$1.00. The value of k is moderately large so that the price of Byties reacts swiftly to any excess demand or supply. In fact, in this example the initial price rise following the change in the cost of ingredients overshoots the new equilibrium price, \$1.00, by a little bit and bounces around a bit before settling down quite quickly.

Using our work above, we modify this model to include a representation of consumers' reaction to changing prices by modifying the demand function.

$$\text{Modified demand} = m(\text{Unmodified demand})$$
$$= m(1000 - 500p)$$

where the inflation multiplier, m is

$$m = 1 + q \left(\frac{p(n) - p(n-1)}{p(n-1)} \right)$$

so that

$$p(n+1) = p(n) + .0008 \, (\text{Modified demand} - \text{supply}).$$

This will be called the *modified change equation*.

We will assume that the price starts out at equilibrium on day 0 and day 1. Notice that we have to know the price for two days before we can get started since the modified demand equation requires knowledge of both the current day's and the previous day's price. To illustrate how to calculate prices using this new change equation, we will work out an example showing the price changes for a few days.

Example

In this example $q = -0.5$. Since q is negative, this is a model in which consumers react to rising prices by buying less than they would if their decisions were based solely on the current price. We start off by assuming that the price is at the equilibrium price:

$p(0) = 0.8667$ (assumption)

$p(1) = 0.8667$ (assumption)

$p(2) = p(1) + .0008(\text{Modified demand} - \text{supply}).$

The first step is to calculate the inflation multiplier, m:

$$m = 1 + q \left(\frac{p(1) - p(0)}{p(0)} \right)$$
$$= 1 + (q)(0)$$
$$= 1.$$

Thus, the modified demand is

$$\text{Modified demand} = m[1000 - (500)(0.8667)]$$
$$= (1)(566.67)$$
$$= 566.67.$$

The supply is

$$\text{Supply} = (1000)(0.8667) - 300$$
$$= 566.67.$$

so,

$$p(2) = p(1) + .0008(\text{Modified demand} - \text{supply})$$
$$= 0.8667 + (.0008)(566.67 - 566.67)$$
$$= 0.8667.$$

The calculations for days 3, 4, and 5 are similar to the ones above. But on day 6, interesting things begin to happen:

$$p(6) = p(5) + .0008(\text{Modified demand} - \text{supply}).$$

First we calculate the inflation multiplier:

$$m = 1 + q\left(\frac{p(5) - p(4)}{p(4)}\right)$$
$$= 1 - 0.5\left(\frac{0.8667 - 0.8667}{0.8667}\right)$$
$$= 1.$$

Thus, the modified demand is

$$\text{Modified demand} = m(1000 - (500)(0.8667)$$
$$= (1)(566.67)$$
$$= 566.67.$$

The supply is

$$\text{Supply} = (1000)(0.8667) - 500$$
$$= 366.67$$

so

$$p(6) = p(5) + .0008(\text{Modified demand} - \text{supply})$$
$$= 0.8667 + .0008(566.67 - 366.67)$$
$$= 1.0267.$$

Notice that the price on day 6 is the same in this modified model as in the original unmodified model. Now things begin to get really interesting:

$$p(7) = p(6) + .0008(\text{Modified demand} - \text{supply}).$$

First we calculate the inflation multiplier

$$m = 1 + q\left(\frac{p(6) - p(5)}{p(5)}\right)$$
$$= 1 - (0.5)\left(\frac{1.0267 - 0.8667}{0.8667}\right)$$
$$= 0.9077.$$

Thus, the modified demand is

$$\text{Modified demand} = m[1000 - (500)(1.0267)]$$
$$= (0.9077)(486.65)$$
$$= 441.7191.$$

The supply is

$$\text{Supply} = (1000)(1.0267) - 500$$
$$= 526.7$$

so

$$p(7) = p(6) + .0008(\text{Modified demand} - \text{supply})$$
$$= 1.0267 + .0008(441.7191 - 526.7)$$
$$= 0.9587.$$

Using the preceding example as a guide, do the following exercises. Be careful to use the correct supply function. Remember that the supply function changes when the cost of the ingredients for Byties goes up. That is why the supply function used in the calculation of the price on day 6 was different from the supply function used in the calculation of the price on days 1, 2, 3, 4, and 5.

Exercises

Exercise 3.4.33   Calculate the price of Byties on day 8.

Exercise 3.4.34   Write a computer program to simulate the model
above for 21 days (for days 0, 1, 2, ..., 20). Your program should be
written so that you can change the values of q and k easily in later
exercises. Run your program using the example above and use it and
the previous exercise to help check your program out.

Table 3.7 and Figure 3.16 show these results (for days 0, 1, 2, ...,
15).

This example shows one possible way that prices might react when
consumers respond to inflation in the most natural way: by buying more
during periods of falling prices and less in periods of rising prices. We
want to compare Figures 3.15 and 3.16 in the context of the behavior
they are intended to model.

In both these graphs the price is at the equilibrium price through day
5. Then a rise in the cost of the ingredients for Byties causes a drop
in the supply of Byties. Thus, on day 5 there is an excess demand for
Byties. The market reacts to this excess demand, and the following

Table 3.7
Price Changes with Consumers Reacting to Inflation ($q = -0.5$)

Day Number	Price
1	0.8667
2	0.8667
3	0.8667
4	0.8667
5	0.8667
6	1.0267
7	0.9587
8	1.0220
9	0.9827
10	1.0113
11	0.9920
12	1.0055
13	0.9962
14	1.0026
15	0.9982

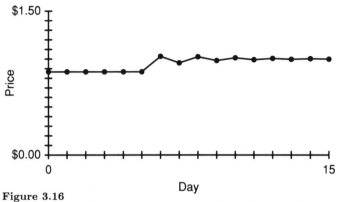

Figure 3.16
Price changes with consumers reacting to inflation $(q = -0.5)$

day, day 6, the price of Byties rises to 1.0267. Now the higher price for
Byties causes a drop in demand. In Figure 3.15 the drop in demand
is sufficient to drive the price down to 0.9947, a little below its new
equilibrium price. But in Figure 3.16 the drop in demand is much more
substantial. Consumers buy less for two reasons: the price of Byties is
high, and it is high in comparison with the preceding day. This much
more substantial drop in demand causes a drop in the price of Byties to
0.9587.

In Figure 3.15 following the rise in the cost of ingredients for Byties,
the price approaches its new equilibrium price quite rapidly. In Figure
3.16 the price approaches its new equilibrium price much more slowly.

This is only one example of what might happen. In fact, this is only
one possible way of modeling how consumers might react to changing
prices. I would like to explore this model further by trying different
values of q. Next let's consider what might happen if consumers react to
changing prices by buying more when prices are rising than one would
expect if they made their decisions on the basis of current price alone.
This corresponds to a positive value of q in our model. We will look at
$q = 0.5$. Table 3.8 and Figure 3.17 show the results of this simulation.

Table 3.8
Price Changes with Consumers Reacting to Inflation

Day Number	Price
0	0.8667
1	0.8667
2	0.8667
3	0.8667
4	0.8667
5	0.8667
6	1.0267
7	1.0306
8	0.9946
9	0.9941
10	1.0011
11	1.0012
12	0.9998
13	0.9998
14	1.0000
15	1.0000

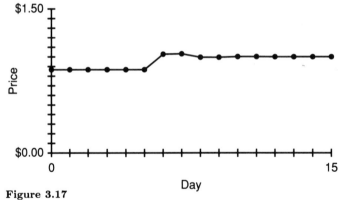

Figure 3.17
Price changes with consumers reacting to inflation ($q = 0.5$)

Exercises

Exercise 3.4.35 Verify the entries in Table 3.8 by using your computer program (after changing q) to simulate this model.

Exercise 3.4.36 Compare the three figures in this section in view of the consumer behavior they are intended to model.

Table 3.9
Comparison of Five Models

Day	$q = -1.0$ Price	$q = -0.5$ Price	$q = 0.0$ Price	$q = 0.5$ Price	$q = 1.0$ Price
0	0.8667	0.8667	0.8667	0.8667	0.8667
1	0.8667	0.8667	0.8667	0.8667	0.8667
2	0.8667	0.8667	0.8667	0.8667	0.8667
3	0.8667	0.8667	0.8667	0.8667	0.8667
4	0.8667	0.8667	0.8667	0.8667	0.8667
5	0.8667	0.8667	0.8667	0.8667	0.8667
6	1.0267	1.0267	1.0267	1.0267	1.0267
7	0.9228	0.9587	0.9947	1.0306	1.0665
8	1.0590	1.0220	1.0011	0.9946	1.0012
9	0.9326	0.9827	0.9998	0.9941	0.9753
10	1.0644	1.0113	1.0000	1.0011	0.9943
11	0.9342	0.9920	1.0000	1.0012	1.0090
12	1.0653	1.0055	1.0000	0.9998	1.0040
13	0.9345	0.9962	1.0000	0.9998	0.9972
14	1.0655	1.0026	1.0000	1.0000	0.9978
15	0.9345	0.9982	1.0000	1.0000	1.0007
16	1.0655	1.0012	1.0000	1.0000	1.0010
17	0.9345	0.9991	1.0000	1.0000	0.9999
18	1.0655	1.0006	1.0000	1.0000	0.9996
19	0.9345	0.9996	1.0000	1.0000	0.9999
20	1.0655	1.0003	1.0000	1.0000	1.0002

You might wonder what might happen if consumers reacted even more strongly to changing prices than in the previous models. We can investigate this by trying larger values of q—for example, $q = 1.0$ and $q = -1.0$. Table 3.9 summarizes five models using five different values of q. Three of these have appeared in Figures 3.15, 3.16, and 3.17. The remaining two are shown in Figures 3.18 and 3.19.

The most interesting of these is Figure 3.19, $q = -1.0$. Since q is negative, this corresponds to the most intuitive kind of consumer behavior: consumers buy less when prices rise than one would expect them to buy if they were making their decisions solely on the basis of the current price. Notice that prices do not seem to be settling down to an equilibrium. Instead they seem to have gotten into a cycle bouncing back and forth between 0.9345 and 1.0655. We do see cycles of this sort in the real world, but usually they are not quite so blatant. In fact, if a cycle this blatant ever appeared, one would expect people to notice it and modify their behavior accordingly.

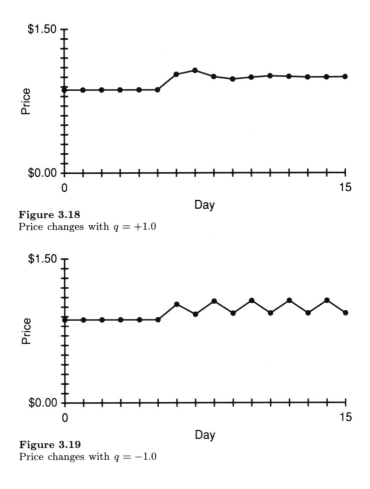

Figure 3.18
Price changes with $q = +1.0$

Figure 3.19
Price changes with $q = -1.0$

Exercises

Exercise 3.4.37 Is the cyclic behavior of prices seen when $q = -1.0$ a fluke? Does it occur only for one very particular value of q? Run your program with $q = -0.8, -0.9, -1.1$ and -1.2 and observe the results. Draw a graph showing the results for $q = -0.8, -0.9, -1.0, -1.1$, and -1.2 on one set of axes. You will probably want to run these simulations for at least 50 days.

Exercise 3.4.38 All of the examples we have examined so far use $k = .0008$. Try some other values of k to see what happens. Try $k = .0006$ with $q = -1.0$ first and then some other combinations of q and k.

Exercise 3.4.39 The model we've been examining is only one of many possible different ways of modeling consumer reaction to inflation. Do you think it is a reasonable model? Can you suggest other possibilities?

3.5 Decisions

As we go through life, we are faced with many choices. Which college should we attend? Or should we skip college altogether? Should we buy a new car or a used car? Should we buy a house? Do we need a new washing machine? Should we get married? Should we use nuclear reactors to produce our electricity, or should we use oil or coal?

Some of the choices are simple. Two stores may offer identical washing machines at two different prices. The obvious choice is the correct choice. As long as the two washing machines are identical, we should choose the one selling for the lower price. But most of our choices are far more complicated. Usually there is an element of uncertainty involved. We may be faced with a choice between two washing machines, one of which is more expensive but also more reliable than the other. If we choose the cheaper machine, we *may* have higher maintenance costs. We don't know for certain what the maintenance costs will be. There is an element of chance involved.

In economics, we are frequently competing against other "economic agents" (other people or business entities) whose decisions may affect us. In this case the element of uncertainty comes from not knowing what these other economic agents will do. This is the realm of game theory—making decisions based in part on the possible decisions of others.

In this section we will study some of the elements of decision making when there is some uncertainty due to chance. In the last two sections we will study game theory—making decisions when we are uncertain about the actions that other people might take.

Table 3.10
Prices of Three Washing Machine Models

Model	Price
Economizer	$225
Standard	$300
Prestige	$350

Example

Suppose that you are planning to buy a washing machine. You have done a lot of research. You've read *Consumer Reports* and talked with friends who have purchased washing machines recently. You have narrowed your decision down to three possible models: the Economizer, the Standard, and the Prestige. The prices of these models are given in Table 3.10.

After talking with your friends, you realize that the purchase price is only part of the expense of owning a washing machine. You should also consider the cost of repairs. The Economizer is cheap but is not well built; in fact, there is a substantial chance that within five years the machine will break. You can expect to pay either $100 for repairs or may have to replace the machine altogether. Thus the possible total cost for the Economizer over a period of five years is:

Total cost of Economizer — $225 or $325 or $450.

The Standard is much better built. It may need repairs, but it was designed so that repairs are fairly easy. Over a period of five years you can expect to pay either $50.00 or $100.00 for repairs. Thus, the possible total cost for the Standard over a period of five years is:

Total cost of Standard — $300 or $350 or $400.

The Prestige comes with a five-year guarantee: the company will make any necessary repairs free. Thus, the total cost for the Prestige over a period of five years will be:

Total cost of Prestige — $350.

We can summarize all this information in Table 3.11. Notice that all the results are negative. This is because all the results involve your paying out money. This table is called the *payoff table*.

Table 3.11
Payoff Table for Three Washing Machine Models

Model	Possible Payoffs		
Economizer	−$225	−$325	−$450
Standard	−$300	−$350	−$400
Prestige	−$350		

Table 3.12
Payoff Table for Three Washing Machine Models

Model	Possible Payoffs		
Economizer	−$225←	−$325	−$450
Standard	−$300←	−$350	−$400
Prestige	−$350←		

In this situation there is no completely clear-cut choice. Different people might make very different choices. You might be an optimist and assume that whatever choice you make, you will have good luck. In this case you would focus on the best possible result or outcome for each of your possible choices. These best possible outcomes are marked by arrows in Table 3.12.

The optimist would ignore everything but the best possible outcomes. He would choose the Economizer, since this is the best choice assuming the best possible outcomes. The optimist's criterion is called the *maximax* (or best-best) criterion. We sometimes say the optimist is using the *maximax strategy*. We can summarize this strategy as follows:

- For each possible action, find the maximum payoff.

- Choose the action with the maximum maximum payoff.

Notice that the numbers in this payoff table are all negative, so, for example, the maximum of −$200 and −$300 is −$200.

A pessimist would assume the worst: whatever choice he made, his bad luck would result in the worst possible outcome. He would concentrate his attention on the results marked by arrows in Table 3.13. He would choose the Prestige because this is the machine that gives him the best worst possible outcome. This strategy is called the *maximin* or best-worst strategy. We can summarize this strategy as follows:

Table 3.13
Payoff Table for Three Washing Machine Models

Model	Possible Payoffs		
Economizer	−$225	−$325	−$450←
Standard	−$300	−$350	−$400←
Prestige	−$350←		

- Identify the minimum possible payoff for each possible action.

- Choose the action that results in the maximum minimum possible payoff.

You might want to think about what personality traits might lead a person to use one strategy or the other. For example, a cautious person might use the maximin strategy. He would be conscious of the risks involved in his actions and seek to minimize risks.

We could do a much better job of decision making if we had more information. We really need to know the likelihood of repairs. Suppose that we had the following additional information:

- Repair records for the Economizer show that 10% of the machines require no repairs within five years, 40% of the machines require repairs costing $100 within five years, and 50% of the machines break down completely and must be replaced at a cost of $225 within five years.

- Repair records for the Standard show that 80% of the machines require no repairs within five years, 15% of the machines require repairs costing $50 within five years, and 5% of the machines require repairs costing $100 within five years.

- Because of the five-year guarantee, the Prestige will require no expenditure of money for repairs for five years.

One way to use this new information is by introducing a new concept called the *expected payoff*. We will illustrate this concept by looking at the Economizer. For the Economizer there are three possible payoffs. These payoffs and their probabilities are summarized in Table 3.14. We compute the expected payoff by multiplying each payoff by its probability and adding up the results as shown in Table 3.15.

We are interested in the expected payoff because it is the average payoff one would expect if he or she bought a very large number of Econ-

Table 3.14
Payoff Table for the Economizer

Payoff	Probability
−$225	0.10
−$325	0.40
−$450	0.50

Table 3.15
Expected Payoff for the Economizer

Payoff	Probability	Product
−$225	0.10	−$22.50
−$325	0.40	−$130.00
−$450	0.50	−$225.00
Expected payoff		−$377.50

omizers. You can illustrate this by running some computer simulations using the methods from Chapter 1.

Exercises

Exercise 3.5.40 Compute the expected payoff for the Standard.

Exercise 3.5.41 Compute the expected payoff for the Prestige.

Exercise 3.5.42 Do a computer simulation that simulates the purchase and repair expenses for 1,000 Economizers. Compute the average payoff for these 1,000 machines. Your results should be close to but not exactly the same as the expected payoff, −$377.50.

Exercise 3.5.43 Do a computer simulation that simulates the purchase and repair expenses for 1,000 Standards. Compute the average payoff for these 1,000 purchases. Your results should be close to but not exactly the same as the expected payoff you computed above.

Over the course of your lifetime, it is unlikely that you will buy a large number of washing machines; however, you will make a large number of decisions. If you make your decisions by choosing the action having the maximum expected payoff, this strategy should work very well. This

Table 3.16
Expected Payoffs

Possible Action	Expected Payoff
Buy Economizer	−$377.50
Buy Standard	−$312.50
Buy Prestige	−$350.00

strategy is called the *maximum expected payoff strategy*. We can summarize it as follows.

- Compute the expected payoff for each possible action.
- Choose the action that has the maximum expected payoff.

For our example, we have already computed the expected payoff for each possible washing machine. The results, summarized in Table 3.16, show that the maximum expected payoff strategy would have us choose the Standard.

This outcome is rather typical of actual problems. There is no one right answer. We have explored three different criteria and gotten three different answers. The correct choice is a matter of philosophy as much as anything else.

Over the long haul, the maximum expected payoff criterion is *usually* the best criterion. It does have some drawbacks. It requires more information. The maximax criterion and the maximin criterion do not require any information about the probabilities of the various possible payoffs. Another problem with the maximum expected payoff criterion is that it may not make much sense when one or more of the possible outcomes is very, very bad or very, very good and has a very, very low likelihood. Consider state lotteries.

Exercises

***Exercise 3.5.44**   The purpose of this exercise is to apply the three decision criteria to a lottery. Suppose that a ticket costs \$2 and that there is a single prize: \$1 million. Suppose the likelihood of winning this prize is 0.000001. Analyze the following possible actions:

- Buy one ticket.
- Don't buy a ticket.

What should you do based on the maximin strategy?

What should you do based on the maximax strategy?

What should you do based on the maximum expected payoff strategy?

Discuss whether you think the maximum expected payoff strategy is a good strategy to use in this case. This is an exercise with no one right answer. We are comparing two possible payoffs—one very likely and also quite small, the other very unlikely but very large. Your own answer to this question will depend more on your philosophy than on mathematics.

For example, one might argue that $2 is barely noticeable, so the risk involved in buying a lottery ticket is negligible. In exchange for this negligible investment, one receives a (admittedly very small) chance at a big prize. One might even assign some value to the pleasure of daydreaming about how to spend the prize. Thus, despite the recommendations of the maximum expected payoff criterion, one might be very willing to buy a lottery ticket *occasionally*. The emphasis here is on the adverb *occasionally*. The return on such a lottery certainly does not justify more than the smallest expenditure.

This is a good place to pause for a little philosophy. We have discussed several possible decision-making strategies, but they all rest on knowing the *dollar value* of the possible payoffs. In real life dollars are sometimes unnatural things to use. For example, suppose that a decision must be reached about whether to build a new coal-fired plant to produce electricity or a nuclear reactor. There are lots of dollar figures floating around—the construction cost, the price of coal, and so on. But some of the most important elements of the problem are not dollars. For example, there is some risk of a major accident involving the nuclear power plant, and such an accident might result in some deaths. How do you assign a dollar value to a death? Similarly how do you assign a dollar value to the health risks assumed by coal miners?

Different individuals might assign dollar values to such risks in different ways. For example, a business might be interested in the cost of liability insurance. Recently there has been a great deal of sound and fury about the cost of liability insurance and the size of judgments in liability suits. This is a complicated subject with many different aspects;

however, at the heart of the discussion is exactly this problem of assigning dollar values to some of the possible results of various activities.

It is extremely important to use all the mathematical tools we have available to help analyze risks and payoffs and make decisions. Nevertheless, all the sophisticated mathematics in the world still rests on basically philosophical decisions about the value of payoffs and risks, and these are often not dollars or, indeed, any other kind of number.

Example

A friend gives you a hot tip on the stock market. She tells you about a company, LoTek, that is just starting up. You can buy 3,000 shares of LoTek stock for $15,000. Your friend is an expert on such startup companies and has determined that there is an 75% chance that the stock will double in value within one year. Unfortunately there is a 25% chance that the company will go bankrupt. You have $15,000 that is in a safe bank account earning 6% interest. You must decide among three possible actions:

1. Leave all your money in the bank account. The payoff after one year will be $900.

2. Leave $7,500 in the bank and invest $7,500 in LoTek stock. In this case there are two possible payoffs. If the stock doubles, you will receive a payoff of $7,500 from it plus $450 from your bank account. The total payoff in this case is $7,950. But if LoTek goes bankrupt, you will lose the $7,500 that you invested in the stock; you will still earn $450 from your bank account. So the total payoff in this case is $-7,050$.

3. Invest all $15,000 in LoTek stock. In this case you will gain $15,000 if the LoTek stock doubles, or you will lose $15,000 if LoTek goes bankrupt.

The payoffs and their probabilities are summarized in Table 3.17. The maximin strategy would be to leave all the money in the bank. The maximax strategy would be to invest all the money in LoTek. Computing the expected payoffs, we obtain the results shown in Table 3.18. We see from Table 3.18 that the maximum expected payoff strategy agrees with the maximax strategy: put all your eggs in the LoTek basket.

Table 3.17
Payoff Table for LoTek Investments

Possible Actions	Stock Doubles	Possible Payoffs Proba- bility	Bank- ruptcy	Proba- bility
All in bank	$900	0.75	−$7,050	0.25
Half and half	$7,950	0.75	−$7,050	0.25
All in LoTek	$15,0000	0.75	−$15,000	0.25

Table 3.18
Expected Payoffs for LoTek Investments

Possible Action	Expected Payoff
All in bank	$900
Half and half	$4,200
All in LoTek	$7,500

But is this really a good idea? If you have only $15,000, then risking it all in one speculative venture may not be a good idea. If you lose, then you will have no money left. In such a case it might make sense to risk only half of your money even though the expected payoff is lower.

The following exercises ask you to experiment with various possible strategies.

Exercises

Exercise 3.5.45   Suppose that your investment counselor finds one investment like LoTek each year. She is extremely good, and her advice is excellent. You are trying to plan a 10-year investment strategy. Suppose that you begin your investment career with $10,000. Write a computer program to simulate each of the following strategies:

- Flamboyant strategy: Each year invest all your money in that year's "LoTek." At the end of the year you've either gone broke, in which case you are no longer an active invester, or you've doubled your money. Repeat the cycle each year, investing all your money in the current LoTek and either doubling your investment or going broke.

Notice there are two possible results of following this strategy. You might be lucky 10 years in a row and double your original $10,000 10 times, winding up with \$10,240,000 after 10 years—or, you might get unlucky one time, lose all your money, and end up a pauper.

Simulate this investment strategy 10,000 times. Keep track of how often you go broke and how often you double your money 10 times. Print out the average amount of money you have at the end of 10 years.

- Conservative strategy: Each year invest half of your money (after cashing in your previous investments) in that year's LoTek. Invest the other half in a bank account earning 6% interest.

  Simulate this strategy 10,000 times. Print out the average amount of money you have at the end of 10 years.

  What is the maximum possible payoff following this strategy?

You were asked to do each simulation 10,000 times. Why do you need such a large number of trials? Do you think that even with 10,000 trials your results are very reliable? Why, or why not? Discuss these two strategies. Which one do you prefer? Why?

There are many possible strategies. For example, you might follow the conservative strategy for nine years and then invest all your money in one huge gamble the last year. Or you might invest 60% of your money each year. Make up a strategy of your own. Simulate it and then discuss it.

3.6   Game Theory, I

In this section we will study a game, as an example of decisions involving competition between several different people or companies.

The game is simple. There are two players, Player A and Player B. Each player picks one side of a coin (heads or tails) and places the coin on a table, chosen side up but covered. **Important:** The players do not flip the coins—they *choose* either heads or tails. Then they count, "One! Two! Three!" and on the count of "Three!" uncover the coins. Depending on the results, money changes hands as shown in Table 3.19.

We begin by looking at the game from the perspective of Player A. Player A has two choices: heads or tails. The payoff table for Player A is shown in Table 3.20. Notice that no matter what Player A does,

Table 3.19
Results of Coin Game

Players' Choices	Results
Both players chose heads	Player A pays player B $0.90
Both players chose tails	Player A pays player B $0.10
One chose heads and the other tails	Player B pays player A $0.50

Table 3.20
Payoffs for Player A

	Payoffs	
	Player B	Player B
Player A's Choice	Chooses Heads	Chooses Tails
Player A chooses heads	−$0.90	$0.50
Player A chooses tails	$0.50	−$0.10

Table 3.21
Payoffs for Player A

	Payoffs	
	Player A	Player A
Player B's Choice	Chooses Heads	Chooses Tails
Player B chooses heads	$0.90	−$0.50
Player B chooses tails	−$0.50	$0.10

he might win $0.50. By playing heads he risks $0.90; by playing tails he risks only $0.10. It looks as if he should play tails—but there is a catch. Player B knows this. We are not dealing with capricious chance but with a thinking opponent!

Table 3.21 shows Player B's payoff table. Notice that no matter what Player B does, she risks $0.50. By playing heads she has the opportunity of winning $0.90; by playing tails she only has a chance of winning $0.10. It looks as if she should play heads more frequently than tails—but there is the same catch. Player A knows this.

With all this in mind what would you do if you were Player A? What would you do if you were Player B?

We want to begin studying this game by experimentation. The first experiment you should do is play the game with a human opponent. Have a friend read the description above and then play the game 20 times with you being Player A and your opponent being Player B. Keep track of your hypothetical winnings or losses. After you've played 20 times, switch sides and play another twenty times. Based on your experimentation, which player would you like to be?

This kind of experimentation is valuable for obtaining a feel for the game; however, it is time-consuming. In order to reach valid conclusions by experimentation, we would have to try out a large number of different possible strategies for each player. In fact, we would have to try out each possible strategy for Player A against each possible strategy for Player B. If we wanted to try out 10 possible strategies for each player, we would have to try 100 different combinations. For each of these different combinations, we would have to play about 1,000 games to get a good idea of what would happen with that combination. Although the game is fun, it's not that much fun. Enter the computer.

We will use the computer to simulate a tournament. Each person in the class will be allowed two entries—one as Player A and one as Player B. Your instructor will also submit two entries. Your entries will be written as True BASIC subroutines. Your instructor will give you more instructions for your particular class.

The computer listing below shows a program that simulates the results of playing one strategy for Player A against another strategy for Player B. In this example, the players use the following strategies:

Player A: Player A reasons that Player B will expect him to play heads very rarely because of the high risk. Therefore, player A decides to play heads quite often—75% of the time. In order to confuse Player B further, Player A decides to make each choice on the basis of pure chance. He chooses heads or tails by using a random number generator. Each time this random number generator is used, it produces a random number between 0 and 1. If this number is less than 0.75, A plays heads. If it is greater than 0.75, A plays tails. This strategy can be implemented by the following True BASIC function:

```
!       Strategy for Player A
!
```

```
DEF PlayerA
IF RND < 0.75 THEN LET PlayerA = 1 ELSE LET PlayerA = 0
END DEF
```

We will be coding heads as 1 and tails as 0. Player A plays heads by returning the number 1 as the value of the function PlayerA. Player A plays tails by returning the number 0 as the value of the function PlayerA. Notice with probability 0.75 the function PlayerA chooses heads (coded as 1) and with probability 0.25 it chooses tails (coded as 0).

Player B: Player B decides to play heads in the first game and thereafter to base her choices on what her opponent is doing. She decides that on each play she will play exactly the opposite of what Player A did the preceding time. These subroutines will be used as part of a program that will keep track of each player's choices. The array A will keep track of A's choices in games $1, \ldots, 1000$, and the array B will keep track of B's choices in games $1, \ldots, 1000$. Thus, for example, A(1) will be 0 if Player A chose tails in game 1 and will be 1 if Player A chose heads in game 1. When Player A makes his choice in game n, he will be able to use the information in $A(1)$, $A(2), \ldots, A(n-1)$ and $B(1), B(2), \ldots, B(n-1)$. Player B will be able to use the same information. The following True BASIC function shows how Player B uses this information to implement her strategy:

```
!    Strategy for Player B
!
DEF PlayerB
IF n = 1 THEN LET PlayerB = 1 ELSE LET PlayerB = 1-A(n-1)
END DEF
```

Notice how Player B makes use of information about the tournament. The variable n keeps track of the current "game number." Player B determines if the current game is the first game with the line

```
IF n = 1 THEN ...
```

Player B also makes use of the record of past games by consulting the variable A(n-1) to see what player A did in the preceding game.

Notice that after the first game (when $n > 1$), A(n - 1) would be
0 if A played tails in the previous game, so B would play heads if
A played tails in the previous game. Similarly, A(n - 1) would be
1 if A played heads in the previous game, so B would play tails if
A played heads in the previous game.

These are only two possible strategies out of many, many possible
strategies you could imagine.

The listing below shows how these two subroutines are incorporated
into a large program that simulates 1,000 plays of the game in which
Players A and B use the strategies described:

```
!       Tournament
!
DIM A(1000), B(1000)    ! Record of games
!
!       Strategy for Player A
!
DEF PlayerA
IF RND < 0.75 THEN LET PlayerA = 1 ELSE LET PlayerA = 0
END DEF
!
!       Strategy for Player B
!
DEF PlayerB
IF n = 1 THEN LET PlayerB = 1 ELSE LET PlayerB = 1-A(n-1)
END DEF
!
!       Run a tournament of 1,000 games
!
LET Awinnings = 0      ! Total winnings for Player A
LET Bwinnings = 0      ! Total winnings for Player B
FOR n = 1 TO 1000      ! Simulate 1,000 games
LET Aplay = PlayerA
LET Bplay = PlayerB
LET A(n) = Aplay       ! Keep record of each play
LET B(n) = Bplay
```

```
IF (Aplay = 1) and (BPlay = 1) THEN
        LET Awinnings = Awinnings - 0.90
        LET Bwinnings = Bwinnings + 0.90
   ELSE IF (Aplay = 0) and (Bplay = 0) THEN
        LET Awinnings = Awinnings - 0.10
        LET Bwinnings = Bwinnings + 0.10
   ELSE
        LET Awinnings = Awinnings + 0.50
        LET Bwinnings = Bwinnings - 0.50
END IF
NEXT n
PRINT USING "A wins $####.##":Awinnings
PRINT USING "B wins $####.##":Bwinnings
END
```

Each person in the class should write two functions. One function, called PlayerA, will implement a strategy for Player A, and the other, called PlayerB, will implement a strategy for Player B. Each person should choose the best strategy that he or she can think up for each player. (The two strategies may be different.) Your instructor will use a program similar to the program above that will simulate 1,000 plays of the game for each combination of strategies.

3.7   Game Theory, II

In this section we will continue studying the same game as in Section 3.6, where we looked at this game experimentally. Now we will investigate it theoretically. We will be able to use some of the ideas from Section 3.5 to find the "best" possible strategies for the two players.

We will be interested in purely mathematical strategies. Some people use psychological clues to help play games. For example, in our game Player B might watch Player A very carefully, hoping to detect a tensing of the muscles as Player A prepared for the big risk of choosing heads. We will ignore all such nonmathematical strategies. We begin by looking at the game from the point of view of player A.

Table 3.22
Possible Outcomes Assuming that Player B Plays Heads

A's Choice	B's Choice	Probability	Payoff (for A)
heads	heads	p	-0.90
tails	heads	$(1-p)$	$+0.50$

Player A

The strategies that we will consider are all very similar. Player A will use a spinner (or some other random device) to choose heads or tails. This spinner will choose heads with some probability, p, and tails with probability $(1-p)$. On each turn Player A will spin the spinner and make the choice indicated by the spinner. Each possible spinner (each possible value of p) corresponds to one possible strategy for Player A.

Suppose that Player A wants to use the maximin strategy. He is a pessimist and supposes the worst—that Player B will somehow manage to choose the strategy that is best for her and worst for him.

We will begin our analysis by assuming that Player B chooses heads. In this case the possible results, their probabilities and payoffs, are given by Table 3.22.

Notice that although we have assumed that B will choose heads there is still an element of chance due to A's use of the spinner. Now, for each of player A's possible strategies (for each choice of p) we can compute the expected payoff for A:

$$\text{Expected payoff for Player A} = p(-0.90) + (1-p)(0.50)$$
$$= 0.50 - 1.40p.$$

Recall from Section 3.5 that the expected payoff is the sum of each possible payoff times its probability. The expected payoff is the average payoff to be expected if a large number of games were played.

If Player B chooses tails, then the possible results, their probabilities and payoffs, are given in Table 3.23 and the expected payoff for A is

$$\text{Expected payoff for Player A} = p(0.50) + (1-p)(-0.10)$$
$$= 0.60p - 0.10.$$

This information is summarized in Figure 3.20.

Table 3.23
Possible Outcomes Assuming that Player B Plays Tails

A's Choice	B's Choice	Probability	Payoff (for A)
heads	tails	p	+0.50
tails	tails	$(1-p)$	−0.10

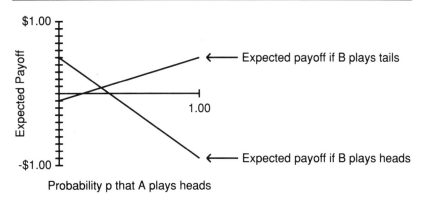

Figure 3.20
Expected payoff for Player A

But now Player A's pessimism comes into the picture. Player A assumes that Player B will always somehow manage to choose the strategy that is best for B and worst for A. In Figure 3.21 I have emphasized with a heavy line the expected payoff from A's pessimistic perspective. Thus, A really considers only the possibilities shown in Figure 3.22—that is, the heavy line from Figure 3.21.

Now A wants to follow the maximin strategy, choosing the strategy with the best possible worst results. Thus, he wants the point of the graph in Figure 3.22. This is the place where the two straight lines in Figure 3.20 crossed. We can find this point by solving the equation:

Expected payoff if B plays heads = Expected payoff if B plays tails

$$0.50 - 1.40p = 0.60p - 0.10$$
$$0.60 = 2.00p$$
$$p = 0.60/2.00$$
$$= 0.30.$$

This is the best strategy for A (best according to the maximin criterion). He should use a spinner that chooses heads with probability 0.30.

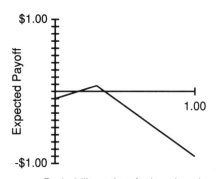
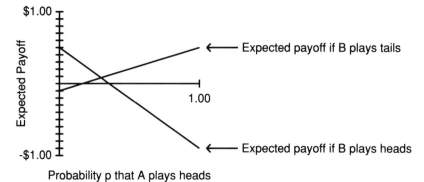

Figure 3.21
Expected payoff for pessimistic Player A

Figure 3.22
Expected payoff for pessimistic Player A

Notice that if he follows this strategy he can expect on the average that his payoff will be:

If B chooses heads: $0.50 - (1.40)(0.30) = 0.08$
If B chooses tails: $(0.60)(0.30) - 0.10 = 0.08$

It doesn't make any difference at all what B chooses to do. In either case the expected payoff will be the same because A chose the point at which the two different expected payoff lines crossed.

We have now discovered A's best possible strategy according to the maximin criterion. It is immune to any mathematical assaults by B. Of course, B might beat this strategy by nonmathematical means. For example, if A felt very nervous each time the spinner told him to play heads and if this nervousness showed on A's face, B might delay making her own choice until A had made his choice and then B could base her choice on whether A looked nervous.

Player A should be feeling pleased with this situation. We have found a strategy that will give him an expected payoff of $0.08 each time the game is played no matter what B does. Verify this experimentally by trying several strategies for B against this best possible strategy for A. Remember that experimental results can be expected to agree only roughly with theoretical results.

Now that we've decided what A should do, we should analyze the game from B's perspective.

Player B

The strategies that we will consider are all similar. Player B will use a spinner (or some other random device) to choose either heads or tails. This spinner will choose heads with some probability, q, and tails with probability $(1 - q)$. On each turn Player B will spin the spinner and make the choice indicated by the spinner. Each possible spinner (each possible value of q) corresponds to one possible strategy.

Player B will also use the maximin strategy. She is a pessimist and supposes the worst—that Player A will somehow manage to choose the strategy that is best for him and worst for player B.

Our analysis for Player B is analogous to that for Player A. We will begin by assuming that her opponent, Player A, plays heads and we will analyze the outcome if Player B uses the strategy described—that is, Player B plays in a completely random fashion, choosing heads with probability q. This leads us to Table 3.24. The expected payoff for B is

Expected payoff for player B $= 0.90q - 0.50(1 - q)$

$$= 1.40q - 0.50.$$

Table 3.24
Results When B Plays Heads with Probability q Assuming A Plays Heads

A's Choice	B's Choice	Probability	Payoff (for B)
heads	heads	q	$+0.90$
heads	tails	$(1 - q)$	-0.50

Table 3.25
Results When B Plays Heads with Probability q Assuming A Plays Tails

A's Choice	B's Choice	Probability	Payoff (for B)
tails	heads	q	−0.50
tails	tails	$(1-q)$	+0.10

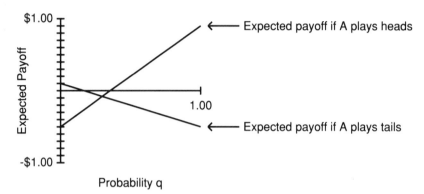

Figure 3.23
Expected payoff for Player B

If Player A chooses tails, then the possible results and their probabilities are shown in Table 3.25, and the expected payoff for B is

$$\text{Expected payoff for player B} = -0.50q + 0.10(1-q)$$
$$= 0.10 - 0.60q.$$

This information is summarized in Figure 3.23.

But now B's pessimism comes into the picture. B assumes that A will always somehow manage to choose the strategy best for A and worst for B. In Figure 3.24 I have emphasized with a heavy line the expected payoff from B's pessimistic perspective. Thus, B really considers only the possibilities shown in Figure 3.25—that is, the heavy line from Figure 3.24.

B wants to follow the maximin strategy, choosing the strategy with the best possible worst results. Thus, she wants the point of the graph in Figure 3.25. This is the place where the two straight lines in Figure 3.23 crossed. We can find this point by solving the equation

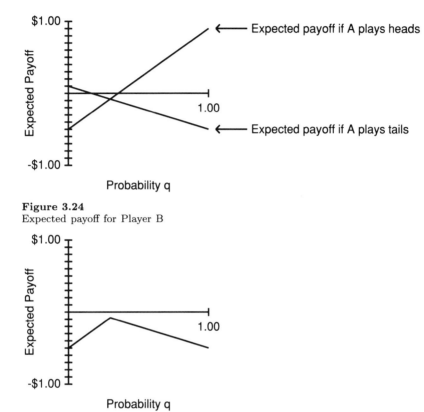

Figure 3.24
Expected payoff for Player B

Figure 3.25
Expected payoff for Player B

Expected payoff if A plays heads = Expected payoff if A plays tails

$$1.40q - 0.50 = 0.10 - 0.60q$$
$$2.00q = 0.60$$
$$q = 0.60/2.00$$
$$= 0.30.$$

This is the best strategy for B (best according to the maximin criterion). She should choose heads in a random fashion with probability $q = 0.30$. If she follows this strategy, she can expect on the average that her payoff will be:

If A chooses heads: $(1.40)(0.30) - 0.50 = -0.08$
If B chooses tails: $0.10 - (0.60)(0.30) = -0.08$

It doesn't make any difference at all what A chooses to do. In either case the expected payoff will be the same because B chose the point at which the two different expected payoff lines crossed.

We have now discovered B's best possible strategy according to the maximin criterion. It is immune to any mathematical assaults by A. Of course, as before, A might beat this strategy by nonmathematical means.

Player B might well be feeling unhappy about this situation. Despite her best efforts, she can expect to lose \$0.08 on the average each time she plays! You can verify this experimentally by trying several strategies for A against this best possible strategy for B. Remember that experimental results can be expected to agree only roughly with theoretical results.

In this particular example, it turned out that the best possible strategy for A and B was the same. Both p and q should be 0.30. That is, both Player A and Player B should choose heads with probability 0.30.

Exercises

****Exercise 3.7.46** Suppose that Player A is greedy and decides to follow the maximax strategy. What value of p should he choose?

****Exercise 3.7.47** If A follows the maximax strategy and B follows the maximin strategy, what will happen?

****Exercise 3.7.48** Suppose that B gets greedy and decides to follow the maximax strategy? What value of q should she choose?

Exercise 3.7.49 If B follows the maximax strategy and A follows the maximin strategy, what will happen?

Exercise 3.7.50   If A follows the maximax strategy and B always chooses the opposite of A's previous choice, what will happen?

Exercise 3.7.51   If A follows the maximin strategy and B always chooses the opposite of A's previous choice, what will happen?

Table 3.26
Payoffs for Exercise 3.7.52

Players' Choices	Results
Both chose heads	A pays B $0.90
Both chose tails	A pays B $0.20
One chose heads and the other chose tails	B pays A $0.50

Table 3.27
Payoffs for Exercise 3.7.53

A's Choice	B's Choice	Results
heads	heads	A pays B $0.90
heads	tails	B pays A $0.40
tails	heads	B pays A $0.60
tails	tails	A pays B $0.10

Table 3.28
Payoffs for Exercise 3.7.54

A's Choice	B's Choice	Results
white	red	A pays B $1.00
white	green	A pays B $0.60
white	blue	B pays A $0.60
black	red	B pays A $0.50
black	green	B pays A $0.40
black	blue	A pays B $0.20

Exercise 3.7.52 Analyze the following game using the methods of this section. A and B each choose either heads or tails. Depending on their choices, money changes hands as shown in Table 3.26.

Exercise 3.7.53 Analyze the following game using the methods of this section. A and B each choose either heads or tails. Depending on their choices, money changes hands as shown in Table 3.27.

Exercise 3.7.54 Consider a game in which Player A chooses white or black and Player B chooses red, green or blue. Depending on their choices, money changes hands as shown in Table 3.28.

If Player A wants to use the maximin strategy what should he do? Would you rather be Player A or Player B?

4 Optics

This chapter is about optics, the study of light, the way it is bent by water and bounced by mirrors. We will study flat mirrors and curved mirrors, the patterns that light makes in coffee cups, and the way that underwater objects appear to be distorted.

The primary reason that this subject is included in this book is to illustrate the way that mathematics can help us understand the physical world. Scientists try to understand the physical world by building up mental images or models of how things work. They go back and forth between experiment and theory. Often mathematics plays a crucial role in the theory. But most important is the interplay between theory and experiment. This interplay motivates my choice of optics—we are surrounded by optical phenomena. You can do many experiments just by keeping your eyes open. Others require some equipment—a mirror, a coffee cup, a swimming pool, or perhaps a rainbow. All the equipment you need is readily available. The exercises in this chapter include a number of optical experiments in addition to the usual computer programs and mathematical exercises.

Our work in this chapter is based on one principle of optics, *Fermat's Principle*. It says that light travels between two points along the fastest path. Philosophically, this is an interesting principle. It does not say why or by what mechanism light "chooses" the fastest path. It is a descriptive principle that seems to summarize a great deal of experimental data. We will use this principle to predict what happens when light strikes a mirror or passes through water and test these predictions by experimentation. In the end we will be able to "explain" a number of seemingly different optical phenomena in terms of this one simple principle. This explanation is limited; it does not answer why or even how. It is just a first step in understanding light and optics, but it is an important first step.

Descriptive principles like Fermat's Principle are enormously important. They help us to organize a large body of knowledge, to summarize lots of seemingly different phenomena as a coherent whole. When physicists search for the how and why of optics and light, they do not have to attempt to explain a myriad of individual observations. Instead they can attempt to explain one principle, Fermat's Principle.

Figure 4.1
An eye and an object in unobstructed air

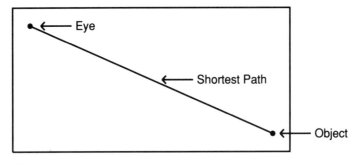

Figure 4.2
The fastest path

4.1   Mirrors and a Mathematical Tool

Fermat's Principle says that light traveling between two points travels along the fastest path. The easiest situation to analyze is when the light is traveling through air with no mirrors or other obstructions. An example is shown in Figure 4.1. We are interested in the fastest path that a light ray might follow if it were to travel from the object shown in the lower right to the eye shown in the upper left. In this situation the fastest path for the light to follow is the shortest path: a straight line between the two points (Figure 4.2.)

The situation is somewhat more complicated if we add a mirror to our picture, as in Figure 4.3. Some light will travel directly between the two points along the straight line connecting them, but there is an additional possibility: light could travel along a straight line from the first point to the mirror and then bounce off the mirror and travel along

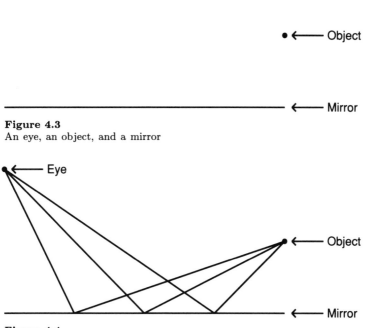

Figure 4.3
An eye, an object, and a mirror

Figure 4.4
Three possible light paths

another straight line from the mirror to the second point. Several paths like this are shown in Figure 4.4.

Figure 4.5 shows a situation like Figure 4.3 except that I have drawn the picture on graph paper and labeled each point with its coordinates. In this figure the mirror lies along the x-axis. We want to examine several possible paths that a light ray might take traveling in a straight line from the object at the point $(200, 50)$ to the mirror along the x-axis and then from the mirror to the eye at the point $(0, 100)$. Figure 4.6 shows two examples of possible paths. One example is drawn with a solid line and the other with a dashed line. We can compute the length of each of these examples.

The solid path goes from point $(0, 100)$ to point $(50, 0)$ and then to point $(200, 50)$. We compute the length of each segment of this path using the Pythagorean Theorem:

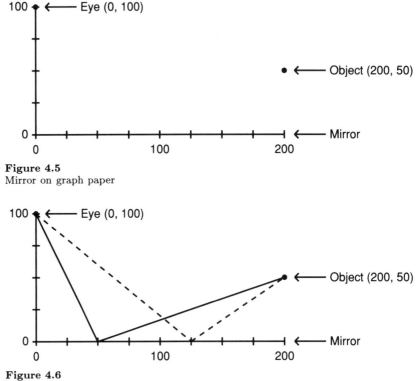

Figure 4.5
Mirror on graph paper

Figure 4.6
Two possible bouncing paths

From $(0, 100)$ to $(50, 0)$:

$$\sqrt{50^2 + 100^2} = \sqrt{12,500} = 111.80.$$

From $(50, 0)$ to $(200, 50)$:

$$\sqrt{150^2 + 50^2} = \sqrt{25,000} = 158.11.$$

The total length of the solid path is $111.80 + 158.11 = 269.91$.

   The dashed path goes from point $(0, 100)$ to $(125, 0)$ and then to $(200, 50)$. We compute the length of each segment of this path using the Pythagorean Theorem:

From $(0, 100)$ to $(125, 0)$:

$$\sqrt{125^2 + 100^2} = \sqrt{25,625} = 160.08.$$

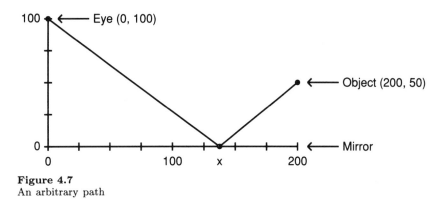

Figure 4.7
An arbitrary path

From $(125, 0)$ to $(200, 50)$:

$$\sqrt{75^2 + 50^2} = \sqrt{8,125} = 90.14.$$

The total length of the dashed path is $160.08 + 90.14 = 250.22$.

Of the two paths, the shorter and, hence, the faster is the solid path. But we actually want to consider all possible paths that start at the point $(0, 100)$, go in a straight line to the mirror (the x-axis), and then in a straight line to the point $(200, 50)$. We will label the point at which such a path hits the mirror $(x, 0)$. See Figure 4.7. We can compute the length of such a path in exactly the same way as the previous examples. First, we compute the length of each segment using the Pythagorean Theorem:

From $(0, 100)$ to $(x, 0)$:

$$\sqrt{x^2 + 100^2} = \sqrt{x^2 + 10,000}.$$

From $(x, 0)$ to $(200, 50)$:

$$\sqrt{(200 - x)^2 + 50^2} = \sqrt{x^2 - 400x + 42,500}.$$

The total length of the entire path is

$$\text{Total length} = \sqrt{x^2 + 10,000} + \sqrt{x^2 - 400x + 42,500}.$$

We have produced a function that describes the length

$$L(x) = \sqrt{x^2 + 10,000} + \sqrt{x^2 - 400x + 42,500}$$

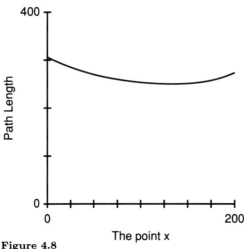

Figure 4.8
Graph of the total length function $L(x)$

of a path that travels in a straight line from the object at the point
$(200, 50)$ to the mirror at the point $(x, 0)$ and then along another straight
line to the eye at the point $(0, 100)$. We want to choose the shortest of
these paths. In order to do this we look at the graph of the function
$L(x)$. This graph is shown in Figure 4.8. We want to find the lowest
point or minimum point on this graph. By looking closely at the graph
you can see that the lowest point is someplace between $x = 100$ and
$x = 150$ and corresponds to a total distance of roughly 250.

We want to find out more precisely the value of x that tells where
the shortest path will hit the mirror. This is one example of a very
general mathematical problem: the problem of finding the minimum
of a function. The remainder of this section will be concerned with
developing a computer program that can be used to find the minimum
of a function.

The first step in finding the minimum of a function is to get a rough
idea of what the function looks like. One way is by using a graphics
program to produce a graph like Figure 4.8. Since graphics is beyond
the scope of this book we will not discuss this approach here. (If you are
using a computer with good graphics capabilities, you can try to pursue
this topic on your own.) Another way is to compile a table showing some
of its values, an easy computer exercise. The next exercise asks you to
compute some values for the function

$$L(x) = \sqrt{x^2 + 10,000} + \sqrt{x^2 - 400x + 42,500}.$$

Exercise

Exercise 4.1.1 Compute the values of the function $L(x)$ for $x = 0, 10, 20, \ldots, 200$.

Table 4.1, which shows the output of a program for making this computation, gives some evidence that the minimum of our function occurs someplace between $x = 120$ and $x = 140$. The function appears to be U-shaped. It is going down from 0 to 130 and then rising from 130 to 200 according to the results in this table. But the table doesn't tell the whole story; it tells only about these particular 21 points. The function might actually reach its minimum anyplace between $x = 120$ and $x = 140$. In fact, the function could do some very bizarre things at any points besides these 21 points, and Table 4.1 would not detect them. Our function really is nicely U-shaped, so the impression given by Table 4.1 and by Figure 4.8 is not misleading.

The mathematical purpose of this section is to develop a method that can be used to find the minimum of a U-shaped function like the function $L(x)$. I will describe a computer algorithm, and you will write a program implementing this algorithm. This program can be applied in the following situation:

Table 4.1
Table of Values of the Function $L(x)$

x	$L(x)$	x	$L(x)$
0	306.1553	110	251.6170
10	296.9676	120	250.5448
20	288.7958	130	250.0354
30	281.6035	140	250.1490
40	275.3338	150	250.9882
50	269.9173	160	252.7109
60	265.2797	170	255.5404
70	261.3495	180	259.7643
80	258.0625	190	265.6993
90	255.3667	200	273.6068
100	253.2248		

Table 4.2
Computer Approximations for the Minimum

Approximation Number	The Minimum Is in the Interval	
	from	to
1	0.00	200.00
2	120.00	140.00
3	132.00	134.00
4	133.20	133.40
5	133.32	133.34

We want to find the minimum value of a function $y = f(x)$ on an interval $[a, b]$. On the interval $[a, b]$ the function is U-shaped. It starts out decreasing on the left side of the interval, then hits a minimum someplace inside the interval and increases on the right side of the interval. In other words, the function is similar to the function $L(x)$ shown in Figure 4.8.

The program will not determine exactly where the minimum is, but it will be able to give extremely good approximations. Its output will be a series of smaller and smaller intervals containing the minimum. The output of this program for the function $L(x)$ is shown in Table 4.2.

This is an example of a common situation in mathematics. We will not be able to find the exact answer to our question—what is the minimum of the function $L(x)$?—but we will be able to find extremely good *estimates* for the answer. In fact, we can find estimates as good as necessary for any particular use.

The key idea behind this program is the following. First the program evaluates the function at 21 equally spaced points in the interval $[a, b]$. For the original interval $[0, 200]$, the program evaluated the function at the points $0, 10, 20, \ldots, 200$. In other words it made the computations shown in Table 4.1 although these computations were not actually printed out. We see in the table that the lowest value for $L(x)$ is 250.0354 when $x = 130$. Table 4.1 corresponds to looking just at the points indicated by dots on the graph of the function $L(x)$ in Figure 4.9.

The point we have found $(130, 250.0354)$ is not necessarily the minimum. After all we have only looked at 21 points, and there is no reason to assume that the minimum is one of those points, but we can deduce that the minimum must be in the interval $[120, 140]$ because the function must be decreasing at $x = 120$ since $L(130)$ is less than $L(120)$ and

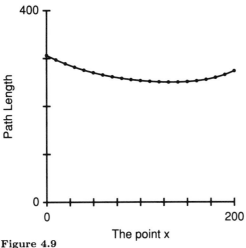

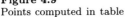

Figure 4.9
Points computed in table

the function must be increasing at $x = 140$ since $L(140)$ is greater than $L(130)$.

This is the whole idea of the program. We started with a large interval $[0, 200]$ containing the sought-for minimum and found a smaller interval $[120, 140]$ containing the minimum. Notice that this is the second interval that the program printed in Table 4.2.

Now we repeat this procedure, finding a smaller interval containing the minimum by evaluating the function $L(x)$ at 21 evenly spaced points in the interval $[120, 140]$. The results of this computation are shown in Table 4.3. Again, the program doesn't actually print out these results. We are looking at these results here in order to understand what the program is doing.

We see in Table 4.3 that the minimum value of $L(x)$ in the table is at $x = 133$, so that the minimum value of $L(x)$ must occur for x someplace in the interval $[132, 134]$. This is the third interval that the program printed out in Table 4.2. We can repeat this procedure with the interval $[132, 134]$ and then again as often as necessary to pin the location of the minimum down as precisely as necessary.

In Table 4.2 this procedure was applied four times until the minimum was trapped inside the interval $[133.32, 133.34]$. Now we know that the minimum value of $L(x)$ occurs when x is approximately 133.3. This gives

Table 4.3
Table of Values of the Function $L(x)$

x	$L(x)$	x	$L(x)$
120	250.5448	131	250.0174
121	250.4678	132	250.0057
122	250.3965	133	250.0004
123	250.3309	134	250.0014
124	250.2710	135	250.0091
125	250.2169	136	250.0233
126	250.1686	137	250.0444
127	250.1263	138	250.0722
128	250.0900	139	250.1071
129	250.0596	140	250.1490
130	250.0354		

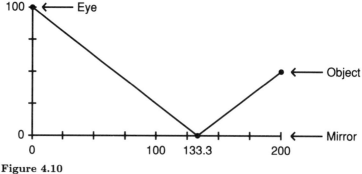

Figure 4.10
The shortest path

us an estimate to the answer to our original question about what path the light would follow in Figure 4.7. This estimate is precise enough for our purposes. If it were not precise enough, we could repeat the procedure as often as necessary to obtain an estimate that was precise enough. The actual path is shown in Figure 4.10.

The next exercise asks you to write a program implementing the algorithm we have discussed. Write your program in such a way that you can modify it easily to work with different functions. You will be applying this program to many different functions and different intervals.

The following step-by-step summary of the algorithm might help you write the program.

Minimizing a Function

This algorithm will find a sequence of estimates for the minimum of a function $f(x)$ on an interval $[a, b]$ provided the function is U-shaped on $[a, b]$. The heart of the algorithm is a procedure for starting with one interval containing the minimum and obtaining a smaller interval containing the minimum. This procedure can be repeated as often as necessary to trap the minimum inside an interval that is sufficiently small for the intended purpose. The basic procedure has two steps:

1. Evaluate the function $f(x)$ at 21 equally spaced points in the interval. These 21 points divide the interval into 20 subintervals of equal size. We will denote these points,

$$x(0), x(1), x(2), \ldots, x(20),$$

and the corresponding values of $f(x)$,

$$f(x(0)), f(x(1)), f(x(2)), \ldots, f(x(20)).$$

2. Find the smallest value of the function $f(x)$ among the 21 values just computed. Call this smallest value $f(x(i))$. The new smaller interval includes the subinterval immediately to the left of the point $x(i)$ and the subinterval immediately to the right of the point $x(i)$). That is, the new smaller interval is $[x(i-1), x(i+1)]$. There are two exceptions to this rule. If the smallest of the 21 values of $f(x)$ is at the point $x(0)$, then the new interval will be $[x(0), x(1)]$. If the smallest of the 21 values of $f(x)$ is at the point $x(20)$, then the new interval will be $[x(19), x(20)]$.

Exercise

Exercise 4.1.2 Write a computer program implementing the algorithm described for finding the minimum of the function $L(x)$.

The remainder of this project will consist of examples and exercises. The examples are meant to be a cooperative effort. Each describes a particular real problem. Solving this problem requires finding the minimum of an appropriate function. This book discusses the function that must be minimized and gives a rough estimate of where the minimum is. You must use your computer program to find the minimum. This will involve making some modifications to your program to minimize the appropriate function on the appropriate interval.

Example 1

Lori Lifeguard is scanning the water when suddenly she sees a swimmer in trouble. Figure 4.11 shows a map of the beach indicating the location of the drowning swimmer and Lori's lifeguard station. Lori grabs her surfboard, runs to the waterline, and paddles on her surfboard out to the swimmer. Lori must decide the fastest way to reach the swimmer. She can run at a speed of 20 feet per second, and she can paddle the surfboard at a speed of 10 feet per second. Figure 4.12 shows one of the many possible routes she might take to reach the swimmer.

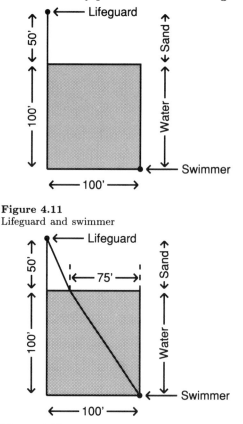

Figure 4.11
Lifeguard and swimmer

Figure 4.12
One possible route

We can compute the length of time it will take her to reach the swimmer if she takes the route shown in Figure 4.12 using the Pythagorean Theorem. Lori will be running

$$\sqrt{50^2 + 25^2} = \sqrt{3,125} = 55.90 \text{ feet}$$

on the beach. Since she runs at a speed of 20 feet per second, this part of her trip will take her

$$\frac{55.90}{20} = 2.80 \text{ seconds.}$$

By the Pythagorean Theorem Lori will be paddling

$$\sqrt{75^2 + 100^2} = \sqrt{15,625} = 125.00 \text{ feet}$$

in the water. This part of her trip will take her

$$\frac{125}{10} = 12.5 \text{ seconds.}$$

Thus, her total travel time will be $2.80 + 12.5 = 15.30$ seconds. Now we want to find the fastest possible route for Lori to follow. The first step is to find a suitable function to work with. Look at Figure 4.13.

Lori will run in a straight line directly from her lifeguard station to a point on the shoreline and from that point will paddle in a straight

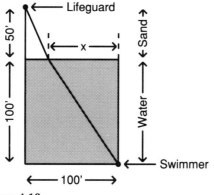

Figure 4.13
Arbitrary route

line directly to the swimmer. Using the notation of Figure 4.13 and the Pythagorean Theorem, we see that the two parts of her trip look like this:

On land:

$$\text{Distance} = \sqrt{50^2 + (100 - x)^2}$$
$$\text{Time} = \frac{\sqrt{50^2 + (100 - x)^2}}{20}$$

On water:

$$\text{Distance} = \sqrt{100^2 + x^2}$$
$$\text{Time} = \frac{\sqrt{100^2 + x^2}}{10}$$

Thus, her total travel time is:

$$T(x) = \frac{\sqrt{50^2 + (100 - x)^2}}{20} + \frac{\sqrt{100^2 + x^2}}{10}.$$

and this is the function we want to minimize. Modify your program to minimize this function.

Notice that x must be between 0 and 100 feet, so it makes sense to start with that interval.

Your program will find the point x to which Lori should run on the shoreline in order to minimize her total travel time.

Example 2

Find the point on the line $y = 2 - 4x/3$ that is closest to the origin (the point $(0,0)$). Look at Figure 4.14. By the Pythagorean Theorem the distance from $(0,0)$ to the point $(x, 2 - 4x/3)$ is

$$D(x) = \sqrt{x^2 + \left(2 - \frac{4x}{3}\right)^2}.$$

This is the function we want to minimize. From Figure 4.14 you can see that x will be somewhere between 0 and 1.5 to minimize $D(x)$.

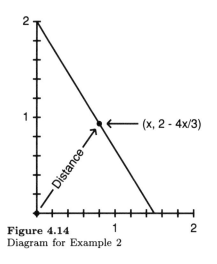

Figure 4.14
Diagram for Example 2

Exercises

*Exercise 4.1.3

a. Use Fermat's Principle to find the path that light would follow traveling from the object to the mirror and then to the eye in Figure 4.15.

b. Draw a graph showing your answer to Part a.

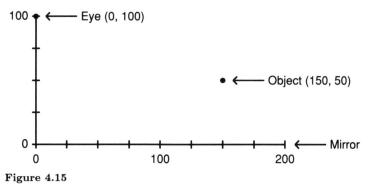

Figure 4.15
Eye, object, and mirror

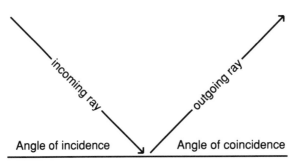

Figure 4.16
Angles of incidence and coincidence

c. You have probably heard that when light bounces off a mirror, the angle of incidence equals the angle of coincidence. Figure 4.16 labels the angles. Check whether in the graph you drew in Part b the angle of incidence equals the angle of coincidence by measuring the angles with a protractor.

Exercise 4.1.4

a. Use Fermat's Principle to find the path that light would follow traveling from the object to the mirror and then to the eye in Figure 4.17.

b. Draw a graph showing your answer to Part a.

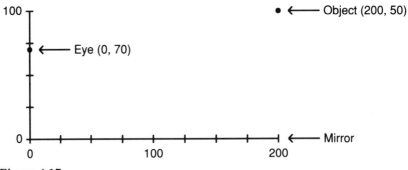

Figure 4.17
Eye, object, and mirror

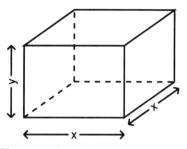

Figure 4.18
Closed box with square base

c. Check whether in the graph you drew in Part b the angle of incidence equals the angle of coincidence by measuring the angles with a
protractor.

*__Exercise 4.1.5__ Nancy Kartun plans to make a closed box with a square
base like the one shown in Figure 4.18. This box will have a volume of
10 cubic feet. Its cost depends on the amount of material she must use
for the four sides plus the top and bottom. The area of the top of the
box is x^2. The area of the bottom of the box is also x^2. Each of the four
sides has an area xy. Thus, the total area of the box and, hence, the
amount of material she will need is $2x^2 + 4xy$. What dimensions should
the box have in order to minimize the cost?
   Hint: The first step in solving this problem is to use the fact that the
volume of the box is 10 cubic feet to find a formula for y in terms of x.

__Exercise 4.1.6__ Find the point on the line $y = 2x + 3$ that is closest to
the point $(10, 5)$.

*__Exercise 4.1.7__ Find the point on the line $y = x$ that is closest to the
point $(7, 10)$.

__Exercise 4.1.8__ Find the point on the line $y = x$ that is closest to the
point $(50, 100)$. Can you make an educated guess for a general formula
giving the point on the line $y = x$ that is closest to the point (a, b)? Try
some more examples to see if your guess seems right.

4.2   Reflections in Flat Mirrors

In this section we will investigate the way that mirrors create reflected or apparent images. We will use two main tools. The first tool is called ray tracing. It involves tracing the path(s) that light follows traveling from one object to another. Section 4.1 developed the basic techniques involved in ray tracing. The second tool comes from Section 1.4, where we discussed linear functions and used them to find the height of a tree or a building. In this section we will use the same methods to investigate mirror images. (You may want to review Section 1.4 before continuing.)

We will use a somewhat simplified model of the way that a person sees an object. One of the advantages of two eyes is that we can perceive how far away an object is. This is called binocular vision and is analogous to the way that we found the height of a building in Section 1.4. A person's two eyes are like the two observers. Each eye has a *line of sight* toward the object. The person's brain computes the point at which the two lines of sight intersect. This point is the "location" of the object. The reason for the quotation marks will become apparent later in this section. Our simplified model of sight has two parts:

1. Each eye reports to the brain its line of sight toward the object.

2. The brain computes the intersection of the two reported lines of sight.

This computing is done almost as a reflex action without any conscious thought. Figure 4.19 shows how this two-step method works most often. When a person looks directly at an object in air, the object is located at the point where the two lines of sight intersect.

The situation is much more interesting when one looks at an object in a mirror. In the case in Figure 4.20 we can use the techniques from Section 4.1 to determine the path followed by two light rays. The first light ray travels from the object to the mirror and then to one of the observer's eyes. The second light ray travels from the object to the mirror and then to the observer's other eye. The brain's reflex computing assumes that each of the incoming light rays is actually a straight line or ray with no corners or bends. We call these assumed lines *apparent light rays*. The result, in Figure 4.20, is misleading. The position computed by the brain, called the *apparent position* of the object, is different from its *actual position*.

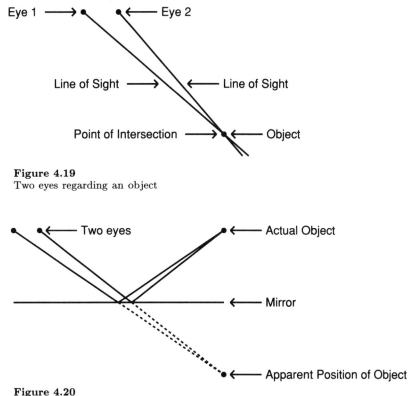

Figure 4.19
Two eyes regarding an object

Figure 4.20
Two eyes, an object, and a mirror

The actual paths followed by the two light rays that travel from the
object to each eye are shown with solid lines. These two paths each make
a sharp turn when the light ray bounces off the mirror. However, at its
reflex level, the brain assumes that each light ray is following a straight
line without any turns. Thus, from the brain's perspective, the light rays
are following the dashed lines. It computes the point of intersection of
the two dashed lines and believes that this is the position of the object.
At a more conscious level, the brain is a bit more sophisticated. It
"knows" there is a mirror and adjusts its first reflex mental image of
the object to compensate for the mirror. We will be working with the
first, reflex level, image. Anybody who has tried to tie a necktie looking

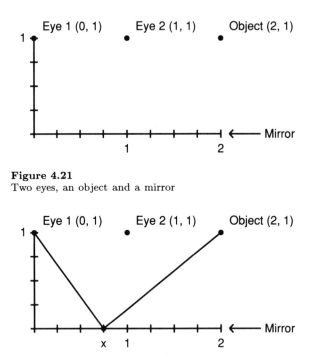

Figure 4.21
Two eyes, an object and a mirror

Figure 4.22
Typical path

in the mirror knows that the brain is less sophisticated in its ability to adjust for the presence of a mirror than one might like.

Now we are ready to use the methods developed earlier to find the apparent position of an object viewed in a flat mirror. (In the next section we will apply these same techniques to investigate curved mirrors.) We will begin by looking at the example pictured in Figure 4.21. We want to find the apparent position of the object located at the point $(2,1)$ as viewed by a person with two rather widely spaced eyes, located at the points $(0,1)$ and $(1,1)$.

The first step is to find the path a light ray would follow traveling from the object at $(2,1)$ to the mirror on the x-axis and then to the eye at $(0,1)$. We begin by looking at a typical path the light ray might possibly follow. We will label the point at which this light ray bounces off the mirror $(x,0)$. See Figure 4.22.

The length of this path is given by the function:

$$P(x) = \sqrt{x^2 + 1^2} + \sqrt{(2-x)^2 + 1^2} = \sqrt{x^2 + 1} + \sqrt{x^2 - 4x + 5}.$$

Fermat's Principle says that the light will follow the path with the shortest length. Thus, to determine which path the light ray will follow we need to find the minimum of $P(x)$. In Section 4.1 you were asked to write a program to find the minimum of a function much like $P(x)$. You should modify that program to find the minimum of $P(x)$.

Exercise

---

*Exercise 4.2.9** Find the shortest path from the point $(2, 1)$ to the x-axis and then to the point $(0, 1)$ by finding the minimum of the function $P(x)$ above. Do this exercise by modifying your program from the previous section.

The minimum value of $P(x)$ is 2.8284, and the corresponding value of x is 1. Thus, a light ray traveling from the point $(2, 1)$ to the mirror on the x-axis and then to the point $(0, 1)$ will follow the path shown in Figure 4.23. The eye at the point $(0, 1)$ will report to the brain that this light ray follows the apparent path shown in Figure 4.24.

It is easy to compute the equation of this apparent path using the techniques of Section 1.4. First, we compute the slope:

$$\text{Slope} = \frac{0 - 1}{1 - 0} = -1.$$

Thus, its equation is $y = -x + b$. We can determine the value of b by substituting the point $(0, 1)$ in the equation, obtaining:

$$1 = -(0) + b$$

So $b = 1$ and the equation of the apparent path is

Apparent path seen by eye 1: $y = -x + 1$.

Next, we want to determine the path followed by a light ray traveling from the object at the point $(2, 1)$ to the mirror on the x-axis and then

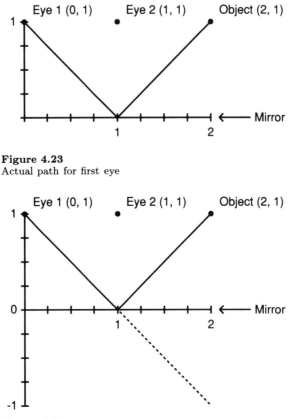

Figure 4.23
Actual path for first eye

Figure 4.24
Apparent path for first eye

to the eye at the point $(1, 1)$. As before, we look at a typical path from the point $(2, 1)$ to the mirror and then to the point $(1, 1)$. We will label the point at which this path bounces off the mirror $(x, 0)$. See Figure 4.25. The length of this path is given by the function:

$$Q(x) = \sqrt{(x-1)^2 + 1^2} + \sqrt{(2-x)^2 + 1^2}$$
$$= \sqrt{x^2 - 2x + 2} + \sqrt{x^2 - 4x + 5}.$$

Fermat's Principle says that the light will follow the shortest path from the point $(2, 1)$ to the mirror on the x-axis and then to the point $(1, 1)$. We find this path by determining the minimum of the function $Q(x)$ in the usual way. This minimum is 2.2361 and occurs when $x = 1.5$.

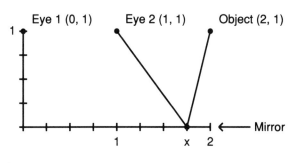

Figure 4.25
Typical path to eye 2

Thus, this light ray follows the path shown in Figure 4.26. The eye at the point $(1, 1)$ reports to the brain that this light ray is following the apparent path shown in Figure 4.27.

We use the same methods as before to find the equation of this apparent path:

Apparent path seen by eye 2: $y = -2x + 3$.

Figure 4.28 combines the results shown in Figures 4.24 and 4.27. We can compute the apparent position of the object by finding the intersection of the two apparent paths shown in Figure 4.28. Exercise 4.2.10 asks you to find this intersection point using the techniques of Section 1.4. The answer is $(2, -1)$.

Exercise

*Exercise 4.2.10   Find the intersection of the two lines $y = -x + 1$ and $y = -2x + 3$.

Notice the apparent position of the object is on the other side of the mirror exactly opposite its real position. This result should match your own experience and give you some confidence in these methods.

The next set of exercises will ask you to compute the apparent position of an object viewed in a flat mirror by two eyes. These exercises will give you lots of "evidence" that an object reflected in a flat mirror always appears to be on the other side of the mirror exactly opposite its real position. We will accumulate this "evidence" by moving the object and

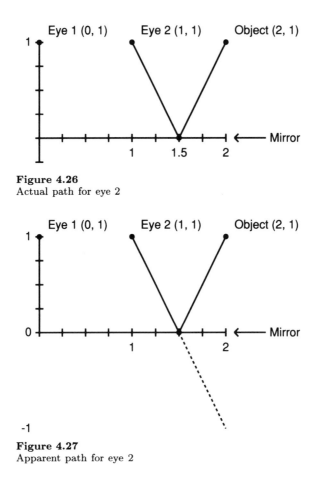

Figure 4.26
Actual path for eye 2

Figure 4.27
Apparent path for eye 2

eyes around to different positions. Thus, we will work with a very general setup as shown in Figure 4.29. The first eye will be located at the point (s, t), the second eye will be located at the point (u, v), and the object will be located at the point (p, q). In other words our program will use the following input:

- s, t: The x- and y-coordinates of the first eye.

- u, v: The x- and y-coordinates of the second eye.

- p, q: The x- and y-coordinates of the object.

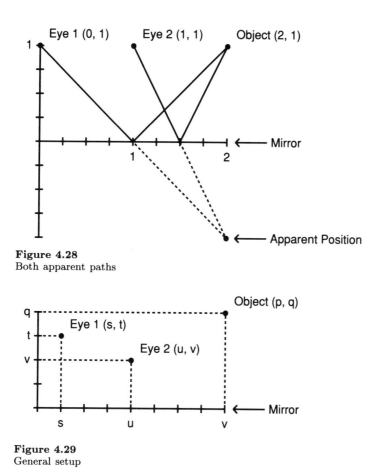

Figure 4.28
Both apparent paths

Figure 4.29
General setup

Our program's output will be the x- and y-coordinates of the apparent position of the object. Because this is a particularly long and complicated program, the entire program is provided rather than being assigned as an exercise. Following the program is an explanation of how it works. In the next section you will have to modify this program, so it is important that you understand it.

```
!   Find the apparent position of an object located
!   at (p, q) as viewed by eyes located at (s, t)
!   and (u, v) with a mirror on the x-axis.
!
```

```
!    Function to find the shortest path from (a, b) to (p, q)
!
DEF bestx(a, b)
LET leftend = a
LET rightend = p
FOR j = 1 TO 5
LET dmin = 999999
LET x = leftend
LET width = (rightend - leftend)/20.0
FOR i = 0 TO 20
LET dist =  SQR((x-a)*(x-a) + b*b) + SQR((x-p)*(x-p) + q*q)
IF dist < dmin THEN
   LET dmin = dist
   LET xmin = x
END IF
LET x = x + width
NEXT i
IF (xmin = leftend) THEN
        LET rightend = leftend + width
    ELSE IF (xmin = rightend) THEN
        LET leftend = rightend - width
    ELSE
        LET leftend = xmin - width
        LET rightend = xmin + width
END IF
NEXT j
LET bestx = (leftend + rightend)/2
END DEF
!
!    Ask user for location of two eyes and object
!
PRINT "Enter location of eye 1: ";
INPUT s, t
PRINT "Enter location of eye 2: ";
INPUT u, v
```

```
PRINT "Enter location of object: ";
INPUT p, q
!
!   Find the points at which the two paths hit the mirror
!
LET mirrorone = bestx(s, t)
LET mirrortwo = bestx(u, v)
!
!   Compute slope and y-intercept for two apparent paths
!
LET slopeone = t/(s - mirrorone)
LET slopetwo = v/(u - mirrortwo)
LET bone = t - s * slopeone
LET btwo = v - u * slopetwo
LET apparentx = (btwo - bone)/(slopeone - slopetwo)
LET apparenty = slopeone * apparentx + bone
PRINT USING "(####.####, ####.####)": apparentx, apparenty
END
```

With a large program like this one, it is important to break the programming task up into smaller and more manageable pieces. There are basically three tasks:

1. Find the path followed by a light ray from the object to the mirror and then to the first eye. Compute the corresponding apparent path.

2. Find the path followed by a light ray from the object to the mirror and then to the second eye. Compute the corresponding apparent path.

3. Compute the point at which these two apparent paths intersect. This point is the apparent location of the object.

In addition, the program needs to read in the appropriate data and to print out the results.

The first two tasks involve the same work. The first step is to find the shortest path from the object to the mirror and then to an eye. We begin by writing a True BASIC function to solve the general problem of finding the shortest path from the object at the point (p, q) to the mirror and then to an eye at the point (a, b). As usual we are interested

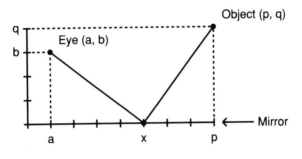

Figure 4.30
Finding the shortest path

in paths that go from the point (a, b) to the x-axis and then to the point (p, q). We will label the point at which such a path hits the x-axis by $(x, 0)$. Look at Figure 4.30. The length of such a path is given by

$$L(x) = \sqrt{(x-a)^2 + b^2} + \sqrt{(p-x)^2 + q^2}.$$

We find the shortest path by computing the minimum of this function. You have already written a program to minimize a function like this. The function **bestx** in the preceding program is a modification of it. This function produces the value of x that minimizes the function $L(x)$. This function is used twice, in the following two lines

```
LET mirrorone = bestx(s, t)
LET mirrortwo = bestx(u, v)
```

to compute the points at which each of the two paths from the object to the two eyes hits the mirror. These two points are called **mirrorone** and **mirrortwo**. The next few lines compute the slope and y-intercept of each of the two apparent paths:

```
LET slopeone = t/(s - mirrorone)
LET slopetwo = v/(u - mirrortwo)
LET bone = t - s * slopeone
LET btwo = v - u * slopetwo
```

Thus, the two apparent paths are described by the equations

$$y = (\texttt{slopeone})x + \texttt{bone}$$

and

$$y = (\texttt{slopetwo})x + \texttt{btwo}$$

The apparent position of the object is the point at which these two lines intersect. We can find this point as follows:

$$(\texttt{slopeone})x + \texttt{bone} = (\texttt{slopetwo})x + \texttt{btwo}$$
$$(\texttt{slopeone} - \texttt{slopetwo})x = \texttt{btwo} - \texttt{bone}$$
$$x = \frac{\texttt{btwo} - \texttt{bone}}{\texttt{slopeone} - \texttt{slopetwo}}$$

or, in True BASIC,

LET apparentx = (btwo - bone)/(slopeone - slopetwo)

This gives us the x-coordinate of the apparent position of the object. We can find the y-coordinate by substituting this value of x into either of our two equations for the two apparent paths:

$$y = (\texttt{slopeone})x + \texttt{bone}$$

or

$$y = (\texttt{slopetwo})x + \texttt{btwo}$$

We chose the first one. This gives us

$$y = (\texttt{slopeone})\texttt{apparentx}) + \texttt{bone}$$

or, in True BASIC,

LET apparenty = slopeone * apparentx + bone

Each of the following exercises asks you to find the apparent position of an object viewed in a mirror by two eyes. Use the preceding program to find the coordinates of this apparent position. Then draw a careful graph.

Exercises

*Exercise 4.2.11

- Object: $(2, 1)$
- First eye: $(0, 1)$
- Second eye: $(0, 0.5)$

Exercise 4.2.12

- Object: (2, 1)
- First eye: (0, 1)
- Second eye: (1.5, 1)

Exercise 4.2.13

- Object: (2, 1)
- First eye: (0, 1)
- Second eye: (4, 2)

Exercise 4.2.14

- Object: (6, 4)
- First eye: (-2, 3)
- Second eye: (4, 5)

Notice that the results of these exercises agree with our experience: an object reflected in a flat mirror always appears to be on the opposite side of the mirror exactly opposite its real position.

4.3   Reflections in Curved Mirrors

Curved mirrors are far more interesting than flat ones. They can be used to make things look closer or farther away, and they can be used to create distorted images, making a reflection tall and thin, or short and fat.

Look at Figures 4.31 and 4.32. Figure 4.31 shows the apparent position of an object reflected in a concave mirror. Figure 4.32 shows the apparent position of an object reflected in a convex mirror. Figures 4.33 and 4.34 are identical to Figures 4.31 and 4.32, respectively, except that I have added coordinate lines. For purposes of comparison, Figures 4.35 and 4.36 are similar to Figures 4.31–4.34 except that they show reflection in a flat mirror.

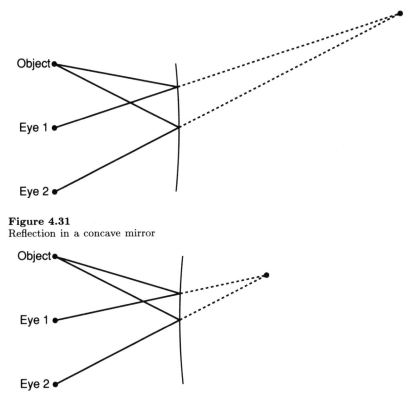

Figure 4.31
Reflection in a concave mirror

Figure 4.32
Reflection in a convex mirror

These six figures show three different situations, each covered by a pair of figures, with and without coordinate lines drawn in. All three situations have two eyes, located at the points $(-4,0)$ and $(-4,-2)$. All three have an object located at the point $(-4,2)$. The only difference in the three situations is the mirror. In Figures 4.31 and 4.33 it is concave with a radius of 20. In Figures 4.32 and 4.34 it is convex, again with a radius of 20. In Figures 4.35 and 4.36 it is flat. In all three situations the mirror is indicated by a heavy line. It is oriented vertically either on the y-axis or tangent to the y-axis at the origin, $(0,0)$.

The flat mirror does exactly what we would expect. The apparent position of the target is at $(4,2)$ behind the mirror at a point directly opposite the object's true position.

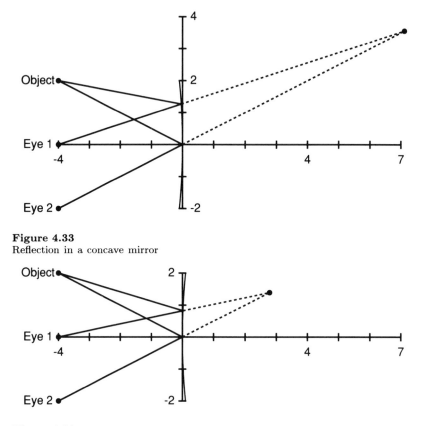

Figure 4.33
Reflection in a concave mirror

Figure 4.34
Reflection in a convex mirror

The concave mirror produces very different results. The apparent
position of the object is much higher and farther away from the mirror
than with the flat mirror. The convex mirror also produces different
results. The apparent position of the object in the convex mirror is
lower and much closer to the mirror than with the flat mirror.

I will begin this section by describing carefully how Figure 4.34 was
produced. In the remainder of this section, you will use these same
techniques to answer some questions about reflections in curved mirrors.
Before we begin, we need to know how to describe a curved mirror
mathematically. Our mirrors will all be sections of circles, so we need
to know how to describe a circle mathematically.

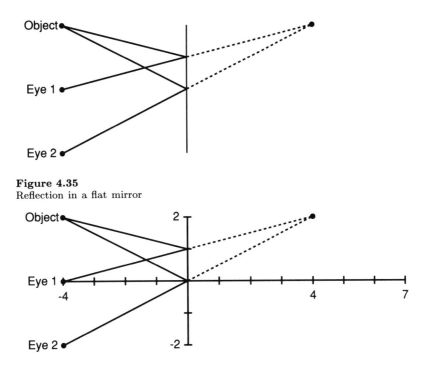

Figure 4.35
Reflection in a flat mirror

Figure 4.36
Reflection in a flat mirror

Figure 4.37 shows a circle of radius 5 with its center at the point $(5, 0)$. Saying that a point (x, y) is on this circle is the same as saying that its distance from the point $(5, 0)$ is 5. In other words, by the Pythagorean Theorem:

$$\sqrt{(x - 5)^2 + y^2} = 5.$$

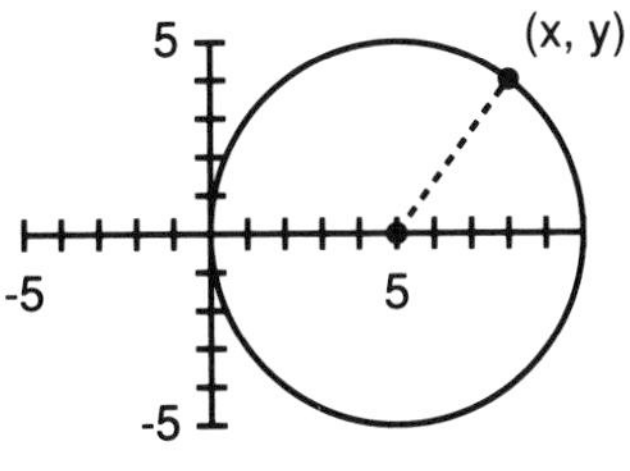

Figure 4.37
Circle of radius 5 centered at $(5, 0)$

Hence

$$(x - 5)^2 + y^2 = 25.$$

We can solve this equation for x:

$$(x - 5)^2 + y^2 = 25$$
$$(x - 5)^2 = 25 - y^2$$
$$x - 5 = \pm\sqrt{25 - y^2}$$
$$x = 5 \pm \sqrt{25 - y^2}.$$

This equation can be expressed as two equations because of the $\pm$ in the last line:

(1) $x = 5 - \sqrt{25 - y^2}$

(2) $x = 5 + \sqrt{25 - y^2}$

Equation 1 corresponds to the left half of the circle, and Equation 2 corresponds to the right half of the circle.

These same calculations can be made for a circle of radius R whose center is at the point $(R, 0)$. See Figure 4.38. The result is the following two equations that describe its left and right halves:

(1) $x = R - \sqrt{R^2 - y^2}$

(2) $x = R + \sqrt{R^2 - y^2}$

Equation 2 describes a convex (looked at from the left) mirror of radius R. This mirror is oriented vertically, and the middle of the mirror

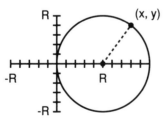

Figure 4.38
Circle of radius R centered at $(R, 0)$

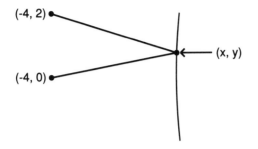

Figure 4.39
An arbitrary path

is resting on the origin, $(0, 0)$. The center of the circle describing this mirror is at the point $(R, 0)$.

Now let us look at the situation described in Figures 4.32 and 4.34. The convex mirror in these figures is given by the formula

$$x = 20 - \sqrt{400 - y^2}.$$

Our work will be completely analogous to the work we did in Section 4.2. The first problem is to find out the path that a light ray will follow traveling from the object at $(-4, 2)$ to the convex mirror and then to the eye at $(-4, 0)$. A typical path that the light ray might follow would bounce off the mirror at a point (x, y) where

$$x = 20 - \sqrt{400 - y^2}.$$

as shown in Figure 4.39.

We can compute the length of this path using the Pythagorean Theorem:

$$L(y) = \sqrt{(4 + x)^2 + (2 - y)^2} + \sqrt{(4 + x)^2 + y^2}$$

and, since $x = 20 - \sqrt{400 - y^2}$

$$L(y) = \sqrt{\left(24 - \sqrt{400 - y^2}\right)^2 + (2 - y)^2 + \sqrt{\left(24 - \sqrt{400 - y^2}\right)^2 + y^2}}.$$

By Fermat's Principle the light ray will follow the fastest path. Thus, we must find the value of y for which $L(y)$ is smallest. This will tell us at what point the light ray will bounce off the mirror. In Section 4.1 you wrote a computer program for finding the minimum of a function. By modifying that program to work with the function $L(y)$, you can find the minimum of $L(y)$. Do so now.

Exercise

*Exercise 4.3.15 Find the path followed by a light ray traveling from the object at the point $(-4, 2)$ to the mirror and then to the eye at the point $(-4, 0)$ in Figure 4.34 by finding the minimum of the function $L(y)$ above. Draw a careful graph showing this path.

The next step is to find the path followed by a light ray traveling from the object at $(-4, 2)$ to the mirror and then to the eye at $(-4, -2)$. See Figure 4.40. The calculations are similar to the preceding ones. In fact it would be a good idea for you to try to do these calculations yourself before reading on. If you run into difficulty, they are described following this exercise.

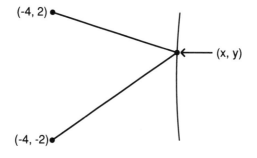

Figure 4.40
An arbitrary path

Exercise

---

*Exercise 4.3.16 Find the path followed by a light ray traveling from the object at the point $(-4, 2)$ to the mirror and then to the eye at the point $(-4, -2)$. Draw a careful graph showing this path.

The length of a typical path as shown in Figure 4.40 is given by:

$$L(y) = \sqrt{(4+x)^2 + (2-y)^2} + \sqrt{(4+x)^2 + (2+y)^2}$$

and, since $x = 20 - \sqrt{400 - y^2}$

$$M(y) = \sqrt{\left(24 - \sqrt{400 - y^2}\right)^2 + (2-y)^2} +$$

$$\sqrt{\left(24 - \sqrt{400 - y^2}\right)^2 + (2+y)^2}.$$

This is the function we want to minimize. As before, you can find the minimum of this function by modifying your program from Section 4.1.

If you have done the last two exercises correctly, you now know that the two paths followed by light rays from the object to the two eyes are as shown in Figure 4.41: the first path bounces off the mirror at the point $(0.0170, 0.8241)$ and the second path bounces off the mirror at the point $(0,0)$ as shown in Figure 4.41.

The point where the two apparent paths intersect can be computed in exactly the same way as in Section 4.2. The first step is to compute the equation for each of the two apparent paths. Refer to Figure 4.41 as we do these computations.

Apparent Path from Eye 1:

We know two points on this line: $(-4, 0)$ and $(0.0170, 0.8241)$. Hence, the slope of this line is

$$\frac{0 - 0.8241}{-4 - 0.0171} = 0.2051.$$

Thus, the equation of this line is

$$y = 0.2051x + b.$$

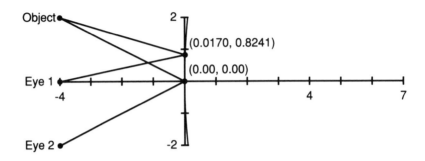

Figure 4.41
Actual paths

We determine the value of b by substituting the point $(-4, 0)$ into this equation:

$$0 = 0.2051(-4) + b$$
$$b = 4(0.2051)$$
$$= 0.8204.$$

So the equation of this line is

$$y = 0.2051x + 0.8204.$$

Apparent Path from Eye 2:

We know two points on this line: $(-4, -2)$ and $(0, 0)$. Hence, the slope of this line is

$$\frac{-2 - 0}{-4 - 0} = 0.5.$$

Thus, the equation of this line is

$$y = 0.5x + b.$$

We determine the value of b by substituting the point $(0, 0)$ into this equation:

$$0 = 0.5(0) + b$$
$$b = 0.$$

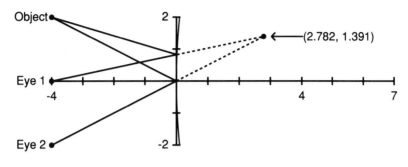

Figure 4.42
Apparent position of object

So the equation of this line is

$$y = 0.5x.$$

Finally, we can compute the apparent position of the object by finding the intersection of the two apparent paths in the usual way:

$$0.5x = 0.2051x + 0.8204$$
$$0.2949x = 0.8204$$
$$x = \frac{0.8204}{0.2949} = 2.782$$

and we can use the equation $y = 0.5x$ to determine y:

$$y = 0.5(2.782) = 1.391.$$

The apparent position of the object as viewed in this convex mirror is $(2.782, 1.391)$, shown in Figure 4.42.

You have a big programming assignment for this section. The assignment is to write a computer program that will do all the calculations above. This program will be similar to the long one in Section 4.2. It will ask for the following input:

- The x- and y-coordinates of the first eye.
- The x- and y-coordinates of the second eye.
- The x- and y-coordinates of an object.
- The radius of a convex mirror. This number is called R.

The program will compute the apparent position of the object as viewed by these two eyes in a convex mirror of radius R with center at $(R, 0)$. (Note: The "middle" of the mirror will be tangent to the y-axis at the origin.) You can check your program by using the calculations that we did above. After you have written and checked out your program, use it to work out the following exercises.

Exercises

This is a long series of exercises whose purpose is to explore reflections in curved mirrors. It will be very useful to draw careful graphs using graph paper and colored pencils. You may have other questions about curved mirrors that can be answered using the techniques of this section. If so, go ahead and experiment.

****Exercise 4.3.17** The purpose of this first experiment is to see whether the position of the observer (the two eyes) makes any difference in the apparent position of the object. Find the apparent position of the object for each of the following two setups. Notice that the only difference between them is the position of the two eyes. There may be some round-off error, so we are looking for a substantial difference between the apparent positions in the two different setups.

1. First setup:
   - Radius: 20
   - Object: $(-5, 5)$
   - Eye 1: $(-5, 2)$
   - Eye 2: $(-5, -2)$

2. Second setup:
   - Radius: 20
   - Object: $(-5, 5)$
   - Eye 1: $(-5, 0)$
   - Eye 2: $(-5, -5)$

****Exercise 4.3.18** The purpose of this exercise is to see whether the radius of the mirror makes any difference. Find the apparent position for each of the following two setups. Notice that the only difference

between them is the radius of the mirror. There may be some round-off error, so we are looking for a substantial difference between the apparent positions in the two different setups.

1. First Setup:
   - Radius: 20
   - Object: $(-5, 5)$
   - Eye 1: $(-5, 0)$
   - Eye 2: $(-5, -5)$
2. Second setup:
   - Radius: 25
   - Object: $(-5, 5)$
   - Eye 1: $(-5, 0)$
   - Eye 2: $(-5, -5)$

Exercise 4.3.19 The purpose of this exercise is to see how a square is distorted by a convex mirror. Find the apparent position for each of the following four setups. Draw all four setups on the same graph using a different color for each. Notice that the four real objects form the corners of a square. What does the apparent image of this square look like?

1. First setup:
   - Radius: 20
   - Object: $(-5, 5)$
   - Eye 1: $(-5, 0)$
   - Eye 2: $(-5, -5)$
2. Second setup:
   - Radius: 20
   - Object: $(-2, 5)$
   - Eye 1: $(-5, 0)$
   - Eye 2: $(-5, -5)$

3. Third setup:

- Radius: 20
- Object: $(-2, 2)$
- Eye 1: $(-5, 0)$
- Eye 2: $(-5, -5)$

4. Fourth setup:

- Radius: 20
- Object: $(-5, 2)$
- Eye 1: $(-5, 0)$
- Eye 2: $(-5, -5)$

For the next series of exercises, we will work with a concave mirror instead of a convex mirror, so you will have to modify your program to reflect this change. We saw that a convex mirror of radius R was described by the formula

$$x = R - \sqrt{R^2 - y^2}.$$

A concave mirror of radius R is described by the formula

$$x = \sqrt{R^2 - y^2} - R.$$

Use this fact to modify your program to work with a concave mirror.

Exercise 4.3.20   The purpose of this experiment is to see whether the position of the observer (the two eyes) makes any difference in the apparent position of the object. Find the apparent position of the object for each of the following two setups. Notice that the only difference between the two is the position of the eyes. There may be some round-off error, so we are looking for a substantial difference between the apparent positions in the two different setups.

1. First setup:

- Radius: 20
- Object: $(-5, 5)$
- Eye 1: $(-5, 2)$
- Eye 2: $(-5, -2)$

2. Second setup:

- Radius: 20
- Object: $(-5, 5)$
- Eye 1: $(-5, 0)$
- Eye 2: $(-5, -5)$

Exercise 4.3.21   The purpose of this exercise is to see whether the radius of the mirror makes any difference. Find the apparent position for each of the following two setups. Notice that the only difference between the two is the radius of the mirror. There may be some round-off error, so we are looking for a substantial difference between the apparent positions in the two different setups.

1. First setup:

- Radius: 20
- Object: $(-5, 5)$
- Eye 1: $(-5, 0)$
- Eye 2: $(-5, -5)$

2. Second setup:

- Radius: 25
- Object: $(-5, 5)$
- Eye 1: $(-5, 0)$
- Eye 2: $(-5, -5)$

Exercise 4.3.22   The purpose of this exercise is to see how a square is distorted by a convex mirror. Find the apparent position for each of the following four setups. Draw all four setups on the same graph using a different color for each. Notice that the four real objects form the corners of a square. What does the apparent image of this square look like?

1. First setup:

- Radius: 20
- Object: $(-5, 5)$

- Eye 1: $(-5, 0)$
- Eye 2: $(-5, -5)$

2. Second setup:

- Radius: 20
- Object: $(-2, 5)$
- Eye 1: $(-5, 0)$
- Eye 2: $(-5, -5)$

3. Third setup:

- Radius: 20
- Object: $(-2, 2)$
- Eye 1: $(-5, 0)$
- Eye 2: $(-5, -5)$

4. Fourth setup:

- Radius: 20
- Object: $(-5, 2)$
- Eye 1: $(-5, 0)$
- Eye 2: $(-5, -5)$

Exercise 4.3.23   Formulate a question of your own about reflections in a curved mirror. Use your program to answer your question.

4.4   Funhouse Mirrors and Light Caustics

Funhouse Mirrors and Other Reflections:

You have probably noticed that curved mirrors can have a magnifying or a reducing effect. Perhaps you have seen funhouse mirrors that make a person look tall and thin or short and fat. You have almost certainly seen convex mirrors used in stores for watching for shoplifters or sometimes as exterior rearview mirrors in cars. These mirrors make objects look much smaller than they actually are. Our first task in this section is to explore these effects.

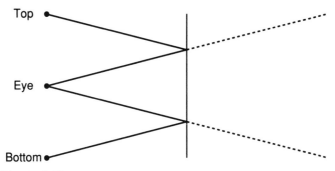

Figure 4.43
Appearance of an object reflected in a flat mirror

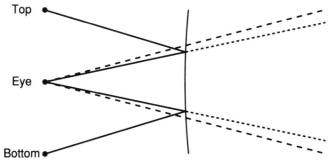

Figure 4.44
Appearance of an object in a convex mirror, $R = 20$

Figure 4.43 examines an image in a flat mirror. If you look at an object in a flat mirror, it appears to be behind the mirror exactly opposite its actual position. Figure 4.43 shows a single eye looking at two targets. Think of these two targets as being the top and bottom of a single object. The solid lines are the two actual paths followed by light rays going from the top of the object to the eye and the bottom of the object to the eye. The dotted lines are the two apparent paths perceived by the eye. This object appears to be "normal" size. We will be comparing this situation with reflections in a curved mirror.

Figure 4.44 is very similar to Figure 4.43 except that I have replaced the flat mirror by a curved mirror. This mirror is convex with a radius $R = 20$. For each target, two lines are shown: a dashed line showing the line of sight the eye would see if the mirror were flat and a dotted line

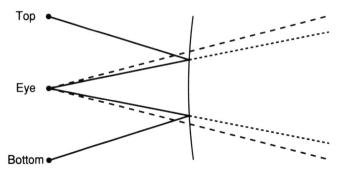

Figure 4.45
Appearance of an object in a convex mirror, $R = 15$

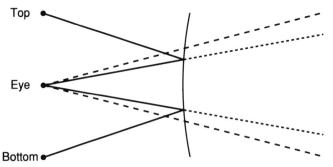

Figure 4.46
Appearance of an object in a convex mirror, $R = 10$

showing the apparent line of sight for the curved mirror. The dashed
lines are identical to the corresponding lines in Figure 4.43. The graphs
of the apparent lines were drawn using the methods from the preceding
sections.

Notice that the two apparent lines are inside the two "normal" lines.
If you think of the two targets as being the top and bottom of an object,
then this object appears to be smaller than normal. Figure 4.45 is
similar to Figure 4.44 except that the radius of the mirror is 15 instead of
20; that is, the mirror is more sharply curved. Notice that the reducing
effect of this mirror is more pronounced than that of the first convex
mirror. Figure 4.46 has a mirror with a radius of 10. Its reducing effect
is even more pronounced.

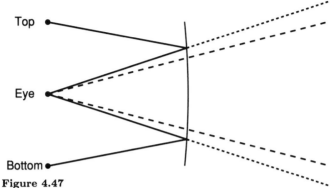

Figure 4.47
Appearance of an object in a concave mirror

Figure 4.48
A cylindrical mirror

Figure 4.47 shows the effect of a concave mirror. In this case the two apparent lines are outside the two normal lines. A concave mirror makes an object look larger than it actually is.

All our work and drawings so far have been two-dimensional. We live in a three-dimensional world (four, if you count time as a dimension). To get a more complete picture of the effect of a curved mirror, we need to think in three dimensions. Funhouse mirrors are usually cylindrical, as shown in Figure 4.48. Suppose that you were standing in front of a convex funhouse mirror looking at your reflection. What would you see? If we were to slice this mirror horizontally, the resulting section would be circular, and it would be convex as shown in Figure 4.49. For this reason this mirror has a reducing effect in the horizontal direction. You would look thinner than usual.

If we were to slice this same mirror vertically, the resulting section would be flat. For this reason this mirror has neither a reducing effect nor a magnifying effect in the vertical direction. Thus, you would look

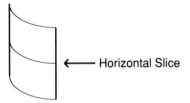

Figure 4.49
Cylindrical mirror with slices

thinner horizontally and normal vertically. You would appear to be
thinner and of normal height.

Exercise

*Exercise 4.4.24 What would your reflection look like in a concave
cylindrical mirror?

The convex mirrors used in some automobiles as outside rearview mirrors and in some stores to help catch shoplifters are sections of spheres.
No matter how you slice a sphere, the slice looks like a circle. For this
reason, the reflection of an object in a convex spherical mirror is smaller
in every direction.

Coffee Cups and Other Light Caustics

Next we want to look at a very common phenomenon involving reflections: light caustics. A light caustic is a bright pattern often produced
by reflected light. They occur frequently and often in unexpected places.
For example, I often see light caustics while bicycling. They are produced by the reflections of the sun off the front wheel of the bicycle onto
the road. You can see light caustics in coffee cups and any other place
that light might be bouncing off a curved surface. Light caustics are
usually produced when a collection of parallel light rays from a bright,
distant light source bounces off a concave surface. Figure 4.50 shows
four parallel light rays hitting a concave mirror. The incoming light
rays from the light source are drawn with dotted lines. The outgoing or
reflected lines are drawn with solid lines.

We can draw the path that each light ray will follow after it bounces
off the mirror by using the fact that when a light ray bounces off a

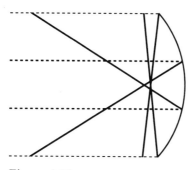

Figure 4.50
Four light rays bouncing off a concave mirror

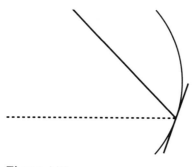

Figure 4.51
A single bouncing ray

surface, the angle of incidence equals the angle of coincidence. Figure 4.51 illustrates how we can draw a typical ray. When a light ray bounces off a curved mirror it acts as if it is bouncing off the tangent to the mirror at the point where it hits the mirror.

Figure 4.52 was drawn by computer. It shows the result when a whole series of parallel light rays bounces off a concave mirror. The incoming parallel light rays are evenly spaced. Notice that the outgoing (after they've bounced) light rays form a dark pattern in the middle of the picture. This pattern is the light caustic. In reality light rays are light rather than black, so this pattern shows up as a very bright pattern. You might compare Figure 4.52 with a real light caustic in a coffee cup or elsewhere.

The light caustics discussed in this section come from cylindrical reflecting surfaces. With other shapes one can see different light caustics.

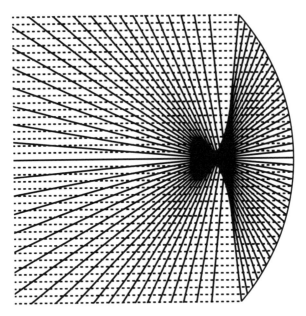

Figure 4.52
Many light rays bouncing off a concave mirror

Just by keeping your eyes open, you will see many different light caustics. You can experiment with light caustics using simple mirrors or the techniques discussed in this chapter.

4.5 Refraction

In this section we will investigate the way that light rays are bent as they pass from one medium (such as water) to another (perhaps air). This phenomenon is called *refraction*. The principles involved can be used to study many different optical phenomena, including microscopes, binoculars, and even rainbows.

Light travels at different speeds in different media. In air it travels at the speed of 30 billion centimeters per second. In water it travels more slowly, at 22.5 billion centimeters per second. Light travels so quickly that it will be more convenient to measure time in nanoseconds. A nanosecond is one-billionth of a second. Thus, light travels in air at a speed of 30 centimeters per nanosecond and in water at a speed of 22.5 centimeters per nanosecond.

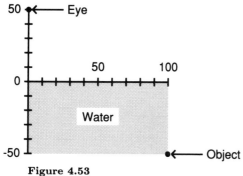

Figure 4.53
Looking at an underwater object

We will begin by looking at the situation shown in Figure 4.53. We have a tank of water 50 centimeters deep and 100 centimeters long. At one end of the tank on the bottom is an object. An observer is looking at this object from a vantage point above the opposite end of the tank. Her eye is 50 centimeters above the surface of the water. We would like to know how the object appears to her.

You will recall that Fermat's Principle says that light will follow the *fastest* path from one point to another. As long as light is traveling in one medium, the fastest path is simply the shortest one. When more than one medium is involved, the fastest path is not necessarily the shortest path. This situation is very similar to that faced by Lori Lifeguard in Example 1 of Section 4.1. Lori was able to run much faster than she could paddle her surfboard, so in order to reach a drowning swimmer as quickly as possible, she did not travel in a straight line directly from her lifeguard station to the swimmer. Instead she followed a more complicated path, running farther on the beach before entering the water.

Figure 4.54 shows one of the possible paths that light might follow traveling from the object to the observer in the situation in Figure 4.53. We can divide this path up into two pieces and compute the length of each of these two pieces in the usual way using the Pythagorean Theorem:

Length of piece $1 = \sqrt{50^2 + 25^2} = 55.9017$

Length of piece $2 = \sqrt{50^2 + 75^2} = 90.1388$

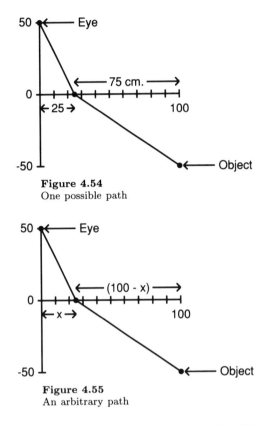

Figure 4.54
One possible path

Figure 4.55
An arbitrary path

Now we can compute the length of time it would take light to travel from the object to the observer along this path:

$$\text{Time for piece } 1 = \frac{55.9017}{30} = 1.8634 \text{ ns.}$$

$$\text{Time for piece } 2 = \frac{90.1388}{22.5} = 4.0062 \text{ ns.}$$

The total travel time for this path would be

$$\text{Total time} = 1.8634 + 4.0062 = 5.8696 \text{ ns.}$$

In order to find the fastest possible path for the light ray to follow, we must look at a general path like that shown in Figure 4.55. As before we can break this path up into two pieces and compute the length of each piece:

Length of piece $1 = \sqrt{50^2 + x^2}$

Length of piece $2 = \sqrt{50^2 + (100 - x)^2}$

and the length of time required to travel each piece:

Time for piece $1 = \dfrac{\sqrt{50^2 + x^2}}{30}$

Time for piece $2 = \dfrac{\sqrt{50^2 + (100 - x)^2}}{22.5}$

The total time required to travel this path is

$$T(x) = \frac{\sqrt{50^2 + x^2}}{30} + \frac{\sqrt{50^2 + (100 - x)^2}}{22.5}.$$

Now we can determine the actual path followed by a light ray traveling from the object to the observer by finding the minimum of the function $T(x)$.

Exercise

*Exercise 4.5.25 Modify your program from Section 4.1 to find the minimum of the function $T(x)$. Make a drawing showing the actual path followed by a light ray traveling from the object to the observer.

Now we will produce a graph like the one shown in Figure 4.56. This graph is analogous to the figures we drew in Section 4.3, except that now we are dealing with refraction rather than reflection. Figure 4.56 shows the actual path followed by light traveling from an object underwater to each of two eyes above water. It also shows the apparent path seen by each of these two eyes and by triangulation shows the apparent position of the object. The work in producing this graph is similar to the work in Section 4.3.

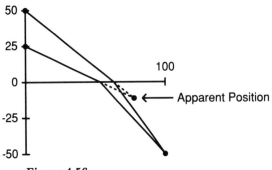
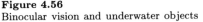

Figure 4.56
Binocular vision and underwater objects

The first step is to compute the actual path followed by the light ray traveling from the object at $(100, -50)$ to the eye at $(0, 50)$. In the previous exercise, you found that this light ray crosses the boundary between air and water (the x-axis) at the point $(63.53, 0)$. Now we know two points on the apparent ray for the eye at $(0, 50)$: $(0, 50)$ and $(63.53, 0)$. We can compute the slope of this line in the usual way:

$$\text{Slope of first apparent ray} = \frac{-50}{63.53} = -0.7870.$$

Thus, the equation of the first apparent line is

$$y = -.7870x + b,$$

and we can determine the value of b by substituting the point $(0, 50)$ into this equation to obtain

$$50 = -0.7870(0) + b.$$

So

$$b = 50$$

and the equation of the first apparent line is

$$y = -.7870x + 50.$$

The computations for the second eye are similar. The first step is to find out where the light ray traveling from the object at $(100, -50)$ to the eye at $(0, 25)$ crosses the boundary between air and water (the x-axis).

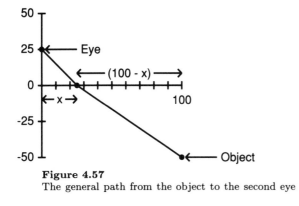

Figure 4.57
The general path from the object to the second eye

Exercises

*Exercise 4.5.26 Write a formula for the time it would take a light ray to travel from the object at $(100, -50)$ to the point $(x, 0)$ on the x-axis and then to the eye at $(0, 25)$. See Figure 4.57.

*Exercise 4.5.27 Find the actual path followed by the light ray traveling from the object at $(100, -50)$ to the eye at $(0, 25)$ by finding the minimum of the function you found in the previous exercise.

If you did the last two exercises correctly, you discovered that the second actual light ray hits the x-axis at the point $(53.65, 0)$. Now you can find the equation of this apparent light ray in the usual way:

$$\text{Slope of the second apparent ray} = \frac{-25}{53.65} = -0.4660.$$

So the equation of this light ray is

$$y = -.4660x + b$$

and we can find the value of b by substituting the point $(0, 25)$ into this equation:

$$25 = -0.4660(0) + b.$$

So

$$b = 25$$

and the equation of the second apparent light ray is

$$y = -.4660x + 25.$$

Now we can find the apparent position of the object by finding the intersection of the two apparent paths:

$$-0.7870x + 50 = -0.4660x + 25$$

$$25 = 0.3210x$$

$$x = \frac{25}{0.3210} = 77.9$$

and, substituting this value of x back into either one of the equations for the apparent rays, we obtain

$$y = -0.4660(77.9) + 25 = -11.3.$$

Thus, the apparent position of the object is at $(77.9, -11.3)$

You have a major programming assignment for this section. Write a computer program that will do all of these calculations. It will be very similar to the long programs in Sections 4.2 and 4.3. It will ask for the following input:

- The x- and y-coordinates of the first eye.

- The x- and y-coordinates of the second eye.

- The x- and y-coordinates of the object.

The program will compute the apparent position of the object as viewed by these two eyes in the situation of Figure 4.53. That is, the area below the x-axis will be filled with water, and the area above the x-axis will be filled with air.

You can check your program by using the calculations we did. After you have written and checked out your program, use it to work out the following exercises.

Exercises

For each of the following find the apparent position of the object. Then draw graphs showing the actual and apparent light rays and the apparent position of the object.

*Exercise 4.5.28

- Eye 1: (0, 50)
- Eye 2: (25, 50)
- Object: (100, -50)

Exercise 4.5.29

- Eye 1: (0, 50)
- Eye 2: (10, 50)
- Object: (100, -50)

Exercise 4.5.30   Formulate your own problem designed to discover whether an object viewed underwater is magnified or reduced. Solve your problem.

4.6   Reality and an Optical Paradox

This section is very much like Section 4.4. We want to look at the real three-dimensional world. We have been working with refraction in two dimensions because it is much easier to visualize two dimensions than three dimensions. However, the world is three-dimensional, and if we try to force it to fit our two-dimensional models, we are forced into some strange contortions. Suppose that you are standing at the end of a swimming pool looking at an object at the bottom of the pool. "Aha!" you say "This situation is exactly like the ones we were looking at in Section 4.5. I know all about the apparent position of an object underwater. Just give me a few measurements, and I'll be able to figure out the apparent position of the object."

You would expect to be able to use your computer program and drafting skills from the previous sections to produce a drawing like Figure 4.56 (p. 298). If you compare that figure with the figures that you drew in the exercises at the end of Section 4.5, you will notice that in all these figures the apparent position of the underwater object is much higher and closer to the observer's two eyes than its actual position. These figures have another similarity. If you try to hold your head to put

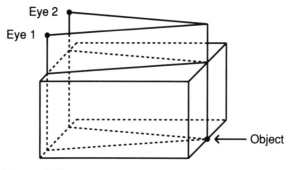

Figure 4.58
A normal person looking at an underwater object

your eyes in any of the positions indicated on these figures, you will find yourself in very strange positions. For example, Figure 4.56 shows the two eyes arranged vertically, with one eye exactly above the other. It is possible to hold your eyes in this position either by lying on your side or by holding your head with a 90 degree tilt to the side, but it is neither comfortable nor usual to do this.

The natural way to look at an underwater object is by holding your head in its normal vertical position with your two eyes on a horizontal line and to look toward the object (Figure 4.58). If you try this, you will notice that the three important points—the two points occupied by your two eyes and the third point occupied by the underwater object—do not all lie in one two-dimensional plane. This means that we cannot draw one figure like the ones at which we have been looking that will contain all three points. We need two planes as shown in Figure 4.58. Each individual plane looks like the plane shown in Figure 4.59. These planes are vertical, and each contains one eye and the underwater object.

By combining two planes like Figure 4.59 into a three-dimensional picture, we obtain Figure 4.60. Notice that the two apparent lines intersect directly above the object. Thus, the apparent position of the object is above its actual position, but in contrast to our two-dimensional work in the previous section, it is directly above the object rather than much closer to the observer.

When I first got a personal computer, this was one of the first experiments I tried. I've always been somewhat mystified by optics and the way that mirrors and lenses can be used to magnify or reduce things.

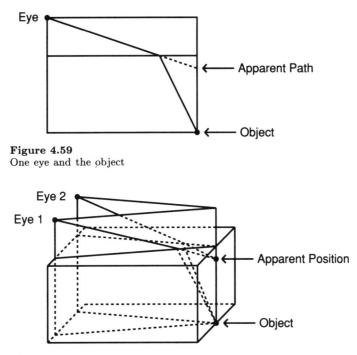

Figure 4.59
One eye and the object

Figure 4.60
Two planes combined

I thought that working out some of these examples would help me understand. It did, but it also produced this somewhat bizarre result. According to our calculations, if you look at an underwater object from a particular point at the side of a swimming pool (let's say your nose is always fixed at one particular spot), then its apparent position depends on how you hold your head. If you hold your head in the usual way, the object will appear to be directly above its actual position. If you hold your head in one of the odd positions necessary to emulate the figures from Section 4.5, then the object will appear to be much closer to you.

These results seemed paradoxical. In fact, I thought I must have made some mistake. So I went to my local swimming pool immediately after it opened before anybody had entered the pool and disturbed the surface. I stood at the edge tilting my head in various positions and looking at a convenient underwater drain. It works. The bizarre results we arrived at above are correct.

5 Local Aid Distribution

One of our main purposes in this course is to use the computer to help understand questions of public policy. Many such questions involve the government. No other noun is less deserving of the definite article *the* than the noun *government*. In fact, we live in the midst of a tangled web of many governments. Our town (or city), state, and federal governments all vie for their share of our tax dollars, and all help to provide various public services. But there are many additional governmental units: county governments, school districts, mass transit districts, port authorities, and others. All raise money either directly or indirectly from us and all provide some public services.

Different public services are provided by different levels of government. For example, national defense is the responsibility of the federal government. The responsibility for some public services is shared by many levels of government. Elementary and secondary education is usually administered at a local level by cities or by school districts; however, its financing is shared by federal, state, and local governments. With this financing comes some measure of regulation from all these levels of government.

Each of our many governments has its own set of resources and responsibilities; however, they are all intimately tied together. The federal government has the broadest resources. It levies taxes on all the citizens of the United States and even raises some revenue from noncitizens (for example, through taxes on income earned in the United States). State governments have more limited resources, and there is a wide variation in these resources among the states. The amount of money a state can raise in taxes is largely determined by the income and wealth of its citizens. Connecticut has a per capita income (1987) of $21,266, more than twice that of Mississippi, $10,292. Some states, most notably Alaska, raise substantial amounts of revenue by taxing the production of oil or other natural resources. Cities and towns are even more limited in their ability to raise money, and there is even more variation in this ability than among states.

One factor that limits a government's ability to raise revenue is the possibility that its citizens and businesses might move away if its taxes are substantially higher than competing areas. This factor is particularly important for cities and towns and less so for states.

Table 5.1 illustrates the variation in revenue resources among the states.* The column labeled "Revenue Resources" estimates each state's revenue resources per capita. It was calculated by first determining a representative tax system (RTS). The RTS includes an income tax that is the "average" of all the state income taxes and treats other taxes similarly. This RTS was applied to each state in order to determine how much money that state would raise if it used this standard tax system. The total RTS tax collection for each state was then divided by that state's population in order to determine its per capita revenue resources.

Notice the huge variation among the states in both population and revenue resources. Figures 5.1, 5.2, and 5.3 present this same information graphically. Figure 5.1 shows population. Figures 5.2 and 5.3 show per capita revenue resources. Figure 5.3 is the same as Figure 5.2 except that I have omitted Alaska. Alaska has huge energy resources and a very small population. As a result, its per capita revenue resources are far bigger than those of the other states. By omitting Alaska, we get a much better picture of the comparative per capita revenue resources for the remaining states.

A state's needs frequently do not match its resources. There is no reason to expect that poorer states would have fewer needs than richer states. In fact, the reverse is often true. For example, welfare needs are much larger in poorer states than in richer ones. During hard times, the same events that cause needs to rise—for example, high unemployment—often cause revenue resources to drop.

The disparities in revenue resources among the states are aggravated by the fact that states are not completely free to determine their tax rates. Businesses often consider tax rates when they make their decisions about where to locate new plants or office buildings. In order to raise the same amount of money as a rich state, a poorer state would have to use a higher tax rate, but this might chase away some existing industry, repel new industry, and result in a weakening of the tax base.

There is a clear national interest in having roughly comparable public services available across the country. Indeed numerous laws and regulations are aimed at ensuring certain minimal standards and a certain

---

*Derived from the article, *The Rich-State-Poor-State Problem in a Federal System*, by Albert Davis and Robert Lucke (National Tax Journal (vol. 35, 1982): 337–363.

Table 5.1
Per Capita Revenue Resources

State	Revenue Resources	Population	State	Revenue Resources	Population
Alabama	$900	3,893,888	New Jersey	$1,257	7,364,823
Alaska	$6,161	401,851	New Mexico	$1,492	1,302,894
Arizona	$1,059	2,718,215	New York	$1,120	17,558,072
Arkansas	$927	2,286,435	North Carolina	$945	5,881,766
California	$1,381	23,667,902	North Dakota	$1,346	652,717
Colorado	$1,325	2,889,964	Ohio	$1,147	10,797,630
Connecticut	$1,338	3,107,576	Oklahoma	$1,339	3,025,290
Delaware	$1,313	594,338	Oregon	$1,220	2,633,105
Dist. of Col.	$1,348	638,333	Pennsylvania	$1,109	11,863,895
Florida	$1,188	9,746,324	Rhode Island	$1,034	947,154
Georgia	$969	5,463,105	South Carolina	$898	3,121,820
Hawaii	$1,252	964,691	South Dakota	$1,050	690,768
Idaho	$1,035	943,935	Tennessee	$943	4,591,120
Illinois	$1,279	11,426,518	Texas	$1,440	14,229,191
Indiana	$1,089	5,490,224	Utah	$1,015	1,461,037
Iowa	$1,217	2,913,808	Vermont	$999	511,456
Kansas	$1,274	2,363,679	Virginia	$1,128	5,346,818
Kentucky	$973	3,660,777	Washington	$1,242	4,132,156
Louisiana	$,379	4,205,900	West Virginia	$1,079	1,949,644
Maine	$954	1,124,660	Wisconsin	$1,117	4,705,767
Maryland	$1,186	4,216,975	Wyoming	$2,399	469,557
Massachusetts	$1,152	5,737,037			
Michigan	$1,155	9,262,078			
Minnesota	$1,201	4,075,970			
Mississippi	$817	2,520,638			
Missouri	$1,104	4,916,686			
Montana	$1,317	786,690			
Nebraska	$1,140	1,569,825			
Nevada	$1,731	800,493			
New Hampshire	$1,154	920,610			

consistency in some public services. Because financial resources vary considerably among the states, the federal government in the past provided a significant part of the financing for many public services. Programs like federal revenue sharing helped support many public services administered at the state or local level. Recently, however, the federal government has largely abandoned this role, creating difficulties for state and local governments that have very limited local resources.

There is an additional reason for maintaining a large federal role in financing locally administered public services. The nation as a whole is

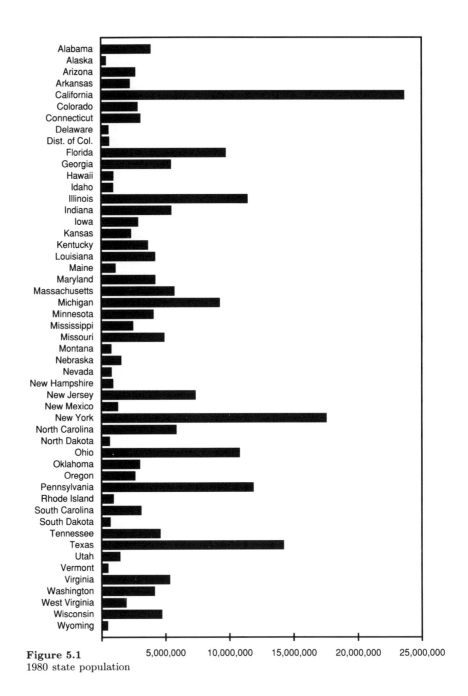

Figure 5.1
1980 state population

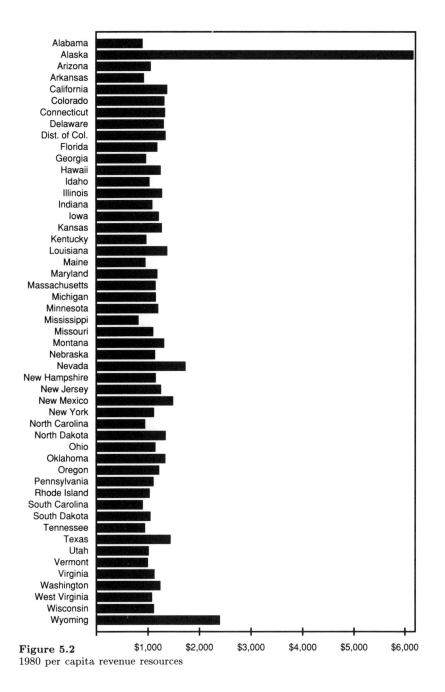

Figure 5.2
1980 per capita revenue resources

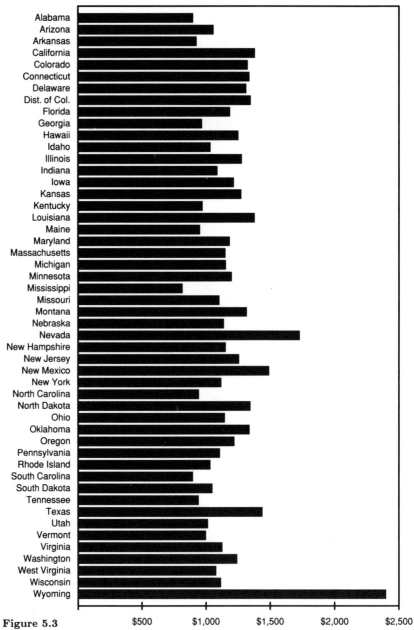

Figure 5.3
1980 per capita revenue resources (Alaska omitted)

much larger and more stable than individual states and localities. Individual states and localities can be very susceptible to economic disasters (for example, a severe downturn in a particular industry) that can lower their financial resources at exactly the time that more money is needed to recover. For this reason federal financing of public services performs some of the same functions as insurance.

We will be concerned with the financial aspect of the relationship of federal, state, and local governments. One of the critical aspects of any government program is the way in which its benefits are apportioned.

The purpose of this chapter is to examine a particular situation in which one government (in this case the Commonwealth of Massachusetts) shares revenue with other governments (the 351 cities and towns in Massachusetts). I chose a particular example so that we can see how the general principles actually work, but the questions that arise, the principles involved, and the mathematical methods we use are extremely general. You can use the knowledge gained in this chapter to become an active and knowledgeable participant in public policy debates on any level of government.

The issues discussed in this chapter have become urgent because of national concern about the quality of education. Education has traditionally been funded from local resources, primarily the property tax. Unfortunately many localities lack adequate local resources to support good schools. It is clear that the existing system of supporting education must change if we are to provide an adequate education to all citizens. One of the critical issues involved in funding education will be determining how to distribute state funds to local school systems.

5.1   The Cities and Towns of Massachusetts

The 351 cities and towns of Massachusetts are primarily responsible for a number of major and very expensive public services. Public education (kindergarten–twelfth grade) is a local responsibility, either directly by the cities and towns or through regional school districts made up of several cities or towns. Public safety (police and fire protection) is a local responsibility. So is the maintenance of roads and snow removal.

Unfortunately, the revenue resources of the cities and towns are very limited. These resources are restricted by three main constraints.

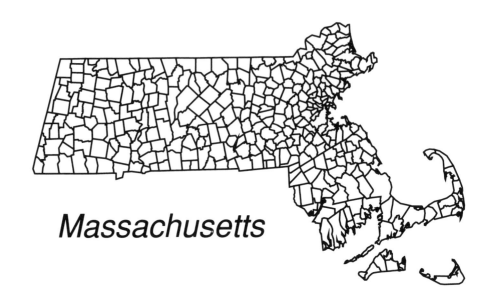

Massachusetts

Figure 5.4
The 351 cities and towns of Massachusetts

First, the cities and towns have only very limited legal authority to raise money. The Commonwealth of Massachusetts levies an income tax and a sales tax, but does not allow cities and towns to levy such taxes. The cities and towns are allowed to raise money in only a few, very strictly proscribed ways. The primary source of revenue for cities and towns is the property tax. In addition there is an excise tax on automobiles, which is levied at a rate fixed by the state but collected by the cities and towns. The only other significant source of locally generated revenue is fees for various town services.

The second constraint is Proposition $2\frac{1}{2}$. In November 1980 voters in Massachusetts passed a severe tax limitation measure called Proposition $2\frac{1}{2}$. The most immediate effect of this measure was to limit the property tax rate in each city and town to $2\frac{1}{2}\%$ of the full and fair market value of the property. Many communities had tax rates above this limit; they were required to reduce their property tax levies by 15% each year until they reached the legal limit. Proposition $2\frac{1}{2}$ also lowered the excise tax on automobiles, so that this relatively insignificant tax became even less significant. In addition, Proposition $2\frac{1}{2}$ restricts the amount by which the total tax levy can rise. The total dollar amount of money each city and town can raise can rise by no more than $2\frac{1}{2}\%$ each year regardless of the rate of inflation or the rate by which property values are rising. Since the rate of inflation is usually more than $2\frac{1}{2}\%$, this means that in terms of buying power, the property tax has fallen considerably since the passage of Proposition $2\frac{1}{2}$.

The third constraint arises from the mobility of our society, especially those in the higher income brackets, and the small size of many cities and towns. If a particular city or town has tax rates that are substantially higher or public services that are substantially worse than those of the surrounding communities, then it may repel new residents and new industry. If the discrepancies are large enough, existing residents and existing industry may leave.

In this context outside revenue becomes exceptionally important. The cities and towns of Massachusetts receive substantial amounts of outside revenue from two sources: the federal government and the state government. The impact of Proposition $2\frac{1}{2}$ was magnified by the fact that it took effect in January 1981 and really began to have an impact with the start of fiscal year 1982 in July 1981. Thus, Proposition $2\frac{1}{2}$ coincided with the radical changes in state and federal relations produced by the Reagan administration. These changes produced a substantial drop in the amount of federal money distributed to cities and towns.

Thus, the distribution of state money to cities and towns has become exceptionally important. To summarize, there are three principal reasons that it is essential that state money be distributed to cities and towns:

1. The state reserves to itself most forms of taxation, leaving cities and towns a limited ability to raise local revenue. Proposition $2\frac{1}{2}$ further restricts this ability.

2. The other major outside source of money, the federal government, has drastically cut the amount of aid distributed to cities and towns.

3. There are substantial differences among the cities and towns regarding local revenue-raising capacity.

The purpose of this chapter is to study the distribution of state aid to cities and towns in Massachusetts. We will begin by looking at some facts. Appendix B contains two tables. Both list the 351 cities and towns

in Massachusetts and each one's 1980 population and 1980 per capita
equalized property valuation (EQV). This latter figure is one good indication of per capita local revenue-raising capacity. Another indication
of local wealth is per capita income. However, per capita income has a
less direct effect on local revenue-raising capacity since localities cannot
levy an income tax. In 1980 different localities used different bases for
evaluating property. Under the impetus of court decisions and Proposition $2\frac{1}{2}$, localities now use full and fair market value. The adjective
equalized in the phrase 'equalized property valuation' means that these
figures have been adjusted to compensate for differences in local valuation practices. We will use per capita EQV for comparing different
communities. The first table in Appendix B lists these data in alphabetic order. The second table lists the same data in order by per capita
EQV with the highest per capita EQV first.

A quick glance at the second table reveals the vast discrepancies in
local revenue-raising capacities among the cities and towns. The highest
per capita EQV figures in this table are enormous: \$392,560 in Rowe
and \$323,108 in Chilmark. But these figures are exceptional. Rowe is
the site of a nuclear power plant, Yankee Station. The value of this
plant together with the very small population (336) of Rowe produce
this extraordinary per capita EQV. The other nuclear power plant in
Massachusetts, Pilgrim Unit 1, is located in Plymouth. Plymouth has
a larger population (35,913), so its per capita EQV (\$27,283), although
fairly high, is not in the same league as Rowe's. Many of the remaining
extremely high per capita EQVs are for cities and towns on Cape Cod.
Chilmark, for example, is on the island of Martha's Vineyard, a few
miles off the southern coast of Cape Cod. The figures for these cities
and towns are inflated by a large number of vacation homes owned by
people whose residence is elsewhere. This results in high total property
values divided by relatively low year-round populations.

When examining tables like those in Appendix B, bear in mind the
reality behind the numbers. For example, the number \$47,087 for the
per capita EQV of the town of Dennis does not tell you that Dennis is
on Cape Cod. It ignores the marvelous beaches and the pounding surf,
the rumble of the hoards of vacationers, the beeps of the cash registers,
and the clicking of the fiddler crabs' "fiddles." Vacation communities on
Cape Cod are fundamentally different from those on the mainland. They
do have large local revenue-raising capacities. Many of their expenses

are much lower than those on the mainland. For example, since the year-round populations are relatively low, there are fewer students per dollar of total EQV. On the other hand, they have some burdens that come with the vacationers. Downtown Hyannis on a summer Sunday has traffic jams worthy of a large city. (You won't find Hyannis in Appendix B. It is a village in the town of Barnstable. Hyannis has no taxing authority of its own, and its public services are provided by Barnstable.) Residents of Cape Cod regard their seasonal inundation by vacationers as a mixed blessing.

At the other end of this table, people who live in Amherst (not surprisingly, the site of the University of Massachusetts at Amherst) may be surprised to discover their town fourth from the bottom in per capita EQV. The reason is the very large number of students who drive up the population but have minimal impact on the total EQV. The result is a very low per capita EQV.

Beginning in Section 5.3 we will be discussing formulas for distributing state aid among the cities and towns. These formulas will be based on numbers like per capita EQV. But we must always be aware of the reality of individual people and very different communities behind these numbers. Sections 5.1–5.4 will analyze the data in Appendix B. You will be writing several computer programs to help in this analysis.

It is a little hard to interpret the data in Appendix B. For example, Rowe's per capita EQV of $392,560 is clearly extremely high, while Chelsea's per capita EQV of $6,209 seems quite low. But what about Leverett at $17,009? Is that high? or low? How high? or how low? In order to find a first basis of comparison, we will compute the "average" per capita EQV. This is a first, very naive basis of comparison. The following True BASIC program computes this average:

```
!   Compute average per capita EQV
!
OPEN #1: NAME "EQVdata"              ! Data file
FOR i = 1 TO 351                     ! Process 351 towns
INPUT #1: name$, population, EQV     ! Read one town
LET sum = sum + EQV                  ! Sum EQV
NEXT i
PRINT USING "Average EQV: $##,###":sum/351
END
```

The information in Appendix B is contained in a disk file called
"EQVdata." Your instructor will give you a copy of this disk file. The
first few lines of this file look like this:

```
Rowe, 336 , 392560
Chilmark, 489 , 323108
Gosnold, 63 , 154651
```

Each line has three pieces of data separated by commas: the town
or city name, the town's per capita EQV in dollars, and the town's
population.

The average per capita EQV computed by this program is $23,499.
But this is a somewhat misleading figure. It is the average of each town's
per capita EQV, but it is not what one would intuitively mean by the
average per capita EQV in the state. The problem with this figure is
that the town of Rowe with 336 residents has been counted equally with
the city of Boston, which has 562,994 residents.

We can see what a drastic impact this has on the "average" PCV by
running the following slight modification of the preceding program. This
modification omits the town of Rowe. Lines marked with an asterisk (*)
have been modified to skip Rowe.

```
!   Compute average per capita EQV omitting Rowe              *
!
OPEN #1: NAME "EQVdata"             ! Data file
INPUT #1: name$, population, EQV   ! Skip Rowe              *
FOR i = 1 TO 350                   ! Process remaining 350 towns *
INPUT #1: name$, population, EQV   ! Read one town
LET sum = sum + EQV                ! Sum EQV
NEXT i
PRINT USING "Average EQV: $##,###":sum/350              !    *
END
```

The average computed by this program is $22,445, a difference of over
$1,000 from our earlier figure.

A more reasonable figure can be obtained by dividing the total EQV
for the whole Commonwealth by the total population of the whole Commonwealth. Table 5.2 illustrates how the total EQV for the whole Commonwealth and the total population for the whole Commonwealth can
be computed from the data in Appendix B.

Table 5.2
Beginning of EQV Computation

City or Town	Population	Per Capita EQV	Total EQV
Abington	13,517	$12,325	$166,597,025
Acton	17,544	$24,419	$428,406,936
⋮	⋮	⋮	⋮

Table 5.3
Beginning of EQV Computation

City or Town	Population	Per Capita EQV
Abington	13,517	$12,325
Acton	17,544	$24,419
Acushnet	8,704	$11,799

Column 4 in Table 5.2 is the product of the per capita EQV for each town and its population (column 3 times column 2). It is the total EQV for that town. By adding up column 2, we get the total population for the Commonwealth. By adding up column 4, we get the total EQV for the Commonwealth. By dividing the total EQV by the total population, we obtain a much more meaningful "average" per capita EQV. Your assignment for this section is to compute this average per capita EQV. In the next section, we will continue our analysis of the data in Appendix B. This average will be very helpful in this analysis.

Before beginning this assignment, we need to consider how a program like this might be checked out. One of the most powerful tools for this is to work out an example. But it is impractical to work out an example using all the data in Appendix B. In fact, the example would require all the work that the program is intended to do. One easy way to check out a program like this is to modify it slightly to use only the first three lines of the data as shown in Table 5.3. In other words we will pretend for this purpose that Massachusetts has only three cities and towns. This pretense can be implemented in your program by changing just one or two lines. This example is short enough so that you can easily work it out by hand.

Exercises

*Exercise 5.1.1 Compute the average per capita EQV using only the data in Table 5.3.

*Exercise 5.1.2 Write, check out, and run a program to compute the average per capita EQV as described for the Commonwealth of Massachusetts. Be sure you check out this program carefully. One way to check out the program is by using the example from the previous exercise.

5.2   Measures of Disparity

A reader casually glancing at the tables in Appendix B will immediately observe the vast disparities in local revenue-raising capacity. The purpose of this section is to examine these disparities more closely. We will develop and use several tools for this examination.

Graphs are useful tools for understanding tables of numbers like those in Appendix B because they can often convey quickly and dramatically an overall picture of a particular situation. For example, consider Table 5.4 and Figure 5.5. There are 45 cities and towns in Massachusetts whose population is over 30,000. Table 5.4 gives the per capita EQV for each of these 45 cities and towns. Figure 5.5 shows exactly the same information in the form of a bar graph. The disparities among these 45 cities and towns are much easier to grasp at a glance by looking at the bar graph than by looking at the table.

We will make heavy use of graphics in this section. Many computers, including virtually all personal computers, have the ability to draw graphs. True BASIC has powerful commands for producing graphs. Although we will not be studying computer graphics in this book, you may want to try to reproduce some of the graphics yourself. The necessary information is available in most books about True BASIC.

To get a picture of the actual numbers of people who are affected by disparities in per capita EQV, we will divide the cities and towns into 26 groups according to their per capita EQVs. It will be convenient

Table 5.4
Per Capita EQV for Cities and Towns With a Population Above 30,000

City or Town	Per Capita EQV	City or Town	Per Capita EQV
Amherst	8,119	Medford	14,336
Arlington	16,278	Melrose	14,171
Attleborough	13,712	Methuen	13,640
Barnstable	38,588	New Bedford	7,535
Beverly	15,082	Newton	23,654
Billerica	14,670	Peabody	15,145
Boston	9,306	Pittsfield	12,381
Braintree	20,998	Plymouth	27,283
Brockton	9,784	Quincy	13,559
Brookline	17,589	Revere	10,831
Cambridge	13,544	Salem	15,780
Chelmsford	17,585	Somerville	8,454
Chicopee	10,401	Springfield	8,633
Everett	23,874	Taunton	9,760
Fall River	6,394	Waltham	17,938
Fitchburg	9,467	Watertown	17,537
Framingham	17,631	Westfield	11,729
Haverhill	10,025	Weymouth	13,156
Holyoke	8,588	Woburn	18,492
Lawrence	8,160	Worcester	8,832
Leominster	11,931		
Lowell	8,239		
Lynn	9,256		
Malden	9,819		
Marlborough	15,044		

to number the groups: 0, 1, 2, ..., 25. These groups are described as follows:

- Group 0: Per capita EQV $0,000–$1,999
- Group 1: Per capita EQV $2,000–$3,999
- Group 2: Per capita EQV $4,000–$5,999
- Group 3: Per capita EQV $6,000–$7,999
- Group 4: Per capita EQV $8,000–$9,999

  ⋮

- Group 24: Per capita EQV $48,000–$49,999
- Group 25: Per capita EQV $50,000–

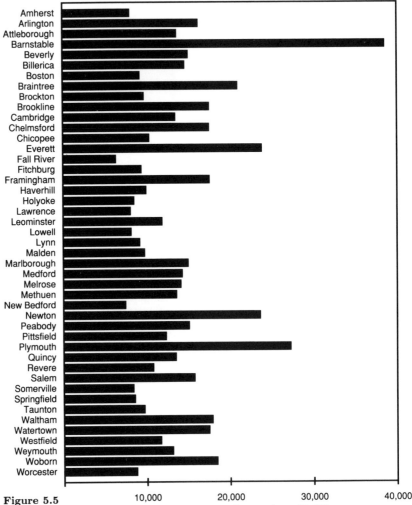

Figure 5.5
Per capita EQV for cities and towns with population above 30,000

We can determine the group in which a city or town falls by dividing its per capita EQV by 2,000. For example, the town of Amherst has a per capita EQV of $8,119. So we divide

$$\frac{8119}{2000} = 4 \text{ with a remainder of } 119.$$

Table 5.5
Numbers of People Living in Towns by EQV

Per Capita EQV	Total Population
$0–1,999	0
$2,000–3,999	0
$4,000–5,999	0
$6,000–7,999	216,483
$8,000–9,999	1,597,420
$10,000–11,999	473,349
$12,000–13,999	810,973
$14,000–15,999	546,124
$16,000–17,999	741,665
$18,000–19,999	313,524
$20,000–21,999	272,246
$22,000–23,999	177,470
$24,000–25,999	118,424
$26,000–27,999	124,389
$28,000–29,999	89,653
$30,000–31,999	60,668
$32,000–33,999	24,531
$34,000–35,999	23,640
$36,000–37,999	21,985
$38,000–39,999	31,716
$40,000–41,999	21,300
$42,000–43,999	0
$44,000–45,999	13,631
$46,000–47,999	21,431
$48,000–49,999	963
$50,000–infinity	35,450

The quotient of this division (ignoring the remainder) is the group in which the city or town falls. Amherst falls into group 4, which has a per capita EQV of $8,000–$9,999.

We are interested in the total population of all the cities and towns in each group. Table 5.5 gives these totals in tabular form, and Figure 5.6 shows the same results in a bar graph. You can see immediately from Figure 5.6 how many people live in relatively poor cities and towns and how many live in richer cities and towns. Table 5.5 was produced by a computer program with the same data used in the exercise at the end of Section 5.1.

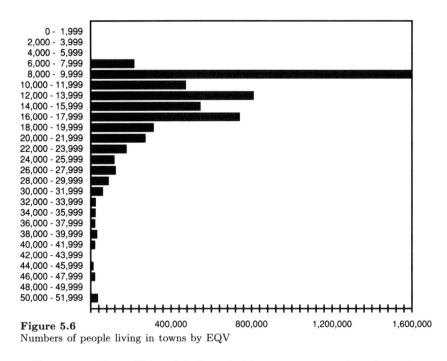

Figure 5.6
Numbers of people living in towns by EQV

You can see from Figure 5.6 that the biggest concentration of people is in towns with a rather small revenue-raising capacity, a per capita EQV of $8,000–$9,999. There are, however, very substantial numbers of people living in much wealthier towns.

Exercise

Exercise 5.2.3 Although it is not directly applicable to our investigation of local aid distribution in Massachusetts, it would be interesting to get an idea of how many people live in cities and towns of various sizes. Make a table and a corresponding bar graph showing how many people live in cities and towns of each of the following sizes:

- Group 0: 0,000–24,999
- Group 1: 25,000–49,999
- Group 2: 50,000–74,999

  ⋮

- Group 10: 250,000 and above.

Use the same disk file that you used for the exercise at the end of Section 5.1. You can draw the bar graph by hand or, if you want to learn something about computer graphics, you can write a program to draw it.

Figure 5.7 is much more difficult to draw without using a computer. It gives a dramatic and concise picture of the disparities in per capita EQV. This graph was made using the data in Table 2 of Appendix B. This table lists each city and town in decreasing order of per capita EQV. Each city and town is represented by a rectangle in Figure 5.7. The height of this rectangle is the community's per capita EQV. The width of this rectangle is the community's population. The widest rectangle represents Boston, the most populous city in Massachusetts. The rectangles representing very small communities are so thin that they look like lines rather than rectangles. The cities and towns appear from left to right in Figure 5.7 in the same order as Table 2 of Appendix B. Rowe, with the highest per

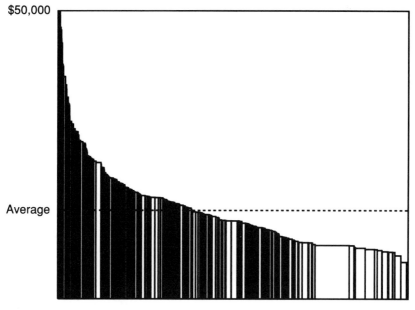

Figure 5.7
How people are affected by per capita EQV

Table 5.6
A Fictitious State

City or Town	Population	Per Capita EQV
Elm	50,000	$10,000
Oak	30,000	$12,000
Maple	40,000	$8,000
Hazel	30,000	$7,000

Table 5.7
A Fictitious State

City or Town	Population	Per Capita EQV
Oak	30,000	$12,000
Elm	50,000	$10,000
Maple	40,000	$8,000
Hazel	30,000	$7,000

capita EQV, is at the far left, and Chelsea, with the lowest per capita EQV, is at the far right.

To see exactly how this graph was made, we will draw a similar graph for a much smaller and more manageable "state," the fictitious state shown in Table 5.6 with only four cities.

The first step in making this graph is rearranging the four cities and towns in order of per capita EQV from highest to lowest, as in Table 5.7.

Figure 5.8 shows a graph similar to that of Figure 5.7 for this fictional state. The total population of the four communities is 150,000. Thus, the x-axis in Figure 5.8 runs from 0 to 150,000. The highest per capita EQV in this state is $12,000. The y-axis in Figure 5.8 runs from $0 to $12,000. Each rectangle in Figure 5.8 represents the community whose name it bears (in Figure 5.7 there is insufficient room to label each rectangle). The rectangles are arranged from left to right in order of per capita EQV, with the highest per capita EQV at the left. The width of each rectangle corresponds to the area of the corresponding community. The total width of all the rectangles corresponds to the total population of the state.

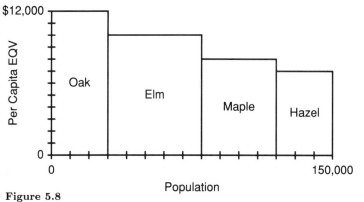

Figure 5.8
How people are affected by per capita EQV, an example

In order to make Figure 5.7 more manageable, it is a procrustean graph. The top of the graph represents an EQV of $50,000, and like Procrustes we shorten the rectangles corresponding to cities and towns like Rowe and Chilmark to fit the graph. The dotted horizontal line about a third of the way up the graph represents the average per capita EQV computed in the exercise at the end of Section 5.1. By looking at this graph, you can see at a glance how many people live in towns with various per capita EQVs.

We Americans and especially those of us who are sports fans seem to have developed an insatiable hunger for numbers. We always want to measure numerically how good our favorite ballplayer is. We compare pitchers by looking up their ERAs (earned run averages) and batters by batting averages. (Some of us even want to rate members of the opposite sex on a numeric scale of 1–10.) Such numeric measures are fundamentally limited; however, they can have some utility if used intelligently and responsibly. In the remainder of this section, we want to develop a numeric measure of disparity. We will apply this measure to per capita EQV in this section. Later we will use it as one measure for comparing the effects of various local aid distribution formulas.

There are many possible ways to measure disparity numerically. Perhaps the most obvious way is the following measure:

Disparity Measure 1: (Average Disparity)

The *average disparity* is computed as follows:

Step 1: Determine the average per capita EQV. For the 1980 per capita EQV in Massachusetts, this average was determined in the exercise at the end of Section 5.1. It is $15,389.

Step 2: For each community the disparity for that community is the absolute value of the difference between its per capita EQV and the average per capita EQV—for example,

City or Town	Per Capita EQV	Disparity
Boston	$9,306	$6,083
Cambridge	$13,544	$1,845
Newton	$23,654	$8,265

Step 3: Compute the average of these 351 community disparities. For example, if the state had only the three cities listed above, the average disparity would be

$$\frac{6,083 + 1,845 + 8,265}{3} = 5,397.67.$$

The problem with this measure is that it focuses on towns and cities rather than people. It fails to distinguish between a town of a few hundred people and a city with half a million residents. Our second measure corrects this flaw.

Disparity Measure 2: (Weighted Average Disparity)

The *weighted average disparity* is computed as follows.

Step 1: Determine the average per capita EQV. For the 1980 per capita EQV in Massachusetts, this average was determined in the exercise at the end of Section 5.1. It is $15,389.

Step 2: For each community the disparity for that community is the absolute value of the difference between its per capita EQV and the average per capita EQV—for example,

City or Town	Per Capita EQV	Disparity
Boston	$9,306	$6,083
Cambridge	$13,544	$1,845
Newton	$23,654	$8,265

Step 3: For each community, multiply its disparity by its population—for example,

City or Town	Population	Per Capita EQV	Disparity	Product
Boston	562,994	$9,306	$6,083	3,424,692,502
Cambridge	18,182	$13,544	$1,845	33,545,790
Newton	83,622	$23,654	$8,265	691,135,830

Step 4: Find the total in column 5 and divide by the total population in the state. For example, if the only three communities in Massachusetts were Boston, Cambridge, and Newton, we would get:

City or Town	Population	Per Capita EQV	Disparity	Product
Boston	562,994	$9,306	$6,083	3,424,692,502
Cambridge	18,182	$13,544	$1,845	33,545,790
Newton	83,622	$23,654	$8,265	691,135,830
Total	664,798			4,149,374,122

The weighted average disparity would be

$$\frac{4,149,374,122}{664,798} = 6,242.$$

This is a much better measure of the disparity than the first one because it takes into account the differing community populations. In effect, it computes for each resident the disparity between the average per capita EQV for the whole state and the per capita EQV in his community and then finds the average of this number for all the residents of the state. Now experiment with this measure of disparity by doing the following exercises.

Exercises

For each of the following fictitious states compute the weighted average disparity. For the last two exercises, you should also make a graph similar to Figures 5.7 and 5.8. (Figure 5.8 is a graph for the state in the first exercise.)

*Exercise 5.2.4

City or Town	Population	Per Capita EQV
Elm	50,000	$10,000
Oak	30,000	$12,000
Maple	40,000	$8,000
Hazel	30,000	$7,000

Exercise 5.2.5

City or Town	Population	Per Capita EQV
Elm	60,000	$10,000
Oak	20,000	$14,000
Maple	10,000	$2,500
Hazel	10,000	$9,500

Exercise 5.2.6

City or Town	Population	Per Capita EQV
Elm	60,000	$10,000
Oak	20,000	$14,000
Maple	10,000	$6,000
Hazel	10,000	$6,000

You should notice something very strange about the last two exercises above: the weighted average disparities for the two states are identical, although the states are very different. In the first, there is one extremely poor community, Maple, with a per capita EQV of only $2,500. In the second, Maple and Hazel are the poorest communities, but their per

capita EQVs are both $6,000, which is nowhere near as low as $2,500.
It is intuitively clear that the first of the two states has a much worse
disparity in per capita EQV than the second. But our measure of disparity, weighted average disparity, says that these two states have the
same disparity.

Our next measure of disparity is better than the weighted average
disparity and will be able to distinguish between these two states. You
should also interpret this example as a warning: any numeric measure
of disparity has flaws. The one we are about to develop is better than
the weighted average disparity but still must be used with care.

Disparity Measure 3: (Disparity Index)

This measure is basically geometric. We will motivate this measure
by looking at an example. Consider two people whose incomes are given
as follows:

- Mr. Smith: $20,000

- Ms. Jones: $50,000

We want to measure the disparity between their incomes. If their incomes were equal, the total income, $70,000, would be divided equally
between them, giving each one $35,000. Figure 5.9 shows this informa-
tion graphically. We can measure the distance between the actual situation (graphically, the point ($50,000, $20,000)) and equality (graphically,

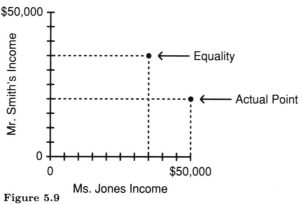

Figure 5.9
Disparity between Mr. Smith and Ms. Jones

the point ($35,000, $35,000)) by using the Pythagorean Theorem:

$$\text{Distance} = \sqrt{(15{,}000)^2 + (15{,}000)^2} = \$21{,}213.$$

This number, $21,213, is the geometric measure of the disparity in the two incomes. It is the geometric distance (in dollars) between equality (in which the total income, $70,000, is divided equally between the two people) and the actual situation.

We can make this measure more meaningful by dividing by the average income. This gives us a number called the *disparity index*.

$$\text{Disparity index} = \frac{\$21{,}213}{\$35{,}000} = 0.6061.$$

Since this measure of disparity is based on geometry, it has many nice mathematical properties. We can adapt this measure to the situation in which we are interested as follows:

Step 1: Determine the average per capita EQV. For the 1980 per capita EQV in Massachusetts, this average was determined in the last exercise in Section 5.1. It is $15,389.

Step 2: For each community, calculate the absolute value of the difference between the average per capita EQV and the community's per capita EQV.

Step 3: Square the number obtained in Step 2.

Step 4: Multiply the number obtained in Step 3 by the community's population.

Step 5: Find the total of all the numbers computed in Step 4.

Step 6: Divide the total obtained in Step 5 by the total state population.

Step 7: Find the square root of the number computed in Step 6.

Step 8: Divide the number obtained in Step 7 by the average per capita EQV. This final number is the *disparity index*.

This disparity index combines all the ideas we've developed so far. Steps 4–6 give the proper weight to each community by incorporating into the disparity index consideration of each community's population. The rest of this method is a straightforward generalization of the measurement of distance using the Pythagorean Theorem. We will see how the disparity index is calculated by working with the following fictitious state:

City or Town	Population	Per Capita EQV
Elm	50,000	$10,000
Oak	30,000	$12,000
Maple	40,000	$8,000
Hazel	30,000	$7,000

Step 1: Determine the average per capita EQV (see Section 5.1).

City or Town	Population	Per Capita EQV	Product
Elm	50,000	$10,000	$500,000,000
Oak	30,000	$12,000	$360,000,000
Maple	40,000	$8,000	$320,000,000
Hazel	30,000	$7,000	$210,000,000
Total	150,000		$1,390,000,000

So the average per capita EQV is

$$\text{Average per capita EQV} = \frac{1,390,000,000}{150,000} = \$9,267.$$

Step 2: Calculate each community's per capita disparity (the absolute value of the difference between its per capita EQV and the statewide average per capita EQV):

City or Town	Population	Per Capita EQV	Disparity
Elm	50,000	$10,000	$733
Oak	30,000	$12,000	$2,733
Maple	40,000	$8,000	$1,267
Hazel	30,000	$7,000	$2,267

Step 3: Square the numbers obtained in Step 2:

City or Town	Population	Disparity	Square
Elm	50,000	$733	537,289
Oak	30,000	$2,733	7,469,289
Maple	40,000	$1,267	1,605,289
Hazel	30,000	$2,267	5,139,289

Step 4: Multiply the number obtained in Step 3 by the community's population:

City or Town	Population	Square	Product
Elm	50,000	537,289	26,864,450,000
Oak	30,000	7,469,289	224,078,670,000
Maple	40,000	1,605,289	64,211,560,000
Hazel	30,000	5,139,289	154,178,670,000

Step 5: Find the total of all the numbers computed in Step 4:

City or Town	Population	Square	Product
Elm	50,000	537,289	26,864,450,000
Oak	30,000	7,469,289	224,078,670,000
Maple	40,000	1,605,289	64,211,560,000
Hazel	30,000	5,139,289	154,178,670,000
Total	150,000		469,333,350,000

Step 6: Divide the total obtained in Step 5 by the total state population.

$$\frac{469,333,350,000}{150,000} = 3,128,889.$$

Step 7: Find the square root of the number computed in Step 6.

$$\sqrt{3,128,689} = 1,769.$$

Step 8: Divide the number obtained in Step 7 by the average per capita EQV. This final number is the disparity index:

$$\frac{1,769}{9267} = 0.1909.$$

Now work out some examples to make sure that you understand the disparity index.

Exercises

*Exercise 5.2.7** Work out the disparity index for the state below:

City or Town	Population	Per Capita EQV
Elm	60,000	$10,000
Oak	20,000	$14,000
Maple	10,000	$2,500
Hazel	10,000	$9,500

Exercise 5.2.8 Work out the disparity index for the state below:

City or Town	Population	Per Capita EQV
Elm	60,000	$10,000
Oak	20,000	$14,000
Maple	10,000	$6,000
Hazel	10,000	$6,000

Note that these are the same two states that we discussed in the last set of exercises. Compare your answers for these two states. Notice that the disparity index gives results more in tune with our intuition. The final exercise in this section asks you to compute the disparity index for the 1980 per capita EQV in Massachusetts.

Exercise 5.2.9 Compute the disparity index for the 1980 per capita EQV in Massachusetts. You will need to write and check out a computer program to work this exercise. Use the same disk file as in the last exercise of Section 5.1.

The answer you obtain for the last exercise will not be very meaningful all by itself; however, it can be useful for comparing different states or, as we shall do later, for comparing the disparity-reducing effects of different local aid distribution formulas. If you enjoy thinking about mathematics, you might want to try the following exercises. They are much more difficult than the usual ones in this book.

Advanced Exercises

Exercise 5.2.10 Intuitively, what is the worst possible distribution of taxable property in a given state?

Exercise 5.2.11 Look at several examples of fictitious states with this worst possible distribution. Compute the disparity index for each of your examples.

Exercise 5.2.12 What can you say about how large the disparity index can be?

5.3   The Lottery Formula

There are vast disparities in revenue-raising capacity among the 351 cities and towns of Massachusetts, and many cities and towns do not have sufficient local resources to support adequate public services. The fiscal disparities are aggravated by the fact that different cities and towns have very different expenses, a factor we examine later in this chapter. In this section we will consider only disparities in revenue resources, that is, in per capita EQV.

Fortunately, cities and towns receive some financial aid from the state and federal governments. Some of it is directed at particular public services. For example, the state provides a significant amount of aid to the public schools. Other kinds of aid are given to the cities and towns with no strings attached. This aid goes into each community's general fund. Federal revenue sharing was one example of this kind of general aid. In addition, the cities and towns of Massachusetts receive some general aid from the state lottery. After Proposition $2\frac{1}{2}$ was passed, it became apparent that there was a need for a substantial amount of additional local aid from the state to help cities and towns meet their public service commitments in the context of the new restrictions on the property tax. We will discuss the distribution of this additional local aid in later sections of this chapter. In this section we will be discussing how the proceeds of the state lottery are distributed. Many states have been relying increasingly on revenue raised through a state lottery. In

Massachusetts, money raised through the state lottery is distributed among the cities and towns to help them meet local expenses. This has become an important source of outside funding for cities and towns.

The question of who gets how much is one of the most important questions in public affairs. It involves many different factors. There is an underlying question of philosophy. Do we believe in an egalitarian society that provides roughly comparable educational opportunities, and fire and police protection to all its citizens, or do we believe in a society where people "vote with their feet" and can choose to live in any one of many different communities offering different levels of public services?

Our philosophical beliefs must face questions of practicality. If people vote with their feet, won't each person seek to live with rich neighbors in a community able to provide excellent public services at a very low tax rate? Since wealthy people are more able than poorer ones to move, wouldn't this aggravate an existing tendency toward communities segregated by economic status?

Based on our philosophy and our sense of how best to implement that philosophy, we will come up with a set of political goals. But now these goals must meet the political realities. Our proposals must be passed by legislatures. This political process involves the balancing of many competing interests and philosophies.

My own philosophy is egalitarian, especially regarding the basic necessities of life like personal safety (police and fire protection) and public health. Right up at the top of my list of egalitarian priorities is public education. I believe strongly in equality of opportunity—the biggest single factor in equality of opportunity is quality education for everyone—and I believe that we all share one world. By working together, we can improve all of our lives. But this requires an intelligent and knowledgeable citizenry. Each of us gains not only from our own individual education but from sharing our world with educated people. We all gain when one of us invents a new medical treatment or develops a tastier tomato, when one of us designs a beautiful and functional building, or when one of us writes a symphony or paints a painting. Finally, in a democracy an investment in high-quality education is an investment in good government.

This does not mean that all of our schools must be identical or that public and private schools cannot coexist. In fact, we have evolved an educational system that in many ways is quite remarkably good. We have both public and private schools. Some schools are particularly well known for wonderful music programs, others for strong science programs. Schools develop their own identities, although all must meet some basic standards. This diversity is possible because schools are locally administered. Schools, however, cannot be entirely locally financed. Because of the huge disparities in local revenue resources, it is impossible for some communities to maintain good schools on their own while others can do so with ease. For this reason we have evolved a system of public finance for education in which the federal and state governments help share the cost of public education.

Education is typical of many other public services: they are locally administered, subject to some state and federal regulation. They are financed by a combination of local, state, and federal funds. Local administration helps make these services responsive to the needs of the communities they serve. State and federal regulation ensure some minimum standards and compatibility. Broad-based financing is necessary for three reasons. First, there is a clear state and national interest in maintaining comparable public services. We all benefit from each other's education. Those of us living downstream or downwind from another community benefit from that community's responsible handling of waste. Second, federal and state governments have preempted many forms of taxation, leaving local governments with limited resources. Third, financial resources vary so widely at the local level that it would be impossible to maintain comparable services if these services had to be financed entirely by local resources.

Thus, it is essential that federal and state governments distribute some of the money that they have collected by taxation back to the local communities. The central topic of this chapter is who gets how much of this money. In this section we will look at the distribution of the proceeds of the state lottery in Massachusetts. We will compare two schemes for distributing this money. Such schemes are called *distribution formulas.*

Distribution formulas are usually mathematical formulas based on numbers, numbers like per capita EQV or school age population. Such formulas are used because they look objective. There are other possible ways of deciding how much money each community should get. For example, in theory one could assemble a team of experts with experience in public finance. This team could study each community carefully and based on its judgment could determine how much money each community should get. Such a team would be able to consider many different factors, both quantitative and qualitative. However, as a practical matter it would be virtually impossible for such a team to balance the competing claims of 351 different cities and towns. Moreover, politically such a team would be extremely vulnerable to charges of favoritism. Formulas based on numbers can be applied to 351 cities and towns with ease, and they have an aura of objectivity.

It is much easier politically and practically to arrive at one formula for dealing with 351 cities and towns at once than to consider 351 individual cases. Communities differ in many qualitative ways, however, ways that are hard to capture purely in terms of numbers. By way of analogy, suppose that one were trying to develop a formula for how many calories a person should eat each day. It is easy to imagine a formula based on height and amount of physical activity. Now suppose that we tried to apply such a formula to animals of different species. We would need a different formula for each species or we would need to develop a much more complicated formula that took into account the large differences among species. There are similar problems in developing distribution formulas. A city like Boston (population 562,994) is very different from a town like Conway (population 1,213). One must be aware of these differences while trying to design a distribution formula that will be fair to both.

We will look at two of the many possible formulas for distributing the proceeds of the state lottery to the cities and towns in Massachusetts. We will examine how effective each of these formulas is in reducing the revenue resource disparities among these communities. One of the goals of the distribution of this money is to offset some of these disparities. We will begin by looking at each formula individually, and then will compare them with each other.

Formula 1

The first formula is based on the idea that the total lottery proceeds should be divided equally among the residents of the state. Thus, this total amount is divided by the total state population to determine each person's share. This number is called the *per capita distribution.* The amount distributed to each town is its population times this per capita distribution.

Mathematically we can express this formula as follows. First, we denote the total amount of money to be distributed by S and the total state population by T. Each person's share, the per capita distribution, is then S/T. Each city and town in Massachusetts is given an identifying number. They are numbered from 1 through 351 in alphabetical order. The population of city or town i will be denoted by $p(i)$. Thus, we can compute the amount of money town i will receive by

$$\text{Share for town } i = p(i) \left(\frac{S}{T} \right).$$

As an example of how this formula works, consider the following mythical state with four towns:

City or Town	Population	Per Capita EQV
Maple	50,000	12,000
Smith	30,000	10,000
Hazel	10,000	6,000
Jones	10,000	14,000

The total state population, T, is 100,000. Suppose this state wants to distribute $S = \$2,500,000$ according to Formula 1. First we compute the per capita distribution:

$$\frac{S}{T} = \frac{\$2,500,000}{100,000} = \$25.$$

Now each town would receive the following amount:

City or Town	Population	Lottery Distribution
Maple	50,000	$1,250,000
Smith	30,000	$750,000
Hazel	10,000	$250,000
Jones	10,000	$250,000

Exercise

Exercise 5.3.13

In fiscal year 1983 Massachusetts distributed $97,051,084 from the state lottery to the 351 cities and towns. Compute how much money each

city and town would have received if this formula had been used. You
will need to write a computer program. Your program should compute
the amount received by each city and town, but to produce output of a
manageable size, it should print out only the amount received by each
of the 45 cities and towns with a population over 30,000. You can use
the same disk file that you used in the exercise at the end of Section 5.1.

Formula 1 makes no attempt to compensate for the disparities among
the cities and towns in revenue resources. The next formula does make
an attempt at this compensation. It is an example of an *equalizing*
formula because it is intended to reduce these disparities.

Formula 2 (The Lottery Formula)

This is the formula that has been used to distribute the proceeds
of the Massachusetts state lottery. It is designed to give more money
to communities having lower revenue resources. This formula uses per
capita EQV as a measure of revenue resources.

The Lottery Formula begins by comparing each community's per capita EQV to the statewide average EQV. We will use the notation $E(i)$
for the per capita EQV of community i and E for the statewide average
EQV. We saw how to compute E in Section 5.1. The next step is to
compute the ratio $E/E(i)$ for each community, i. For a resource-rich
community, this ratio will be less than 1 since its per capita EQV, $E(i)$,
will be above the state average, E. For a resource-poor community this
ratio will be bigger than 1 since its per capita EQV will be below the
state average. For example, for Chelsea, the ratio is $15{,}389/6{,}209 =
2.4785$, and for Rowe, it is $15{,}389/392{,}560 = 0.0392$.

The Lottery Formula is designed to give more aid per capita to poorer
communities than to richer ones. The per capita distribution, $L(i)$, for
each community, i, is given by the formula

$$L(i) = A\left(\frac{E}{E(i)}\right).$$

The first factor on the right, A, is the per capita amount a community
would receive if its per capita resources were exactly the same as the
statewide average. We will determine the value of A later.

The second factor, $E/E(i)$, is the ratio we computed. If a community's
per capita EQV is average, then $E(i) = E$, and the second factor is 1.

Thus, it receives A dollars per capita. If a community's per capita revenue resources are below average, then $E(i) < E$, and $E/E(i)$ is greater than 1, so it receives more than A dollars per capita. If a community's per capita EQV is above average, then $E(i) > E$, and $E/E(i)$ is less than 1, so it receives less than A dollars per capita. Thus, this formula achieves its intended purpose: it allocates more money to those communities that are resource poor and less money to those communities that are resource rich.

Now we are ready to determine the value of the number A. If A is too large, then the Lottery Formula will distribute too much money—more than is available from the proceeds of the lottery. If A is too small, some of the proceeds of the lottery will be left over. We want to determine the value of A that will exactly use up all the proceeds of the lottery. Let S be the total amount of money available for distrubution. For each town, the Lottery Formula calls for

$$\text{Allocation to town } i = P(i)A\left(\frac{E}{E(i)}\right).$$

Thus, the total amount of money called for by the Lottery Formula is

$$P(1)A\left(\frac{E}{E(1)}\right) + P(2)A\left(\frac{E}{E(2)}\right) + \cdots + P(351)A\left(\frac{E}{E(351)}\right)$$

$$= A\left[P(1)\left(\frac{E}{E(1)}\right) + P(2)\left(\frac{E}{E(2)}\right) + \cdots + P(351)\left(\frac{E}{E(351)}\right)\right].$$

We want this total to be equal to S; that is, we want to choose A so that

$$S = A\left[P(1)\left(\frac{E}{E(1)}\right) + P(2)\left(\frac{E}{E(2)}\right) + \cdots + P(351)\left(\frac{E}{E(351)}\right)\right].$$

Solving this equation for A, we see that A must be

$$A = \frac{S}{P(1)\left(\frac{E}{E(1)}\right) + P(2)\left(\frac{E}{E(2)}\right) + \cdots + P(351)\left(\frac{E}{E(351)}\right)}.$$

To illustrate the Lottery Formula, we will compute the distribution of $2,500,000 (the same figure used to illustrate Formula 1) for the same mythical state we examined in the example above.

Step 1: Compute the statewide average per capita EQV, E, using the method of Section 5.1.

City or Town	Population	Per Capita EQV	Total EQV
Maple	50,000	12,000	600,000,000
Smith	30,000	10,000	300,000,000
Hazel	10,000	6,000	60,000,000
Jones	10,000	14,000	140,000,000
Total	100,000		1,100,000,000

Thus, the average per capita EQV is

$$E = \text{average per capita EQV} = \frac{1,100,000,000}{100,000} = \$11,000.$$

Step 2: Compute the sum

$$\frac{P(1)}{E(1)} + \frac{P(2)}{E(2)} + \frac{P(3)}{E(3)} + \frac{P(4)}{E(4)}.$$

(Notice that because our mythical state has only four towns, this sum has only four terms.)

City or Town	Population $(P(i))$	$E(i)$	$P(i)/E(i)$
Maple	50,000	12,000	4.1667
Smith	30,000	10,000	3.0000
Hazel	10,000	6,000	1.6667
Jones	10,000	14,000	0.7143
Sum			9.5476

Step 3: Compute

$$A = \frac{S}{E\left(\frac{P(1)}{E(1)} + \frac{P(2)}{E(2)} + \frac{P(3)}{E(3)} + \frac{P(4)}{E(4)}\right)}$$

$$= \frac{2,500,000}{(11,000)(9.5476)}$$

$$= 23.8041.$$

Step 4: Compute each community's per capita share of the lottery proceeds:

City or Town	$E/E(i)$	A	Per Capita Lottery Distribution
Maple	0.9167	23.8041	21.82
Smith	1.1000	23.8041	26.18
Hazel	1.8333	23.8041	43.64
Jones	0.7857	23.8041	18.70

Notice that the Lottery Formula accomplishes its intended purpose, channeling more money (per capita) to poorer communities and less money to richer ones. (Recall that under Formula 1 each community received $25.00 per capita.)

The following exercise asks you to compute the results of applying the Lottery Formula in Massachusetts.

Exercise

Exercise 5.3.14 Massachusetts distributed $97,051,084 from the state lottery to the 351 cities and towns using the Lottery Formula in fiscal year 1983.. Compute the per capita distribution of lottery money using the usual disk file from the exercise at the end of Section 5.1. You will need to write a computer program to do this. Your program should compute the per capita amount received by each of the 351 cities and towns, but to produce output of a manageable size, it should only print out the results for each of the 45 cities and towns with a population over 30,000.

Compare the results of this exercise with the per capita results using Formula 1.

Comparisons

Now we want to compare the results of these two formulas. We are particularly interested in how effective each formula is in reducing the disparities among the cities and towns in revenue resources. For purposes of comparison, we will assume that each city and town taxes property

Table 5.8
Comparison of Two Distribution Formulas

| City or Town | Original Per Capita Revenue Resources | Per Capita Distribution | |
		Formula 1	Lottery Formula
Maple	300.00	25.00	21.82
Smith	250.00	25.00	26.18
Hazel	150.00	25.00	43.64
Jones	350.00	25.00	18.70

Table 5.9
Comparison of After-Distribution Resources

| City or Town | Total Per Capita Resources after | |
	Formula 1	Lottery Formula
Maple	325.00	321.82
Smith	275.00	276.18
Hazel	175.00	193.64
Jones	375.00	368.70

at the same rate, 2.5%. Thus, a town with a per capita EQV of $10,000 would raise $250 per capita from the property tax.

We will illustrate our ideas by looking at our mythical state. The results of our two distribution formulas are shown in Table 5.8. We are interested in the total per capita revenue resources available to each city and town after the lottery proceeds have been distributed. Table 5.9 shows these figures. The column headed "Original Per Capita Revenue Resources" in Table 5.8 lists the per capita amount of money each city or town would raise locally based on the property tax. The entries in column 2 of Table 5.9 were computed by adding the per capita distributions using Formula 1 to the original per capita revenue resources. The entries in column 3 were computed by adding the per capita distributions using the Lottery Formula to the original per capita revenue resources.

Now we can apply all our analytical tools from Section 5.2 to examine the disparities in total per capita revenue resources after the distribution of money using Formula 1 and after using the Lottery Formula. We will begin by looking at graphs similar to Figures 5.7 and 5.8. Figure 5.10 is analogous to Figure 5.8. You may want to reread the discussion of Figure 5.8 before continuing. This figure illustrates the disparities in per capita

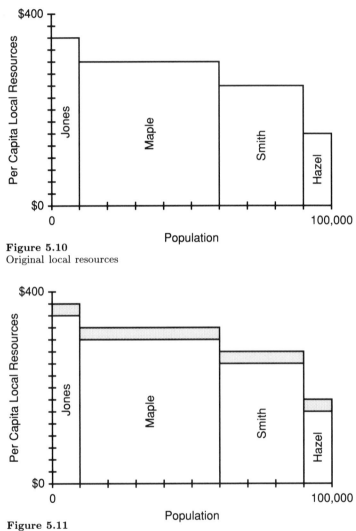

Figure 5.10
Original local resources

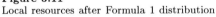

Figure 5.11
Local resources after Formula 1 distribution

revenue resources before any lottery money is distributed. Figure 5.11 is
similar to Figure 5.10 except that I have added the $25 per capita that
each community would receive under Formula 1. This $25 increment is
represented by the shaded area in Figure 5.11. Figure 5.12 is identical to
Figure 5.10 except that I have added the per capita amounts of lottery

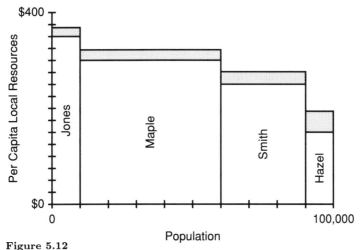

Figure 5.12
Local resources after Lottery Formula distribution

money each community would receive under the Lottery Formula instead of Formula 1.

You can get a good visual impression of the disparity-reducing effects of the Lottery Formula by comparing these three figures. Notice in Figure 5.12 that the poorer communities receive more money per capita than the richer communities.

We can also compute the disparity index for these three situations. The results are as follows:

- Original per capita revenue resources: 0.1863.

- Per capita revenue resources including the lottery money each community would receive under Formula 1: 0.1708.

- Per capita revenue resources including the lottery money each community would receive under the Lottery Formula: 0.1495.

This last analysis also indicates that the Lottery Formula does a much more effective job of reducing disparities than Formula 1 does. Notice that even though Formula 1 is not designed to reduce revenue resource disparities, it does result in a small disparity reduction. This result can be understood by looking at an exaggerated example. Suppose that there are only two towns in a state, Richtown and Poortown. Richtown has $400 per capita local resources, and Poortown has $100 per capita

local resources. Thus, Richtown is four times as rich as Poortown. Now
suppose that both towns receive $200 per capita from the lottery. After
the distribution of this money, Richtown will have $600 per capita, and
Poortown will have $300 per capita. Now Richtown is only twice as rich
as Poortown.

<hr>

Exercises

The following exercises ask you to apply the two formulas to a mythical
state and to analyze the results using figures similar to Figures 5.10,
5.11, and 5.12. They refer to the following state.

Town	Population	Per Capita EQV
Westville	15,000	15,000
Northville	25,000	10,000
Southville	50,000	7,000
Eastville	20,000	12,000

*Exercise 5.3.15 Suppose $3 million were distributed among these four
communities using Formula 1. How much money would each community
receive per capita? What is the total amount of money each community
would receive?

*Exercise 5.3.16 Suppose $3 million were distributed among these four
communities using the Lottery Formula. How much money would each
community receive per capita?

Exercise 5.3.17 Draw graphs similar to Figures 5.10, 5.11, and 5.12
for this state.

Exercise 5.3.18 Compute the disparity index for this state for:

- The original per capita revenue resources.

- The per capita revenue resources including the money distributed by
  Formula 1.

- The per capita revenue resources including the money distributed by
  the Lottery Formula.

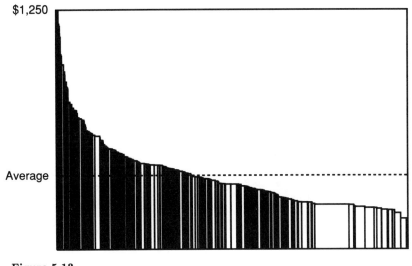

Figure 5.13
Original resources

Finally look at the real data for Massachusetts. You have already computed the results of distributing the fiscal year 1983 lottery proceeds ($97,051,084) using Formula 1 and using the Lottery Formula. Now we want to compare these results. We will begin by drawing figures analogous to Figures 5.10, 5.11, and 5.12. Figure 5.13 is analogous to Figure 5.10. It shows the original per capita revenue resources before any lottery money is distributed. This figure is identical to Figure 5.7 except that the y-axis shows per capita revenue resources rather than per capita EQV.

Figures 5.14 and 5.15 are analogous to Figures 5.11 and 5.12, respectively. They show the per capita revenue resources including the lottery proceeds distributed by Formula 1 (Figure 5.14) or the Lottery Formula (Figure 5.15). It takes a sharp eye to discern the differences between Figures 5.14 and 5.15 because the proceeds of the lottery are quite small compared to the total amount of money raised by the property tax. These figures give a good visual impression of the disparity-reducing effects of Formula 1 and the Lottery Formula.

As final exercises compute the disparity index after these two different distributions of the FY 1983 lottery proceeds.

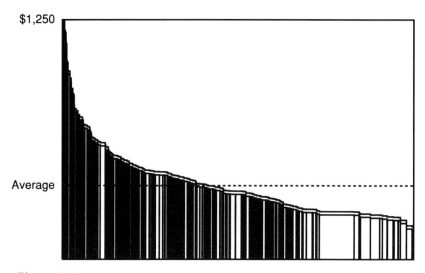

Figure 5.14
Resources, including Formula 1 distribution

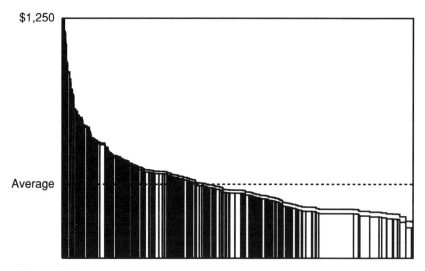

Figure 5.15
Resources, including Lottery Formula distribution

Exercises

Exercise 5.3.19   Compute the disparity index for the total per capita revenue resources for Massachusetts, including the FY 1983 lottery proceeds ($97,051,084) distributed using Formula 1.

Exercise 5.3.20   Compute the disparity index for the total per capita revenue resources for Massachusetts, including the FY 1983 lottery proceeds ($97,051,084) distributed using the Lottery Formula.

5.4   Target Formulas

In this section we will discuss a particularly interesting type of distribution formula called a *target formula*. We will illustrate the main idea involved by looking at a particular example. Consider the following mythical state from Section 5.3.

City or Town	Per Capita Revenue Resources	Population
Maple	$300	50,000
Smith	$250	30,000
Hazel	$150	10,000
Jones	$350	10,000

The idea behind a target formula is that we establish a minimum goal, or *target,* for each community's total per capita revenue resources. Then we allocate to each community enough money to bring its per capita revenue resources up to that target. For example, we might decide to bring each community's per capita revenue resources up to the statewide average. In Section 5.3 we computed the statewide average per capita revenue resources for this state to be $275. In order to reach this target, we would have to allocate the following amounts of money to each community:

City or Town	Population	Per Capita Allocation	Total Allocation
Maple	50,000	$0	$0
Smith	30,000	$25	$750,000
Hazel	10,000	$125	$1,250,000
Jones	10,000	$0	$0
Total			$2,000,000

Each community's allocation was computed as follows. First, if the community's per capita resources are already greater than or equal to the target, its per capita allocation is $0. If the community's per capita revenue resources are below the target, then its per capita allocation is equal to the difference between the target and its per capita revenue resources. Each community's total allocation is equal to its per capita allocation multiplied by its population.

Notice that in our example, two towns, Maple and Jones, would receive no money at all under this formula since they already have above-average per capita resources. This would be a political problem for this formula since the residents of Maple and Jones would be likely to object to a formula that gave them no money at all.

One way to respond to this criticism is to set a higher target. For example, suppose that we chose a target of $325. In order to reach this target, we would have to allocate the following amounts of money to each community:

City or Town	Population	Per Capita Allocation	Total Allocation
Maple	50,000	$25	$1,250,000
Smith	30,000	$75	$2,250,000
Hazel	10,000	$175	$1,750,000
Jones	10,000	$0	$0
Total			$5,250,000

This new formula makes more people happy than the first formula. Except for Jones, everybody gets some money, and the poorest towns get even more money than with our first target formula. However, there is a catch: the cost of this second target formula is enormous. In practice, there are two stages involved in a target formula. The first stage is the one shown above. We establish a target and then calculate how much money each city or town *should* receive in order to reach its target. The second stage is finding the money to pay the bill. This stage frequently falls short. For example, suppose that the state can only afford to distribute $1 million to the cities and towns. For our first target formula, we needed $2 million. The state has only half the required sum. In this situation a state commonly responds by paying each city or town half its *computed* or *target* allocation. Thus, the actual amount of money each city or town would receive would be only half that needed to bring its per capita resources up to the target:

City or Town	Per Capita Allocation	Target Allocation	Actual Allocation
Maple	$0	$0	$0
Smith	$25	$750,000	$375,000
Hazel	$125	$1,250,000	$625,000
Jones	$0	$0	$0
Total		$2,000,000	$1,000,000

The second target formula required $5.25 million. The state has only $1 million or $1,000,000/$5,250,000 = 4/21$ of the required sum. Therefore, each community would receive $4/21$ of its target allocation:

City or Town	Per Capita Allocation	Target Allocation	Actual Allocation
Maple	$25	$1,250,000	$238,095.24
Smith	$75	$2,250,000	$428,571.43
Hazel	$175	$1,750,000	$333,333.33
Jones	$0	$0	$0.00
Total		$2,000,000	$1,000,000.00

Thus, in practice, a target formula works as follows:

Step 1: Establish a target for per capita revenue resources.

Step 2: For each community, calculate the total amount of money needed to bring its per capita revenue resources up to the target. This number, $T(i)$, for community i, is called its *target allocation*.

Step 3: Find the total amount of money needed to bring all the communities up to the target. This number is

$$\text{TOT} = T(1) + T(2) + \cdots + T(351).$$

Note: This formula is for the state of Massachusetts which has 351 communities. In our examples above since there were only four communities, TOT $= T(1) + T(2) + \cdots + T(4)$.

Step 4: Divide the actual amount of money available by TOT. The result is called R:

$$R = \frac{\text{Actual Amount of Money to Be Distributed}}{\text{TOT}}.$$

Step 5: The actual allocation for community i, $A(i)$, is given by

$$A(i) = R \cdot T(i).$$

If we compare the two examples that we worked out above, we see the following:

City or Town	Actual Allocation Using	
	$275 Target	$325 Target
Maple	$0	$238,095.24
Smith	$375,000	$428,571.43
Hazel	$625,000	$333,333.33
Jones	$0	$0.00
Total	$1,000,000	$1,000,000.00

Some communities receive more money with the higher target, and others receive less money. Using target formulas involves some interesting political and practical considerations. There are two good reasons for setting a high target: more communities will receive some money with a higher target, and a higher target establishes a more ambitious goal. It sounds better. But if the same total amount of money is distributed using a higher target, then some communities will receive more money, and others will receive less money than with a lower target. It is important to consider these practical consequences of a higher target.

The following exercises ask you to compute the results of distributing the fiscal year 1983 lottery proceeds using two different target formulas and to compare these results with each other and with our earlier formulas. As usual use the same disk file as in the exercise at the end of Section 5.1. Although these target formulas were not actually used, the basic ideas are part of several different distribution formulas that are used. We will see these ideas reappear in later sections of this chapter.

Exercises

Exercise 5.4.21 In Section 5.3 we computed the statewide average per capita revenue resources for Massachusetts to be $384.73. Suppose we use this average as a target.

- What is the total allocation required to bring every community's per capita revenue resources up to this target?

- Suppose that the fiscal year 1983 lottery proceeds ($97,051,084) were distributed using this target. How much money per capita would each community receive? Although your program should compute the results for all 351 communities, it should print out only the results for the 45 cities and towns whose population is over 30,000. How many communities would receive no money at all? What is the total population of these communities?

Exercise 5.4.22 Repeat the previous exercise using a target of $500.

Exercise 5.4.23 Make a large table showing for each of the 45 cities and towns whose population is over 30,000 the per capita amounts of money they would receive if the fiscal year 1983 lottery proceeds were distributed under each of the following formulas:

- Formula 1 from Section 5.3.
- The Lottery Formula from Section 5.3.
- The target formula with a target of $384.73 as computed above.
- The target formula with a target of $500.00 as computed above.

Try to make your output as easy to read as possible.

Using this table and any other information you care to compile, discuss and compare these four formulas. What is each formula's good points? bad points?

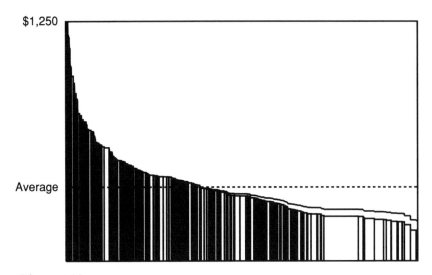

Figure 5.16
Per capita revenue resources, including $384.73 target

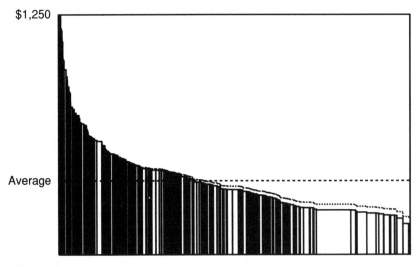

Figure 5.17
Per capita revenue resources, including $500.00 target

Figures 5.16–5.18 can help us compare the two different target formula. Figure 5.16 shows the results of distributing the fiscal year 1983
lottery proceeds using a target formula with a target of $384.73. Figure

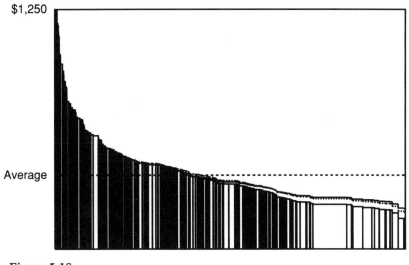

Figure 5.18
Comparison of different targets

5.17 uses a target of $500. Figure 5.18 superimposes these two graphs
on the same figure. We use a dotted line for the target formula using
a target of $500. By looking at Figure 5.18, you can see the impact of
a higher target. The communities with the lowest per capita revenue
resources lose money when the higher target is used, while communities with higher per capita revenues gain money. Compare these three
figures with Figures 5.14 and 5.15.

   In practice, the fact that target formulas allocate no money at all
to some communities (unless an enormously high target is used) is a
grave political liability. One way that this problem can be avoided is to
modify the formula so that each community receives a certain minimum
per capita allocation, a common political compromise. For example, one
might begin by giving each community a $5 per capita allocation. If this
were done in Massachusetts, $28,685,185 would be required since Mas-
sachusetts' total population is 5,737,037. This would leave $68,365,899
to be distributed using the target formula. The final exercise asks you
to compute the results of this modification.

Exercise

Exercise 5.4.24 Compute the results of distributing the fiscal year 1983 lottery proceeds under the modified target formula described. More specifically,

1. Give each community $5 per capita from the lottery proceeds.

2. Distribute the remaining money as follows:

   a. Compute the new per capita revenue resources for each community. This number is equal to the original per capita revenue resources plus $5.

   b. Compute the new average per capita revenue resources. This number is the old average plus $5.

   c. Now distribute the remaining money using the new per capita revenue resources and the new average per capita revenue resources as the target.

3. Compare the results of this exercise with the previous results.

We have discussed a number of different formulas for distributing money to the 351 cities and towns in Massachusetts. Before continuing, think about this problem. What do you think of the formulas used so far? Do you see any shortcomings? How might they be corrected? In the remaining sections, we will be discussing some of these shortcomings and more sophisticated formulas aimed at correcting some of them.

5.5   The Gap

So far we have discussed the disparities among communities in resources, but there are many other ways in which communities differ. Some communities have far greater needs for public services than others. In this section we will discuss a more sophisticated distribution formula that attempts to take into account differences among communities in *both resources and needs*. The basic formula estimates two different quantities for each city and town:

- Per capita resources: The per capita amount of money available to the city or town to support public services.

- Per capita needs: The per capita amount of money needed by the city or town to support a standard level of public services. This figure can be thought of as an individualized target. In Section 5.4 we were interested in formulas aimed at providing each community with a standard level of resources. Here we consider the fact that different communities may require different amounts of money in order to sustain the same standard level of services.

The difference between these two figures is called the *gap*. The local aid formula allocates money to each community on the basis of this gap. Ideally each community would be given enough money to fill this gap, making up the difference between its needs and its resources. However, as in Section 5.4 this goal is too ambitious. Typically the state does not have enough money to achieve this ideal goal. As a result, each community usually receives an amount of aid per capita that is roughly proportional to its gap.

Two complications prevent the local aid distribution formula from being quite this straightforward. First, for many communities, the gap is negative; they have more than enough local resources to support a standard level of public services. For political reasons, it is difficult to pass legislation that gives no money at all to some communities. A common compromise is to give each community a minimum amount per capita even if its local resources are sufficient to meet its needs.

The second complication arises from the fact that each year the legisature must operate in the context of the recent past. It is very difficult to give a city or town less money than it received the previous year. When I first became interested in local aid, the Massachusetts economy was booming and state tax revenues were increasing as a result. At the same time local tax revenues were suffering from the constraints of Proposition $2\frac{1}{2}$. Moreover, certain local expenses were rising rapidly. The cities and towns had increased needs, and, fortunately, the state had increased resources, so it responded by increasing the amount of local aid each year. Thus, it was possible to guarantee each city and town each year an amount of aid that was no less than the preceding year. In effect, each year the state used a different formula to distribute the *increase* in local aid while the previous years' distributions were left

the same. Now state revenues are plummeting, a situation that brings
up a whole new set of problems. I will base much of the discussion here
on the Massachusetts local aid distribution formula as it operated in the
1980s during a period when state revenues were increasing. The ideas
are applicable to many other situations.

This section will emphasize a discussion of the ideas, especially the
philosophical and political ideas involved in the local aid distribution
formula. Part of the value of discussing a particular distribution formula
is that this will help us to focus our theoretical ideas about what a
fair distribution of local aid is. In later sections I will introduce some
mathematical tools that can be used to help implement our political and
philosophical intentions. Our discussion will be divided into two parts
corresponding to the two parts in the computation of the gap. We will
begin with a discussion of local needs.

Per Capita Local Needs for Public Services

We want to make a distinction between the per capita *costs* of providing public services and the per capita *needs* for public services. We
will begin by discussing a more familiar situation that has some of the
same elements. Suppose we wanted to compare the food needs of two
families: the Smiths and the Joneses.

There are five Smiths: two adult Smiths and three teenagers. The
three teenagers eat enormous quantities of food. Mr. Smith is 6' 4" and
a lumberjack and eats even more than the three teenaged children. Mrs.
Smith is 5' 10" and teaches aerobic dancing; she is another big eater!
The Smiths live in a farming community. They are able to buy lots of
produce and fresh meat at good prices. They cook almost all of their
own meals, including bag lunches. They usually eat moderately priced
food—lots of potatoes and spaghetti, hamburger, pot roast, and stews.

There are four Joneses: two adult Joneses and two children aged 5 and
7. Mr. Jones is an average-sized actuary, and Mrs. Jones is an average-
sized economist. Neither occupation entails lots of physical work. They
are both average consumers of food. Their children don't eat anywhere
near as much as they will as teenagers. The Joneses live in the middle of
a large city. The cost of food is more expensive than in the Smiths' home
town. The Joneses eat all of their lunches out and many dinners. When
they do cook their own dinners, they eat expensive food: chateaubriand,
prime ribs of beef, and often prepared gourmet foods.

There are a number of differences between the two families that will have a bearing on how much they actually spend for food.

- Demographics: The Smith family is larger than the Jones family. This factor would tend to increase the amount of money spent by the Smiths on food. But it is not enough simply to count mouths. The Smiths are big eaters: each family member requires considerably more food than the average person.

- Local Costs of Food: Some food items are more expensive for the Joneses than the Smiths. During the summer, for example, the Smiths can buy wonderful fresh-picked corn for about 25% less than the Joneses can buy fresh corn.

- Family Preferences: The Smiths choose to eat less expensive food than the Joneses. Furthermore, the Joneses eat many meals in restaurants and when they do eat at home, they frequently eat expensive prepared foods.

We want to determine how much money each family needs for food. Our determination will be based on a mental image or model explaining how much money different families might spend on food. This model will have to take into account a variety of different factors. The first and most obvious are the demographic ones. How many people are there in the family? Are there any reasons that any of the family members might require more than an average amount of food? There is no question that these factors have a bearing on the actual *needs* for food.

There are other factors that have a tremendous bearing on expenditures for food but are not relevant factors for *need*. The Joneses eat many meals out in restaurants, and when they eat at home, they eat fancier and more expensive food. The frequently eat more expensive prepared foods at home because they often lack the time to cook. These choices increase their expenditures for food. However, this increased expenditure is due to personal preference and not to any increased need for food.

Here is the beginning of a formula for determining a family's food needs:

Step 1: The purpose of this step is to estimate the number of "standard" eaters in the family. We will invent a new unit called the SEE (standard eater equivalent). One SEE represents one person with average food requirements. For example, each of Mr. Jones and Mrs. Jones is one SEE. We will use a standard table for estimating each person's SEE equivalent. For example, a 6' 4" lumberjack might be 1.8 SEEs; an average-sized teenager might be 1.4 SEEs. (These numbers are made up. If this were a serious exercise rather than an example, some research would be needed to come up with realistic numbers.)

Step 2: The purpose of this step is to estimate the cost of feeding one SEE a standard diet. We might ask a dietitian to design a standard diet for one SEE. Then we would go to various stores and determine the price of the necessary ingredients. The resulting number would be a standard cost per SEE.

Step 3: For each family, multiply the number of SEEs by the standard cost per SEE. The result is the estimated needs for food for that family.

This mechanism makes a very sharp distinction between two different kinds of factors. The first group of factors, those considered in Step 1, might be called *uncontrollable* factors because there is nothing the family can do to change them. In this example, these factors were all demographic factors: the number of people in the family and their relative needs for food.

The second group of factors might be called *preference* factors. They influence a family's expenditures on food but are matters of personal preference rather than necessity. In Step 2, we computed the cost per SEE on the basis of a standard diet. This method specifically excludes from consideration factors like the number of meals eaten in restaurants or the kind of food eaten. Each family's needs are estimated on the basis of the same, standard diet.

You may have started shaking your head in disagreement some time ago, and you may still be shaking it. Unfortunately, in matters of public policy, things are rarely so clear cut. Here are some possible objections to what has been said so far:

- Mr. Smith chose to be a lumberjack. Thus, this factor is not entirely an uncontrollable demand factor. If Mr. Smith were a food critic whose job required him to eat expensive meals in restaurants at least five nights a week, would this be an uncontrollable demand factor?

- Both Mr. and Mrs. Jones work full time. The uncontrollable astronomical limit of 24 hours in a day forces them to eat some of their meals out and to use more expensive prepared foods when they eat at home.

- Some factors weren't mentioned at all in the formula. Local costs of food vary quite considerably. There are several possibilities for determining the standard cost per SEE. One possibility would be to find a national average by shopping in supermarkets across the country and using average prices. Another possibility would be to determine the cost per SEE for each community.

- Now about this dietitian determining the "standard diet." If the dietitian's name is Jones, she is likely to choose a very different standard than if her name is Smith. Who is going to determine the standard?

Before we turn to the real problem, determining a city or town's needs for public services, pause and think about the example and about the coming real problem.

Exercises

Exercise 5.5.25 How would you determine a family's needs for food?

Exercise 5.5.26 List some of the factors that might be relevant in determining local expenditures for public services.

Exercise 5.5.27 Consider each factor on your list. Is it a legitimate uncontrollable demand factor for determining need or a matter of preference?

The biggest item in city and town budgets is education. One of the principal reasons for variation in per capita educational needs is simply the per capita number of students. The situation here is somewhat analogous to the number of eaters being fed in our example above—some students are more expensive to educate than others. For this reason we will look at weighted full time equivalent students (WFTEs). One WFTE represents one student with average educational needs. Certain students, for example, special needs students, count as more than one WFTE. The per capita number of WFTEs varies widely among the cities

Table 5.10
Per Capita Weighted Full Time Equivalent Students

City or Town	Pop.	WFTE	City or Town	Pop.	WFTE
Amherst	33,229	0.104854	Medford	58,076	0.174161
Arlington	48,219	0.167496	Melrose	30,055	0.218067
Attleborough	34,196	0.252404	Methuen	36,701	0.224879
Barnstable	30,898	0.203534	New Bedford	98,478	0.224464
Beverly	37,655	0.204825	Newton	83,622	0.169766
Billerica	36,727	0.308833	Peabody	45,976	0.230944
Boston	562,994	0.148309	Pittsfield	51,974	0.219841
Braintree	36,337	0.246501	Plymouth	35,913	0.242845
Brockton	95,172	0.259852	Quincy	84,743	0.177465
Brookline	55,062	0.138624	Revere	42,423	0.210772
Cambridge	95,322	0.125324	Salem	38,220	0.173846
Chelmsford	31,174	0.282813	Somerville	77,372	0.163955
Chicopee	55,112	0.207256	Springfield	152,319	0.218837
Everett	37,195	0.186700	Taunton	45,001	0.212273
Fall River	92,574	0.201304	Waltham	58,200	0.178261
Fitchburg	39,580	0.176933	Watertown	34,384	0.173985
Framingham	65,113	0.212770	Westfield	36,465	0.198333
Haverhill	46,865	0.233165	Weymouth	55,601	0.233064
Holyoke	44,678	0.210672	Woburn	36,626	0.216775
Lawrence	63,175	0.226914	Worcester	161,799	0.199179
Leominster	34,508	0.207027			
Lowell	92,418	0.212008			
Lynn	78,471	0.222362			
Malden	53,386	0.191146			
Marlborough	30,617	0.228657			

and towns. Table 5.10 lists the WFTEs per capita for the 45 cities and towns whose population is over 30,000.

Notice the tremendous variation in WFTEs per capita. Amherst has the lowest number: 0.104854. Amherst is often statistically exceptional because of the large number of college and university students. Billerica has the highest number: 0.308833. If we were to include smaller towns, the variation would be even wider. The lowest number would be Harvard (0.097937) and the highest number Ayer (0.432032).

The per capita WFTEs is the most important factor in the part of the local formula that determines per capita needs, although there are a number of other factors, for example,

- Road Mileage. For many small rural communities, road maintenance and snow removal is a substantial part of the town budget. The amount of money needed for these services is directly related to the number of miles of roads in the community.

- Infrastructure Age. An important part of a town's budget is maintenance and upkeep for the infrastructure. This includes maintenance of schools and other public buildings and the sewage and water supply systems. It is generally cheaper to maintain newer items than older ones.

- Population Density. Some public services are more costly for high-density areas than for low-density areas. Some are cheaper for high-density areas than lower ones.

- Residents' Income. This is a tricky factor. As we saw for the Smiths and the Joneses, income certainly has an impact on expenditures. Richer people and richer towns are more likely to spend more money because they have more money to spend. On the other hand, poorer people might be expected to require more of certain kinds of public services than richer ones. The model underlying the local aid distribution formula in Massachusetts involves several factors related to residents' income.

Think about the factors that might be involved in the determination of local expenditures and local needs for public services. Think once again about the questions raised in the previous exercises.

Per Capita Local Resources

This half of the local aid formula should be much easier than the need half; however, it still raises some extremely interesting questions of public policy.

The biggest single factor in determining per capita local resources is per capita equalized valuation. This is the tax base to which the property tax is applied. Proposition $2\frac{1}{2}$ limits the property tax in two ways:

1. The property tax rate is limited absolutely to 2.5%. No city or town may exceed this limit.

2. The total tax levy (that is, the total amount of property taxes raised) by a city or town may not grow by more than 2.5% each year. Because the rate of inflation has been above 2.5%, this is an extremely significant limitation. In fact, this limitation is more significant than the

first one. Most cities and towns currently have tax rates well below
2.5%. Although this limitation is usually expressed as a limit on the
total tax levy, it implies a limit on the tax rate. That limit is equal to
the total levy limit divided by the total EQV for all taxable property.
There are two exceptions to this limit:

a. If there is new construction in a city or town, this new construction
   may be taxed. That is, the tax levy limit is raised to include the
   taxes that could be raised from this new construction. In other
   words, Proposition $2\frac{1}{2}$ limits to 2.5% levy increases due to increased
   values of existing property but does allow communities to add new
   property to the tax rolls.

b. Voters in a city or town can vote to override this second clause of
   Proposition $2\frac{1}{2}$ provided that the new tax rate does not exceed the
   absolute 2.5% limit of the first clause. Historically voters have been
   reluctant to approve overrides.

In fiscal years 1985 and 1986 the per capita resource computation
included 2.5% of per capita EQV. This figure is based on the assumption
that communities could tax property at the full 2.5% rate; however, a
number of objections have been raised.

In fact the property tax is restricted by both clauses of Proposition
$2\frac{1}{2}$. For many communities, the second clause is the significant one.
Several people have suggested that instead of using 2.5% of per capita
EQV, the formula should use the limit implied by the second clause. I
am opposed to this change for two reasons:

1. It favors communities that have taxed themselves at a lower rate than
   other communities. Historically communities with greater needs and
   lower resources have had to tax themselves at a higher rate. Thus,
   this change would favor the wrong communities.

2. The primary benefits and primary responsibility for the provision of
   local public services reside with the cities and towns. For the reasons
   already discussed, the state must play a significant part in financing
   local public services. However, local communities do have an obligation to do their part. Several people, including me, have argued that
   one factor that ought to be taken into account in the allocation of
   local aid is local effort. More money should be channeled to communities taxing themselves at a higher rate. The proposed change goes

in exactly the opposite direction: it would reward communities that are taxing themselves at a lower rate.

I have discussed a few of the elements involved in the current local aid distribution formula and touched on some of the controversy. In the next sections we will develop some mathematical tools that will be extremely helpful for further discussion. However, first we want to work out some examples illustrating the impact of the change considered above. At the same time these examples will illustrate the way that the current formula works. These examples are much simpler than the actual formula.

Examples

Consider a mythical state with two communities:

Town	Population	Per Capita Needs	Per Capita EQV
Town A	10,000	$1,200	$25,000
Town B	10,000	$800	$30,000

Suppose the state has $1 million to distribute in local aid.

Example 1

Suppose the state calculates per capita local resources as 2.5% of per capita EQV:

Town	Per Capita EQV	Per Capita Resources
Town A	$25,000	$625
Town B	$30,000	$750

Then the gap is computed by:

Town	Per Capita Need	Per Capita Resources	Gap
Town A	$1,200	$625	$575
Town B	$800	$750	$50

Ideally, we would like to allocate enough money to each town to fill the gap. This would require the following allocations:

Town	Gap	Population	Ideal Allocation
Town A	$575	10,000	$5,750,000
Town B	$50	10,000	$500,000
Total			$6,250,000

This situation is analogous to the situation in Section 5.4. The state has only $1 million to distribute, not enough to fill the gap completely for every community. Thus we make a final adjustment, multiplying each allocation by the factor

$$R = \frac{\text{Available Money}}{\text{Total Ideal Allocation}}.$$

In this case $R = \$1,000,000/\$6,250,000 = 0.16$. We have the final allocations:

Town	Ideal Allocation	Actual Allocation
Town A	$5,750,000	$920,000
Town B	$500,000	$80,000

Example 2

Now suppose that the effective Proposition $2\frac{1}{2}$ tax limits due to the second clause for each town are the following:

Town	Effective Rate Limit
Town A	2.00%
Town B	1.50%

These are realistic numbers. Notice that Town B has lower needs and higher resources per capita than Town A, so historically it would have been able to tax itself at a lower rate. Now we can repeat all the previous calculations using this new limit:

Town	Per Capita EQV	Per Capita Resources
Town A	$25,000	$500
Town B	$30,000	$450

Then the gap is computed by:

Town	Per Capita Needs	Per Capita Resources	Gap
Town A	$1,200	$500	$700
Town B	$800	$450	$350

Ideally, we would like to allocate enough money to each town to fill the gap. This would require the following allocations:

Town	Gap	Population	Ideal Allocation
Town A	$700	10,000	$7,000,000
Town B	$350	10,000	$3,500,000
Total			$10,500,000

This situation is analogous to the situation in Section 5.4. The state has only $1 million to distribute—not enough to fill the gap completely for every community. Thus we make a final adjustment, multiplying each allocation by the factor

$$R = \frac{\text{Available money}}{\text{Total ideal allocation}}.$$

In this case $R = \$1,000,000/\$10,500,000 = 0.095238$. We have the final allocations:

Town	Ideal Allocation	Actual Allocation
Town A	$7,000,000	$666,667
Town B	$3,500,000	$333,333

Notice how this change shifts money from Town A to Town B.

We have been considering only part of the formula thus far. Both the computations of need and resources are more complicated than we have seen up to this point.

Exercise

*Exercise 5.5.28** One possible compromise would be to compute per capita resources as a fixed but lower percentage of per capita EQV. For example, one could use 1.5% of per capita EQV. This figure is closer to the actual tax rates in effect now, it would be a better estimate of resources. Work out the resulting allocation in the preceding examples using this modification.

5.6   Data Snooping and Sigma Notation

We need to find a way of estimating each city and town's per capita needs for public services. There are basically two different ways to go about this. One possibility would be analogous to the suggestion in the last section that a professional dietitian might design a standard diet for an SEE. That is, we could commission a large study that would determine a standard bundle of public services and then determine the cost of providing that bundle. This approach, however, is extraordinarily difficult (but not necessarily impossible). There is a great deal of controversy about the composition of such a standard bundle. Moreover, our ideas about that composition change. Thus, our commission would have a difficult and unending task. The second approach is to analyze actual expenditures of cities and towns. This is the approach that we shall use.

We will begin by looking at some data about per capita expenditures. This data can help us to understand per capita needs, although there is a big difference between needs and expenditures. We will be using fiscal year 1980 data, the best data available. Fiscal year 1980 was the last year before Proposition $2\frac{1}{2}$. Prior to Proposition $2\frac{1}{2}$, if the price of heating oil rose (and it did rather frequently), cities and towns could respond to that increased price by raising additional revenue. After Proposition $2\frac{1}{2}$, many communities were unable to respond to such price increases by raising revenue. Their only option was to cut something out of the budget. Thus, after fiscal year 1980, city and town budgets were determined more by the limits imposed by Proposition $2\frac{1}{2}$ than by actual needs.

Table 3 in Appendix B includes, for each of the 351 cities and towns in Massachusetts, population and per capita expenditures in fiscal year 1980. The list is in population order, with the smallest town (Gosnold) first and the largest city (Boston) last.

In this section we will look at these data to see if we can detect any obvious patterns relating population and per capita expenditures. In the next section we will develop a more sophisticated tool for analyzing data. Before looking to see if there is any obvious relationship between per capita expenditures and population, think about what you might expect.

Exercises

Exercise 5.6.29   Relying on educated guesswork without looking too carefully at Table 3 of Appendix B, do you think smaller communities tend to spend less or more money per capita on public services than larger communities? Give some reasons that you might expect their per capita expenditures to be lower or higher.

Exercise 5.6.30   Do any numbers in Table 3 of Appendix B look out of line? Can you offer any explanation?

Each of the cities and towns in Massachusetts will be identified by a number called its *population rank*. Cities and towns are numbered from 1 to 351, with the smallest town, Gosnold, first and the largest city, Boston, last. Thus, Gosnold is number 1 and Boston is number 351. These numbers are indicated in Table 3 of Appendix B. Notice that this numbering is different from the alphabetical numbering used earlier. For our purposes in this section, numbering communities in order of population will be more convenient. We will denote the population of community number i by $p(i)$ and the per capita fiscal year 1980 expenditures of town number i by $e(i)$. Thus, for Boston we see that

$$p(351) = 562,994 \quad \text{and} \quad e(351) = \$1,325.56.$$

Now suppose that we wanted to find the average per capita expenditures of the three cities whose population is over 100,000: Springfield, Worcester, and Boston. We would add up their per capita expenditures and divide by 3. Using our new notation, we can write this as

$$\frac{e(349) + e(350) + e(351)}{3} = \frac{849.58 + 1060.06 + 1325.56}{3} = 1078.40.$$

We will frequently be interested in sums like the one that appears in the numerator above, so we will use a special notation, called sigma notation. Sigma (written Σ) is the Greek letter that corresponds to our letter "S." The notation

$$\sum_{i=349}^{351} e(i)$$

means the sum

$$e(349) + e(350) + e(351).$$

More generally, we write

$$\sum_{i=a}^{b} e(i)$$

for

$$e(a) + e(a+1) + \cdots + e(b).$$

This notation is analogous to a True BASIC FOR ... NEXT loop. In True BASIC the same sum would be computed by

```
LET sum = 0
FOR i = a TO b
LET sum = sum + e(i)
NEXT i
```

Exercises

Compute each of the following sums:

***Exercise 5.6.31**

$$\sum_{i=1}^{5} e(i)$$

***Exercise 5.6.32**

$$\sum_{i=1}^{10} e(i)$$

*Exercise 5.6.33

$$\sum_{i=6}^{10} e(i)$$

Now suppose that we are interested in computing the average per capita expenditures of the towns whose population is under 5,000. Looking at Table 3 in Appendix B, we see that there are 125 towns (Gosnold, ..., Hampden) whose population is under 5,000. We want to compute

$$\sum_{i=1}^{125} e(i)$$

and divide the result by 125. This requires a lot of addition, so we will write a quick computer program to do the calculations. The necessary data are available in a disk file called "EXPdata." Your instructor will give you a copy of this disk file. The first two lines of EXPdata look like this:

```
1, Gosnold, 63, 2196
2, Mount Washington, 93, 1495
```

This file contains one line for each city and town. Each line has four items: the community's population rank, its name, its population, and its per capita fiscal year 1980 expenditures. A program for computing the average expenditures for the first 125 cities and towns on this file is given below. The result is $860.60.

```
!     Compute the average per capita expenditures
!     for first 125 cities and towns
!
OPEN #1: NAME "EXPdata"
LET sum = 0.0
FOR i = 1 TO 125
INPUT #1: n, name$, pop, exp
LET sum = sum + exp
NEXT i
LET average = sum/125
```

```
PRINT USING "Average per capita expenditures $#,###.##":average
END
```

Your main assignment for this section is to write a computer program whose input will be two numbers—a and b—and whose output will be the average per capita expenditures for the towns numbered a through b. After you have written this program, use it to solve the following exercises. Use the computation above for towns 1 through 125 to check out your program.

Exercises

Exercise 5.6.34 Find the average per capita expenditures for all the cities and towns whose population is between 5,000 and 15,000.

Exercise 5.6.35 Find the average per capita expenditures for all the cities whose population is over 50,000.

Exercise 5.6.36 Find the average per capita expenditures for all 351 cities and towns in Massachusetts.

Exercise 5.6.37 Do some exploration. Can you discover any relationship between population and per capita expenditures?

Exercise 5.6.38 Find the total expenditures by all the city and town governments in Massachusetts. Note that the total expenditures for each city and town can be found by multiplying its per capita expenditures by its population. That is, the expenditures for town i are $p(i)e(i)$. Thus, we want to find the sum

$$\sum_{i=1}^{351} p(i)e(i).$$

That is,

$$p(1)e(1) + p(2)e(2) + \cdots + p(351)e(351).$$

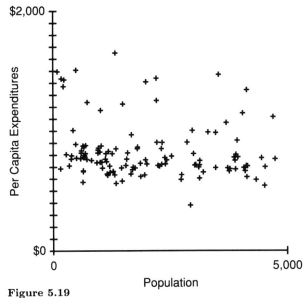

Figure 5.19
Scatter plot per capita expenditures vs. population

One way to look for patterns in data is to make a scatter plot. Figures 5.19–5.21 are scatter plots for the data in Table 3 of Appendix B. The x-axis on each of these figures represents population. The y-axis represents per capita expenditures. Each city and town is represented by a plus sign: the x-coordinate of this plus sign is population, and its y-coordinate is per capita expenditures. Figure 5.19 shows the cities and towns whose population is under 5,000. One town is omitted from this figure, Rowe. The per capita expenditures of Rowe are $3,202, well above any other community. (Why?)

Figure 5.20 shows cities and towns whose population is in the range 5,000–15,000. Figure 5.21 shows cities and town whose population is in the range 15,000–100,000. The three largest cities—Springfield, Worcester, and Boston—are not shown in any of these figures. Notice that there does not seem to be any recognizable pattern.

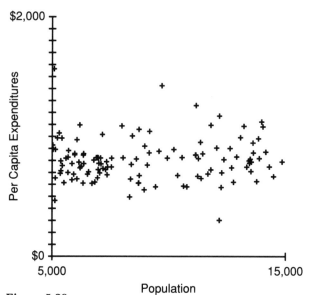

Figure 5.20
Scatter plot per capita expenditures vs. population

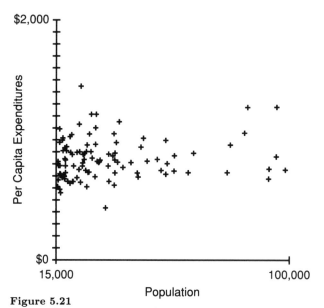

Figure 5.21
Scatter plot per capita expenditures vs. population

5.7   Linear Regression

In this section we will study a powerful and commonly used method for searching for patterns in data like the data we have available for studying municipal needs. This method is called *linear regression*.

Scatter plots can be useful for discovering patterns in data; however, they have some limitations. They rely too much on the eye of the beholder. Sometimes it is difficult to detect a pattern. The actual model used in the Massachusetts local aid distribution formula involves 19 variables. There is no way to draw a scatter plot showing the relationships among so many variables. Scatter plots can be useful when two or three variables are involved, but for larger numbers of variables, we must use analytic techniques like linear regression and its offspring, multiple regression (discussed in Section 5.8).

The idea behind linear regression is that we are attempting to detect a possible linear relationship between two variables. Eventually we will develop a formula for detecting such a relationship, but we will begin our study of linear regression in a more leisurely way. Consider the data shown in Table 5.11. This table shows per capita expenditures and per capita EQV for the seven cities whose population is between 50,000 and 60,000. These same data are shown in the scatter plots in Figures 5.22 and 5.23. The two figures are identical except for the city names in Figure 5.22.

Looking at Figure 5.23 we can see a rough pattern. Higher expenditures seem to be associated with higher EQVs. This is exactly what we would expect. Richer cities (those with higher EQVs) would be expected to spend more. (Note: It is always important to compare results with

Table 5.11
EQV and Per Capita Expenditure Data for Seven Communities

City or Town	Per Capita EQV	Per Capita Expenditures
Brookline	$17,589	$997
Chicopee	$10,401	$715
Malden	$9,819	$747
Medford	$14,336	$742
Pittsfield	$12,381	$838
Waltham	$17,938	$869
Weymouth	$13,156	$803

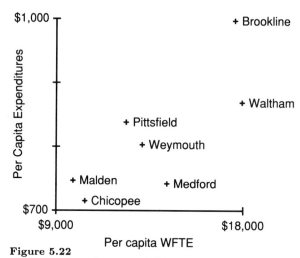

Figure 5.22
Per capita expenditures vs. EQV for seven cities

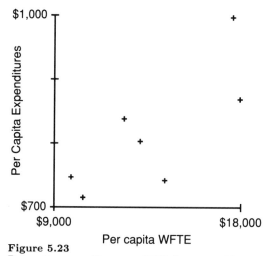

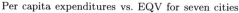

Figure 5.23
Per capita expenditures vs. EQV for seven cities

your educated intuition. If they don't agree, you should try to resolve the discrepancy. Perhaps you've made an error, or perhaps your intuition can be changed and strengthened in the light of this new information.)

We might try to draw a linear function approximating this apparent relationship between EQV and expenditures. Figures 5.24 and 5.25

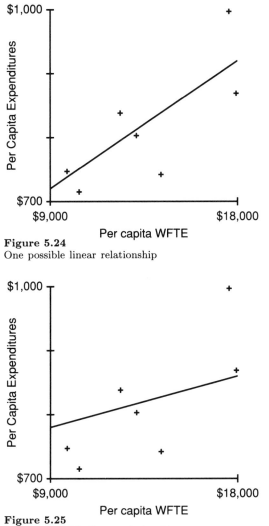

Figure 5.24
One possible linear relationship

Figure 5.25
Another possible linear relationship

show two linear functions that have been added to this scatter plot.
They were obtained by pure guesswork. I tried to draw linear functions
that "looked like" the scatter plot.

The equation of the linear function in Figure 5.24 is

Expenditures $= 0.022222 \cdot$ EQV $+ 520.$

Table 5.12
Comparison of Predicted and Actual Per Capita Expenditures

City or Town	EQV	Actual Exp.	Predicted Exp.	Difference	Squared
Brookline	17,589	997.00	910.86	86.14	7,420
Chicopee	10,401	715.00	751.13	−36.13	1,305
Malden	9,819	747.00	738.20	8.80	77
Medford	14,336	742.00	838.57	−96.57	9,327
Pittsfield	12,381	838.00	795.13	42.87	1,838
Waltham	17,938	869.00	918.62	−49.62	2,462
Weymouth	13,156	803.00	812.35	−9.35	87
Sum of squares					22,516

The equation of the linear function in Figure 5.25 is

$$\text{Expenditures} = 0.008889 \cdot \text{EQV} + 700.$$

These two equations give us two different models (which we will call Model 1 and Model 2, respectively) relating per capita EQV and per capita expenditures. We need to have a method for judging such models to determine which is the better one. One way to judge such a model is to put it to its intended use and see how well it performs. The intended use of these models is to predict or estimate per capita expenditures on the basis of per capita EQV.

Table 5.12 shows the results we obtain if we use Model 1 to predict expenditures on the basis of EQV. All we are doing is plugging EQV into the Model 1 equation:

$$\text{Expenditures} = 0.022222 \cdot \text{EQV} + 520.$$

The first three columns of Table 5.12 repeat the original data: the name, per capita EQV, and per capita expenditures for the seven towns whose population is between 50,000 and 60,000. The next column, "Predicted Exp.," uses Model 1 to predict per capita expenditures on the basis of per capita EQV. For example, the prediction for Brookline is

$$\text{Predicted expenditures} = (0.022222)(17,589) + 520 = 910.86.$$

The next column shows the difference between the actual per capita expenditures and the value predicted by Model 1. We want to find a

Table 5.13
Comparison of Predicted and Actual Per Capita Expenditures

City or Town	EQV	Actual Exp.	Predicted Exp.	Difference	Squared
Brookline	17,589	997.00	856.35	140.65	19,783
Chicopee	10,401	715.00	792.45	−77.45	5,999
Malden	9,819	747.00	787.28	−40.28	1,623
Medford	14,336	742.00	827.43	−85.43	7,299
Pittsfield	12,381	838.00	810.05	27.95	781
Waltham	17,938	869.00	859.45	9.55	91
Weymouth	13,156	803.00	816.94	−13.94	194
Sum of squares					35,770

model that makes these differences as small as possible, but we must decide what we mean by the phrase "differences as small as possible." There are several possible interpretations for this phrase. For example,

- We could add up the absolute value of all of these differences. This sum would be one possible measure of how good a model was.

- We could look for the worst difference (the difference with the largest absolute value). This is looking at the worst "mistake" made by a model. The best model would be the one whose worst mistake was smallest.

- Motivated by our discussion of the disparity index in Section 5.2 we could compute the square of each difference and add up these squares. These calculations are made for Model 1 in the last column and bottom line of Table 5.12.

It turns out that this last approach—using the sum of the squares of the differences between the predicted and actual per capita expenditures—is the one most often used. It has many very nice properties. It is closely related to the formula for measuring distance obtained from the Pythagorean formula. This relationship gives it many nice mathematical properties. From our point of view, it has other useful properties. For example, it penalizes large errors much more severely than small errors. Because the errors are squared, an error of 20, for example, counts four times as heavily as an error of 10. Table 5.13 duplicates the calculations of 5.12 for Model 2. The bottom line for these tables is:

Model 1: Sum of squares: 22,516 (Table 5.12)

Model 2: Sum of squares: 35,770 (Table 5.13)

On the basis of this criterion, we conclude that Model 1 is better than Model 2.

This criterion is the most frequently used criterion for this kind of problem, and we will use it from now on. It is important to note that other criteria are possible. The study of such criteria is an active area of statistics.

One of the nicest things about this criterion is that there is an easy formula for finding the best linear model. This formula is called the *linear regression formula*. (If you are interested in how this formula is obtained you can find an explanation in almost any book on statistics.)

Linear Regression Formula

Suppose we have two variables, x and y. The variable x will be called the *explanatory* or *independent* variable, and the variable y will be called the *dependent* variable. We are seeking a linear model for estimating the dependent variable, y, on the basis of the explanatory variable, x. That is, we are looking for a relationship of the form

Predicted-$y = mx + b$

that can be used to estimate y given x. (I am using the terms *estimating* and *predicting* interchangeably.) In the example above, the explanatory variable was per capita EQV, and the dependent variable was per capita expenditures.

We will be given data for n cases (in the example above, each city was a "case" and n was 7). For each case we will be given the value of x and the value of y. Thus, we are given

- $x(1)$: The value of x for case 1. $y(1)$: The value of y for case 1.
- $x(2)$: The value of x for case 2. $y(2)$: The value of y for case 2.

  $\vdots$

- $x(n)$: The value of x for case n. $y(n)$: The value of y for case n.

To find m and b we proceed as follows:

Step 1: Compute

$$S_x = \sum_{i=1}^{n} x(i).$$

Step 2: Compute

$$S_y = \sum_{i=1}^{n} y(i).$$

Step 3: Compute

$$S_{xy} = \sum_{i=1}^{n} x(i)y(i).$$

Step 4: Compute

$$S_{x^2} = \sum_{i=1}^{n} x^2(i).$$

Step 5:

$$m = \frac{S_x S_y - n S_{xy}}{S_x S_x - n S_{x^2}}$$

$$b = \frac{S_y - m S_x}{n}$$

We will use these five steps as a recipe without any explanation. (If you are interested in an explanation of how this recipe is derived, you can consult almost any statistics book.)

The calculations for our example are shown below:

i	City or Town	$x(i)$	$y(i)$	$x(i)y(i)$	$x(i)^2$
1	Brookline	17,589	997	17,536,233	309,372,921
2	Chicopee	10,401	715	7,436,715	108,180,801
3	Malden	9,819	747	7,334,793	96,412,761
4	Medford	14,336	742	10,637,312	205,520,896
5	Pittsfield	12,381	838	10,375,278	153,289,161
6	Waltham	17,938	869	15,588,122	321,771,844
7	Weymouth	13,156	803	10,564,268	173,080,336
	Sum	95,620	5,711	79,472,721	1,367,628,720

Thus

$$S_x = 95,620$$
$$S_y = 5,711$$
$$S_{xy} = 79,472,721$$
$$S_{x^2} = 1,367,628,720$$
$$n = 7$$

So

$$
\begin{aligned}
m &= \frac{S_x S_y - n S_{xy}}{S_x S_x - x S_{x^2}} \\
&= \frac{(95,620)(5,711) - (7)(79,472,721)}{(95,620)(95,620) - (7)(1,367,628)} \\
&= 0.023763
\end{aligned}
$$

and

$$
\begin{aligned}
b &= \frac{S_y - m S_x}{n} \\
&= \frac{(5,711) - (0.023763)(95,620)}{7} \\
&= 491.25.
\end{aligned}
$$

Linear regression gives the following linear model relating per capita EQV and per capita expenditures:

Predicted expenditures $= 0.023763 \cdot$ EQV $+ 491.25$.

This linear function is shown in Figure 5.26.

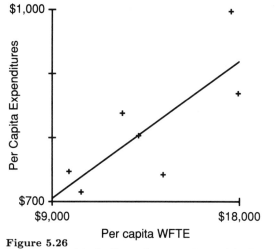

Figure 5.26
Scatter plot with the linear function obtained by linear regression

---

Exercises

*__Exercise 5.7.39__   Use the linear model that we obtained above,

Predicted expenditures $= 0.023763 \cdot \text{EQV} + 491.25$,

to estimate per capita expenditures for Brookline, Chicopee, Malden, Medford, Pittsfield, Waltham, and Weymouth on the basis of per capita EQV.

Exercise 5.7.40   Using your results from the preceding exercise compute

- The difference between the predicted and actual expenditures for each of these seven cities.
- The square of each of these differences.
- The sum of these squares.

Verify that this model (the one obtained by linear regression) is indeed better than our two earlier "guesswork" models, Models 1 and 2.

Exercise 5.7.41   The following table gives per capita EQV and expenditures for the 12 communities in Massachusetts whose population is between 35,000 and 45,000. Use the linear regression formula to find the best linear model for predicting expenditures on the basis of EQV for these 12 communities.

City or Town	EQV	Expenditures
Beverly	$15,082	$815
Billerica	$14,670	$890
Braintree	$20,998	$1,051
Everett	$23,874	$978
Fitchburg	$9,467	$771
Holyoke	$8,588	$725
Methuen	$13,640	$725
Plymouth	$27,283	$867
Revere	$10,831	$812
Salem	$15,780	$1,153
Westfield	$11,729	$623
Woburn	$18,492	$833

We have just scratched the surface of linear regression, an extremely important and interesting subject. As one indication of its popularity, note that many hand calculators have the capability of performing linear regression. (You can read more about linear regression and its uses in any good statistics book.)

For the rest of this chapter we will use linear regression to study the local aid distribution problem in Massachusetts. We will start by studying the data shown in Table 4 in Appendix B. This table gives population, per capita expenditures, per capita EQV, and per capita WFTE students for each of the 351 cities and towns in Massachusetts. We will eventually discuss many more data, but this is a good place to start. One of these variables, EQV, is a good indication of the resources of a community. As we discussed earlier, there are other factors that might be used, for example, per capita income. Another variable, WFTE, is an obvious example of a factor that influences the needs of a community. Education is very expensive. The more students there are per capita, the higher are the educational needs per capita. The impact of the final variable, population, is harder to understand without further study. Some arguments seem to indicate that per capita needs in larger cities are greater than those in smaller towns, and some arguments indicate the reverse.

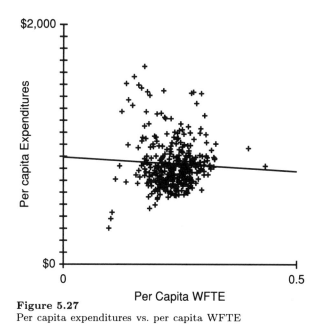

Figure 5.27
Per capita expenditures vs. per capita WFTE

Your instructor will give you a disk file containing the data in Table 4 of Appendix B. Your assignment for this section will be to write and use a program that can be used to analyze these data using linear regression, but first we will discuss some analysis that I did using a similar program.

The first thing I did was based on my strong intuition that per capita costs depend strongly on the per capita number of WFTE students. There is a considerable variation in the amount of money each community spends on each student, but for every community, education is a large part of the budget. I ran a linear regression using per capita WFTE as the explanatory variable and per capita expenditures as the dependent variable. The result was the following linear model:

Predicted expenditures $= -235 \cdot$ WFTE $+ 894$.

This result is shown in Figure 5.27. This figure includes a scatter plot showing the data points together with the linear function obtained above. Notice that the results are completely contrary to intuition: per capita expenditures are predicted to fall as per capita WFTE rises. Before continuing, we must resolve this conflict. One of the problems with linear regression is that it is sensitive to each individual data point.

If even one single data point is unusual, it can have a dramatic impact
on the results obtained by linear regression. Our data have a number of
unusual data points. For example, I have already mentioned the town
of Rowe, which has a nuclear power plant and a very small population.
As a result, its resources are very high—a per capita EQV of $393,560.
Not surprisingly, Rowe's per capita expenditures are also very high. In
fact, they are so high ($3,202) that the data point for Rowe doesn't
even fit on the scatter plot in Figure 5.27. One other town, Gosnold,
has per capita expenditures that are too large to fit in Figure 5.27. Both
towns have below-average per capita WFTEs. For these two data points
the combination of very high per capita expenditures and lower-than-
average WFTE tries to lower the slope of the linear equation relating
per capita expenditures to per capita WFTE. They are both unusual
towns. Both have very low populations. In fact, small towns can easily
have unusual data because all our data are per capita.

I thought it would be interesting to try another linear regression using
the same two variables and data only for cities and towns whose population was over 500. There are 15 towns whose population is under 500,
leaving 336 cities and towns whose population is over 500. The following
equation was obtained by linear regression using these 336 data points:

Predicted expenditures $= 88 \cdot \text{WFTE} + 798$.

Figure 5.28 shows this linear equation and the scatter plot for these
336 cities and towns. This linear equation is a little better. At least now
the slope is positive and per capita expenditures are predicted to rise as
per capita WFTE increases. The slope is still surprisingly low, however.
The amount of money that each community spends on the education
of each WFTE student varies quite considerably; however, this amount
is in the neighborhood of several thousand dollars. Thus, per capita
expenditures for education should be roughly several thousand dollars
times WFTE per capita. In other words, we would expect the slope to
be several thousand rather than only 88.

I suspected that the problem might lie with the fact that local resources have such a strong influence on per capita expenditures that the
influence of per capita WFTE is obscured, so I tried another experi-

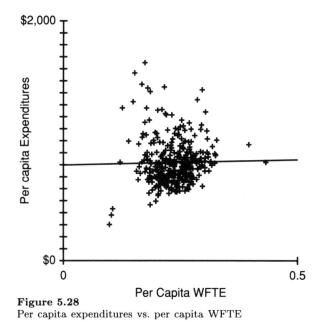

Figure 5.28
Per capita expenditures vs. per capita WFTE

ment. I ran another linear regression using the same variables but this time used only cities and towns that met the following two criteria:

1. Population at least 500.

2. Per capita EQV between $15,000 and $25,000.

There are 152 cities and towns that meet these criteria. The linear model obtained was:

Predicted expenditures $= 578 \cdot \text{WFTE} + 681$.

This linear model and the 152 data points are shown in Figure 5.29 This result looks a lot better. Notice that the slope of the line is much larger than in earlier experiments.

The True BASIC program I used to find this linear model using linear regression is given below. Study it and make sure that you understand how it works. Understanding this program will be very helpful to you when you write your own program a little later.

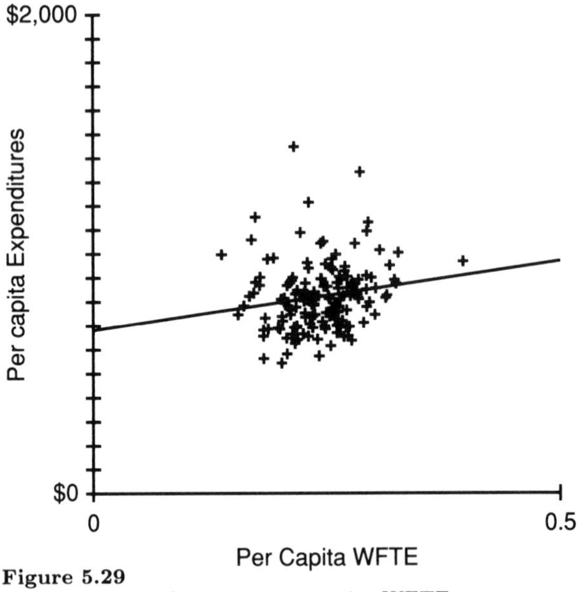

Figure 5.29
Per capita expenditures vs. per capita WFTE

```
!               This Program runs a linear regression
!
!               Dependent Variable:    Per Capita Expenditures
!               Explanatory Variable:  Per Capita WFTE
!
!               Only cities and towns meeting the following
!               criteria are included.
!
!                   Population >= 500
!                   $15,000 <= Per Capita EQV ,= $25,000
!
OPEN #1: NAME "THREEVAR"
LET sumx = 0.0
LET sumy = 0.0
LET sumxsq = 0.0
LET sumxy = 0.0
LET n = 0
```

```
FOR i = 1 TO 351      ! Read 351 cases
INPUT #1: name$, pop, exp, eqv, wfte
IF ((pop > 500) AND (15000 < eqv) AND (eqv < 25000)) THEN
    LET n = n + 1        ! Count number of cases
    LET sumx = sumx + wfte
    LET sumy = sumy + exp
    LET sumxsq = sumxsq + wfte*wfte
    LET sumxy = sumxy + wfte*exp
END IF
NEXT i
LET m = (sumx * sumy - n * sumxy)/(sumx * sumx - n * sumxsq)
LET b = (sumy - m * sumx)/n
PRINT USING "Number of cases ###":n
PRINT USING "Slope        ####.##":m
PRINT USING "Constant b   ####.##":b
END
```

Next I wondered if the differences between large and small communities might be significant enough to obscure the dependence of expenditures on WFTE, so as an experiment, I ran another linear regression with the same two variables but this time included only cities and towns whose population was between 10,000 and 50,000. There are 130 communities that meet this criterion. The result was the following linear model:

Predicted expenditures $= 1,211 \cdot \text{WFTE} + 543$.

This model shows a much stronger relationship between the two variables than any of our earlier models. This model and the associated scatter plot are shown in Figure 5.30.

So far, we have discovered a number of things. First, as we suspected, there does seem to be a relationship between per capita WFTE and per capita expenditures. Second, per capita expenditures depend on a number of factors, which can obscure this dependence. Your assignment is to explore these ideas. You will need to do some programming. Write one program to do the first exercise below and then modify it to do the second exercise, or write a more general program for both exercises by asking the user appropriate questions. In addition to these exercises, you may want to do some experimentation on your own.

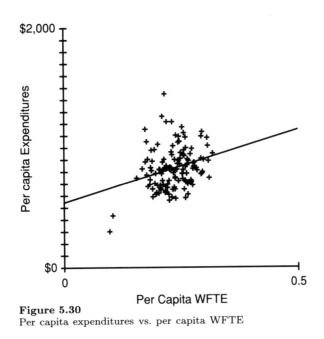

Figure 5.30
Per capita expenditures vs. per capita WFTE

Exercises

Exercise 5.7.42 Intuitively, one would expect that per capita expenditures would be higher in communities with higher per capita EQV. Try a linear regression using per capita EQV as the independent variable and per capita expenditures as the dependent variable. Use all 351 cities and towns.

Exercise 5.7.43 The dependence expected might be obscured by the differences between small towns and large cities. Run a regression similar to that of the previous exercise except use only cities whose population is between 10,000 and 50,000.

Exercise 5.7.44 Do you think that the slopes you obtained in the previous two exercises are intuitively reasonable? Why or why not?

5.8 Multiple Regression and THE FORMULA

Ideally in this section we would talk about the actual formula used to
distribute local aid in Massachusetts. This formula is very sophisticated.
Yet we now have enough background to discuss the main ideas behind it
and to understand in general how it works. However, there are a large
number of details. As you can imagine, local finance is quite complicated, partly because of the large variety of public services provided by
cities and towns and partly because of all the factors that make cities
and towns different from one another and that have an impact on local spending. In addition to these fundamental complications, the local
aid formula has changed from one year to the next, so it is incorrect to
speak of "the" local aid formula. Each fiscal year the formula has been
somewhat different. Thus, we will discuss the local aid distribution formula in somewhat general terms, including enough of the details to give
an accurate picture of how it works and the main ideas involved but
stopping far short of including all the details.

In Section 5.7 we looked at two factors that might influence a community's per capita expenditures for public services. First, we looked
at the possible dependence of per capita expenditures on per capita
WFTE students. We expected communities with larger per capita numbers of WFTE students to spend more money per capita because of
the increased per capita demand for education. Then we looked at the
possible dependence of per capita expenditures on per capita EQV. We
expected wealthier communities to spend more per capita.

Both expectations were confirmed using linear regression. We also
found evidence that the situation is somewhat more complicated than
this. We discovered that there were some very significant differences
among communities that could obscure these relationships. For example, we found a much stronger relationship between per capita WFTE
students and per capita expenditures when we looked only at communities whose population was between 10,000 and 50,000 than when we
looked at all communities.

Clearly a large number of factors can influence per capita expenditures. We need a tool to investigate the dependence of per capita expenditures on several variables all at once. There is such a tool: *multiple
regression*. In this section we will use multiple regression to study the
combined influence of WFTE students and EQV on expenditures. The

idea behind multiple regression is that it attempts to detect a linear dependence of one variable on several other variables. In our case we are looking for a linear dependence of per capita expenditures on per capita EQV and per capita WFTE students. More precisely, we are looking for a formula of the form

Predicted expenditures $= A \cdot$ WFTE $+ B \cdot$ EQV $+ C$.

The number A is called the *coefficient* for WFTE, the number B is called the *coefficient* for EQV, and the number C is called the *constant term*. Such a formula determines a linear model. One example of such a formula is given below:

Pred. expenditures $= 1,467.85 \cdot$ WFTE $+ 0.0101 \cdot$ EQV $+ 254.71$.   (5.1)

The intended use of such a formula is to predict or estimate per capita expenditures on the basis of per capita WFTE and per capita EQV. For example, in Table 4 of Appendix B, we read that Auburn has a per capita EQV of \$15,864 and a per capita WFTE of 0.234402. Formula 5.1 predicts that Auburn's per capita expenditures would be

$$\text{Pred. expenditures} = (1,467.85)(0.234402) + (0.0101)(15,864) + 254.71$$
$$= 759.01.$$

This happens to be fairly close to Auburn's actual per capita expenditures (\$790).

Exercise

Exercise 5.8.45 Pick three communities from Table 4 in Appendix B and use Formula 5.1 to estimate per capita expenditures on the basis of per capita EQV and WFTE. Choose communities whose population is between 5,000 and 25,000. Compare your estimates with actual per capita expenditures.

As in Section 5.7 we want to choose the best linear formula for estimating per capita expenditures. As in Section 5.7 there are several possible meanings of the word best. And as in Section 5.7, we will use the one most commonly used: minimizing the sum of the squares of the differences between actual and predicted per capita expenditures. There is a simple formula for finding the best linear formula. (I will not discuss this formula here. It can be found in any statistics book.) I wrote a program that uses this formula to find the best linear formula for estimating per capita expenditures on the basis of per capita EQV and WFTE and ran it using several different groups of cities and towns. Some of the results follow:

- Cities and towns whose population is above 500:

  Pred. expenditures $= 588.25 \cdot$ WFTE $+ 0.0080 \cdot$ EQV $+ 517.34$.

- Cities and towns whose population is between 1,000 and 25,000:

  Pred. expenditures $= 1,420.85 \cdot$ WFTE $+ 0.0095 \cdot$ EQV $+ 260.71$.

- Cities and towns whose population is above 25,000:

  Pred. expenditures $= -446.35 \cdot$ WFTE $+ 0.0096 \cdot$ EQV $+ 815.60$.

- Cities and towns whose population is between 5,000 and 25,000:

  Pred. expenditures $= 1,467.85 \cdot$ WFTE $+ 0.0101 \cdot$ EQV $+ 254.71$.

- Cities and towns whose popuation is above 10,000:

  Pred. expenditures $= 209.74 \cdot$ WFTE $+ 0.0116 \cdot$ EQV $+ 595.14$.

I was somewhat surprised at these results. The intuitive connection between per capita WFTE and per capita demand for public services is very strong. The third model, for cities whose population is above 25,000, is quite startling. For these cities, the linear model forecasts lower per capita expenditures for cities with higher per capita WFTEs. There must be some additional factors that are obscuring the expected relationship between WFTE and expenditures. The second and fourth models are much more in agreement with expectations. They forecast higher per capita expenditures in communities with higher per capita

WFTEs and higher per capita expenditures in communities with more
money (higher per capita EQVs).

In order to build a reasonable model for forecasting the cost of providing public services, we will have to consider more factors, including
those that are causing the surprising results for cities and towns whose
population is above 25,000. First we want to use the following very simple model (the fourth one in the list above) to see how a model of this
kind could be used to estimate needs:

Pred. expenditures $= 1,467.85 \cdot \text{WFTE} + 0.0101 \cdot \text{EQV} + 254.71.$

This is the same model we considered earlier: Formula 5.1. This
model is designed to estimate per capita expenditures for public services.
However, we want to allocate local aid on the basis of per capita *needs*
rather than per capita *expenditures*.

In Section 5.5 we introduced an analogy. We discussed two families,
the Smiths and the Joneses, and the problem of determining each family's food needs. We discussed these two families' actual expenditures on
food and noticed that several kinds of factors influenced expenditures.
One kind was called an *uncontrollable* factor. A good example of such
a factor is the number of people in a family. The per capita number of
WFTE students in a community is exactly this kind of factor. Cities
and towns have a legal obligation to provide an education for every student. The per capita number of WFTE students is one of the factors
that determines per capita needs.

Another important kind of factor influencing expenditures might be
called a *resource* factor. Richer families might spend more money on
food than poorer families because they can afford to do so. Per capita
EQV is a good example of a resource factor for municipal spending.

The model above relates expenditures to two factors:

- WFTE, an uncontrollable factor.
- EQV, a resource factor.

We want to use this model (just as an example) to estimate the per
capita needs of each community. The model used as is estimates per
capita *expenditures*; however, we can use it to estimate per capita *needs*
as follows.

For a given community, say, Auburn, estimate needs by applying the
model to the actual per capita WFTE of that community (for Auburn,

WFTE $= 0.234402$) and the statewide average per capita EQV. The model we are using was determined using cities and towns whose population was between 5,000 and 25,000. The average per capita EQV for such municipalities is \$18,972.* Thus, for Auburn, we obtain

Estimated needs $= 1,467.86 \cdot \text{WFTE} + 0.0101 \cdot \text{EQV} + 254.71$

$$= (1,467.85)(0.234402) + (0.0101)(18,972) + 254.71$$

$$= \$790.40.$$

The rationale for this calculation is that we are computing what Auburn's per capita expenditures would have been given its actual demographics (per capita WFTE) if it had average resources (per capita EQV). In this example, it turns out that Auburn's estimated needs are somewhat higher than its estimated expenditures.

Exercise

Exercise 5.8.46 In the first exercise you were asked to select three communities and use Formula 5.1 to estimate per capita expenditures. Use the method above to estimate per capita needs for those same three communities.

The Massachusetts local aid distribution formula is based on a linear model of municipal expenditures similar to the one discussed above. The model was obtained by multiple regression. However, it is based on many more factors (18 in fiscal year 1987) than the simplified example. Some of these factors are uncontrollable factors like WFTE. Others are factors measuring local resources or local preferences. This linear model is used to estimate municipal needs. This estimate is then used to compute the gap and the amount of local aid for each community as discussed in Section 5.5. We will close this chapter by discussing just a few of the complexities of the actual formula.

Estimating Per Capita Needs

We will divide the factors involved in estimating local needs into three groups.

---

*This is a simple average obtained by summing the per capita EQV for the cities and towns whose population is between 5,000 and 25,000 and dividing by the number of such communities.

Group 1: Uncontrollable Factors

- WFTE Students per Capita.

- Population Density. High population density can have an impact
  on municipal expenditures in various ways. There is considerable
  variation of population density among the 351 cities and towns of
  Massachusetts. For example, Somerville (population 77,372) has a
  population density of 20,306 people per square mile, and Plymouth
  (population 35,913) has a population density of only 479.55 people
  per square mile. The lowest population density in the state belongs
  to Gosnold—5.02 people per square mile. The model obtained using
  multiple regression has a coefficient for the density variable of 0.01157.
  Since this coefficient is positive, expenditures rise with increasing density.

- Road Mileage. We would expect that most public services are more
  expensive to provide in densely populated areas than in more thinly
  popuated areas. However, there are several exceptions, including snow
  removal and road maintenance. Thinly populated communities may
  have very large per capita expenses for road maintenance because
  they have relatively many more miles of roads to maintain. Thus,
  road mileage is an important factor to consider for estimating per
  capita needs for public services.

- Manufacturing Employment. Commuters place a significant burden
  on public services. Cities and towns must provide roads, police and
  fire protection, traffic control, and other services for people who work
  in the city even if they do not reside there. In addition, they have
  to provide water and sewage and other services for their places of
  employment. This variable helps to estimate these increased costs.

- Nonmanufacturing Employment. This variable is similar to manufacturing employment. Nonmanufacturing employment includes people
  employed in retail sales and service industries. These kinds of economic activity draw additional people (for example, shoppers) into a
  community and thus generate additional needs for public services.

- Percentage of Housing Units Built before 1940. Maintenance is a
  large part of municipal budgets—road maintenance, building maintenance, maintenance of the water and sewage systems, and so forth.
  It is generally more expensive to maintain older buildings and

equipment. This variable attempts to measure the age of a community's infrastructure to reflect the increased cost of maintaining an older infrastructure.

- Percentage of Population below the Poverty Level. This variable is included to help account for the increased needs of people below the poverty line.

This first group of variables includes demographic factors that have a significant impact on the local per capita costs of providing public services. They are uncontrollable factors. When each community's per capita needs are estimated, its own value for each of these factors is used.

Group 2: Resource Factors

This next group of variables includes a number of variables that measure a community's resources:

- Per Capita EQV.
- Per Capita Personal Income.
- Per Capita State Aid.
- Per Capita Local Receipts.
- Per Capita Federal Revenue Sharing.
- Other Federal Aid per Capita.
- Per Capita Regional School Aid. Regional school districts receive some aid directly. Thus, communities that are part of regional school districts receive some aid indirectly. This variable accounts for this indirect aid.

These variables require little explanation. All measure resources available to each community. When each community's needs are estimated, the statewide average value is used for each of these variables. Thus, we are estimating what per capita expenditures would have been if the community had average resources.

Group 3: Preference Factors

This group contains factors that are thought of as measuring preferences for public services. I am not completely comfortable with the distinction between these factors and the first group. This group includes:

- Percentage of the Population over 65. Intuition would lead one to expect that increased numbers of people over 65 would lead to increased needs for public services. However, multiple regression yields a negative coefficient for this variable. In order to understand this result, we need to remember that the linear regression attempts to predict expenditures using actual fiscal year 1980 expenditure data.

  There are several possible reasons that fiscal year 1980 expenditures might actually be lower for communities with a larger percentage of their population over 65. First, in 1980 there was a large concern in Massachusetts about the level of the property tax. The property tax is particularly burdensome for retired people on fixed incomes. Thus, communities with higher percentages of elderly people might sacrifice some public services in order to keep property taxes lower.

  Second, many of the increased needs for public services associated with the elderly are largely picked up by the federal or state governments. For example, medical care is largely a federal and state responsibility.

- Government Employment per Capita. This is a puzzling variable. I would have expected it to have a positive coefficient for two reasons. First, government employees might be expected to be more likely than other people to support increased public expenditures. Second, like the other employment variables, this one might be expected to measure increased costs due to commuters. However, surprisingly, the coefficient for this variable is negative. I don't entirely understand this.

These variables are thought of as preference variables that have an impact on the kind and level of public services chosen by town residents. When each community's needs are estimated, statewide average values are used for these variables.

Using all of these factors and multiple regression applied to all cities and towns whose population is over 500, a linear model is obtained that does a surprisingly good job of estimating fiscal year 1980 per capita expenditures. As one indication of how good this model is, note that the coefficient on the number of WFTE students turns out to be 1,296.52.

This number seems a little low to me based on looking at actual per pupil expenditure figures; however, it is in the ballpark. Certainly it is much better than the coefficient on WFTE obtained in Model 1 using only two variables and all cities and towns whose population is over 500.

In fiscal year 1987 this model was used as described earlier to estimate per capita needs for public services. Although the model was obtained using fiscal year 1980 data for the reasons explained earlier, it is applied using the most recent data available. Thus, the estimates of needs are based as nearly as possible on each community's current circumstances. Of course, costs for everything, including public services, are higher in fiscal year 1987 than they were in fiscal year 1980. Thus, the costs obtained from the formula are multiplied by an inflation factor to account for this inflation.

Estimating Resources

Now we must return to the resource side of our considerations. Recall that the formula involves several steps:

- Determine for each community the per capita uncontrollable costs for public services.

- Determine for each community the per capita resources available for providing public services.

- Find the gap: the difference between per capita costs and per capita resources. Per capita aid is proportional to this gap except that each community receives at least $5 per capita even if its gap is negative.

We have already discussed some of the resources available as part of our discussion of the linear model for estimating expenditures. The calculation of each community's resources in this part of the formula involves the following:

- Per capita property tax resources: This resource is estimated at 2.0% of per capita EQV. This percentage was close to the statewide average property tax rate in fiscal year 1987.

- Per capita receipts from the motor vehicle excise tax.

- Per capita state aid.

- Net free cash: Free cash is a measure of how much money a community has in the bank available to meet unusual needs. The inclusion of this factor in the resource calculations is extremely controversial. Small towns argue that they must maintain substantially more free cash per capita than larger communities because their per capita expenditures fluctuate more widely than those of larger communities. Cities and towns that are financially strapped often look at neighbors with substantial free cash reserves and argue that those free cash reserves lessen their owners' financial difficulties. On the other hand, communities with substantial free cash reserves argue that they ought not to be penalized for past prudent financial management.

One of the changes between fiscal year 1986 and fiscal year 1987 was an attempt to respond to some of these criticisms. The word *net* in "net free cash" refers to an attempt to allow for the fact that some cities and towns regularly spend more of their free cash reserves than others. This is acomplished by subtracting from free cash reserves the average amount spent from free cash over the last three years.

This concludes our discussion of the Massachusetts local aid formula. This formula, like all other such formulas, is not perfect, but it does a remarkably good job. As you can imagine, the process by which a formula for allocating local aid is enacted into law is very complicated. It involves a good deal of economics, mathematics, and statistics—and it also involves questions of public policy and of politics. The mathematician or the economist who approaches this problem looking for a formal theorem that will determine the unique best way to allocate local aid is doomed to failure. There is no one best way. In fact, each person involved is likely to have his or her own idea of what "best" means.

On the other hand, the mayor or town manager who approaches the problem with only a vague feeling that his or her municipality should get more money is also doomed to failure. One of the values of the approach discussed is the interplay between theory and reality. This requires participants in the debate to be more specific. For example, a number of rural communities claimed that despite their small population, they often had lots of road mileage to maintain. Thus, they argued that their per capita needs for road maintenance were higher than those of larger urban communities. This kind of claim can be and was verified by analyzing the data using multiple regression. As a result the formula for estimating needs makes use of this factor. At its best, the process of designing a local aid distribution formula uses economics, mathematics, and statistics to focus public policy concerns in a fruitful way.

The need side of the formula is the most quantitative. This is the side of the formula where economics, statistics, and mathematics provide the most help to public policy makers. If one suspects that a particular factor may influence needs, then the numbers can help. One can look at the data to see whether that factor is of significant help in estimating expenditures. Of course, this is not the whole answer since there may still be some debate about whether the factor is a legitimate uncontrollable one as opposed to a preference or resource one.

The resource side of the formula is also quantitative, but here the numbers provide much less help to policymakers. For example, in fiscal year 1986 the resource side included 2.5% of per capita EQV; in fiscal year 1987 the resource side included 2.0% of per capita EQV. This change makes a significant difference, but economics, statistics, and mathematics provide little help in choosing between the two alternatives. The choice depends essentially on philosophy, not mathematics.

Nonetheless, a sound knowledge of practical economics and mathematics is needed to understand the implications of such choices. This chapter has introduced some of the most important concepts and techniques involved in allocating aid from one government to its subunits. You can use these ideas to help understand the debate about allocation formulas like the local aid distribution formula in Massachusetts or your own state's local aid programs.

6 Population Models

We share the earth's finite resources with bumblebees and elephants, with turnips and our fellow human beings. From day to day and year to year, our numbers and the numbers of our earthly neighbors vary. Some years there are zillions of annoying mosquitos, other years very few mosquitos. This chapter is about population models. We want to study some of the ways in which populations vary, a very complex field of study. There are many different species, all interacting in complex ways. There are many other factors that can cause populations to change (for example, the weather). We will be able to investigate only some very simple models, but even these will be able to give us some insight into population changes.

We will begin by studying single species models—models with only one species in a finite habitat. Even this simple situation will lead to some surprising complexity. For example, we will see that it is possible for the population of a single species to vary as shown in the graph in Figure 6.1. You might guess that this kind of cyclical variation must be caused by some external factor, perhaps sunspots or harvesting by farmers, but we shall see in Section 6.3 that this kind of variation can occur without any outside interference. In the last half of this chapter we will investigate models of population change for two species sharing the same habitat.

Regard this chapter as a sampler, a teaser giving a hint of some of the possibilities of mathematical modeling for population dynamics and ecology. You may want to explore some of your own ideas and build some of your own models after you've completed this chapter.

6.1 Exponential Models

We will begin by studying some extremely simple models of population growth. In fact, these models are so simple that we will soon discover they are almost completely useless. Nevertheless, they are the obvious starting point in our study of population growth. This is typical of mathematical modeling. The first, most obvious model is frequently not very good, but its shortcomings are very important. They help us to understand the phenomenon we are trying to model and to discover more realistic models.

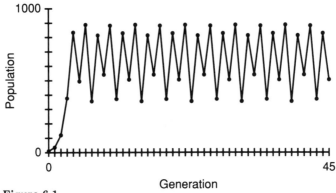

Figure 6.1
One example of the population growth of a single species

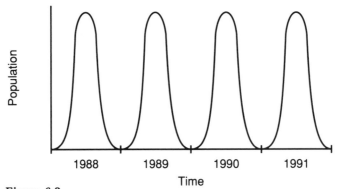

Figure 6.2
Population changes for a temperate zone insect

In the first few sections of this chapter we will be studying a single
species and ignore any interactions that it might have with any other
species sharing its habitat. Later we will investigate models that include
interactions among different species.

Some animals, like temperate-zone insects, have very distinct generations. For temperate-zone insects, each generation hatches in the spring,
lives for a while, lays eggs, and dies. Other animals, like people, do not
have distinct generations. At any given time there is a mixture of people
of different ages in different stages of their life cycle. We will be studying
a species with very distinct generations.

The population of such a species might look something like the graph shown in Figure 6.2. Notice that during each year (or each generation) the population varies considerably. In the winter the population is zero. (Actually there are a bunch of eggs, but eggs are not shown in this graph.) In the spring the population rises quite rapidly as eggs hatch. During the summer the population declines as some individuals are eaten or otherwise expire. Then the population drops very rapidly until the population returns to zero for the winter.

Our first simplification will be to measure the population in each generation by a single number. This number could be any one of several possible numbers. For example, one could choose the peak (largest) number of individuals alive at one time during each generation, or one could choose a particular day, say June 13, and always measure the population on that day. The particular measure used for the population of each generation is not too important. Using the same measure consistently is important.

We will number the generations: Generation 0, Generation 1, Generation 2, and so forth. This does not imply that Generation 0 is the first generation to exist but simply that it is the first generation in which we are interested. The population of Generation 0 will be denoted $p(0)$, the population of Generation 1, $p(1)$, and so on. Thus, our model is described by the sequence of numbers $p(0), p(1), p(2), \ldots$

We are interested in how the population changes from one generation to the next. If we were to examine these changes in detail, we might see a record like this:

Time	Population
Winter	1,000 eggs.
Spring	500 eggs hatch. 500 eggs fail to hatch.
Summer	300 individuals survive the summer and reach egg-laying age.
Fall	150 individuals actually lay eggs. Each one of these lays ten eggs, for a total of 1,500 eggs. 300 eggs are eaten by predators.
Winter	1,200 eggs.
Spring	600 eggs hatch. 600 eggs fail to hatch.

For our simplified model we are looking at a single number describing the population of each generation. For example, suppose we were to measure the population for each generation in the spring immediately after the eggs hatch. In this case the record above would be simplified to:

Time	Population
Spring	500
Spring	600

If these two generations were the first two generations, we would write this:

$$p(0) = 500$$

$$p(1) = 600$$

Notice that the net population growth from Generation 0 to Generation 1 is 20%.

Our first model is called an *exponential* model. In an exponential model the rate of population growth from one generation to the next stays constant. For example, an exponential model based on the data above would predict that the population would continue to grow by 20% each year. Thus, we would expect that

$$p(2) = p(1) + 0.20p(1)$$
$$= 1.20p(1)$$
$$= 1.20(600)$$
$$= 720$$

$$p(3) = p(2) + 0.20p(2)$$
$$= 1.20p(2)$$
$$= 1.20(720)$$
$$= 864$$

We can describe this model by the *change equation*

$$p(n + 1) = 1.20p(n).$$

This equation describes how the population of each generation may be computed based on the population of the preceding generation. More generally, an exponential model may be described by a change equation of the form

$$p(n + 1) = Rp(n)$$

where R is a constant that does not vary from generation to generation. In the example, the constant R was 1.20. If the population is growing, R will be bigger than 1. If the population is declining, R will be less than 1. We can completely describe a particular exponential model if we know two things:

- The population of the first generation, $p(0)$.
- The rate at which the population is increasing. This is usually expressed either as the value of the constant R or in terms of a percentage. In the example, we could describe the rate at which the population grew either by saying that the population grew by 20% each generation or by saying

$$p(n+1) = 1.20p(n)$$

(that $R = 1.20$). The two descriptions are equally good.

Example

Suppose that the population growth of a particular species is described by an exponential model and that

- $p(0) = 800$
- The population is declining at a rate of 10% per year.

Predict the population for Generations 1, 2, 3, and 4.

Answer:

$$
\begin{aligned}
p(1) &= p(1) - 0.10p(1) \\
&= 0.90p(1) \\
&= 0.90(800) \\
&= 720
\end{aligned}
$$

More generally,

$$
\begin{aligned}
p(n+1) &= p(n) - 0.10p(n) \\
&= 0.90p(n),
\end{aligned}
$$

so that

$$p(2) = 0.90p(1)$$
$$= 0.90(720)$$
$$= 648;$$
$$p(3) = 0.90p(2)$$
$$= 0.90(648)$$
$$= 583.20;$$
$$p(4) = 0.90p(3)$$
$$= 0.90(583.20)$$
$$= 524.88.$$

For mathematical simplicity and to compete with television violence, we have allowed fractional individuals. In practice, ecologists often measure population size by biomass rather than the number of individuals. It is much easier to weigh a colony of insects than to count the number of individuals. In terms of biomass, fractional numbers make sense.

Example

Suppose that the newspapers report that a new pest appeared in your area last year. Last year the population of this pest was 1,200, and this year the population is 1,500. Assume that the population of this pest grows according to an exponential model. What would you expect the population to be next year? in three years?

Answer:

Let $p(0)$ be the population last year so that $p(1)$ is the population this year. According to the exponential model,

$$p(1) = Rp(0).$$

But we know that $p(0) = 1,200$ and that $p(1) = 1,500$. So

$$1,500 = R1,200$$

and

$$R = 1,500/1,200 = 1.25.$$

Thus, we are dealing with the model

- $p(0) = 1,200$
- $p(n+1) = 1.25p(n)$

and can make the following predictions based on this model:

$$p(2) = 1.25(1,500)$$
$$= 1,875;$$
$$p(3) = 1.25(1,875)$$
$$= 2,343.75;$$
$$p(4) = 1.25(2,343.75)$$
$$= 2,929.69.$$

This answers our questions. Next year the population will be 1,875. The following year it will be 2,343.75, and the year after that 2,929.69.

Exercises

*Exercise 6.1.1   Assume that the population change for a particular species is described by an exponential model. Given the following data, predict the population for generations 1, 2, ..., 10:

- $p(0) = 100$.
- The population is increasing by 30% each year.

*Exercise 6.1.2   Assume that the population change for a particular species is described by an exponential model. Given the following data, predict the population for generations 1, 2, ..., 10:

- $p(0) = 1,000$.
- The population is decreasing by 20% each year.

*Exercise 6.1.3   Assume that the population change for a particular species is described by an exponential model. Given the following data, predict the population for generations 2, 3, ..., 10:

- $p(0) = 1,000$.
- $p(1) = 900$.

*Exercise 6.1.4   Assume that the population change for a particular species is described by an exponential model. Given the following data, predict the population for generations 4, 5, ..., 10:

- $p(2) = 800$.
- $p(3) = 900$.

What was the population for generations 0 and 1?

Now let's look at three different exponential models, with $R = 0.9$, $R = 1.0$, and $R = 1.2$. All three models will start with $p(0) = 1,000$. The population for each of these models for the following 10 generations is shown in Table 6.1. Figure 6.3 shows these same three models graphically. Notice that when $R = 1$, the population doesn't change. However, when R is less than 1 (for example when $R = 0.9$), the population declines. When R is bigger than 1, the population grows.

The most dramatic situation is when R is bigger than 1. If we continued computing, we would see, for example, that $p(30) = 237,376$ and that $p(60) = 56,347,514$. For R greater than 1, the population will continue to increase. It will rise very rapidly to very high levels. Clearly something is seriously wrong here. It is true that sometimes the population rises rapidly to very high levels, but this can't go on forever. Sooner or later the population predicted by an exponential model with R greater than 1 would be far higher than could possibly be supported by the environment. There wouldn't be enough food for all these individuals.

Table 6.1
Comparison of Three Exponential Models

Generation	$R = 0.9$	$R = 1.0$	$R = 1.2$
0	1,000.00	1,000.00	1,000.00
1	900.00	1,000.00	1,200.00
2	810.00	1,000.00	1,440.00
3	729.00	1,000.00	1,728.00
4	656.10	1,000.00	2,073.60
5	590.49	1,000.00	2,488.32
6	531.44	1,000.00	2,985.98
7	478.30	1,000.00	3,583.18
8	430.47	1,000.00	4,299.82
9	387.42	1,000.00	5,159.78
10	348.68	1,000.00	6,191.74

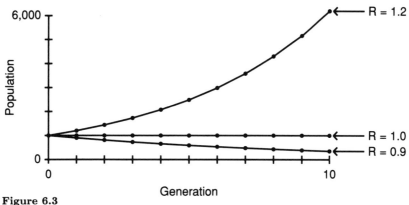

Figure 6.3
Comparison of three exponential models

Exponential models with R greater than 1 can be realistic for a short while. If a new species is introduced into an environment of plenty, then for a short time its population may grow exponentially. Sooner or later, however, the limits of the environment will begin to have an effect. In the next section we will look at some models that attempt to incorporate the limiting effects of a finite environment.

If R is exactly equal to 1, the exponential model will predict zero population growth; the population will remain unchanged from generation to generation. There is nothing wrong, mathematically, with such a model; however, it relies on a fluke of nature. One would not expect that R would be exactly equal to 1. Let's try to think about such a species. One possibility would be a species in which each individual lived forever with no births and no deaths. This is clearly unstable. An occasional disaster would inevitably wipe out the species. The same flaw would apply to any species in which R was exactly equal to 1. It would be on the razor's edge of survival, at the mercy of the occasional disaster and would eventually die out.

If R is less than 1, the population will die out. This can be realistic, but we don't see such species very often. They have all died out.

We have accomplished our first goal. We have studied the most naive model of population growth and have seen why it is unrealistic. In the next section we will look at some better models. Before continuing, you might want to try out some ideas of your own. Start with the following exercise.

Exercises

Exercise 6.1.5   One rarely sees species whose population growth can be described by an exponential model with R less than 1; however, one does see a variation on this theme. Consider an island with very harsh living conditions that is inhabited by a single species. Left by itself, such a population might be modeled by an exponential model with R less than 1 because of the harsh living conditions. Now suppose that the island is near a more hospitable mainland inhabited by the same species and some individuals from the mainland migrate to the island. Suppose that on the island $p(0) = 1,000$ and that if there were no immigration from the island, the population would drop by 25% each generation. That is, without immigration we would have

$$p(n + 1) = 0.75p(n).$$

However, suppose that each generation 100 individuals migrate to the island from the mainland. This situation can be modeled by

$$p(n + 1) = 0.75p(n) + 100.$$

- Compute $p(1), p(2), \ldots, p(10)$.
- Do you see a pattern? Can you make any long range predictions?

Exercise 6.1.6   Do some calculations for modifications of the model in the previous exercise. Try different Rs and different immigration rates. Do you detect any pattern?

6.2   The Logistic Model

In Section 6.1 we discussed exponential models of population growth. In these models the rate of population growth is constant; however, in practice it is not constant. The rate of population growth depends on both the birth rate and the death rate. These rates can be affected by many different factors, for example, by the weather or by competition from

another species. In this section we will be considering a single species
living in a finite habitat. In this situation the most important factor
influencing the rate of population growth is the size of the population
itself. If there is a relatively small population, there will be lots of food,
water, and shelter. The animals will be healthy with a high birth rate
and a low death rate. As a result, the rate of population growth will be
high. However, if there is a relatively large population, then there will
be lots of competition for the available food, water, and shelter. The
animals will be less healthy. Birth rates will go down, and death rates
will rise. As a result the rate of population growth will be lower.

The species we will discuss is a mythical species called flugel flies.
Flugel flies inhabit a tropical island. They have a relatively pleasant
life cycle. Each year on April 1 a new generation of flugel flies hatches.
Throughout the summer they have nothing to do but eat, drink, and
grow. At the end of the summer the female flugel flies lay eggs and die.
The following year on April 1 a new generation of flugel flies is born and
the life cycle starts anew.

As usual we will keep track of the flugel fly population with a sequence:
$p(0)$, $p(1)$, ... If $p(k)$ was the actual number of individuals, then we
would be working with some extremely large numbers. In order to keep
our numbers conveniently small, we will often work with thousands or
even millions of individuals. Thus, for example, $p(k) = 3.412$ might
mean that there are 3,412,000 individuals. We will be interested in how
the flugel fly population changes from one generation to the next. The
simplest model for population change is the exponential model. In an
exponential model, the population changes according to an equation like

$$p(n + 1) = Rp(n)$$

where R is a constant, called the *population multiplier*. It is a number
that depends on both the birth rate and the death rate.

This is not a very realistic model. It ignores the effects of crowding.
There is only a certain amount of food, water, and shelter available. As
the population rises, there will be more and more individuals competing
for the same limited supplies of food, water, and shelter. Eventually
some of the individuals will not be getting enough food or water or
finding suitable shelter. Health will start to suffer. The death rate will
go up, and the birth rate will decline. Thus, the population multiplier

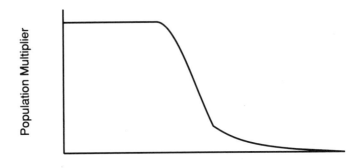

Population

Figure 6.4
The population multiplier as a function of population

will not be constant. It will be a function of the population. This function, denoted $R(p)$, will look roughly like the graph in Figure 6.4.

Notice that the function pictured in Figure 6.4 starts out relatively high and then falls as the population grows. This corresponds to the observation that with a relatively small population, there is plenty of food, water, and shelter, the animals are healthy, the birth rate is high, and the death rate is low. When the population is higher, there is less food and shelter per individual, the animals are less healthy, the birth rate falls, and the death rate rises, so that the rate of population growth falls.

In this section we will work with particularly simple examples of population multipliers, linear functions. We will assume, for simplicity, that $R(p)$ is given by an equation like

$$R(p) = a(1 - bp).$$

The graph of this function looks like Figure 6.5.

With this function describing the population multiplier, the population changes from year to year according to the equation

$$p(n + 1) = a(1 - bp(n))p(n).$$

Models like this are called *logistic models*. We will begin our discussion of logistic models with an example.

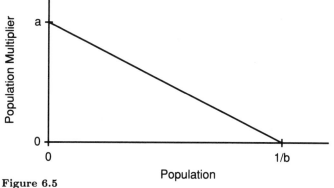

Figure 6.5
$R = a(1 - bp)$

Example

In this example the initial flugel fly population, $p(0)$, is 10. The population changes from year to year according to the equation

$$p(n + 1) = 2.8(1 - .001p(n))p(n).$$

(Using the notation above, $a = 2.8$ and $b = .001$.)
We can calculate the population for the first few years as follows:

$$p(0) = 10$$
$$p(1) = (2.8)(1 - .001(10))(10)$$
$$\quad = 27.72$$
$$p(2) = (2.8)(1 - .001(27.72))(27.72)$$
$$\quad = 75.46.$$

It is a simple matter to write a computer program to carry out these calculations. Some results are shown in Table 6.2. Figure 6.6 shows these results in graphical form.

The results of these calculations are very interesting. For the first few years, the population rises very quickly, almost like an exponential model, but then the population seems to hit some sort of natural bound. When the population is 600 or 700, it stops its rapid growth and seems to stutter around, finally settling down to a population of about 642.8. Frequently one observes exactly this phenomenon when a new species is introduced into an environment. The population initially rises

Table 6.2
The Logistic Model $p(n + 1) = 2.8(1 - .001p(n))p(n)$

Generation	Population	Generation	Population	Generation	Population
0	10.0000				
1	27.7200	16	638.7213	31	643.0014
2	75.4645	17	646.1179	32	642.7417
3	195.3549	18	640.2188	33	642.9495
4	440.1358	19	644.9483	34	642.7833
5	689.9656	20	641.1719	35	642.9162
6	598.9566	21	644.1974	36	642.8099
7	672.5812	22	641.7799	37	642.8950
8	616.6040	23	643.7157	38	642.8269
9	661.9298	24	642.1683	39	642.8813
10	626.5805	25	643.4069	40	642.8378
11	655.1367	26	642.4165	41	642.8726
12	632.6113	27	643.2091	42	642.8447
13	650.7599	28	642.5752	43	642.8671
14	636.3601	29	643.0825	44	642.8492
15	647.9366	30	642.6767	45	642.8635

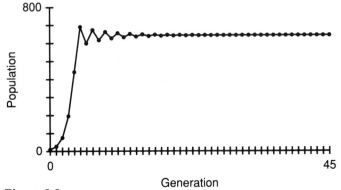

Figure 6.6
The logistic model $p(n + 1) = 2.8(1 - .001p(n))p(n)$

dramatically until it begins to fill the environment, at which point the population levels off.

This model brings up two very important concepts. The first is the idea of an *equilibrium population* or an *equilibrium point*. The second concept is the idea of a *limit*. An equilibrium population is a population that doesn't change. We will denote an equilibrium population by p_*.

The population in this model changes according to the equation

$$p(n+1) = 2.8(1 - .001p(n))p(n).$$

If p_* is an equilibrium population, then if we put p_* into the right side of the change equation in place of $p(n)$, the result will be $p(n+1) = p_*$. In other words an equilibrium population is a solution of the equation

$$p_* = 2.8(1 - .001p_*)p_*.$$

We can solve this equation as follows:

$$p_* = 2.8(1 - .001p_*)p_*$$
$$p_* = 2.8p_* - .0028p_*^2$$
$$0 = 1.8p_* - .0028p_*^2$$
$$0 = p_*(1.8 - .0028p_*)$$

This equation has two solutions:

$$p_* = 0 \quad \text{and} \quad p_* = \frac{1.8}{.0028} = 642.8571$$

So we see that there are two equilibrium populations: 0 and 642.8571. The first equilibrium population, $p_* = 0$, is not particularly interesting. If we start with a population of zero, then (ignoring spontaneous generation and divine intervention) the population will stay zero. The second equilibrium population, $p_* = 642.8571$, is more interesting. This is the level at which resources exactly balance the needs of the species. With the population at this level, the population multiplier is exactly 1, so the population stays constant.

Looking at Table 6.2 and Figure 6.6, we see that the population seems to be approaching the equilibrium level of 642.8571. Notice that the population doesn't rise directly to the equilibrium level and stop. Instead it seems to be bouncing around a bit, tending to get closer and closer to the equilibrium level. This is the second concept brought out by this model: the idea of a limit. I use the word *limit* here in a different way from ordinary English. In ordinary English the word *limit* usually has the following meaning: "1. the final or furthest bound or point as to extent, amount, continuance, procedure, etc. the limit of his experience;

the limit of vision. 2. a boundary or bound, as of a country, tract, district, etc."*

Mathematicians, however, use this word in a different way. This leaves us without a word for the usual meaning of *limit*, so we use the word *bound* instead of *limit* for the meaning above.

The mathematical meaning of *limit* is illustrated by the numbers in Table 6.2. These numbers are getting closer and closer to the number 642.8571. When this happens, we say that the population is approaching the limit, 642.8571.

These two concepts, equilibrium and limit, are quite different. An equilibrium population is a level at which the population remains constant. The population approaches a limit if, as time goes on, the population is getting closer and closer to that limit. We can see the difference between these two concepts by considering another logistic model.

Example

In this model the initial flugel fly population will again be 10. The population will change according to the equation

$$p(n+1) = 3.4(1 - .001p(n))p(n).$$

Table 6.3 and Figure 6.7 show the results of following this model for 30 years.

Notice that this population is not approaching any limit. For the first few years, it rises quickly, but then it starts bouncing around, swinging wildly back and forth between about 450 and 840. There are two equilibrium populations that we can calculate as follows:

$$p_* = 3.4(1 - .001p_*)p_*$$
$$p_* = 3.4p_* - .0034p_*^2$$
$$0 = 2.4p_* - .0034p_*^2$$

So

$$p_* = 0 \quad \text{or} \quad p_* = \frac{2.4}{.0024} = 705.8824.$$

---

* *The Random House Dictionary of the English Language* (New York: Random House, 1967).

Table 6.3
The Logistic Model $p(n+1) = 3.4(1 - .001p(n))p(n)$

Generation	Population	Generation	Population	Generation	Population
0	10.0000				
1	33.6600	11	449.8276	21	452.5124
2	110.5918	12	841.4413	22	842.3328
3	334.4283	13	453.6207	23	451.5481
4	756.7924	14	842.6865	24	842.0182
5	625.7960	15	450.7243	25	452.2800
6	796.1963	16	841.7445	26	842.2575
7	551.7104	17	452.9164	27	451.7232
8	840.9085	18	842.4627	28	842.0758
9	454.8567	19	451.2457	29	452.1461
10	843.0711	20	841.9183	30	842.2140

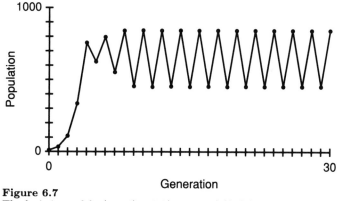

Figure 6.7
The logistic model $p(n+1) = 3.4(1 - .001p(n))p(n)$

Besides illustrating the difference between our two new concepts, an equilibrium point and approaching a limit, this model unveils a surprising possibility for such a simple model. The model appears to be settling down into a pattern with the population oscillating back and forth between roughly 450 and roughly 840. This surprising mathematical behavior is actually seen in the real world. Some populations do exhibit this cyclic behavior. Intuitively, these populations have naturally high birth rates that can result in very large populations. But these very large populations produce famines and shelter shortages, which result in high death rates. Thus, a very large population one year produces a

very small population the following year. The population bounces back
and forth between too large and too small.

Logistic models are very simple, but they demonstrate a rich variety
of behavior. We will discuss these models further in the next section.
Before continuing, it is important for you to explore these models yourself. You should do at least the following exercises. You may want to
experiment with additional logistic models of your own.

Exercises

Write a computer program to compute the first 60 years for each of
the following logistic models. For each exercise, compute the equilibrium
population.

*Exercise 6.2.7

- $p(0) = 10$
- $p(n + 1) = 2.9(1 - .001p(n))p(n)$

Exercise 6.2.8

- $p(0) = 20$
- $p(n + 1) = 2.9(1 - .001p(n))p(n)$

Exercise 6.2.9

- $p(0) = 1$
- $p(n + 1) = 2.9(1 - .001p(n))p(n)$

Exercise 6.2.10

- $p(0) = 10$
- $p(n + 1) = 3.3(1 - .001p(n))$

Exercise 6.2.11

- $p(0) = 20$
- $p(n + 1) = 3.3(1 - .001p(n))p(n)$

Exercise 6.2.12

- $p(0) = 10$
- $p(n + 1) = 3.3(1 - .005p(n))p(n)$

Exercise 6.2.13

- $p(0) = 10$
- $p(n+1) = 3.4(1 - .001p(n))p(n)$

Exercise 6.2.14

- $p(0) = 10$
- $p(n+1) = 3.5(1 - .001p(n))p(n)$

Exercise 6.2.15

- $p(0) = 10$
- $p(n+1) = 3.55(1 - .001p(n))p(n)$

Exercise 6.2.16

- $p(0) = 10$
- $p(n+1) = 3.9(1 - .001p(n))p(n)$

Exercise 6.2.17

- $p(0) = 11$
- $p(n+1) = 3.9(1 - .001p(n))p(n)$

Exercise 6.2.18

- $p(0) = 10.01$
- $p(n+1) = 3.9(1 - .001p(n))p(n)$

Exercise 6.2.19

- $p(0) = 10$
- $p(n+1) = 4.1(1 - .001p(n))p(n)$

Come to the next class meeting prepared to discuss your experiences with logistic models.

6.3 The Surprising Complexities of a Simple Model

In Section 6.2 we looked at an apparently very simple model for population growth called the logistic model. We wanted a model in which the

Table 6.4
The Logistic Model $p(n + 1) = 1.8(1 - .001p(n))p(n)$

Generation	Population	Generation	Population	Generation	Population
0	10.0000	7	321.2843	14	444.4387
1	17.8200	8	392.5092	15	444.4433
2	31.5044	9	429.2023	16	444.4442
3	54.9214	10	440.9778	17	444.4444
4	93.4290	11	443.7295	18	444.4444
5	152.4601	12	444.3005	19	444.4444
6	232.5888	13	444.4156	20	444.4444

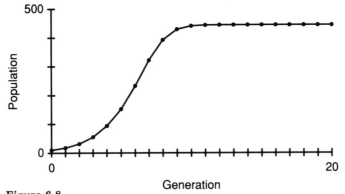

Figure 6.8
The logistic model $p(n + 1) = 1.8(1 - .001p(n))p(n)$

population multiplier depended on the population. The logistic model uses the simplest possible such multiplier—a linear function of the form $R(p) = a(1 - bp)$. If you did the exercises at the end of Section 6.2, you have already discovered that this very simple model can produce some strikingly complex behavior. We begin this section by looking at five of these models illustrating some of this surprising behavior:

- $p(n + 1) = 1.80(1 - .001p(n))p(n)$ Table 6.4 and Figure 6.8.
- $p(n + 1) = 2.80(1 - .001p(n))p(n)$ Table 6.5 and Figure 6.9.
- $p(n + 1) = 3.40(1 - .001p(n))p(n)$ Table 6.6 and Figure 6.10.
- $p(n + 1) = 3.52(1 - .001p(n))p(n)$ Table 6.7 and Figure 6.11.
- $p(n + 1) = 3.55(1 - .001p(n))p(n)$ Table 6.8 and Figure 6.12.

Table 6.5
The Logistic Model $p(n + 1) = 2.8(1 - .001p(n))p(n)$

Generation	Population	Generation	Population	Generation	Population
0	10.0000	11	655.1367	22	641.7799
1	27.7200	12	632.6113	23	643.7157
2	75.4645	13	650.7599	24	642.1683
3	195.3549	14	636.3601	25	643.4069
4	440.1358	15	647.9366	26	642.4165
5	689.9656	16	638.7213	27	643.2091
6	598.9566	17	646.1179	28	642.5752
7	672.5812	18	640.2188	29	643.0825
8	616.6040	19	644.9483	30	642.6767
9	661.9298	20	641.1719	31	643.0014
10	626.5805	21	644.1974	32	642.7417

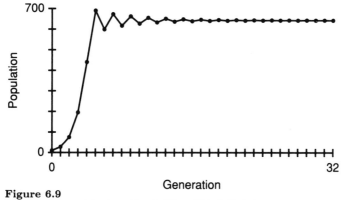

Figure 6.9
The logistic model $p(n + 1) = 2.8(1 - .001p(n))p(n)$

All of these models start with the same initial population, $p(0) = 10$. The only difference among the five models is the value of the constant a.

These models show five very different kinds of behavior. The first model (Table 6.4 and Figure 6.8) is the most straightforward. The population starts out at 10 and rises steadily to the equilibrium population.

The second model (Table 6.5 and Figure 6.9) is somewhat more interesting. Again the population starts out at 10 and starts rising. However, it overshoots the equilibrium population, then undershoots the equilibrium population, then overshoots, and so forth. The population oscil-

Table 6.6
The Logistic Model $p(n+1) = 3.4(1 - .001p(n))p(n)$

Gener-ation	Population	Gener-ation	Population	Gener-ation	Population
0	10.0000	11	449.8276	22	842.3328
1	33.6600	12	841.4413	23	451.5481
2	110.5918	13	453.6207	24	842.0182
3	334.4283	14	842.6865	25	452.2800
4	756.7924	15	450.7243	26	842.2575
5	625.7960	16	841.7445	27	451.7232
6	796.1963	17	452.9164	28	842.0758
7	551.7104	18	842.4627	29	452.1461
8	840.9085	19	451.2457	30	842.2140
9	454.8567	20	841.9183	31	451.8245
10	843.0711	21	452.5124	32	842.1090

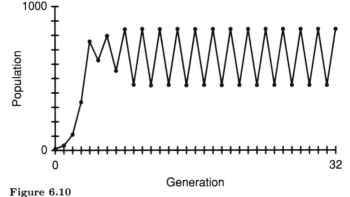

Figure 6.10
The logistic model $p(n+1) = 3.4(1 - .001p(n))p(n)$

lates back and forth, but the oscillations become smaller and smaller and the population approaches the equilibrium population as a limit.

The third model (Table 6.6 and Figure 6.10) is very interesting. It is somewhat similar to the second model, but in this case the oscillations settle down into a pattern, bouncing back and forth between about 840 and about 450. We call this a *2-cycle* because the population repeats the same two numbers over and over again.

The fourth model (Table 6.7 and Figure 6.11) is even more surprising. After a few generations, the population settles into a *4-cycle*, repeating a sequence of four numbers over and over again.

Table 6.7
The Logistic Model $p(n+1) = 3.52(1 - .001p(n))p(n)$

Gener-ation	Population	Gener-ation	Population	Gener-ation	Population
0	10.0000	16	823.8530	32	823.3256
1	34.8480	17	510.8196	33	512.0212
2	118.3903	18	879.5879	34	879.4913
3	367.3967	19	372.8138	35	373.0719
4	818.1056	20	823.0593	36	823.2902
5	523.8071	21	512.6271	37	512.1018
6	878.0049	22	879.4388	38	879.4845
7	377.0352	23	373.2123	39	373.0902
8	826.7764	24	823.4156	40	823.3065
9	504.1246	25	511.8163	41	512.0646
10	879.9401	26	879.5085	42	879.4876
11	371.8722	27	373.0260	43	373.0817
12	822.2131	28	823.2491	44	823.2990
13	514.5491	29	512.1952	45	512.0818
14	879.2549	30	879.4765	46	879.4862
15	373.7033	31	373.1115	47	373.0856

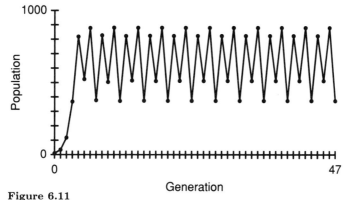

Figure 6.11
The logistic model $p(n+1) = 3.52(1 - .001p(n))p(n)$

The fifth model (Table 6.8 and Figure 6.12) is truly startling. After a few generations it settles into an *8-cycle*, repeating a sequence of eight numbers over and over again.

Our next two models exhibit another kind of strange behavior. Table 6.9 and Figure 6.13, and Table 6.10 and Figure 6.14 look at two models that are almost identical. The population changes from year to year according to the equation $p(n+1) = 3.9(1 - .001p(n))p(n)$. The only

Table 6.8
The Logistic Model $p(n + 1) = 3.55(1 - .001p(n))p(n)$

Gener-ation	Population	Gener-ation	Population	Gener-ation	Population
0	10.0000	16	812.6412	32	812.6528
1	35.1450	17	540.5070	33	540.4813
2	120.3799	18	881.6751	34	881.6825
3	375.9044	19	370.3506	35	370.3306
4	832.8310	20	827.8282	36	827.8098
5	494.2434	21	505.9768	37	506.0197
6	887.3824	22	887.3732	38	887.3714
7	354.7689	23	354.7942	39	354.7992
8	812.6232	24	812.6492	40	812.6544
9	540.5470	25	540.4892	41	540.4777
10	881.6636	26	881.6802	42	881.6835
11	370.3818	27	370.3368	43	370.3278
12	827.8569	28	827.8154	44	827.8072
13	505.9100	29	506.0065	45	506.0257
14	887.3760	30	887.3719	46	887.3711
15	354.7864	31	354.7976	47	354.7999

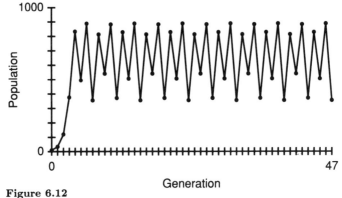

Figure 6.12
The logistic model $p(n + 1) = 3.55(1 - .001p(n))p(n)$

difference between these two models is that the first one starts with an initial population of 10, and the second starts with an initial population of 10.01.

Neither of these two models exhibits any apparent pattern. If you look at the two models together, you will see an even stranger phenomenon. The initial populations of these two models are very close, 10.00 and 10.01. The models start out close to each other but after a few years

Table 6.9
The Logistic Model $p(n+1) = 3.9(1 - .001p(n))p(n)$ $p(0) = 10.00$

Generation	Population	Generation	Population	Generation	Population
0	10.0000	16	966.3652	32	897.1938
1	38.6100	17	126.7636	33	359.7246
2	144.7651	18	431.7089	34	898.2590
3	482.8520	19	956.8117	35	356.4201
4	973.8532	20	161.1600	36	894.6008
5	99.3063	21	527.2312	37	367.7320
6	348.8338	22	972.1080	38	906.7701
7	885.8803	23	105.7447	39	329.6984
8	394.2760	24	368.7949	40	861.8897
9	931.4075	25	907.8623	41	464.2398
10	249.1615	26	326.2284	42	970.0127
11	729.6122	27	857.2334	43	113.4434
12	769.3850	28	477.2989	44	392.2386
13	691.9836	29	972.9902	45	929.7112
14	831.2549	30	102.4932	46	254.8585
15	547.0537	31	358.7544	47	740.6319

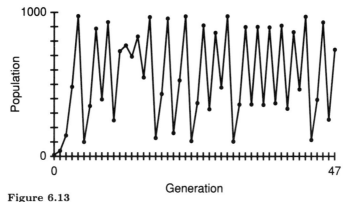

Figure 6.13
The logistic model $p(n+1) = 3.9(1 - .001p(n))p(n)$ $p(0) = 10.00$

look completely different. The word *chaos* is sometimes used to describe this kind of behavior. "Chaos" has two aspects. First, it appears as if there is no pattern and, second, two models that start out close to each other often diverge and become quite different.

So far we have looked at some examples of the strange behavior that can occur with logistic models. When people first noticed this strange behavior, they were quite startled. The logistic model is very simple.

Table 6.10
The Logistic Model $p(n + 1) = 3.9(1 - .001p(n))p(n)$ $p(0) = 10.01$

Generation	Population	Generation	Population	Generation	Population
0	10.0100	16	925.1710	32	157.6234
1	38.6482	17	269.9957	33	517.8351
2	144.9027	18	768.6822	34	973.7594
3	483.2330	19	693.4585	35	99.6528
4	973.9036	20	829.0378	36	349.9161
5	99.1200	21	552.7630	37	887.1519
6	348.2515	22	964.1427	38	390.4424
7	885.1923	23	134.8292	39	928.1888
8	396.3448	24	454.9360	40	259.9519
9	933.0969	25	967.0800	41	750.2699
10	243.4657	26	124.1614	42	730.7234
11	718.3416	27	424.1067	43	767.3903
12	789.0751	28	952.5368	44	696.1596
13	649.0987	29	176.3207	45	824.9336
14	888.3014	30	566.4036	46	563.2309
15	386.9660	31	957.8032	47	959.4072

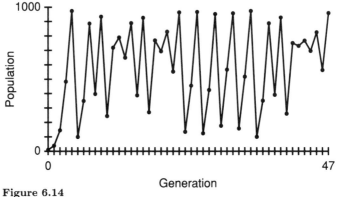

Figure 6.14
The logistic model $p(n + 1) = 3.9(1 - .001p(n))p(n)$ $p(0) = 10.01$

The formula that tells us how to compute $p(n + 1)$ from $p(n)$ is simple, yet these models can exhibit very complicated behavior. One is tempted to say "very unusual behavior." But there are further surprises in store. It turns out that this behavior, far from being unusual, is very common.

This is an active area of current research within mathematics and also in fields like physics and ecology where these models look promising. Research in this area is going on in three directions: the accumulation of experimental evidence by using the computer to simulate models, theoretical work on mathematical phenomena like those observed above, and applications of these models in many different areas. The exercise below asks you to do some research of your own by investigating another mathematical model of population growth. You may also want to design and investigate your own model.

Exercise

Exercise 6.3.20   The purpose of this exercise is to investigate a model that is designed with the same biology in mind as the logistic model. In this model the population multiplier will be the function shown in Figure 6.15. The idea behind this function is that we are looking at an environment in which the effects of crowding will not be felt until the population reaches 500. When the population is over 500, the population multiplier begins to drop off until at a population of 1,500, the multiplier is 0 and the population abruptly dies out.

This population multiplier can be described by:

$$R(p) = \begin{cases} a & \text{if } p \le 500; \\ a\left(\frac{1500-p}{1000}\right) & \text{if } 500 \le p \le 1500; \\ 0 & \text{if } 1500 \le p. \end{cases}$$

For this exercise you should experiment with the model

$$p(n+1) = R(p(n))p(n).$$

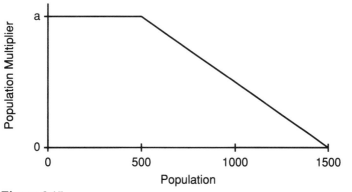

Figure 6.15
Population multiplier

Try using different values of a and different initial populations. You should do a number of different experiments of your own choice, but include among them the following:

- $a = 1.5,\quad p(0) = 10$
- $a = 1.8,\quad p(0) = 10$
- $a = 2.1,\quad p(0) = 10$
- $a = 2.2,\quad p(0) = 10$
- $a = 2.3,\quad p(0) = 10$
- $a = 2.4,\quad p(0) = 10$
- $a = 2.5,\quad p(0) = 10$

You may also want to design your own population multiplier and try some experiments with it.

Logistic models exhibit a large variety of intriguing behavior. In the rest of this section and Section 6.4, we investigate two particular aspects, equilibrium points and 2-cycles, of this behavior in more detail. You have probably noticed from your experiments that the most crucial factor in changing the behavior of these models is the constant a. For this reason we will now concentrate on logistic models of the form

$$p(n + 1) = a(1 - .001p(n))p(n).$$

We will be interested in what happens for different values of the constant a. Another way of writing this model is

$$p(n + 1) = f(p(n))$$

where

$$f(p) = a(1 - .001p)p.$$

We think of the function $f(p)$ as a machine that given the old population, $p(n)$, will compute the new population, $p(n + 1)$. See Figure 6.16.

Notice that $f(p)$ is a quadratic function:

$$f(p) = ap - .001p^2$$

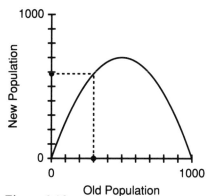

Figure 6.16
The function $f(p)$ computing the new population from the old

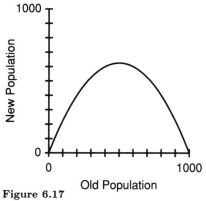

Figure 6.17
$f(p) = 2.5(1 - .001p)p$

The graph of $f(p)$ looks like an upside-down U. Figure 6.17 shows a graph of $f(p) = 2.5p(1 - .001p)$, a typical example of the functions at which we are looking.

Figure 6.18 shows graphs of the function $f(p) = a(1 - .001p)p$ for $a = 0.5, 1.5, 2.5, 3.5, 4.0$. Notice that for $a = 4.0$ the graph just barely fits inside the frame $0 \le f(p) \le 1000$. For this reason we will confine our attention to models in which a is less than or equal to 4.0. If a is bigger than 4.0, it is possible for the population to become larger than 1,000, and then the next population of the generation would be negative. This corresponds to the species dying out—an interesting phenomenon but one that we will not study.

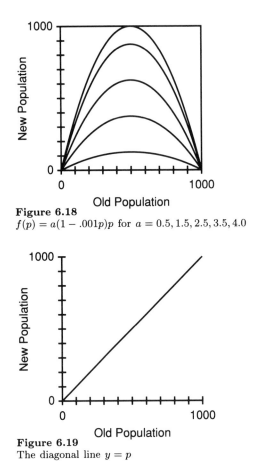

Figure 6.18
$f(p) = a(1 - .001p)p$ for $a = 0.5, 1.5, 2.5, 3.5, 4.0$

Figure 6.19
The diagonal line $y = p$

We will investigate these functions by looking closely at their graphs. The first phenomenon to investigate is equilibrium values. An equilibrium value is a population level that does not change. That is, p_* is an equilibrium value if $f(p_*) = p_*$. Sometimes such a point is called a *fixed point* for the function f. There is a very neat way to visualize fixed points. First, we draw the diagonal line—New Population = Old Population—on the graph. See Figure 6.19.

A point is on this diagonal line if and only if its horizontal and vertical coordinates are the same. The point p_* is a fixed point if and only if $f(p_*) = p_*$—in other words, if the point $(p_*, f(p_*))$ is on the diagonal. Therefore, we can find the fixed points for the function $f(p)$ by looking

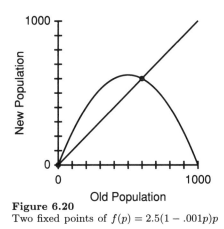

Figure 6.20
Two fixed points of $f(p) = 2.5(1 - .001p)p$

at its graph to see where it crosses the diagonal line. For example (see Figure 6.20), the function $f(p) = 2.5(1 - .001p)$ has two fixed points. They can be calculated by

$$p_* = 2.5(1 - .001p_*)p_*$$
$$p_* = 2.5p_* - .0025p_*^2$$
$$0 = 1.5p_* - .0025p_*^2$$
$$0 = p_*(1.5 - .0025p_*)$$

So

$$p_* = 0 \quad \text{or} \quad p_* = \frac{1.5}{.0025} = 600.$$

Thus, the two fixed points are $p_* = 0$ and $p_* = 600$. These two points are indicated by dots in Figure 6.20. This figure is identical to Figure 6.17 except that we have added the diagonal line—New Population = Old Population—and marked the two fixed points, that is, the two points where the graph of the function $f(p)$ crosses the diagonal line.

Figure 6.21 is the same as Figure 6.18 except that we have added the diagonal line—New Population = Old Population—and marked the nonzero fixed point for each function by a dot. Notice that 0 is always an equilibrium point. For small values of a, 0 is the only equilibrium point. For large values of a, there are two equilibrium points: 0 and a non-0 point.

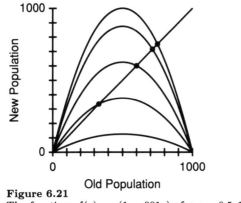

Figure 6.21
The functions $f(p) = a(1 - .001p)p$ for $a = 0.5, 1.5, 2.5, 3.5, 4.0$

Exercises

*__Exercise 6.3.21__ Find a general formula for the nonzero fixed point of
the function $f(p) = a(1 - .001p)p$ in terms of the constant a.

*__Exercise 6.3.22__   Using the formula you obtained in the preceding
exercise can you explain why our models have a nonzero equilibrium
point for "large" values of a but not for "small" values of a?

*__Exercise 6.3.23__   Using the same formula, can you determine the di-
viding line between "large" and "small" values of a?

Now we want to develop an extremely useful graphical method of
visualizing the sequence

$$p(0), p(1), p(2), \ldots$$

We can visualize the calculation of $p(1)$ from $p(0)$ on our graphs as
follows:

- Locate $p(0)$ on the horizontal (or "Old Population") axis.
- Go up vertically to the graph of the function $y = f(p)$ from the point
  $p(0)$ on the horizontal axis. This takes you to the point $(p(0), p(1))$
  since $p(1) = f(p(0))$.

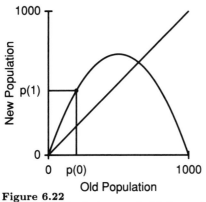

Figure 6.22
A "graphical" calculation of $p(1)$ from $p(0)$

- Move horizontally to the vertical (or "New Population") axis. This takes you to the point $p(1)$ on the vertical axis.

This process is pictured in Figure 6.22. Now suppose that we want to calculate the next year's population, $p(2)$. We can modify the procedure as follows:

- Locate $p(0)$ on the horizontal axis.
- Go up vertically to the graph of the function $f(p)$. This takes you to the point $(p(0), p(1))$ since $p(1) = f(p(0))$.
- Move horizontally to the diagonal line—New Population = Old Population. This takes you to the point $(p(1), p(1))$.
- Move vertically to the graph of the function $f(p)$. This takes you to the point $(p(1), p(2))$ since $p(2) = f(p(1))$.

This process is pictured in Figure 6.23. By repeating the last two steps—going horizontally to the diagonal line and then vertically to the graph of the function $f(p)$—we can "compute"

$$p(3), p(4), p(5), \ldots$$

Figure 6.24 shows a few more steps of this graphical computation.

In the next section we will use these graphical techniques to gain some insight into equilibrium points and 2-cycles.

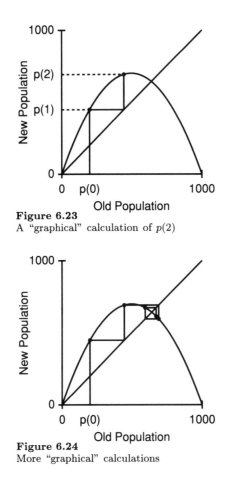

Figure 6.23
A "graphical" calculation of $p(2)$

Figure 6.24
More "graphical" calculations

Exercise

Exercise 6.3.24   Calculate $p(1), p(2), p(3), p(4)$, and $p(5)$ graphically on each of the graphs shown in Figures 6.25 − 6.28.

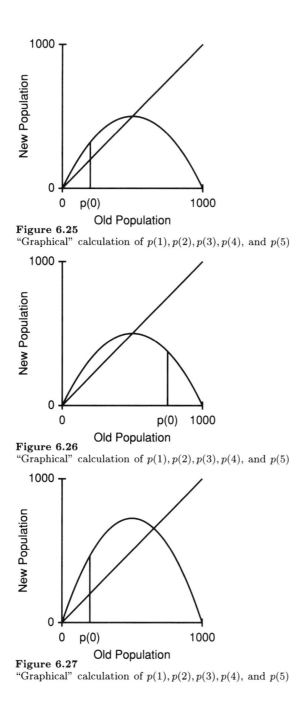

Figure 6.25
"Graphical" calculation of $p(1), p(2), p(3), p(4)$, and $p(5)$

Figure 6.26
"Graphical" calculation of $p(1), p(2), p(3), p(4)$, and $p(5)$

Figure 6.27
"Graphical" calculation of $p(1), p(2), p(3), p(4)$, and $p(5)$

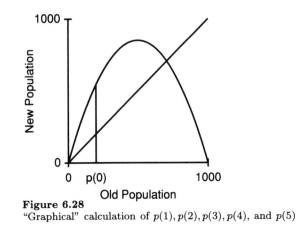

Figure 6.28
"Graphical" calculation of $p(1), p(2), p(3), p(4)$, and $p(5)$

6.4   Equilibrium Points and 2-Cycles

In this section we will continue to explore some of the behavior of logistic models. Since this is not a theoretical mathematics course, we will not prove any general theorems. We will simply look at a number of examples; however, these examples are very typical. The behavior we will see in these examples is not unusual; it is the rule rather than the exception. In the preceding section we discovered that the behavior of a logistic model of the form

$$p(n + 1) = a(1 - .001p(n))p(n)$$

depended strongly on the value of the constant a. Zero is always an equilibrium point for such a model. In the exercises, we discovered that if a is greater than 1, there is a second equilibrium point:

$$p_* = \frac{a - 1}{.001a}.$$

We have seen examples in which the population approached this equilibrium point as a limit and examples in which the population did other things (for example, settle into a 2-cycle) rather than approach a limit. In this section we will use the graphical techniques we developed in the last section to explore these ideas further. We will look at models in which a is greater than 1 so there is a nonzero equilibrium point. We start by looking at the logistic model

$$p(n + 1) = 1.9(1 - .001p(n))p(n).$$

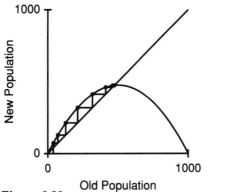

Figure 6.29
The model $p(n+1) = 1.9(1 - .001p(n))p(n)$ $p(0) = 40$

Table 6.11
The Model $p(n+1) = 1.9(1 - .001p(n))p(n)$ $p(0) = 40$

Generation	Population	Generation	Population
0	40.0000		
1	72.9600	6	460.3704
2	128.5100	7	472.0160
3	212.7908	8	473.5121
4	318.2707	9	473.6669
5	412.2515	10	473.6825

Figure 6.29 illustrates the first ten years of this model with an initial population $p(0) = 40$. A quick calculation (see Section 6.2) shows that the nonzero equilibrium point for this model is

$$p_* = \frac{0.9}{.0019} = 473.684.$$

Table 6.11 shows numeric calculations for this same model.

In this model we see that the population moves directly toward the equilibrium point. In fact, a close look at Figure 6.29 will convince you that if we start with any initial population less than the equilibrium population, then the population will approach the equilibrium population directly as a limit.

Figure 6.30 shows the same function but now with a very large initial population, $p(0) = 950$. Notice in this case that the population first

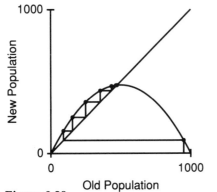

Figure 6.30
The model $p(n+1) = 1.9(1 - .001p(n))p(n)$ $p(0) = 950$

Table 6.12
The Model $p(n+1) = 1.9(1 - .001p(n))p(n)$ $p(0) = 950$

Generation	Population	Generation	Population
0	950.0000		
1	90.2500	6	467.1742
2	155.9994	7	472.9527
3	250.1608	8	473.6100
4	356.4027	9	473.6768
5	435.8217	10	473.6835

drops dramatically and then rises toward the equilibrium population. Table 6.12 shows numeric calculations for this same model.

There are two key points on a graph like Figure 6.29 or Figure 6.30. The first of these key points is the nonzero equilibrium point, in this case the point $p_* = 473.684$. The second key point is the point $p = 500$ at which the function $f(p)$ is at its maximum. When the constant a is less than 2, then the equilibrium point is to the left of the point $p = 500$. When the constant a is greater than 2, then the equilibrium point is to the right of the point $p = 500$. Figure 6.31 illustrates this point. The lower graph is a graph of the function

$$f(p) = 1.9(1 - .001p)p$$

and the upper graph is a graph of the function

$$f(p) = 2.1(1 - .001p)p.$$

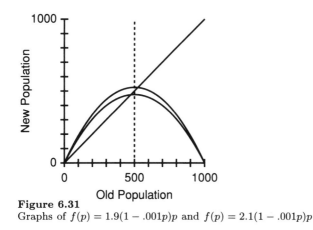

Figure 6.31
Graphs of $f(p) = 1.9(1 - .001p)p$ and $f(p) = 2.1(1 - .001p)p$

We begin by examining the various possibilities for logistic models in which the constant a is less than 2 so that the equilibrium point is to the left of the maximum.

Figure 6.29 is typical of what happens when the initial population is less than the equilibrium and a is less then 2. In this situation the population rises steadily toward the equilibrium. Figure 6.30 is typical of what happens when the initial population is greater than the maximum (when $p(0) > 500$) and a is less 2. In this situation the population at first falls but then rises steadily toward the equilibrium. There is a third possibility: the initial population might be between the equilibrium population and the maximum. To see what happens in this case, we will look at the model

$$p(n + 1) = 1.2(1 - .001p(n))p(n)$$

with $p(0) = 490$. This function behaves exactly the same way as the model

$$p(n + 1) = 1.9(1 - .001p(n))p(n)$$

except that it is easier to see what happens on the graph. Figure 6.32 shows a graph of this example. Table 6.13 shows the results of numeric calculations for the same example.

In this case the population drops steadily toward the equilibrium population. In fact a close look at Figure 6.32 will convince you that with

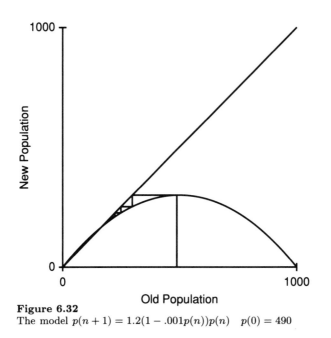

Figure 6.32
The model $p(n + 1) = 1.2(1 - .001p(n))p(n)$ $p(0) = 490$

Table 6.13
The Model $p(n + 1) = 1.2(1 - .001p(n))p(n)$ $p(0) = 490$

Generation	Population	Generation	Population
0	490.0000		
1	299.8800	6	191.3439
2	251.9424	7	185.6777
3	226.1609	8	181.4418
4	210.0146	9	178.2248
5	199.0901	10	175.7529

any initial population between the equilibrium population and the maximum ($p = 500$), the population will drop directly toward the equilibrium population as a limit.

Exercise

Exercise 6.4.25 Look at the function

$$f(p) = 1.9(1 - .001p)p.$$

Let $p(0) = 495$ and calculate $p(1), p(2), \ldots, p(10)$. Notice that the results are similar to Figure 6.32. The population drops steadily toward the equilibrium population.

We have now looked at all the possibilities for a logistic model in which the constant a is less than 2. The population always approaches the equilibrium population more or less directly. Next we want to look at what can happen if a is greater than 2. Figure 6.33 shows what happens for the model

$$p(n + 1) = 2.5(1 - .001p(n))p(n) \quad p(0) = 100,$$

and Table 6.14 shows numeric computations for the same model.

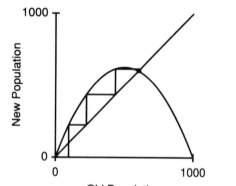

Figure 6.33
The model $p(n + 1) = 2.5(1 - .001p(n))p(n) \quad p(0) = 100$

Table 6.14
The Model $p(n + 1) = 2.5(1 - .001p(n))p(n) \quad p(0) = 100$

Generation	Population	Generation	Population
0	100.0000		
1	225.0000	6	598.0639
2	435.9375	7	600.9587
3	614.7400	8	599.5184
4	592.0868	9	600.2402
5	603.8000	10	599.8797

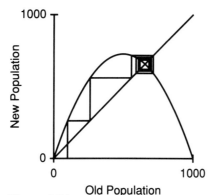

Figure 6.34
The model $p(n+1) = 2.9(1 - .001p(n))p(n)$ $p(0) = 100$

Table 6.15
The Model $p(n+1) = 2.9(1 - .001p(n))p(n)$ $p(0) = 100$

Generation	Population	Generation	Population	Generation	Population
0	100.0000				
1	261.0000	11	678.3062	21	663.2329
2	559.3491	12	632.8001	22	647.7296
3	714.7853	13	673.8560	23	661.7103
4	591.2151	14	637.3448	24	649.1644
5	700.8714	15	670.2955	25	660.4750
6	607.9869	16	640.8983	26	650.3186
7	691.1826	17	667.4282	27	659.4726
8	619.0027	18	643.7066	28	651.2487
9	683.9312	19	665.1104	29	658.6591
10	626.8910	20	645.9418	30	651.9991

Figure 6.34 and Table 6.15 look at the model

$$p(n+1) = 2.9(1 - .001p(n))p(n) \quad p(0) = 100.$$

In these new examples the population overshoots, then undershoots, then overshoots, then undershoots the equilibrium population. It oscillates around the equilibrium population, but it does approach the equilibrium population as a limit. You may want to compare this behavior with some of the graphs in earlier sections.

So far in this section our examples have the population approaching the equilibrium population as a limit. In the case of Figures 6.33 and 6.34, the population approached the equilibrium population in a

rather roundabout fashion, but eventually it did approach the equilibrium population. Notice that as the constant a changed, the behavior of our model changed. When a is between 1 and 2, there is a nonzero equilibrium population and the population always approaches this equilibrium population more or less directly. When a is between 2 and 3, the population approaches the equilibrium population in a roundabout fashion, but it still approaches the equilibrium population.

In the exercises that follow, you will investigate models with a less than 1.

Exercises

Exercise 6.4.26 Consider the model

$$p(n + 1) = 0.95(1 - .001p(n))p(n).$$

- Calculate the population for the first 20 generations starting with an initial population $p(0) = 450$.

- Calculate the population for the first 20 generations starting with an initial population $p(0) = 750$.

- Indicate on Figure 6.35 what happens starting with an initial population $p(0) = 450$.

- Indicate on Figure 6.35 what happens starting with an initial population $p(0) = 750$.

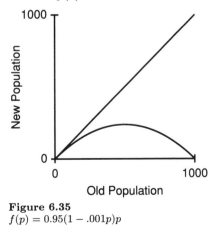

Figure 6.35
$f(p) = 0.95(1 - .001p)p$

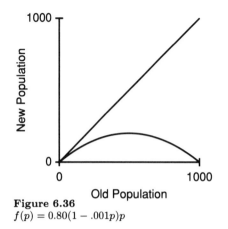

Figure 6.36
$f(p) = 0.80(1 - .001p)p$

Exercise 6.4.27   Repeat the four parts of the preceding exercise for the model

$$p(n + 1) = 0.80(1 - .001p(n))p(n).$$

Use Figure 6.36.

Exercise 6.4.28   Based on your results above, what can you say about logistic models in which the constant a is less than 1?

We now want to make a distinction between two kinds of equilibria. An equilibrium is called *attracting* if the population tends to approach it as a limit. If $a < 1$, then 0 is an attracting equilibrium. If $1.0 < a < 3.0$, then there are two equilibria, 0 and $(a - 1)/(.001a)$ (see Section 6.2); the equilibrium $(a - 1)/(.001a)$ is attracting, and the equilibrium 0 is *not attracting*.

Next we want to look at what might happen when a is bigger than 3. Figure 6.37 and Table 6.16 both examine the model

$$p(n + 1) = 3.1(1 - .001p(n))p(n) \quad p(0) = 100.$$

Figure 6.38 and Table 6.17 both examine the model

$$p(n + 1) = 3.3(1 - .001p(n))p(n) \quad p(0) = 100.$$

These examples exhibit the same kind of behavior; in each the population settles down into a 2-cycle. That is, the population bounces back and

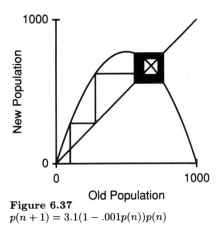

Figure 6.37
$p(n + 1) = 3.1(1 - .001p(n))p(n)$

Table 6.16
$p(n + 1) = 3.1(1 - .001p(n))p(n)$

Generation	Population	Generation	Population	Generation	Population
0	100.0000				
1	279.0000	11	752.2517	21	763.3119
2	623.5929	12	577.7442	22	560.0672
3	727.6469	13	756.2631	23	763.8150
4	614.3484	14	571.4206	24	559.2451
5	734.4658	15	759.1872	25	764.1190
6	604.5800	16	566.7482	26	558.7475
7	741.0954	17	761.1885	27	764.3011
8	594.8064	18	563.5197	28	558.4493
9	747.1364	19	762.4923	29	764.4094
10	585.6631	20	561.4032	30	558.2718

forth between two numbers. We will examine the first model

$$p(n + 1) = 3.1(1 - .001p(n))p(n)$$

in more detail. We will let $f(p)$ be the function

$$f(p) = 3.1p(1 - .001p)$$

so that

$$p(n + 1) = f(p(n))$$

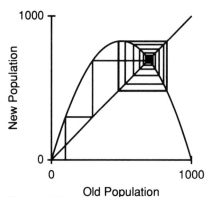

Figure 6.38
$p(n + 1) = 3.3(1 - .001p(n))p(n)$

Table 6.17
$p(n + 1) = 3.3(1 - .001p(n))p(n)$

Generation	Population	Generation	Population	Generation	Population
0	100.0000				
1	297.0000	11	768.9725	21	823.6273
2	689.0103	12	586.2576	22	479.3758
3	707.1079	13	800.4468	23	823.5963
4	683.4509	14	527.1147	24	479.4419
5	713.9410	15	822.5738	25	823.6053
6	673.9565	16	481.6222	26	479.4227
7	725.1391	17	823.8855	27	823.6027
8	657.7308	18	478.8241	28	479.4283
9	742.8993	19	823.5202	29	823.6035
10	630.2998	20	479.6044	30	479.4267

and

$$p(n + 2) = f(p(n + 1)) = f(f(p(n))).$$

We are looking for 2-cycles. Thus we are looking for population levels p such that $f(f(p)) = p$. We could solve the equation $f(f(p)) = p$ algebraically. However, it is just as instructive to look at the graph of the function $y = f(f(p))$ to see where this graph crosses the diagonal. This is exactly analogous to our earlier work in Section 6.3. In that section we examined the graph of

New population $= f$(Old population)

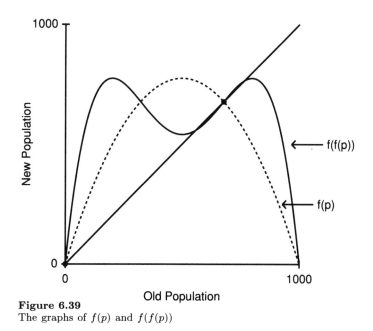

Figure 6.39
The graphs of $f(p)$ and $f(f(p))$

or, better yet,

Next year's population $= f$(This year's population).

The points at which that graph crossed the diagonal were equilibrium populations. Now the points at which

Year after next's population $= f(f$(This year's population))

cross the diagonal are points in a 2-cycle, since for a point in a 2-cycle, we must wait two years (or two generations) to return to the same point.

Figure 6.39 shows both the function $f(p)$ (the dashed line) and the function $f(f(p))$ (the solid line) for the function $f(p) = 3.1(1 - .001p)p$. Notice that there are four points at which the graph of the function $f(f(p))$ crosses the diagonal. The points marked with dots are the same points at which the function $f(p)$ crosses the diagonal. These are the two equilibrium points. The equilibrium points always show up as fixed points of $f(f(p))$. The other two points form a 2-cycle. Figure 6.40 combines Figures 6.37 and 6.39. Notice that the population settles down into a 2-cycle that alternates back and forth between these two points.

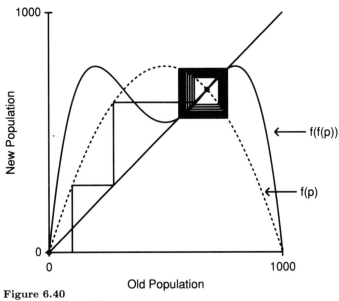

Figure 6.40
The 2-cycle revealed

This is typical behavior. When the constant a is a little bit larger than 3, the population will settle into a 2-cycle. But if a gets even bigger, then we begin to see even more complicated behavior.

This is the end of our work in this section and of our work on logistic models. We have only begun to scratch the surface of these models.*

6.5   Continuous Models

We have been looking at organisms like temperate-zone insects that have very distinct generations. Many organisms do not have distinct generations. At any given moment there may be a mixture of individuals with different ages. At any given moment some individuals are dying and some are being born. For this kind of organism we must describe the population by a function $p(t)$ that gives the population at each time, t. The graph of this function will appear at first glance to be continuous,

---

*If you would like to read more, the following articles are very interesting: Robert M. May, "Simple mathematical models with very complicated dynamics," *Nature,* 261, June 10, 1976, p. 459,and Robert M. May and George F. Oster, "Bifurcations and dynamic complexity in simple ecological models," *The American Naturalist,* 110, July-August 1976: p. 573.

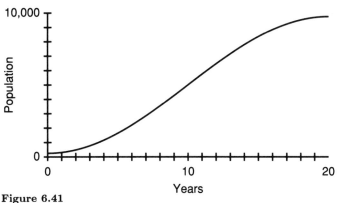

Figure 6.41
A continuously changing population

like Figure 6.41. If we were to examine this graph closely with a high-powered microscope, we would not see a continuous unbroken line. We would see a broken line with many small jumps—one jump each time an individual was born or died.

In Sections 6.1–6.4 we were able to describe the population dynamics using a formula like

$$p(n + 1) = f(p(n))$$

that described the population of each generation in terms of the population of the preceding generation.

In this section we want to model population growth for organisms that do not have a rigid life cycle and distinct generations. Instead of calculating this population for each generation, we will calculate it for a series of times. For example, we might calculate the population each half-year to get a sequence of numbers like

$$p(0), p(0.5), p(1.0), p(1.5), \ldots$$

or we might calculate the population each tenth of a year to get a sequence of numbers like

$$p(0), p(0.1), p(0.2), p(0.3), \ldots$$

How frequently we calculate the population will depend on the organisms and their environment. For example, with human populations the population changes relatively slowly, and it would be quite sufficient under normal circumstances to calculate the population each month. In unusual circumstances, for example, during a plague or a war, it might be necessary to calculate the population more frequently. For bacteria it would be necessary to calculate the population much more frequently. For California redwood trees, it would be sufficient to calculate the population much less frequently.

The models we will examine in this section are called *continuous* models, since we think of the population changing continuously rather than in discrete jumps. Neither our models nor the actual populations change continuously. Both change in discrete jumps. Our models change in discrete jumps because we are calculating the population at a sequence of discrete times. In reality, populations change in jumps because a whole individual is either born or dies at a time.

We will begin each model in this section by choosing a unit of time. This unit will tell us how frequently we will calculate the population. We will call this unit T. It must be small enough so that during each period of time of length T, the population change is relatively small. We will call T the *fundamental unit of time*. Our models in this section will change according to the equation

$$p(t + T) = R(p(t))p(t)$$

where $p(t)$ is the population at time t and $p(t+T)$ is the population one fundamental unit of time later. The function $R(p)$ is analogous to the population multiplier we used in the first four sections of this chapter. However, usually $R(p)$ will be very close to 1 since the population will change relatively little during each fundamental unit of time.

We will begin by looking at continuous logistic models. For these models the function $R(p)$ is a linear function of the form

$$R(p) = a(1 - bp).$$

This is exactly the same kind of population multiplier used for the discrete logistic models in Sections 6.1–6.4, The difference is that for continuous logistic models, the constant a will always be slightly above 1 because the population changes very little during each fundamental unit of time. For this reason we won't see any of the surprising behavior (such as 2-cycles) for continuous models that we saw for discrete models. Notice that if $p = 1/b$, then $R(p) = 0$. Zero is not a realistic value of $R(p)$ for these models because we do not expect such large changes in the population during one fundamental unit of time. In all our models, the population will stay well below $1/b$ so that we do not run into this problem. Now we are ready to look at some examples of continuous models.

Example

In this model the fundamental unit of time, T, will be one-tenth of a year. That is $T = 0.1$ year, so that we will calculate the population at times $t = 0.0, 0.1, 0.2, 0.3, \ldots$

The population multiplier is

$$R(p) = (1.1)(1 - .001p)$$

so that the population changes according to the equation

$$p(t + T) = 1.1(1 - .001p(t))p(t).$$

The initial population will be $p(0) = 10.0$. Table 6.18 shows $p(t)$ for the first two years.

Although we must calculate the population for this model at intervals of 0.10 year, we are really interested in long-term behavior. We would like to see what happens over a period of 10 years. If we printed out

Table 6.18
Two Year Population Record

Time (years)	Population	Time (years)	Population
.0	10.0000		
.1	10.8900	1.1	24.0067
.2	11.8485	1.2	25.7734
.3	12.8790	1.3	27.6200
.4	13.9844	1.4	29.5429
.5	15.1677	1.5	31.5371
.6	16.4314	1.6	33.5968
.7	17.7776	1.7	35.7148
.8	19.2077	1.8	37.8832
.9	20.7227	1.9	40.0929
1.0	22.3226	2.0	42.3340

Table 6.19
Population Record for Ten Years

Time (years)	Population
0.0	10.0000
1.0	22.3226
2.0	42.3340
3.0	64.0882
4.0	79.0974
5.0	86.3681
6.0	89.2666
7.0	90.3288
8.0	90.7058
9.0	90.8381
10.0	90.8843

the results of simulating this model for 10 years, we would have a huge table. We can make the output more manageable by printing out the results after every year. The calculations remain the same. We calculate the population each tenth of a year but print out the results only every year. Table 6.19 gives these results for the first 10 years. Notice the entries for time 0.0, 1.0, and 2.0 agree with the same entries in Table 6.18.

Exercises

Write quick computer programs to simulate the following models.

Exercise 6.5.29   For this model, the fundamental unit of time is .25 year. The population changes according to the equation

$$p(t + T) = 1.05(1 - .0002p(t))p(t)$$

and the initial population $p(0) = 25$. Print out a table giving the population for the first 50 years.

Exercise 6.5.30   This exercise is identical to the first except that the population changes according to the equation

$$p(t + T) = 1.05(1 - .0005p(t))p(t)$$

We can ask the same questions about these models that we asked about the models in Sections 6.1–6.4. For example, we can look for equilibrium populations. Remember that an equilibrium population is a population level p_* that does not change. In other words if $p(t) = p_*$ then $p(t + T)$ will also be equal to p_*. In our example above the population changed according to the equation

$$p(t + T) = 1.1(1 - .001p(t))p(t).$$

We look for an equilibrium population by trying to solve the equation

$$p_* = 1.1(1 - .001p_*)p_*$$
$$p_* = 1.1p_* - .0011p_*^2$$
$$0 = 0.1p_* - .0011p_*^2$$
$$0 = p_*(0.1 - .0011p_*)$$

So

$$p_* = 0 \quad \text{or} \quad p_* = \frac{0.1}{.0011} = 90.9091.$$

and we see that there are two equilibria, 0 and 90.9091. Zero is always an equilibrium population since if we start out with no members of a particular species we will not get any new individuals. (Of course, there are other models, for example models that include immigration, in which new individuals could appear.) However, 90.9091 is a more interesting equilibrium population. Notice from Table 6.19 that in this model the population appears to be approaching this equilibrium population as a limit.

We want to examine when the population is rising and when it is falling. We continue looking at the same example with the population changing according to the equation

$$p(t + T) = 1.1(1 - .001p(t))p(t).$$

It is worthwhile to think of this as

$$p(t + T) = R(p(t))p(t)$$

where $R(p)$ is the population multiplier

$$R(p) = 1.1(1 - .001p).$$

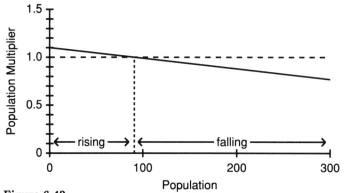

Figure 6.42
The population multiplier function, $R(p)$

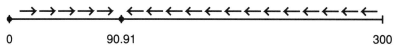

Figure 6.43
Direction in which p will change

The population will rise if $R(p(t))$ is bigger than 1, and it will fall
if $R(p(t))$ is less than 1. If $R(p(t))$ is equal to 1, then $p(t)$ is at an
equilibrium point and will remain there. Figure 6.42 shows a graph of
the population multiplier $R(p)$ with these regions indicated.

We can summarize this information as shown in Figure 6.43. The
equilibrium points are indicated by dots in this figure. Arrows pointing
to the right and left indicate whether p is falling (leftward arrows) or
rising (rightward arrows).

Think of Figure 6.43 as being analogous to the map of a river. Each
point on the graph corresponds to a point in the river and to a possible
value of p. The arrows indicate the direction in which the current is
flowing. Simulating a model with an initial population $p(0) = a$ is
analogous to following a cork after it is placed in the river at the point
a. For example, if $p(0) = 20$, the cork is placed in the river at the spot
indicated on Figure 6.44. The current then carries the cork (analogous
to the population) toward the equilibrium population 90.91. In Figure
6.43 we can see graphically that wherever the cork is put into the river,
it will be carried by the current toward the equilibrium 90.91.

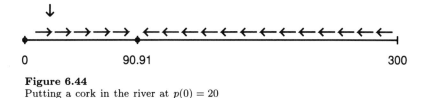

Figure 6.44
Putting a cork in the river at $p(0) = 20$

Exercises

*Exercise 6.5.31   Find the equilibrium populations and draw a figure analogous to Figure 6.43 for the population model

$$p(t + T) = 1.1(1 - .0002p(t))p(t).$$

Exercise 6.5.32   Find the equilibrium populations and draw a figure analogous to Figure 6.43 for the population model

$$p(t + T) = 1.1(1 - .0005p(t))p(t).$$

We could have drawn figures like Figure 6.43 for the models in Sections 6.1–6.4 but they might have been misleading. When we drop a cork in a river, it moves in a continuous way. The models in Sections 6.1–6.4 change in large jumps. Thus, the analogy to a cork in a river is not appropriate.

So far all the models we have considered have had population multipliers that were decreasing. When p was low, the population multiplier $R(p)$ was high. As p increased, $R(p)$ decreased. The motivation behind this is that as the population increases, there is less food, water, and shelter for each individual. Thus, the birth rate falls, the death rate rises, and the population multiplier drops. However, there may be other factors involved. For example, suppose we are considering a species whose members cooperate in some way; perhaps they hunt in packs. In this case if the population were quite low, the individuals might not be as efficient at catching prey for food. Thus, a very low population might result in a low population multiplier. Our next example is a model of this kind.

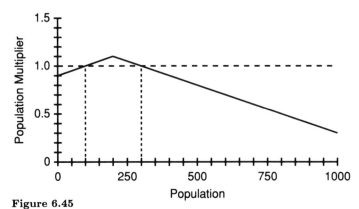

Figure 6.45
A population multiplier for a species that hunts in packs

Example

For this example our fundamental unit of time is .125 year and the population changes according to the equation

$$p(t + T) = R(p(t))p(t)$$

where $R(p)$ is the function

$$R(p) = \begin{cases} 0.9 + .001p, & \text{if } 0 \le p \le 200; \\ 1.3 - .001p, & \text{if } 200 \le p. \end{cases}$$

Figure 6.45 shows a graph of the population multiplier $R(p)$. Note that we calculate $R(p)$ as shown in the following examples.

To calculate $R(50)$, notice that 50 is between 0 and 200, so the first clause of the definition of $R(p)$ applies. Thus,

$$R(50) = 0.9 + (.001)(50) = 0.9 + .05 = 0.95.$$

To calculate $R(320)$, notice that 320 is greater than 200, so the second clause of the definition of $R(p)$ applies. Thus,

$$R(320) = 1.3 - (.001)(320) = 1.3 - .320 = 0.98.$$

Table 6.20 shows the results of simulating this model for 10 years starting with $p(0) = 150$.

Table 6.20
Simulation of Pack Hunter Model with $p(0) = 150$

Year	Population
1	150.000
2	257.977
3	297.040
4	299.827
5	299.990
6	299.999
7	300.000
8	300.000
9	300.000
10	300.000

We can find the equilibrium populations for this model as follows. First, as always, 0 is an equilibrium population. Next we look at Figure 6.45. Notice there are two points at which the graph of the population multiplier $R(p)$ crosses the line $R(p) = 1$. To find the first point, we look at the first clause of the definition of $R(p)$:

$$0.9 + .001p = 1$$
$$.001p = 0.1$$
$$p = \frac{0.1}{.001}$$

$$= 100$$

Thus, the first equilibrium point is at $p = 100$.

To find the second point we look at the second clause of the definition of $R(p)$

$$1.3 - .001p = 1$$
$$-.001p = -0.3$$
$$.001p = 0.3$$
$$p = \frac{0.3}{.001}$$

$$= 300.$$

Therefore there are three equilibrium points: 0, 100, and 300. Figure 6.46 is a "river map" analogous to Figure 6.43. It indicates the flow of

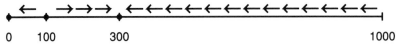

Figure 6.46
Direction of population change for a species that hunts in packs

the current in the river. The direction in which the current flows was
found by examining Figure 6.45. The current flows right (population
increases) when $R(p) > 1$ and flows left (population decreases) when
$R(p) < 1$.

Notice that if the initial population is less than 100, then Figure 6.46
predicts that the population will die out.

Exercises

Exercise 6.5.33 Simulate the model in the preceding the example with
an initial population of 80 for 10 years. Explain your results.

Exercise 6.5.34 Consider the following model.

The fundamental unit of time T is .25 year and the population changes
according to the equation

$$p(t + T) = R(p(t))p(t)$$

where

$$R(p) = \begin{cases} 0.8 + .001p, & \text{if } 0 \le p \le 500; \\ 1.55 - .0005p, & \text{if } 500 < p \le 3100. \end{cases}$$

- Sketch a graph of the function $R(p)$.

- Find the equilibrium populations for this model.

- Sketch a "river map" (analogous to Figures 6.43 and 6.46) for this
  model.

- Simulate this model for 10 years with $p(0) = 180$.

- Simulate this model for 10 years with $p(0) = 220$.

- Simulate this model for 10 years with $p(0) = 1500$.

- Make sure your results match the predictions of your "river map."

- Simulate this model for 10 years with $p(0) = 3000$. What went wrong?

6.6   Two Interacting Species

So far in this chapter we have been considering one single species living alone in its own habitat. In the real world many different species share the same space. They often compete for the same food and water supplies and for the same shelter. In this section and Section 6.7 we will consider models of two species sharing the same habitat.

We will call these two species the Ps and the Qs. The population of each species will be represented by a function. The P population will be represented by the function $p(t)$, and the Q population will be represented by the function $q(t)$. Each species has its own population multiplier function. For the Ps this function will be denoted $R_p(p, q)$, and for the Qs it will be denoted $R_q(p, q)$. Each of the population multipliers depends on *both* populations. This is exactly what we would expect because the two species interact with each other in various ways. For example, they might compete for the same food. The two populations will change according to the equations

$$p(t + T) = R_p(p(t), q(t))p(t)$$
$$q(t + T) = R_q(p(t), q(t))q(t).$$

Two examples of these kinds of equations are given below:

$$p(t + T) = (1.2 - .01p(t) - .001q(t))p(t)$$
$$q(t + T) = (1.1 - .001p(t) - .01q(t))q(t)$$

or

$$p(t + T) = (1.3 - .002p(t) - .01q(t))p(t)$$
$$q(t + T) = (1.2 - .01p(t) - .003q(t))q(t)$$

The population multipliers reflect information about how the two species interact with each other. For example, let's compare the two population multipliers.

$$R_p(p, q) = 1.1 - .01p - .001q$$

and

$$R_q(p, q) = 1.1 - .001p - .01q.$$

We can get some idea of these two functions by making some sample calculations:

$R_p(1, 0) = 1.09$

$R_p(10, 0) = 1.00$

$R_p(100, 0) = 0.1$

$R_p(0, 1) = 1.009$

$R_p(0, 10) = 1.09$

$R_p(0, 100) = 1.00$

Notice that the function $R_p(p, q)$ decreases much more rapidly when p increases than it does when q increases. For example, $R_p(100, 0) = 0.1$ but $R_p(0, 100) = 1.00$. This is because the coefficient of p is $-.01$, while the coefficient of q is $-.001$, which is much closer to 0. We say that $R_p(p, q)$ is *more sensitive* to p than to q.

If we look at the following sample calculations for $R_q(p, q)$, we see exactly the opposite pattern:

$R_q(1, 0) = 1.009$

$R_q(10, 0) = 1.09$

$R_q(100, 0) = 1.00$

$R_q(0, 1) = 1.09$

$R_q(0, 10) = 1.0$

$R_q(0, 100) = 0.1$

The function $R_q(p, q)$ is more sensitive to q than to p. Do the following exercises before continuing.

Exercises

Determine whether each of the following functions is more sensitive to p or to q.

*__Exercise 6.6.35__ $R(p, q) = 1.2 - .005p - .001q$.

*__Exercise 6.6.36__ $R(p, q) = 1.15 - .001p - .002q$.

__Exercise 6.6.37__ $R(p, q) = 1.25 - .005p - .002q$.

Now we want to investigate a particular example.

Example 1

   This example involves two very different species sharing the same habitat. The basic time interval for this model is $T =$ one month. These species have very different life-styles. They compete for some things but not other things. They share the same water supply and eat some of the same foods but seek shelter in different places, and each species has an alternative food supply not used by the other species. The two populations change according to the equations

$$p(t + T) = (1.2 - .005p(t) - .001q(t))p(t)$$
$$q(t + T) = (1.3 - .001p(t) - .006q(t))q(t)$$

   Notice that the population multiplier for the species P,

$$1.2 - .005p - .001q,$$

is more sensitive to p than to q. This corresponds to the fact that each individual of the species P must compete with every other individual of the species P for everything—food, water, and shelter—while each individual of the species P competes with each individual of the species Q only for some things—water and some food. Similarly, the population multiplier for the species Q,

$$1.3 - .001p - .006q,$$

is more sensitive to q than to p.
   This model is an example of two *competitive species*. Competitive species compete for some of the resources of their habitat. They are more sensitive to the effects of crowding from individuals of their own species than from individuals of the other species.
   You may want to write a quick computer program to simulate this model for several generations, trying several different initial populations. Recall $T =$ one month is the basic time interval. You should simulate nine years. Some output from a program that I wrote is given in Tables 6.21 and 6.22.
   Notice that in both of these simulations, the population seems to approach a limiting equilibrium population with $p = 31.0345$ and

Table 6.21
Simulation of Two Competitve Species

Year	Species P	Species Q
0	10.0000	20.0000
1	24.6521	44.9785
2	29.8856	45.1668
3	30.8527	44.8904
4	31.0063	44.8376
5	31.0301	44.8291
6	31.0338	44.8278
7	31.0344	44.8276
8	31.0345	44.8276
9	31.0345	44.8276

Table 6.22
Simulation of Two Competitve Species

Year	Species P	Species Q
0	30.0000	1.0000
1	37.8243	12.9540
2	33.9415	40.5031
3	31.5567	44.5563
4	31.1166	44.7962
5	31.0472	44.8230
6	31.0364	44.8269
7	31.0348	44.8275
8	31.0345	44.8276
9	31.0345	44.8276

$q = 44.8276$. This is the kind of thing that we often see in nature. Different species often do share the same environment.

We would like to visualize the changing population in this kind of situation with two species. For this purpose we will use a graph like those shown in Figures 6.47 and 6.48. These graphs show the results of simulating two models for nine years. Figure 6.47 shows the model with the initial condition $p(0) = 10$ and $q(0) = 20$. Figure 6.48 shows the model with the initial condition $p(0) = 30$ and $q(0) = 1$. Compare these two figures with Tables 6.21 and 6.22.

These figures show the way in which both populations are changing at the same time. Each point on these graph has two coordinates: the "p-coordinate," indicated on the horizontal axis, and the "q-coordinate," indicated on the vertical axis (Figure 6.49). The p-coordinate represents the population of the species P, and the q-coordinate represents the

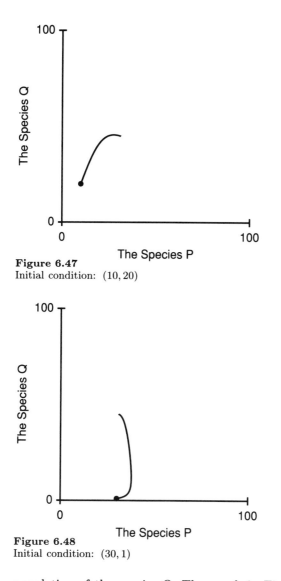

Figure 6.47
Initial condition: $(10, 20)$

Figure 6.48
Initial condition: $(30, 1)$

population of the species Q. The graph in Figure 6.47 represents the same model as Table 6.21. The curve represents the history of the P and Q populations from time $t = 0$ to time $t = 9$. The initial population is $p(0) = 10$ and $q(0) = 20$. This point is indicated by a dot on the curve. Its coordinates are (10, 20). Nine years later the population is

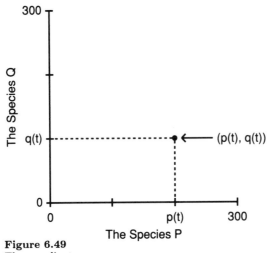

Figure 6.49
The coordinates

$p(9) = 31.0345$ and $q(9) = 44.8276$. This point is the top end of the curve in Figure 6.47. Its coordinates are $(31.0345, 44.8276)$. Figure 6.48 represents graphically the data of Table 6.22.

Now we want to develop a method for finding the equilibrium points for this kind of model. For this model an equilibrium point is a particular value p_* for the P population and a particular value q_* for the Q population such that the following two equations are satisfied:

$$p_* = (1.2 - .005p_* - .001q_*)p_*$$
$$q_* = (1.3 - .001p_* - .006q_*)q_*$$

These two equations will be called the *equilibrium equations*. They say that if $p(t) = p_*$ and $q(t) = q_*$, then $p(t+T)$ will also equal p_* and $q(t+T)$ will equal q_*. That is, once the population reaches the equilibrium point (p_*, q_*) it will stay there.

We can solve the two equilibrium equations as follows. The first equation yields

$$p_* = (1.2 - .005p_* - .001q_*)p_*$$
$$p_* = 1.2p_* - .005p_*^2 - .001p_*q_*$$
$$0 = 0.2p_* - .005p_*^2 - .001p_*q_*$$
$$0 = p_*(0.2 - .005p_* - .001q_*)$$

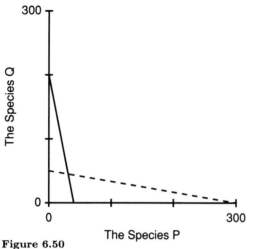

Figure 6.50
Solutions of the equilibrium equations

Therefore,

$$p_* = 0 \quad \text{or} \quad 0.2 - .005p_* - .001q_* = 0.$$

Thus, this first equation is satisfied if and only if the point (p_*, q_*) is located on one of the two lines

$$p_* = 0 \quad \text{and} \quad 0.2 - .005p_* - .001q_* = 0.$$

These two lines are drawn with heavy solid lines in Figure 6.50.

The second equation yields

$$q_* = (1.3 - .001p_* - .006q_*)q_*$$
$$q_* = 1.3q_* - .001p_*q_* - .006q_*^2$$
$$0 = 0.3q_* - .001p_*q_* - .006q_*^2$$
$$0 = q_*(0.3 - .001p_* - .006q_*)$$

Therefore,

$$q_* = 0 \quad \text{or} \quad 0.3 - .001p_* - .006q_* = 0.$$

Thus, the second of the equilibrium equations is satisfied if and only if the point (p_*, q_*) on one of the two lines

$$q_* = 0 \quad \text{and} \quad 0.3 - .001p_* - .006q_* = 0.$$

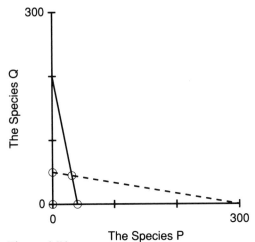

Figure 6.51
Solutions of the equilibrium equations

These two lines are indicated using heavy dashed lines in Figure 6.50.

The equilibrium points are the four points at which a solid line intersects a dashed line. These four points are circled in Figure 6.51. (Figure 6.51 is identical to Figure 6.50 except that these four points have been circled.)

Next we want to calculate the four equilibria shown in Figure 6.51. The first one is easy. It is the point $(0,0)$ $(p_* = 0$ and $q_* = 0)$ where the two axes intersect.

The second equilibrium point is at the intersection of the lines

$$p_* = 0 \quad \text{and} \quad 0.3 - .001p_* - .006q_* = 0.$$

Substituting $p_* = 0$ into the second of these equations we obtain

$$0.3 - .006q_* = 0$$
$$.006q_* = 0.3$$
$$q_* = \frac{0.3}{.006}$$
$$= 50.$$

The second equilibrium point is the point $(0, 50)$.

The third equilibrium point is at the intersection of the lines

$$q_* = 0 \quad \text{and} \quad 0.2 - .005p_* - .001q_*.$$

Substituting $q_* = 0$ into the second equation we get,

$$0.2 - .005p_* = 0$$
$$.005p_* = 0.2$$
$$p_* = \frac{0.2}{.005}$$
$$= 40.$$

The third equilibrium point is the point $(40, 0)$.

The last and most interesting equilibrium point is at the intersection of the two lines

$$0.2 - .005p_* - .001q_* = 0$$
$$0.3 - .001p_* - .006q_* = 0$$

Multiplying the second equation by 5, we obtain

$$1.5 - .005p_* - .030q_* = 0,$$

and subtracting this from the first equation, we obtain

$$-1.3 + .029q_* = 0$$
$$.029q_* = 1.3$$
$$q_* = \frac{1.3}{.029}$$
$$= 44.8276.$$

Substituting $q_* = 44.8276$ into the second equation, we obtain

$$0.3 - .001p_* - .006(44.8276) = 0$$
$$0.3 - .001p_* - .2689656 = 0$$
$$.001p_* = .0310345$$
$$p_* = \frac{.0310345}{.001}$$
$$= 31.0345.$$

Thus, this last equilibrium point is the point $(31, 0345, 44.8276)$.

Both simulations (Tables 6.21 and 6.22) resulted in the population approaching this last equilibrium as a limit.

Notice that in this example we have four equilibria:

- (0, 0): corresponding to no Ps and no Qs.
- (0, 50): corresponding to no Ps but some Qs.
- (40, 0): corresponding to no Qs but some Ps.
- (31.0345, 44.8276): corresponding to some Ps and some Qs.

Both simulations went to this last equilibrium as a limit. At this equilibrium the two species are coexisting. This behavior is very typical of competitive species. In the next section we will develop some graphical techniques for determining which equilibrium is likely to be the limit population, but first we want to investigate another population model. The exercises for this section will ask you to carry out the same kind of analysis for this model that we have just completed for the competitive model.

Example 2

This model describes two very aggressive species called Montagues and Capulets. The basic time interval for this model will be $T =$ three years. Montagues and Capulets are bitter enemies. Whenever a Montague meets a Capulet, they fight. They often injure each other and sometimes even kill one another. At the very least a Montague is a constant irritant to a Capulet, distracting him or her from the necessary business of gathering food. Capulets are a similar distraction for Montagues. These facts are reflected in the equations that describe the way these two populations change,

$$m(t + T) = (1.3 - .001m(t) - .002c(t))m(t)$$

$$c(t + T) = (1.3 - .002m(t) - .001c(t))c(t)$$

where $m(t)$ represents the Montague population at time t and $c(t)$ represents the Capulet population a time t. Notice that the population multiplier for Montagues is more sensitive to Capulets than to Montagues. This is exactly the opposite of what occurred in the competitive model. It is caused by the fact that while Montagues compete with each other for food, shelter, and so forth, they actually fight with Capulets. Similarly, the population multiplier for Capulets is more sensitive to Montagues than to Capulets.

This kind of situation is called two *aggressive species*. Your assignment for this section is to analyze this model.

Exercises

Exercise 6.6.38 Write a computer program to simulate this model. Use it to calculate tables similar to Tables 6.21 and 6.22. Try your program with several different initial populations.

Exercise 6.6.39 Draw a graph similar to Figure 6.51 indicating graphically any equilibrium points.

Exercise 6.6.40 Calculate the four equilibrium points.

Exercise 6.6.41 Based on your work above, what conjectures would you make about this kind of situation?

6.7   Graphical Analysis of Equilibrium Points

Figure 6.52 shows some population models involving the same example of two competitive species examined in the previous section. The populations of the two species in these models all change according to the equations

$$p(t + T) = (1.2 - .005p(t) - .001q(t))q(t)$$
$$q(t + T) = (1.3 - .001p(t) - .006q(t))q(t).$$

The only differences among the different models are the initial conditions. Each curved line in Figure 6.52 represents the record of one model. Such a graphical record for a model of this type is called a *trajectory*. The dot at the beginning of each curved line is placed at the initial point. Notice that all of these trajectories seem to be tending toward the same limit. As you can guess, this limit is the equilibrium population $(31.0345, 44.8276)$.

So far we have looked at two different kinds of two species population models. The first one, modeling the behavior of two competitive species, was worked out in Section 6.6 and is shown in Figure 6.52. The second one, modeling the behavior of two aggressive species, was the assignment at the end of Section 6.6. Figure 6.53 is analogous to Figure 6.52 and shows several trajectories for two aggressive species whose populations

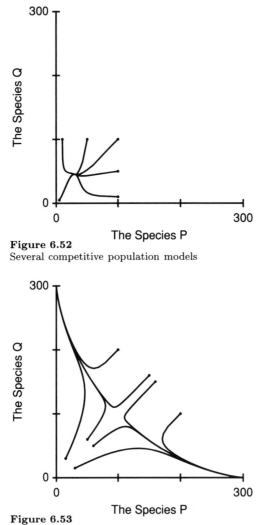

Figure 6.52
Several competitive population models

Figure 6.53
Several aggressive population models

change according to the equations

$$p(t + T) = (1.3 - .001p(t) - .002q(t))p(t)$$
$$q(t + T) = (1.3 - .002p(t) - .001q(t))q(t)$$

Figures 6.52 and 6.53 exhibit different behavior. In Figure 6.52 the population always tends toward the equilibrium point $(31.0345, 44.8276)$

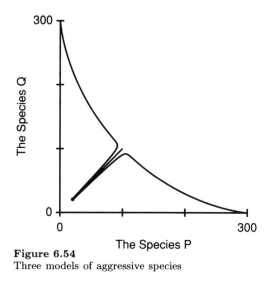

Figure 6.54
Three models of aggressive species

at which the two species coexist. However, in Figure 6.53 (and in your simulations in the exercises at the end of Section 6.6) usually one or the other species dies out. There are exceptions, however. With this particular model, if we start out with the two populations exactly equal, then they will reach an equilibrium at which they both coexist. However, this is a very uneasy (the technical term is *unstable*) equilibrium. If either species acquires the slightest advantage, it will wipe the other species out. Figures 6.54 and 6.55 illustrate this. Figure 6.54 shows three trajectories, with the initial populations $(20, 20)$, $(20, 21)$, and $(21, 20)$. Figure 6.55 shows two trajectories, with the initial populations $(100, 101)$ and $(101, 100)$.

Our goal in this section is to develop some graphical techniques that will help us understand the difference in behavior between the competitive species model and the aggressive species model.

The basic idea is exactly the same as in Section 6.5 where we developed "river" diagrams. You might want to look back at Section 6.5 and particularly Figure 6.43. In Section 6.5 we thought of the population of one species as being represented by a point in a river. For each population we drew an arrow pointing leftward if the population was decreasing and rightward if the population was increasing. These arrows indicated the flow of the "current" in the river. In Figure 6.43 we observed that

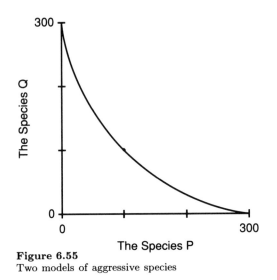

Figure 6.55
Two models of aggressive species

the current was always flowing toward the equilibrium point 90.91. This picture represented graphically the fact that in this model if we start with any initial population, the population will tend toward 90.91 as a limit. We visualized the population change like a cork carried along by the currents in the river.

We will draw a similar picture for our two species models. Instead of a river, we will now think of a lake. Figures 6.52–6.55 can be thought of as maps of a lake. Each trajectory can be thought of as the history of a cork that is dropped into the lake at the point (marked with a dot) that corresponds to the initial population.

We will draw a map of this lake with arrows at each point indicating the direction in which the current is flowing. Figures 6.56 and 6.57 are computer-generated maps of this kind. We will discuss these figures and then show how somewhat cruder but equally useful maps can be developed without computer graphics. Drawings like Figures 6.56 and 6.57 that show the direction in which the "current" is flowing are called *phase diagrams*. If you have a computer capable of nice graphics, an extra project would be the development of a program to generate graphs like Figures 6.56 and 6.57.

Figure 6.56 is a phase diagram for our model of two competitive species. The arrows in this figure indicate the direction in which the current

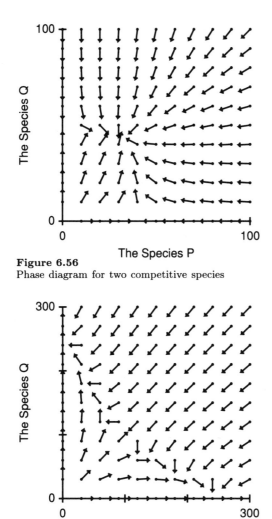

Figure 6.56
Phase diagram for two competitive species

Figure 6.57
Phase diagram for two aggressive species

is flowing. Notice in this figure that the arrows lead generally toward
the central equilibrium point (31.0345, 44.8276). If you compare Figures
6.52 and 6.56 you will see that the population histories shown in Figure
6.52 are being carried by the currents shown in Figure 6.56 toward the
equilibrium point (31.0345, 44.8276).

Figure 6.57 is a phase diagram for our model of two aggressive species. The arrows in this figure indicate a very different situation from Figure 6.56. Here many of the arrows are pointing away from the equilibrium at the center of the picture. Do some experiments with this figure. Try putting the point of a pencil down at various places on the graph and then visualizing how it would be carried by the currents. Then compare your observations with Figures 6.53, 6.54, and 6.55, which show actual population histories. Notice that usually the population is carried by the current to one of the two equilibrium points $(300, 0)$ and $(0, 300)$. Only if the original P and Q populations are exactly equal will the currents carry the population toward the central equilibrium $(100, 100)$.

These phase diagrams depict dramatically what kind of behavior one can expect from competitive species and from aggressive species. Competitive species will tend to coexist. All the arrows are pointing toward the central equilibrium, which corresponds to coexistence. With two aggressive species, one species will usually wipe out the other one. Looking at the currents depicted in Figure 6.57, we can see that unless the initial population of P is exactly equal to that of Q, the population will tend toward one of the equilibria $(0, 300)$ and $(300, 0)$.

Now we want to develop some rough methods for sketching phase diagrams like Figures 6.56 and 6.57. We will use the aggressive species model as an example. For this model the populations change according to the equations

$$p(t + T) = (1.3 - .001p(t) - .002q(t))p(t)$$
$$q(t + T) = (1.3 - .002p(t) - .001q(t))q(t).$$

We will concentrate first on the P population. For species P the population multiplier is the function

$$R_p(p, q) = 1.3 - .001p - .002q.$$

We want to find out three things.

1. For what values of p and q is $R_p(p, q) = 1$? In other words, for what values of p and q will the P population remain unchanged during the next unit of time?

2. For what values of p and q is $R_p(p, q) < 1$? In other words, for what values of p and q will the P population decrease during the next unit of time?

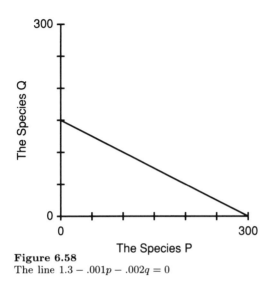

Figure 6.58
The line $1.3 - .001p - .002q = 0$

3. For what values of p and q is $R_p p, q) > 1$? In other words, for what values of p and q will the P population increase during the next unit of time?

We can answer the first question by graphing the equation

$1.3 - .001p - .002q = 1$

$0.3 - .001p - .002q = 0.$

This is the equation of a straight line. When $p = 0$ we get

$0.3 - .002q = 0$

$$q = \frac{0.3}{.002}$$

$$= 150.$$

This straight line intersects the q-axis at $(0, 150)$.

When $q = 0$ we get

$0.3 - .001p = 0$

$$p = \frac{0.3}{.001}$$

$$= 300.$$

This straight line intersects the p-axis at the point $(300, 0)$. This straight line is shown in Figure 6.58. Table 6.23 gives some sample calculations for $R_p(p, q)$.

Table 6.23
Sample Values of $R_p(p, q)$

p	q	$R_p(p, q)$	p	q	$R_p(p, q)$
0	0	1.30	150	0	1.15
0	50	1.20	150	50	1.05
0	100	1.10	150	100	.95
0	150	1.00	150	150	.85
0	200	.90	150	200	.75
0	250	.80	150	250	.65
50	0	1.25	200	0	1.10
50	50	1.15	200	50	1.00
50	100	1.05	200	100	.90
50	150	.95	200	150	.80
50	200	.85	200	200	.70
50	250	.75	200	250	.60
100	0	1.20	250	0	1.05
100	50	1.10	250	50	.95
100	100	1.00	250	100	.85
100	150	.90	250	150	.75
100	200	.80	250	200	.65
100	250	.70	250	250	.55

Notice that as p and q increase, the population multiplier $R_p(p, q)$ goes down. Thus if (p, q) is above the line

$$1.3 - .001p - .002q = 1,$$

then $R_p(p, q)$ is less than 1. This means that the population of P will be going down. We indicate this by drawing arrows pointing to the left since this is the direction of decreasing p. Similarly, if (p, q) is below the line

$$1.3 - .001p - .002q = 1,$$

then $R_p(p, q)$ is greater than 1, and the population of P will be rising. We indicate this with arrows pointing to the right since this is the direction of increasing p. In Figure 6.59 we have added arrows to Figure 6.58 to indicate the direction in which the P population is going.

Next we want to consider the Q population. The Q population multiplier is

$$R_q(p, q) = 1.3 - .002p - .001q.$$

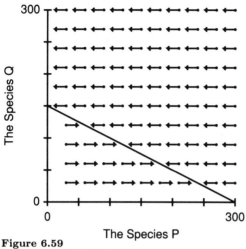

Figure 6.59
Direction in which p is changing

Again, we want to determine three things:

1. For what values of p and q will the Q population remain unchanged during the next unit of time?

2. For what values of p and q will the Q population decrease over the next unit of time?

3. For what values of p and q will the Q population increase over the next unit of time?

   We can answer the first question by graphing the equation

$$1.3 - .002p - .001p = 1$$
$$0.3 - .002p - .001p = 0.$$

This is the equation of a straight line that intersects the p-axis at the point $(150, 0)$ and the q-axis at the point $(0, 300)$. Its graph is shown in Figure 6.60.

Arrows have been placed on Figure 6.60 to indicate the direction in which the Q population is changing. These arrows are analogous to those in Figure 6.59. The arrows below the line—$1.3 - .002p - .001q = 1$— are pointing up since for (p, q) in this region, the Q population will rise during the next unit of time. The arrows above the line—$1.3 - .002p - .001q$—are pointing down since the Q population will fall during

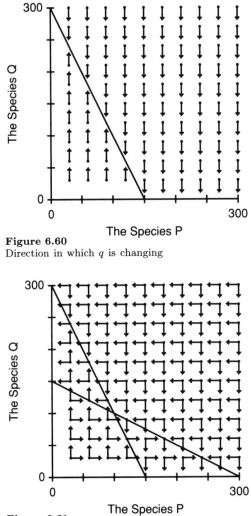

Figure 6.60
Direction in which q is changing

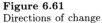

Figure 6.61
Directions of change

the next unit of time. Figures 6.59 and 6.60 can be superimposed to
produce Figure 6.61.

Notice that the two lines

$$1.3 - .001p - .002q = 1 \quad \text{and} \quad 1.3 - .002p - .001q = 1$$

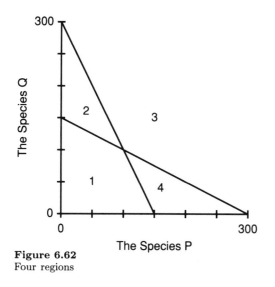

Figure 6.62
Four regions

have divided the graph into four regions, labeled 1, 2, 3, and 4 in Figure 6.62:

- In region 1 the arrows are pointing up and to the right.
- In region 2 the arrows are pointing up and to the left.
- In region 3 the arrows are pointing down and to the left.
- In region 4 the arrows are pointing down and to the right.

These directions are indicated in Figure 6.63. Figure 6.63 is the crude phase diagram that we have been trying to produce. It is not as precise as the computer-generated phase diagrams in Figure 6.56 and 6.57, but it does capture the essence of those diagrams. We can see that the central equilibrium is unstable and that most often the population will tend toward one of the equilibria $(0, 300)$ and $(300, 0)$.

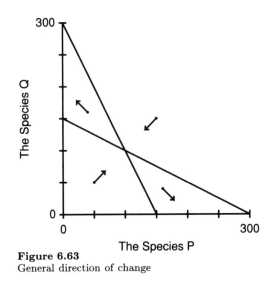

Figure 6.63
General direction of change

Exercises

For each of the following models, draw a crude phase diagram using the methods of this section. Check your work by comparing the predictions made from your phase diagram with the results of computer simulations of these models. You can probably use your program from Section 6.6 with slight modifications.

Exercise 6.7.42

$$p(t + T) = (1.2 - .005p(t) - .001q(t))p(t)$$
$$q(t + T) = (1.3 - .001p(t) - .006q(t))q(t)$$

(This is the competitive species model from Section 6.5.)

Exercise 6.7.43

$$p(t + T) = (1.2 - .004p(t) - .002q(t))p(t)$$
$$q(t + T) = (1.3 - .001p(t) - .002q(t))q(t)$$

A A Brief True BASIC Reference Manual

True BASIC is a powerful and flexible language. It deserves an entire book of its own, and, in fact, there are several excellent books on the market. One such book is the *True BASIC Reference Manual* published by True BASIC, Inc. This appendix should suffice as a brief reference manual for this course, but if you continue to use True BASIC, you will certainly want to take advantage of the many features not covered in this brief introduction.

A.1 The Basics

A.1.1 Constants

True BASIC works with two different kinds of data: numeric and alphabetic data. A piece of numeric datum, or a *number*, can be written with the usual decimal notation. For example,

```
123
4.12
-34
-.123
```

are all valid numbers. True BASIC does not accept commas or dollar signs as part of a number.

Numbers can also be written in True BASIC using a variant of scientific notation. Scientific notation was designed to make it easier to represent very small or very large numbers. Numbers written in scientific notation are written with a power of 10. For example, 1.23×10^6 represents the number 1,230,000. In True BASIC one would write the same number as follows

```
1.23E6
```

or

```
1.23e+06
```

Either a capital or lowercase E can be used, and the power of 10 following the E may or may not have a plus sign (of course, if the power of 10 is negative, the minus sign must be included) and may or may not have leading zeroes.

Alphabetic data are represented in True BASIC by a *string*. A string uses all the ordinary letters (both capital and lowercase) and symbols. A string constant is always enclosed by quotation marks—for example,

```
"This is a string"
"Hello, world"
```

A.1.2 Variables

A *variable* is a small unit of the computer's RAM or memory that can hold either numeric or alphabetic data. Each variable has a name. There are two kinds of variables corresponding to the two kinds of data. The name of a numeric variable must begin with a letter. It may not have any spaces, but it may have numbers and the "underscore" character. The following are all valid names for variables:

```
x
Joe_Smith
p3
```

The name of a string variable (a variable that can contain alphabetic data) is exactly the same as the name of a numeric variable except that a dollar sign ($) is added to the end. The following are all valid names for string variables:

```
Name$
Joe$
x$
Joe_Smith$
```

A.1.3 Arrays

An array is a way of organizing information or variables. It may contain alphabetic or numeric information. In fact, an array is just an organized group of variables. Any valid name for a numeric variable may be used as a name for an array of numeric variables. Any valid name for an alphabetic (or string) variable may be used as the name of an array of string variables. Before using an array, it must be declared so that True BASIC knows how much information is involved and how it is organized. This is accomplished by means of a "Dimension," or `DIM` statement. True BASIC recognizes both one-dimensional and many-dimensional arrays. A one-dimensional array is declared by means of a statement like

```
DIM count(14)
```

which declares a group of 14 variables that can be referred to as

```
count(1), count(2), ..., count(14)
```

or by a statement like

```
DIM count (5 to 15)
```

which declares a group of 11 variables that can be referred to as

```
count(5), count(6), ..., count(15).
```

More generally, a DIM statement of the form

```
DIM count(firstnumber to lastnumber)
```

declares a group of (lastnumber - firstnumber + 1) variables that can be referred to as

```
count(firstnumber), ..., count(lastnumber).
```

A DIM statement of the form

```
DIM count(lastnumber)
```

is exactly the same as

```
DIM count (1 to lastnumber)
```

True BASIC also recognizes arrays that have several dimensions. For example, the statement

```
DIM count(3, 5)
```

declares an array that has three rows, each with five columns. The elements of this array are referred to as count(1,1), count(1,2), ..., count(1,5), count(2,1), ..., count(3,5). The total size of an array is limited by the amount of memory (RAM) available.

A.1.4   The LET Statement

The LET statement places information into a variable. It consists of four elements

1. The word LET.

2. The name of the variable into which the information will be placed.

3. An equal sign (=).

4. The information to be placed into the variable.

The following are all valid LET statements:

```
LET name$ = "George Jones"
LET age = 21
LET net_salary = salary - tax
```

The variable must be the appropriate type for the information on the right side of the equal sign. Numeric information can only be put into a numeric variable, and alphabetic information (a string) can only be put into a string variable. The information on the right side of the equal sign can be a simple constant (like 12.34 or "Joe"), another variable, or a more complex expression. If the information on the right side of the equal sign is another variable, then the information will be read from the variable on the right and copied into the variable on the left. After the LET statement is executed, the same information will be in both variables. This is an example of a general principle—information may be read any number of times from a variable without destroying the information; however, writing information into a variable causes any old information that had been in the variable to be lost.

A.1.5 Expressions

True BASIC recognizes three kinds of expressions: numeric or "arithmetic" expressions, logical expressions, and string or "alphabetic" expressions. (We will discuss logical expressions later under the section on IF...THEN...ELSE statements.)

A numeric expression uses the usual algebraic symbols "+", "−", and "/" for addition, subtraction and division. It uses the symbols "*" for multiplication and "^" for exponentiation. The usual conventions for the use of parentheses are followed. The following are valid numeric expressions:

```
x * y - 14
(high - low)/2
2*x^2
```

Just as numeric expressions are used to express computations involving numbers, string expressions are used to express computations involving alphabetic information—for example,

```
LET Formal_Name$ = "Mr. " & Last_Name$
LET Full_Name$ = First$ & " " & Middle$ & " " & Last$
```

The symbol "&" is used in an alphabetic expression for concatenation. For example, the expression `"Joe" & "Smith"` will produce the result `"JoeSmith"`. One can also extract part of a string by an expression like the one on the right in the following statement:

```
Let Title$ = Name$[1:3]
```

This statement extracts the first three letters from the string in the variable `Name$` and puts them into the variable `Title$`. More generally, the expression `stringname$[i:j]` extracts the part of the string in the variable `stringname$` starting with the ith position and continuing up through the jth position. For example, the result of the code

```
LET Bill$ = "123456789Arnold"
LET One$ = Bill$[3:6]
LET Two$ = Bill$[9:11]
```

would be to put the string `"3456"` into the variable `One$` and the string `"9Ar"` into the variable `two$`.

A.2   Reading and Writing in True BASIC

A.2.1   The INPUT Statement

One way that a person can enter information into the computer is by typing it at the keyboard. The True BASIC `INPUT` statement is used to read information from the keyboard. We will see later on that it can also be used to read information from a disk file. The `INPUT` statement has two elements:

1. The word `INPUT`.

2. A list of variables separated by commas.

When True BASIC executes this statement, it will pause and display a flashing question mark on the screen indicating that it is waiting for the user to type information. The user must type one constant or piece of information for each variable in the variable list. The variable names in the variable list are separated by commas, and the user must separate the items typed in by commas. Numeric information is typed in exactly the same way that a numeric constant is written—for example,

```
12345
12.345
-34.78
```

Notice in particular the first number above, "12345." The most natural way for an english-speaking human to type this number would have been "12,345." However, a numeric item may not contain a comma. True BASIC uses commas to separate items in lists and would interpret

```
12,345
```

as a list of two numbers, "12" and "345."

Generally alphabetic information may be typed in with or without surrounding quotation marks—for example,

```
George
```

and

```
"George"
```

are both perfectly good ways of typing the string `"George"`. However, there are some differences. True BASIC would interpret the input

```
Smith, Susan
```

as two strings `"Smith"` and `"Susan"` because of the comma. If one wants to enter the single string `"Smith, Susan"` one should type

```
"Smith, Susan"
```

In addition, True BASIC will ignore spaces at the beginning or the end of a string that is not enclosed in quotes.

A.2.2   The PRINT Statement

The `PRINT` statement displays information on the computer screen. We will see later that it can also be used to write information into a disk file. The True BASIC `PRINT` statement is an extremely powerful and flexible statement. For example, it can be used to print a numeric item using the usual format for dollars and cents, for example, 12345.67 can be `PRINT`ed as $12,345.67. The simplest `PRINT` statement consists of two elements:

1. The word `PRINT`.

2. A list of items to be printed. Each item can be a numeric or string
   variable or constant or a more complicated numeric or string expression. The items are usually separated by commas—for example,

```
PRINT "The total is", Total
PRINT a, b, c
PRINT "Average",(a + b + c)/3
```

Even this simple statement has several options. Most often one sepa-
rates items in the list by commas; however, one can also separate them
by semicolons. If two items are separated by a comma, then True BA-
SIC will place a tab between them so they are separated by some space.
If two items are separated by a semicolon, then True BASIC will print
the two items side by side with no intervening space. Usually there is no
punctuation after the last item in the list. When True BASIC prints a
list in which the last item has no following punctuation, then it will automatically print a "carriage return" following the last item so that any
subsequent output will appear on a new line. If the last item is followed
by a semicolon, then the carriage return is omitted, and any subsequent
printing will appear on the same line. If the last item is followed by a
comma, then the carriage return is replaced by a tab and subsequent
information will appear on the same line with an intervening tab. In
every case True BASIC will automatically print on the next line once a
line is full.

True BASIC also has an extremely powerful method, the PRINT US-
ING statement, of producing nicely formatted output. A PRINT USING
statement has the following elements:

- The words "PRINT USING".

- A string, which may be either a string constant or a string variable.
  This string is called a *format string* and serves as a template for the
  output.

- A colon (:).

- A list of items to be printed. In a PRINT USING statement the items in
  this list must be separated by commas. The last item may be followed
  by a semicolon or not. If a semicolon is present, True BASIC will not
  perform an automatic carriage return. If a semicolon is not present,

True BASIC will perform an automatic carriage return so that any subsequent output will appear on a new line.

The new element involved in a PRINT USING statement is the format string. The format string describes precisely how the output, both numeric and alphabetic output, should appear. The format string is made up of pieces that specify how each item will be formatted and any information that might appear between items. We will call each piece a *subtemplate*. A subtemplate for printing numeric data uses the symbols "#", ".", ",", "^" and "$". Each # indicates a position in the printed output that can be occupied by a digit of the output or by a minus sign. The decimal point indicates where the decimal point should appear in the output. For example, the statement

```
PRINT USING "##.###":12.3456
```

will print

```
12.346
```

Notice that each of the # symbols in the format string has been replaced by one digit of the output. Notice also that the output was rounded off to fit into the space indicated by the template. Commas in the template show up as commas in the output. In the United States we usually write large numbers with commas separating each group of three digits to the left of the decimal point. For example, the code

```
PRINT USING "##,###,###,###.##":12345678901.23
```

will produce

```
12,345,678,901.23
```

If an item does not need all the space indicated by a template blanks will be used to fill the unneeded space on the left. True BASIC will not print any unnecessary commas. The symbol "$" is used to indicate that the item should be preceded by a dollar sign. For example, the code

```
PRINT USING "$##,###.##":12345.678
```

produces the output

```
$12,345.68
```

The symbols "^^^^" indicate that the number should be printed using True BASIC's version of scientific notation. This part of the template is replaced by the "power of 10" part of the output. For example, the code

```
PRINT USING "#.###^^^^":123456789
```

produces the output

```
1.235e+08
```

The subtemplate for an alphabetic or string item uses the symbols "#", "<" and >". Each # is replaced by one character of the string. The symbols "<" and ">" are optional. They indicate to True BASIC how to justify the string if the item to be printed does not fill up the allotted space. If the subtemplate begins with the symbol "<", then the item will be left justified. If the subtemplate begins with the symbol ">", then the item will be right justified. If neither symbol is present the item will be printed in the center of the allotted space.

Between the subtemplates that indicate how each item is to be formatted, one can use either space or text. Text will be printed verbatim, as will space. This is helpful both for labeling output and for producing nicely spaced output.

A.3 IF...THEN...ELSE

Sometimes a program must make a decision and perform one of several different possible actions on the basis of such a decision. This kind of situation is often called *branching*. True BASIC uses the construction IF...THEN...ELSE to express branching. The simplest such construction has the following elements (the first three elements are written on one line):

- The word IF.
- A condition that will determine which of two possible actions should be taken. This condition is a logical expression—for example, the expression

  Salary $<$ 20000
- The word THEN
- The first possible action—the one to be taken if the condition is met. This might be a single line of code or several lines of code.
- The word ELSE all by itself on one line.

- The second possible action—the one to be taken if the condition is not met. This might be a single line of code or several lines of code.
- The words END IF all by themselves on one line.

The condition is most often a numeric condition and is expressed using the usual arithmetic expressions plus the symbols "=", "<" and ">" used in the usual way to express equality, less than, and greater than. For example, the code

```
IF age < 21 THEN
    PRINT "Sorry, you are not eligible to vote."
    PRINT "You must be at least 21 to vote."
ELSE
    PRINT "You are eligible to vote."
END IF
```

will print the message, "Sorry, you are not eligible to vote. You must be at least 21 to vote." if age is less than 21 and the message "You are eligible to vote" otherwise.

In addition to these familiar symbols, the two symbol sequences "<>", "<=" and ">=" are used to express "unequal," "less than or equal to," and "greater than or equal to," respectively. More complicated expressions can be formed using the words "NOT", "AND", and "OR" in the usual way. An expression of this sort is frequently called a *logical expression*. A logical expression can involve both numbers and strings. For example, the expression

a$ < b$

checks whether a$ is before b$ in the usual alphabetic order. In the system used by True BASIC, all capital letters come before lowercase letters. Thus, for example, the string "Z" is less than the string "a".

The basic IF...THEN...ELSE statement has many variations. For example, if there are three or more possible actions, one can use a construction like

```
IF score < 60 THEN
    PRINT "Grade is E"
  ELSE IF score < 70 THEN
    PRINT "Grade is D"
```

```
    ELSE IF score < 80 THEN
      PRINT "Grade is C"
    ELSE IF score < 90 THEN
      PRINT "Grade is B"
    ELSE
      PRINT "Grade is A"
END IF
```

One can even have branches inside branches—for example,

```
IF age < 65 THEN
   IF salary < 3000 THEN
        PRINT "No tax"
      ELSE
        PRINT USING "Tax = $##,###.##": 0.05 * (salary - 3000)
   END IF
 ELSE
   IF salary < 2000 THEN
        PRINT "No tax"
      ELSE
        PRINT USING "Tax = $##,###.##": 0.05 * (salary - 2000)
   END IF
END IF
```

A.4 Loops

Often one would like to repeat a portion of a program several times. This is called a *loop*. True BASIC provides two ways of doing this: "FOR...NEXT" loops and "DO" loops.

A.4.1 FOR...NEXT Loops

A FOR...NEXT loop uses an "index" or "counting" variable to keep count of how many times the loop has been executed. The value of this variable changes as the loop is executed. A FOR...NEXT loop always has three elements:

1. A FOR statement describing how many times the following block of code should be executed.

2. A block of code to be executed one or more (usually more) times.

3. A NEXT statement indicating the end of the block of code in the loop.

The simplest kind of FOR statement looks like

```
FOR i = 1 TO 100
```

This statement will execute the following block of code (all the code up to the matching NEXT statement) 100 times using the index variable i to monitor the execution of the loop. The first time the loop is executed, i will be 1. The second time it will be 2, the third time 3, and the last time i will be 100. This statement allows two variations. First, the index variable can start with a number other than 1, for example,

```
FOR i = 5 to 25
FOR i = -5 to 5
```

are both valid FOR statements. True BASIC also provides the possibility of incrementing the index variable by something other than 1. For example, the statement

```
FOR x = -4 to 4 step 0.5
```

will cause the following block of code to be executed 17 times for $x = -4, -3.5, -3.0, \ldots, 3.5, 4$.

This option should be used very cautiously because it can sometimes produce surprising and unwanted results. The difficulty arises from the fact that the index variable, like any other variable, is allocated only a finite amount of space. Hence, round-off error can produce undesired results. For example, the code

```
For x = 0 TO 1 STEP 1/9
PRINT x
NEXT x
```

might be expected to produce the output

```
0
 .111111
 .222222
 .333333
 .444444
 .555556
```

```
 .666667
 .777778
 .888889
1.000000
```

However, it actually produces

```
0
 .111111
 .222222
 .333333
 .444444
 .555556
 .666667
 .777778
 .888889
```

The reason for this unexpected behavior is that the last time we expected the loop to be executed, the value of the index variable x was actually slightly bigger than 1. Hence, True BASIC did not execute the loop that one last time.

The NEXT statement at the end of the block of code to be repeated has two elements:

1. The word NEXT.

2. The name of the index variable.

For example, the following code might ease an errant student's punishment by printing "I will not talk in Mr. Jones' class." 500 times:

```
FOR i = 1 to 500
PRINT i; "I will not talk in Mr. Smith's Class"
NEXT i
```

FOR. . .NEXT loops may be used inside FOR. . .NEXT loops. In fact, this is very common. For example, the following code would print 10 lines, each with 30 stars.

```
FOR line = 1 to 10
   FOR column = 1 to 50
   PRINT "*";
```

```
    NEXT column
PRINT                          ! carriage return
NEXT line
```

A.4.2 DO Loops

Like a FOR...NEXT loop a DO loop has three elements:

1. A DO WHILE statement that marks the beginning of a block of code to be repeated and describes how often it is to be repeated.

2. A block of code to be repeated.

3. A LOOP statement that marks the end of the block of code to be repeated.

The DO WHILE statement has two elements:

1. The words DO WHILE.

2. A condition. This condition can be any logical expression. The following block of code will be repeated as long as (while) this logical expression is true.

For example, the code

```
PRINT "What is the sum of 3 and 4?"
INPUT answer
DO WHILE (answer <> 7)
   PRINT "Your answer is incorrect.  Please try again."
   INPUT answer
LOOP
PRINT "That's right."
```

would pose a simple arithmetic problem and ask for the answer. It would keep asking for the answer until the user supplied the correct one. Notice that if the user supplies the correct answer on the first try the block of code within the DO loop will never be executed. True BASIC also recognizes another kind of DO loop that begins with the statement DO UNTIL instead of DO WHILE. It behaves exactly as expected. That is, it repeats the following block of code until the condition is true. For example, the following code accomplishes exactly the same purpose as the preceding code:

```
PRINT "What is the sum of 3 and 4?"
INPUT answer
DO UNTIL (answer = 7)
   PRINT "Your answer is incorrect.  Please try again."
   INPUT answer
LOOP
PRINT "That's right."
```

It is perfectly permissible—indeed, quite common—to have DO loops inside of FOR...NEXT loops, or vice versa, or DO loops inside of DO loops, or FOR...NEXT loops inside of FOR...NEXT loops.

A.5 Functions and Subroutines

A.5.1 Built-in Functions

True BASIC includes a number of built-in functions for many common tasks. Each function accepts one or more pieces of input, called arguments, and returns one piece of output. The following functions do numeric computations involving one argument:

Function Name	Example of Use	Result
abs	abs(x)	absolute value of x
sqr	sqr(x)	square root of x
exp	exp(x)	e^x
log	log(x)	natural log of x
log10	log10(x)	common log of x
log2	log2(x)	log base two of x
sin	sin(x)	sine of x
cos	cos(x)	cosine of x
tan	tan(x)	tangent of x
atn	atn(x)	arctangent of x
int	int(x)	integer part of x

The trigonometric functions assume that the angle is measured in *radians.* If you want to use angles measured in degrees, you must begin your program with the following statement:

OPTION ANGLE degrees

The following functions do numeric computations involving two arguments:

Function Name	Example of Use	Results
min	min(x, y)	the smaller of x and y
max	max(x, y)	the larger of x and y
mod	mod(x, y)	the remainder of x divided by y

True BASIC also includes several functions that do computations involving strings. The most important is the function len, which computes the length of a string. For example, the code

```
PRINT "What is your name?"
INPUT name$
IF len(name$) > 50 THEN
   PRINT "Wow, you have a very long name!"
END IF
```

offers gratuitous comments to persons with unusually long names.

A.5.2   Defining Your Own Functions

The simplest user-defined functions can be expressed in a single line. For example,

```
DEF cube(x) = x*x*x
```

defines a new function cube that computes the cube of a number. A one-line user-defined function has five elements:

1. The word "DEF".

2. The name of the function.

3. A list of arguments enclosed in parentheses and separated by commas.

4. An equal sign.

5. An expression computing the result using the given arguments.

For example, the following function will compute the smallest of three numbers:

```
DEF smallest(x, y, z) = min(x, min(y, z))
```

Many functions would be difficult or impossible to define in a single line. For these functions True BASIC accepts multiline definitions. A multiline definition has three elements:

1. A DEF statement.

2. The body of the definition.

3. An END DEF statement marking the end of the definition of the function.

The DEF statement has three elements:

1. The word DEF.

2. The name of the function.

3. A list of arguments enclosed in parentheses and separated by commas.

The body of the definition must have at least one LET statement with the name of the function on the left side of the equal sign. This statement computes the value of the function. The name of the function may not occur on the right side of a LET statement. (The last sentence is a simplification. The function being defined *may* be used on the right side of a LET statement. This allows a very powerful technique called *recursion*, which is beyond the scope of this book.)

As an example of a multiline function, the following function will count the number of times the letter e (either lowercase or capital) occurs in a string.

```
DEF counte(a$)
LET count = 0
FOR i = 1 TO len(a$)
IF a$[i:i] = "e" OR a$[i:i] = "E" THEN
   LET count = count + 1
END IF
NEXT i
LET counte = count
END DEF
```

A.5.3   Subroutines

A subroutine is very much like a function. It performs some task, possibly using one or more arguments. The difference between a subroutine and a function is that a function returns one simple result, the value of the function, whereas a subroutine performs a task. Both subroutines and functions can be especially useful as ways of organizing a program.

One of the most effective strategies for solving a problem is to break it into smaller, more manageable problems. Suppose that you want to travel from your house to another house across the country. If you were to think of the whole trip at once in all its minute detail, the problem might be overwhelming. In fact, most people conceptualize a problem at several levels. At the highest level one thinks of the problem in broad terms. At this level one might say the trip consists of three parts: driving from your house to the nearest interstate highway, driving on the interstate highway system across the country, and then driving from the appropriate exit of the interstate highway system to your final destination. These individual parts form the next level. Then one might break each of these parts down into smaller parts. At the bottom level each part should be a small, manageable chunk.

Subroutines and functions facilitate exactly this approach to programming. The phrase *top-down programming* is often used to describe this strategy for programming. A subroutine is a block of code that accomplishes a particular task. A large program often uses many different subroutines. Indeed subroutines themselves often use other subroutines. Subroutines frequently improve a programmer's life in other ways as well. Different programs often have some of the same needs. Frequently a programmer can use a subroutine that he or she has used before in a new program. This has two advantages. First, it simplifies programming. The amount of new code that must be written for a new program is smaller. Second, it simplifies debugging. By using a subroutine that has already been checked out, the programmer avoids having to check out that much new code.

A subroutine has three elements:

1. The first statement of every subroutine begins with the word "SUB" followed by the name of the subroutine and a list of its arguments (sometimes called parameters) enclosed in parentheses and separated by commas.

2. The body of the subroutine. This is the section of code that does all the actual work of the subroutine.

3. The statement END SUB. This marks the end of the subroutine for True BASIC.

One common task a programmer faces is to print out the contents of a two-dimensional array in tabular format. Here is an example of a subroutine that accomplishes this task. The subroutine has four arguments: the name of the array, the subtemplate to be used for printing each item, the number of rows, and the number of columns in the array.

```
SUB PrintArray (a(,), template$, rows, columns)
FOR i = 1 TO rows
    FOR j = 1 TO columns
        PRINT USING template$: a(i, j);   ! Print one item
        PRINT " ";                        ! Interitem space
    NEXT j
    PRINT                                 ! Carriage return
NEXT i
END SUB
```

The first argument of the subroutine PrintArray is a two-dimensional array. This fact is indicated by the parentheses and single comma after this argument. A one-dimensional array would be indicated by notation like "a()".

A program or another subroutine or function makes use of a subroutine with a CALL statement. A call statement consists of the word CALL followed by the name of the subroutine and a list of parameters enclosed in parentheses and separated by columns. Some subroutines don't use parameters. In this case the list of parameters and the parentheses are omitted from both the CALL statement and the SUB statement. Here is an example of a statement that calls the subroutine PrintArray:

```
CALL PrintArray (tax, "$##,###.##", 5, 5)
```

A.6   Disk Files

We have already described how information can be read into the computer from the keyboard using the INPUT statement and how information may be "printed" on the monitor using the PRINT and PRINT USING statements. There is another way in which we often move information around. Your computer almost certainly has a disk drive. In fact, it may have several different disk drives. Large amounts of information are frequently stored on disks. This provides a way of saving information and also a way of moving information around. For example, a disk is available with all the programs and data used in this book. This is my way of communicating information to readers.

The basic unit of information on a disk is a *file*. A typical disk may contain many files. In fact some of the bigger hard drives may contain thousands of files. Each file has a name by which it is known. A True BASIC program can read a file using a slight variation on the INPUT statement, and it can write a file using slight variations of either the PRINT or PRINT USING statements.

A.6.1   Reading a Disk File

The first step in reading a file is to "open" it. Think of this as pulling a file folder out of a file cabinet, opening it up, and placing it on your desk ready to be read. This is accomplished by means of an OPEN statement. A typical OPEN statement is shown below:

OPEN #1: NAME "TaxData", ACCESS INPUT

This statement has six elements.

1. The word OPEN.

2. A "pound sign" (#) followed by a number or numeric expression. This number is called a *channel number*. From now on this file will be referred to by this channel number within the program.

3. The word NAME.

4. The name of the file. This must be a string giving the name of the file on the disk. Different computer systems allow different kinds of names. The Macintosh allows names with blanks ("Tax Data"), whereas some other systems do not allow blanks within file names. The file name is always followed by a comma.

5. The word ACCESS.

6. The word INPUT. This indicates to True BASIC that the program will read this file.

Once the file has been opened, it can by read by a slight variation of the usual INPUT statement. The only difference between a normal INPUT statement that reads from the keyboard and an INPUT statement that reads from a disk file is the addition of a channel number followed by a colon. For example, the statement

```
INPUT #1:a, b, c
```

will read three items from the disk file associated by a previous OPEN statement with channel number 1.

Finally, when a program is done reading from a file, it should "close" it. This is accomplished by a statement like

```
CLOSE #1
```

having two elements: the word CLOSE and the channel number preceded by a pound sign (#).

A.6.2   Writing a Disk File

The basic elements involved in writing information on a disk file are the same as for reading a disk file. The first thing one must do is to open the file. This is accomplished with an OPEN statement having the following elements:

- The word OPEN.

- A "pound sign" (#) followed by a number or numeric expression. This number is called a *channel number*. From now on this file will be referred to by this channel number within the program.

- The word NAME.

- The name of the file followed by a comma. This must be a string giving the name of the file on the disk. Different computer systems allow different kinds of names. For example, the Macintosh computer allows names with blanks ("Tax Data") whereas some other systems do not.

- The word ACCESS.

- The word OUTPUT followed by a comma. This indicates to True BASIC that the program will write this file.

- The word CREATE.

- One of the three words NEW, OLD, or NEWOLD. These words are used to help you manage your files. The basic problem is that there may already be a file on the disk whose name is the same as the file that you want to write. This can occur in one of two circumstances: either the existing file is there for some other purpose, or it is an older version of the file that you now want to write. In the first case you do not want to destroy the old file. Writing a new file with the same name would destroy this old file. In the second case you do want to replace this old file by a new one. These three words tell True BASIC what to expect in the way of an old file with the same name and how to handle the situation if such an old file exists. The word NEW tells True BASIC that there should not be an old file with the same name. If such a file exists, the program will halt. This is an important aspect of the way that True BASIC uses files. It can prevent you from inadvertently destroying an important file. The word OLD tells True BASIC that there should be an old file with the same name. The old file will be replaced by the new file. If such an old file does not exist, then the program will halt. The word NEWOLD tells True BASIC that there may or may not be an old file with the same name. If there is, it will be replaced by the new file. If there is not, then a new file will be written.

A typical OPEN statement is shown below:

```
OPEN #1: NAME "FirstReport", ACCESS OUTPUT, CREATE NEW
```

One writes onto a disk file using either a modified PRINT or a modified PRINT USING statement. The modification consists of a pound sign # followed by the channel number associated with the file by a previous OPEN statement and either a colon (for a PRINT statement) or a comma (for a PRINT USING statement)—for example,

```
PRINT #1: a, b, c
PRINT #1, USING "## ## ##":a, b, c
```

Finally, the CLOSE statement is used to close the file after one is through writing it.

B Local Aid Data

B.1 Population and Per Capita EQV

The following table contains 1980 data on population and per capita equalized property valuation (EQV) for the 351 cities and towns in Massachusetts. This table is in alphabetical order.

Table 1
Population, Per Capita EQV (Alphabetic Order)

City or Town	Population	EQV	City or Town	Population	EQV
Abington	13,517	12,325	Bourne	13,874	24,168
Acton	17,544	24,419	Boxborough	3,126	21,491
Acushnet	8,704	11,799	Boxford	5,374	26,833
Adams	10,381	11,617	Boylston	3,470	15,965
Agawam	26,271	13,452	Braintree	36,337	20,998
Alford	394	32,690	Brewster	5,226	44,374
Amesbury	13,971	10,772	Bridgewater	17,202	11,295
Amherst	33,229	8,119	Brimfield	2,318	17,407
Andover	26,370	24,638	Brockton	95,172	9,784
Arlington	48,219	16,278	Brookfield	2,397	10,776
Ashburnham	4,075	14,562	Brookline	55,062	17,589
Ashby	2,311	14,055	Buckland	1,864	12,983
Ashfield	1,458	21,132	Burlington	23,486	24,785
Ashland	9,165	18,167	Cambridge	95,322	13,544
Athol	10,634	9,045	Canton	18,182	20,702
Attleborough	34,196	13,712	Carlisle	3,306	30,339
Auburn	14,845	15,864	Carver	6,988	14,611
Avon	5,026	18,729	Charlemont	1,149	20,766
Ayer	6,993	12,354	Charlton	6,719	12,483
Barnstable	30,898	38,588	Chatham	6,071	64,882
Barre	4,102	12,823	Chelmsford	31,174	17,585
Becket	1,339	33,988	Chelsea	25,431	6,209
Bedford	13,067	27,512	Cheshire	3,124	14,011
Belchertown	8,339	12,292	Chester	1,123	15,699
Bellingham	14,300	11,559	Chesterfield	1,000	18,060
Belmont	26,100	22,789	Chicopee	55,112	10,401
Berkley	2,731	14,072	Chilmark	489	323,108
Berlin	2,215	14,894	Clarksburg	1,871	10,839
Bernardston	1,750	15,109	Clinton	12,771	10,078
Beverly	37,655	15,082	Cohasset	7,174	25,746
Billerica	36,727	14,670	Colrain	1,552	18,454
Blackstone	6,570	9,779	Concord	16,293	29,031
Blandford	1,038	19,027	Conway	1,213	18,805
Bolton	2,530	26,672	Cummington	657	21,157
Boston	562,994	9,306	Dalton	6,797	15,227

City or Town	Popu-lation	EQV	City or Town	Popu-lation	EQV
Danvers	24,100	20,303	Granby	5,380	12,100
Dartmouth	23,966	16,870	Granville	1,204	22,782
Dedham	25,298	19,804	Great Barrington	7,405	17,542
Deerfield	4,517	20,795	Greenfield	18,436	12,790
Dennis	12,360	47,087	Groton	6,154	19,841
Dighton	5,352	18,296	Groveland	5,040	15,802
Douglas	3,730	14,686	Hadley	4,125	27,055
Dover	4,703	44,333	Halifax	5,513	13,120
Dracut	21,249	12,057	Hamilton	6,960	21,106
Dudley	8,717	13,112	Hampden	4,745	14,485
Dunstable	1,671	20,347	Hancock	643	28,165
Duxbury	11,807	22,741	Hanover	11,358	18,463
East Bridgewater	9,945	12,559	Hanson	8,617	12,649
East Brookfield	1,955	13,555	Hardwick	2,272	9,696
East Longmeadow	12,905	18,582	Harvard	12,170	8,907
Eastham	3,472	60,023	Harwich	8,971	40,363
Easthampton	15,580	11,374	Hatfield	3,045	16,493
Easton	16,623	14,823	Haverhill	46,865	10,025
Edgartown	2,204	123,094	Hawley	280	19,286
Egremont	1,311	31,732	Heath	482	31,535
Erving	1,326	61,003	Hingham	20,339	21,869
Essex	2,998	22,158	Hinsdale	1,707	16,251
Everett	37,195	23,874	Holbrook	11,140	12,738
Fairhaven	15,759	12,260	Holden	13,336	16,512
Fall River	92,574	6,394	Holland	1,589	22,442
Falmouth	23,640	34,966	Holliston	12,622	17,969
Fitchburg	39,580	9,467	Holyoke	44,678	8,588
Florida	730	44,616	Hopedale	3,905	15,198
Foxborough	14,148	16,766	Hopkinton	7,114	21,127
Framingham	65,113	17,631	Hubbardston	1,797	15,314
Franklin	18,217	12,626	Hudson	16,408	13,091
Freetown	7,058	18,362	Hull	9,714	12,930
Gardner	17,900	10,737	Huntington	1,804	14,279
Gay Head	220	103,227	Ipswich	11,158	17,387
Georgetown	5,687	16,388	Kingston	7,362	16,979
Gill	1,259	16,481	Lakeville	5,931	15,896
Gloucester	27,768	20,055	Lancaster	6,334	12,624
Goshen	651	27,143	Lanesborough	3,131	15,050
Gosnold	63	154,651	Lawrence	63,175	8,160
Grafton	11,238	12,903	Lee	6,247	14,016

Notes: Table 1 continued

City or Town	Population	EQV	City or Town	Population	EQV
Leicester	9,446	10,544	Monson	7,315	11,398
Lenox	6,523	17,231	Montague	8,011	16,502
Leominster	34,508	11,931	Monterey	818	38,545
Leverett	1,471	17,009	Montgomery	637	19,152
Lexington	29,479	30,785	Mount Washington	93	86,065
Leyden	498	24,839	Nahant	3,947	22,865
Lincoln	7,098	30,389	Nantucket	5,087	122,155
Littleton	6,970	20,201	Natick	29,461	19,351
Longmeadow	16,301	20,968	Needham	27,901	27,006
Lowell	92,418	8,239	New Ashford	159	51,987
Ludlow	18,150	13,471	New Bedford	98,478	7,535
Lunenburg	8,405	14,539	New Braintree	671	15,604
Lynn	78,471	9,256	New Marlborough	1,160	41,250
Lynnfield	11,267	26,050	New Salem	688	16,468
Malden	53,386	9,819	Newbury	4,529	20,722
Manchester	5,424	33,831	Newburyport	15,900	13,604
Mansfield	13,453	17,305	Newton	83,622	23,654
Marblehead	20,126	29,062	Norfolk	6,363	14,840
Marion	3,932	33,800	North Adams	18,063	8,171
Marlborough	30,617	15,044	North Andover	20,129	19,996
Marshfield	20,916	16,934	North Attleborough	21,095	13,050
Mashpee	3,700	55,730	North Brookfield	4,150	10,988
Mattapoisett	5,597	20,976	North Reading	11,455	19,005
Maynard	9,590	17,716	Northampton	29,286	12,415
Medfield	10,220	18,767	Northborough	10,568	18,263
Medford	58,076	14,336	Northbridge	12,246	10,542
Medway	8,447	17,095	Northfield	2,386	20,930
Melrose	30,055	14,171	Norton	12,690	12,041
Mendon	3,108	18,063	Norwell	9,182	20,377
Merrimac	4,451	11,144	Norwood	29,711	17,835
Methuen	36,701	13,640	Oak Bluffs	1,984	59,526
Middleborough	16,404	12,625	Oakham	994	17,948
Middlefield	385	25,790	Orange	6,844	8,248
Middleton	4,135	21,640	Orleans	5,306	56,672
Milford	23,390	13,647	Otis	963	49,107
Millbury	11,808	10,205	Oxford	11,680	10,548
Millis	6,908	16,807	Palmer	11,389	12,020
Millville	1,693	9,492	Paxton	3,762	18,607
Milton	25,860	17,251	Peabody	45,976	15,145
Monroe	179	31,397	Pelham	1,112	17,968

Notes: Table 1 continued

City or Town	Population	EQV	City or Town	Population	EQV
Pembroke	13,487	16,735	Shrewsbury	22,674	16,565
Pepperell	8,061	14,167	Shutesbury	1,049	22,574
Peru	633	21,722	Somerset	18,813	30,325
Petersham	1,024	24,326	Somerville	77,372	8,454
Phillipston	953	19,570	South Hadley	16,399	12,001
Pittsfield	51,974	12,381	Southampton	4,137	15,371
Plainfield	425	20,184	Southborough	6,193	27,079
Plainville	5,857	17,142	Southbridge	16,665	9,871
Plymouth	35,913	27,283	Southwick	7,382	14,413
Plympton	1,974	19,650	Spencer	10,774	9,718
Princeton	2,425	19,357	Springfield	152,319	8,633
Provincetown	3,536	36,340	Sterling	5,440	18,132
Quincy	84,743	13,559	Stockbridge	2,328	33,484
Randolph	28,218	13,541	Stoneham	21,424	15,921
Raynham	9,085	14,706	Stoughton	26,710	14,680
Reading	22,678	17,788	Stow	5,144	23,328
Rehoboth	7,570	17,768	Sturbridge	5,976	19,294
Revere	42,423	10,831	Sudbury	14,027	27,468
Richmond	1,659	24,177	Sunderland	2,929	14,442
Rochester	3,205	19,261	Sutton	5,855	16,806
Rockland	15,695	10,634	Swampscott	13,837	20,814
Rockport	6,345	33,712	Swansea	15,461	14,656
Rowe	336	392,560	Taunton	45,001	9,760
Rowley	3,867	16,126	Templeton	6,070	10,705
Royalston	955	16,262	Tewksbury	24,635	14,987
Russell	1,570	17,599	Tisbury	2,972	45,121
Rutland	4,334	12,224	Tolland	235	111,830
Salem	38,220	15,780	Topsfield	5,709	25,398
Salisbury	5,973	19,973	Townsend	7,201	12,337
Sandisfield	720	33,458	Truro	1,486	87,618
Sandwich	8,727	46,625	Tyngsborough	5,683	14,936
Saugus	24,746	19,037	Tyringham	344	47,442
Savoy	644	18,913	Upton	3,886	15,008
Scituate	17,317	18,929	Uxbridge	8,374	12,778
Seekonk	12,269	20,776	Wakefield	24,895	16,827
Sharon	13,601	19,285	Wales	1,177	13,772
Sheffield	2,743	26,187	Walpole	18,859	17,647
Shelburne	2,002	13,227	Waltham	58,200	17,938
Sherborn	4,049	33,984	Ware	8,953	10,239
Shirley	5,124	8,134	Wareham	18,457	16,146

Notes: Table 1 continued

City or Town	Popu-lation	EQV	City or Town	Popu-lation	EQV
Warren	3,777	10,527	Westminster	5,139	21,522
Warwick	603	23,997	Weston	11,169	40,675
Washington	587	18,910	Westport	13,763	18,775
Watertown	34,384	17,537	Westwood	13,212	29,004
Wayland	12,170	28,406	Weymouth	55,601	13,156
Webster	14,480	10,228	Whately	1,341	21,126
Wellesley	27,209	29,501	Whitman	13,534	11,829
Wellfleet	2,209	77,637	Wilbraham	12,053	17,888
Wendell	694	18,256	Williamsburg	2,237	14,283
Wenham	3,897	20,570	Williamstown	8,741	14,529
West Boylston	6,204	16,344	Wilmington	17,471	21,573
West Bridgewater	6,359	16,009	Winchendon	7,019	9,765
West Brookfield	3,026	14,359	Winchester	20,701	24,260
West Newbury	2,861	19,416	Windsor	598	27,676
West Springfield	27,042	16,552	Winthrop	19,294	10,682
West Stockbridge	1,280	22,969	Woburn	36,626	18,492
West Tisbury	1,010	88,228	Worcester	161,799	8,832
Westborough	13,619	21,316	Worthington	932	22,597
Westfield	36,465	11,729	Wrentham	7,580	15,567
Westford	13,434	16,131	Yarmouth	18,449	37,119
Westhampton	1,137	21,416			

Notes: Table 1 continued

B.2   Population and Per Capita EQV (EQV Order)

The following table contains the same data as Table 1, but is arranged by per capita EQV instead of alphabetically.

Table 2
Population, Per Capita EQV (EQV Order)

City or Town	Popu-lation	EQV	City or Town	Popu-lation	EQV
Rowe	336	392,560	Erving	1,326	61,003
Chilmark	489	323,108	Eastham	3,472	60,023
Gosnold	63	154,651	Oak Bluffs	1,984	59,526
Edgartown	2,204	123,094	Orleans	5,306	56,672
Nantucket	5,087	122,155	Mashpee	3,700	55,730
Tolland	235	111,830	New Ashford	159	51,987
Gay Head	220	103,227	Otis	963	49,107
West Tisbury	1,010	88,228	Tyringham	344	47,442
Truro	1,486	87,618	Dennis	12,360	47,087
Mount Washington	93	86,065	Sandwich	8,727	46,625
Wellfleet	2,209	77,637	Tisbury	2,972	45,121
Chatham	6,071	64,882	Florida	730	44,616

City or Town	Population	EQV	City or Town	Population	EQV
Brewster	5,226	44,374	Sheffield	2,743	26,187
Dover	4,703	44,333	Lynnfield	11,267	26,050
New Marlborough	1,160	41,250	Middlefield	385	25,790
Weston	11,169	40,675	Cohasset	7,174	25,746
Harwich	8,971	40,363	Topsfield	5,709	25,398
Barnstable	30,898	38,588	Leyden	498	24,839
Monterey	818	38,545	Burlington	23,486	24,785
Yarmouth	18,449	37,119	Andover	26,370	24,638
Provincetown	3,536	36,340	Acton	17,544	24,419
Falmouth	23,640	34,966	Petersham	1,024	24,326
Becket	1,339	33,988	Winchester	20,701	24,260
Sherborn	4,049	33,984	Richmond	1,659	24,177
Manchester	5,424	33,831	Bourne	13,874	24,168
Marion	3,932	33,800	Warwick	603	23,997
Rockport	6,345	33,712	Everett	37,195	23,874
Stockbridge	2,328	33,484	Newton	83,622	23,654
Sandisfield	720	33,458	Stow	5,144	23,328
Alford	394	32,690	West Stockbridge	1,280	22,969
Egremont	1,311	31,732	Nahant	3,947	22,865
Heath	482	31,535	Belmont	26,100	22,789
Monroe	179	31,397	Granville	1,204	22,782
Lexington	29,479	30,785	Duxbury	11,807	22,741
Lincoln	7,098	30,389	Worthington	932	22,597
Carlisle	3,306	30,339	Shutesbury	1,049	22,574
Somerset	18,813	30,325	Holland	1,589	22,442
Wellesley	27,209	29,501	Essex	2,998	22,158
Marblehead	20,126	29,062	Hingham	20,339	21,869
Concord	16,293	29,031	Peru	633	21,722
Westwood	13,212	29,004	Middleton	4,135	21,640
Wayland	12,170	28,406	Wilmington	17,471	21,573
Hancock	643	28,165	Westminster	5,139	21,522
Windsor	598	27,676	Boxborough	3,126	21,491
Bedford	13,067	27,512	Westhampton	1,137	21,416
Sudbury	14,027	27,468	Westborough	13,619	21,316
Plymouth	35,913	27,283	Cummington	657	21,157
Goshen	651	27,143	Ashfield	1,458	21,132
Southborough	6,193	27,079	Hopkinton	7,114	21,127
Hadley	4,125	27,055	Whately	1,341	21,126
Needham	27,901	27,006	Hamilton	6,960	21,106
Boxford	5,374	26,833	Braintree	36,337	20,998
Bolton	2,530	26,672	Mattapoisett	5,597	20,976

Notes: Table 2 continued

City or Town	Population	EQV	City or Town	Population	EQV
Longmeadow	16,301	20,968	Woburn	36,626	18,492
Northfield	2,386	20,930	Hanover	11,358	18,463
Swampscott	13,837	20,814	Colrain	1,552	18,454
Deerfield	4,517	20,795	Freetown	7,058	18,362
Seekonk	12,269	20,776	Dighton	5,352	18,296
Charlemont	1,149	20,766	Northborough	10,568	18,263
Newbury	4,529	20,722	Wendell	694	18,256
Canton	18,182	20,702	Ashland	9,165	18,167
Wenham	3,897	20,570	Sterling	5,440	18,132
Norwell	9,182	20,377	Mendon	3,108	18,063
Dunstable	1,671	20,347	Chesterfield	1,000	18,060
Danvers	24,100	20,303	Holliston	12,622	17,969
Littleton	6,970	20,201	Pelham	1,112	17,968
Plainfield	425	20,184	Oakham	994	17,948
Gloucester	27,768	20,055	Waltham	58,200	17,938
North Andover	20,129	19,996	Wilbraham	12,053	17,888
Salisbury	5,973	19,973	Norwood	29,711	17,835
Groton	6,154	19,841	Reading	22,678	17,788
Dedham	25,298	19,804	Rehoboth	7,570	17,768
Plympton	1,974	19,650	Maynard	9,590	17,716
Phillipston	953	19,570	Walpole	18,859	17,647
West Newbury	2,861	19,416	Framingham	65,113	17,631
Princeton	2,425	19,357	Russell	1,570	17,599
Natick	29,461	19,351	Brookline	55,062	17,589
Sturbridge	5,976	19,294	Chelmsford	31,174	17,585
Hawley	280	19,286	Great Barrington	7,405	17,542
Sharon	13,601	19,285	Watertown	34,384	17,537
Rochester	3,205	19,261	Brimfield	2,318	17,407
Montgomery	637	19,152	Ipswich	11,158	17,387
Saugus	24,746	19,037	Mansfield	13,453	17,305
Blandford	1,038	19,027	Milton	25,860	17,251
North Reading	11,455	19,005	Lenox	6,523	17,231
Scituate	17,317	18,929	Plainville	5,857	17,142
Savoy	644	18,913	Medway	8,447	17,095
Washington	587	18,910	Leverett	1,471	17,009
Conway	1,213	18,805	Kingston	7,362	16,979
Westport	13,763	18,775	Marshfield	20,916	16,934
Medfield	10,220	18,767	Dartmouth	23,966	16,870
Avon	5,026	18,729	Wakefield	24,895	16,827
Paxton	3,762	18,607	Millis	6,908	16,807
East Longmeadow	12,905	18,582	Sutton	5,855	16,806

Notes: Table 2 continued

City or Town	Popu-lation	EQV	City or Town	Popu-lation	EQV
Foxborough	14,148	16,766	Easton	16,623	14,823
Pembroke	13,487	16,735	Raynham	9,085	14,706
Shrewsbury	22,674	16,565	Douglas	3,730	14,686
West Springfield	27,042	16,552	Stoughton	26,710	14,680
Holden	13,336	16,512	Billerica	36,727	14,670
Montague	8,011	16,502	Swansea	15,461	14,656
Hatfield	3,045	16,493	Carver	6,988	14,611
Gill	1,259	16,481	Ashburnham	4,075	14,562
New Salem	688	16,468	Lunenburg	8,405	14,539
Georgetown	5,687	16,388	Williamstown	8,741	14,529
West Boylston	6,204	16,344	Hampden	4,745	14,485
Arlington	48,219	16,278	Sunderland	2,929	14,442
Royalston	955	16,262	Southwick	7,382	14,413
Hinsdale	1,707	16,251	West Brookfield	3,026	14,359
Wareham	18,457	16,146	Medford	58,076	14,336
Westford	13,434	16,131	Williamsburg	2,237	14,283
Rowley	3,867	16,126	Huntington	1,804	14,279
West Bridgewater	6,359	16,009	Melrose	30,055	14,171
Boylston	3,470	15,965	Pepperell	8,061	14,167
Stoneham	21,424	15,921	Berkley	2,731	14,072
Lakeville	5,931	15,896	Ashby	2,311	14,055
Auburn	14,845	15,864	Lee	6,247	14,016
Groveland	5,040	15,802	Cheshire	3,124	14,011
Salem	38,220	15,780	Wales	1,177	13,772
Chester	1,123	15,699	Attleborough	34,196	13,712
New Braintree	671	15,604	Milford	23,390	13,647
Wrentham	7,580	15,567	Methuen	36,701	13,640
Southampton	4,137	15,371	Newburyport	15,900	13,604
Hubbardston	1,797	15,314	Quincy	84,743	13,559
Dalton	6,797	15,227	East Brookfield	1,955	13,555
Hopedale	3,905	15,198	Cambridge	95,322	13,544
Peabody	45,976	15,145	Randolph	28,218	13,541
Bernardston	1,750	15,109	Ludlow	18,150	13,471
Beverly	37,655	15,082	Agawam	26,271	13,452
Lanesborough	3,131	15,050	Shelburne	2,002	13,227
Marlborough	30,617	15,044	Weymouth	55,601	13,156
Upton	3,886	15,008	Halifax	5,513	13,120
Tewksbury	24,635	14,987	Dudley	8,717	13,112
Tyngsborough	5,683	14,936	Hudson	16,408	13,091
Berlin	2,215	14,894	North Attleborough	21,095	13,050
Norfolk	6,363	14,840	Buckland	1,864	12,983

Notes: Table 2 continued

City or Town	Population	EQV	City or Town	Population	EQV
Hull	9,714	12,930	Templeton	6,070	10,705
Grafton	11,238	12,903	Winthrop	19,294	10,682
Barre	4,102	12,823	Rockland	15,695	10,634
Greenfield	18,436	12,790	Oxford	11,680	10,548
Uxbridge	8,374	12,778	Leicester	9,446	10,544
Holbrook	11,140	12,738	Northbridge	12,246	10,542
Hanson	8,617	12,649	Warren	3,777	10,527
Franklin	18,217	12,626	Chicopee	55,112	10,401
Middleborough	16,404	12,625	Ware	8,953	10,239
Lancaster	6,334	12,624	Webster	14,480	10,228
East Bridgewater	9,945	12,559	Millbury	11,808	10,205
Charlton	6,719	12,483	Clinton	12,771	10,078
Northampton	29,286	12,415	Haverhill	46,865	10,025
Pittsfield	51,974	12,381	Southbridge	16,665	9,871
Ayer	6,993	12,354	Malden	53,386	9,819
Townsend	7,201	12,337	Brockton	95,172	9,784
Abington	13,517	12,325	Blackstone	6,570	9,779
Belchertown	8,339	12,292	Winchendon	7,019	9,765
Fairhaven	15,759	12,260	Taunton	45,001	9,760
Rutland	4,334	12,224	Spencer	10,774	9,718
Granby	5,380	12,100	Hardwick	2,272	9,696
Dracut	21,249	12,057	Millville	1,693	9,492
Norton	12,690	12,041	Fitchburg	39,580	9,467
Palmer	11,389	12,020	Boston	562,994	9,306
South Hadley	16,399	12,001	Lynn	78,471	9,256
Leominster	34,508	11,931	Athol	10,634	9,045
Whitman	13,534	11,829	Harvard	12,170	8,907
Acushnet	8,704	11,799	Worcester	161,799	8,832
Westfield	36,465	11,729	Springfield	152,319	8,633
Adams	10,381	11,617	Holyoke	44,678	8,588
Bellingham	14,300	11,559	Somerville	77,372	8,454
Monson	7,315	11,398	Orange	6,844	8,248
Easthampton	15,580	11,374	Lowell	92,418	8,239
Bridgewater	17,202	11,295	North Adams	18,063	8,171
Merrimac	4,451	11,144	Lawrence	63,175	8,160
North Brookfield	4,150	10,988	Shirley	5,124	8,134
Clarksburg	1,871	10,839	Amherst	33,229	8,119
Revere	42,423	10,831	New Bedford	98,478	7,535
Brookfield	2,397	10,776	Fall River	92,574	6,394
Amesbury	13,971	10,772	Chelsea	25,431	6,209
Gardner	17,900	10,737			

Notes: Table 2 continued

B.3   Per Capita Expenditures

The following table shows 1980 data on population and per capita expenditures for the 351 cities and towns in Massachusetts. This table is in population order.

Table 3
Per Capita Expenditures

Rank	City or Town	Pop.	Exp ($)	Rank	City or Town	Pop.	Exp ($)
1	Gosnold	63	2,196	31	Worthington	932	736
2	Mount Washington	93	1,495	32	Phillipston	953	817
3	New Ashford	159	686	33	Royalston	955	841
4	Monroe	179	1,436	34	Otis	963	858
5	Gay Head	220	1,372	35	Oakham	994	825
6	Tolland	235	1,427	36	Chesterfield	1,000	739
7	Hawley	280	805	37	West Tisbury	1,010	1,172
8	Rowe	336	3,202	38	Petersham	1,024	876
9	Tyringham	344	711	39	Blandford	1,038	740
10	Middlefield	385	767	40	Shutesbury	1,049	691
11	Alford	394	795	41	Pelham	1,112	766
12	Plainfield	425	1,006	42	Chester	1,123	812
13	Heath	482	890	43	Westhampton	1,137	745
14	Chilmark	489	1,508	44	Charlemont	1,149	642
15	Leyden	498	775	45	New Marlborough	1,160	630
16	Washington	587	771	46	Wales	1,177	830
17	Windsor	598	818	47	Granville	1,204	708
18	Warwick	603	836	48	Conway	1,213	656
19	Peru	633	573	49	Gill	1,259	811
20	Montgomery	637	877	50	West Stockbridge	1,280	664
21	Hancock	643	663	51	Egremont	1,311	634
22	Savoy	644	669	52	Erving	1,326	1,650
23	Goshen	651	780	53	Becket	1,339	852
24	Cummington	657	868	54	Whately	1,341	562
25	New Braintree	671	796	55	Ashfield	1,458	692
26	New Salem	688	813	56	Leverett	1,471	581
27	Wendell	694	880	57	Truro	1,486	1,225
28	Sandisfield	720	764	58	Colrain	1,552	713
29	Florida	730	1,240	59	Russell	1,570	765
30	Monterey	818	755	60	Holland	1,589	817

Rank	City or Town	Pop.	Exp ($)	Rank	City or Town	Pop.	Exp ($)
61	Richmond	1,659	641	101	Eastham	3,472	985
62	Dunstable	1,671	968	102	Provincetown	3,536	1,470
63	Millville	1,693	677	103	Mashpee	3,700	1,068
64	Hinsdale	1,707	698	104	Douglas	3,730	691
65	Bernardston	1,750	692	105	Paxton	3,762	665
66	Hubbardston	1,797	852	106	Warren	3,777	684
67	Huntington	1,804	865	107	Rowley	3,867	780
68	Buckland	1,864	730	108	Upton	3,886	755
69	Clarksburg	1,871	620	109	Wenham	3,897	681
70	East Brookfield	1,955	633	110	Hopedale	3,905	803
71	Plympton	1,974	759	111	Marion	3,932	921
72	Oak Bluffs	1,984	1,409	112	Nahant	3,947	783
73	Shelburne	2,002	724	113	Sherborn	4,049	1,148
74	Edgartown	2,204	1,439	114	Ashburnham	4,075	694
75	Wellfleet	2,209	1,254	115	Barre	4,102	667
76	Berlin	2,215	905	116	Hadley	4,125	709
77	Williamsburg	2,237	712	117	Middleton	4,135	1,342
78	Hardwick	2,272	707	118	Southampton	4,137	615
79	Ashby	2,311	852	119	North Brookfield	4,150	708
80	Brimfield	2,318	721	120	Rutland	4,334	592
81	Stockbridge	2,328	903	121	Merrimac	4,451	775
82	Northfield	2,386	778	122	Deerfield	4,517	543
83	Brookfield	2,397	725	123	Newbury	4,529	701
84	Princeton	2,425	759	124	Dover	4,703	1,116
85	Bolton	2,530	790	125	Hampden	4,745	767
86	Berkley	2,731	594	126	Avon	5,026	928
87	Sheffield	2,743	635	127	Groveland	5,040	892
88	West Newbury	2,861	906	128	Nantucket	5,087	1,565
89	Sunderland	2,929	381	129	Shirley	5,124	466
90	Tisbury	2,972	1,003	130	Westminster	5,139	654
91	Essex	2,998	810	131	Stow	5,144	892
92	West Brookfield	3,026	715	132	Brewster	5,226	988
93	Hatfield	3,045	719	133	Orleans	5,306	1,029
94	Mendon	3,108	699	134	Dighton	5,352	693
95	Cheshire	3,124	605	135	Boxford	5,374	797
96	Boxborough	3,126	717	136	Granby	5,380	714
97	Lanesborough	3,131	753	137	Manchester	5,424	986
98	Rochester	3,205	657	138	Sterling	5,440	758
99	Carlisle	3,306	989	139	Halifax	5,513	613
100	Boylston	3,470	693	140	Mattapoisett	5,597	819

Notes: Table 3 continued

Rank	City or Town	Pop.	Exp ($)	Rank	City or Town	Pop.	Exp ($)
141	Tyngsborough	5,683	700	181	Montague	8,011	1,088
142	Georgetown	5,687	827	182	Pepperell	8,061	823
143	Topsfield	5,709	882	183	Belchertown	8,339	495
144	Sutton	5,855	638	184	Uxbridge	8,374	645
145	Plainville	5,857	775	185	Lunenburg	8,405	768
146	Lakeville	5,931	686	186	Medway	8,447	1,005
147	Salisbury	5,973	847	187	Hanson	8,617	813
148	Sturbridge	5,976	858	188	Acushnet	8,704	610
149	Templeton	6,070	646	189	Dudley	8,717	613
150	Chatham	6,071	973	190	Sandwich	8,727	1,059
151	Groton	6,154	786	191	Williamstown	8,741	675
152	Southborough	6,193	1,096	192	Ware	8,953	555
153	West Boylston	6,204	739	193	Harwich	8,971	920
154	Lee	6,247	751	194	Raynham	9,085	762
155	Lancaster	6,334	610	195	Ashland	9,165	864
156	Rockport	6,345	845	196	Norwell	9,182	1,043
157	West Bridgewater	6,359	857	197	Leicester	9,446	580
158	Norfolk	6,363	774	198	Maynard	9,590	877
159	Lenox	6,523	686	199	Hull	9,714	1,425
160	Blackstone	6,570	706	200	East Bridgewater	9,945	820
161	Charlton	6,719	608	201	Medfield	10,220	892
162	Dalton	6,797	803	202	Adams	10,381	676
163	Orange	6,844	619	203	Northborough	10,568	825
164	Millis	6,908	824	204	Athol	10,634	586
165	Hamilton	6,960	655	205	Spencer	10,774	580
166	Littleton	6,970	825	206	Holbrook	11,140	846
167	Carver	6,988	725	207	Ipswich	11,158	847
168	Ayer	6,993	820	208	Weston	11,169	1,260
169	Winchendon	7,019	776	209	Grafton	11,238	669
170	Freetown	7,058	697	210	Lynnfield	11,267	817
171	Lincoln	7,098	821	211	Hanover	11,358	952
172	Hopkinton	7,114	772	212	Palmer	11,389	650
173	Cohasset	7,174	1,017	213	North Reading	11,455	856
174	Townsend	7,201	734	214	Oxford	11,680	689
175	Monson	7,315	725	215	Duxbury	11,807	1,094
176	Kingston	7,362	790	216	Millbury	11,808	723
177	Southwick	7,382	681	217	Wilbraham	12,053	905
178	Great Barrington	7,405	746	218	Harvard	12,170	302
179	Rehoboth	7,570	746	219	Wayland	12,170	1,171
180	Wrentham	7,580	820	220	Northbridge	12,246	575

Notes: Table 3 continued

Rank	City or Town	Pop.	Exp ($)	Rank	City or Town	Pop.	Exp ($)
221	Seekonk	12,269	699	261	Acton	17,544	909
222	Dennis	12,360	808	262	Gardner	17,900	701
223	Holliston	12,622	901	263	North Adams	18,063	695
224	Norton	12,690	740	264	Ludlow	18,150	676
225	Clinton	12,771	619	265	Canton	18,182	933
226	East Longmeadow	12,905	831	266	Franklin	18,217	843
227	Bedford	13,067	991	267	Greenfield	18,436	784
228	Westwood	13,212	1,086	268	Yarmouth	18,449	833
229	Holden	13,336	746	269	Wareham	18,457	727
230	Westford	13,434	799	270	Somerset	18,813	909
231	Mansfield	13,453	780	271	Walpole	18,859	943
232	Pembroke	13,487	812	272	Winthrop	19,294	654
233	Abington	13,517	710	273	Marblehead	20,126	1,026
234	Whitman	13,534	789	274	North Andover	20,129	639
235	Sharon	13,601	947	275	Hingham	20,339	895
236	Westborough	13,619	864	276	Winchester	20,701	1,044
237	Westport	13,763	625	277	Marshfield	20,916	878
238	Swampscott	13,837	982	278	North Attleborough	21,095	653
239	Bourne	13,874	818	279	Dracut	21,249	653
240	Amesbury	13,971	1,122	280	Stoneham	21,424	783
241	Sudbury	14,027	1,082	281	Shrewsbury	22,674	685
242	Foxborough	14,148	871	282	Reading	22,678	896
243	Bellingham	14,300	748	283	Milford	23,390	753
244	Webster	14,480	667	284	Burlington	23,486	1,131
245	Auburn	14,845	790	285	Falmouth	23,640	900
246	Swansea	15,461	611	286	Dartmouth	23,966	647
247	Easthampton	15,580	610	287	Danvers	24,100	1,448
248	Rockland	15,695	819	288	Tewksbury	24,635	782
249	Fairhaven	15,759	666	289	Saugus	24,746	808
250	Newburyport	15,900	786	290	Wakefield	24,895	879
251	Concord	16,293	1,093	291	Dedham	25,298	837
252	Longmeadow	16,301	979	292	Chelsea	25,431	886
253	South Hadley	16,399	589	293	Milton	25,860	746
254	Middleborough	16,404	718	294	Belmont	26,100	902
255	Hudson	16,408	786	295	Agawam	26,271	610
256	Easton	16,623	713	296	Andover	26,370	957
257	Southbridge	16,665	560	297	Stoughton	26,710	730
258	Bridgewater	17,202	686	298	West Springfield	27,042	732
259	Scituate	17,317	998	299	Wellesley	27,209	1,049
260	Wilmington	17,471	1,016	300	Gloucester	27,768	901

Notes: Table 3 continued

Rank	City or Town	Pop.	Exp ($)	Rank	City or Town	Pop.	Exp ($)
301	Needham	27,901	1,214	341	Lynn	78,471	958
302	Randolph	28,218	848	342	Newton	83,622	1,058
303	Northampton	29,286	693	343	Quincy	84,743	1,273
304	Natick	29,461	963	344	Lowell	92,418	676
305	Lexington	29,479	1,102	345	Fall River	92,574	758
306	Norwood	29,711	1,214	346	Brockton	95,172	861
307	Melrose	30,055	821	347	Cambridge	95,322	1,274
308	Marlborough	30,617	812	348	New Bedford	98,478	751
309	Barnstable	30,898	819	349	Springfield	152,319	850
310	Chelmsford	31,174	831	350	Worcester	161,799	1,060
311	Amherst	33,229	433	351	Boston	562,994	1,326
312	Attleborough	34,196	783				
313	Watertown	34,384	881				
314	Leominster	34,508	655				
315	Plymouth	35,913	867				
316	Braintree	36,337	1,051				
317	Westfield	36,465	623				
318	Woburn	36,626	833				
319	Methuen	36,701	725				
320	Billerica	36,727	890				
321	Everett	37,195	978				
322	Beverly	37,655	815				
323	Salem	38,220	1,153				
324	Fitchburg	39,580	771				
325	Revere	42,423	812				
326	Holyoke	44,678	725				
327	Taunton	45,001	692				
328	Peabody	45,976	940				
329	Haverhill	46,865	1,014				
330	Arlington	48,219	823				
331	Pittsfield	51,974	838				
332	Malden	53,386	747				
333	Brookline	55,062	997				
334	Chicopee	55,112	715				
335	Weymouth	55,601	803				
336	Medford	58,076	742				
337	Waltham	58,200	869				
338	Lawrence	63,175	728				
339	Framingham	65,113	890				
340	Somerville	77,372	729				

Notes: Table 3 continued

B.4   Weighted Full-Time Equivalent Students

The following table shows 1980 data on population, per capita equalized property valuation (EQV), per capita expenditures, and per capita weighted full-time equivalent (WFTE) students for the 351 cities and towns in Massachusetts.

Table 4
Weighted Full-Time Equivalent Students

City or Town	Population	EQV	Exp ($)	WFTE
Abington	13,517	12,325	709.76	0.2707
Acton	17,544	24,419	909.22	0.2929
Acushnet	8,704	11,799	610.15	0.2430
Adams	10,381	11,617	675.90	0.1795
Agawam	26,271	13,452	610.00	0.2244
Alford	394	32,690	794.81	0.1746
Amesbury	13,971	10,772	1,122.08	0.2557
Amherst	33,229	8,119	433.04	0.1049
Andover	26,370	24,638	957.09	0.2488
Arlington	48,219	16,278	823.33	0.1675
Ashburnham	4,075	14,562	694.14	0.2770
Ashby	2,311	14,055	851.89	0.2942
Ashfield	1,458	21,132	692.20	0.2178
Ashland	9,165	18,167	863.98	0.2505
Athol	10,634	9,045	585.78	0.2310
Attleborough	34,196	13,712	782.76	0.2524
Auburn	14,845	15,864	789.57	0.2344
Avon	5,026	18,729	928.48	0.2691
Ayer	6,993	12,354	820.37	0.4320
Barnstable	30,898	38,588	818.89	0.2035
Barre	4,102	12,823	666.72	0.2463
Becket	1,339	33,988	851.96	0.2114
Bedford	13,067	27,512	991.30	0.2728
Belchertown	8,339	12,292	495.32	0.1972
Bellingham	14,300	11,559	748.17	0.3106
Belmont	26,100	22,789	902.32	0.1788
Berkley	2,731	14,072	594.03	0.2673
Berlin	2,215	14,894	904.69	0.3067
Bernardston	1,750	15,109	691.81	0.2353
Beverly	37,655	15,082	814.79	0.2048
Billerica	36,727	14,670	889.89	0.3088

City or Town	Population	EQV	Exp ($)	WFTE
Blackstone	6,570	9,779	705.89	0.2592
Blandford	1,038	19,027	740.49	0.2535
Bolton	2,530	26,672	789.64	0.2719
Boston	562,994	9,306	1,325.56	0.1483
Bourne	13,874	24,168	817.71	0.2261
Boxborough	3,126	21,491	716.51	0.2457
Boxford	5,374	26,833	796.56	0.3165
Boylston	3,470	15,965	693.19	0.2155
Braintree	36,337	20,998	1,051.46	0.2465
Brewster	5,226	44,374	987.77	0.2054
Bridgewater	17,202	11,295	685.96	0.2058
Brimfield	2,318	17,407	720.85	0.2669
Brockton	95,172	9,784	860.80	0.2599
Brookfield	2,397	10,776	725.23	0.2547
Brookline	55,062	17,589	996.55	0.1386
Buckland	1,864	12,983	730.40	0.2489
Burlington	23,486	24,785	1,131.24	0.2949
Cambridge	95,322	13,544	1,274.33	0.1253
Canton	18,182	20,702	933.44	0.2564
Carlisle	3,306	30,339	989.38	0.2673
Carver	6,988	14,611	724.60	0.2727
Charlemont	1,149	20,766	642.39	0.2405
Charlton	6,719	12,483	608.31	0.2653
Chatham	6,071	64,882	972.81	0.1603
Chelmsford	31,174	17,585	831.37	0.2828
Chelsea	25,431	6,209	886.33	0.1886
Cheshire	3,124	14,011	604.80	0.2303
Chester	1,123	15,699	812.04	0.2644
Chesterfield	1,000	18,060	739.47	0.2352
Chicopee	55,112	10,401	714.78	0.2073
Chilmark	489	323,108	1,507.86	0.1350
Clarksburg	1,871	10,839	619.68	0.2970
Clinton	12,771	10,078	619.00	0.2030
Cohasset	7,174	25,746	1,016.94	0.2518
Colrain	1,552	18,454	712.72	0.2898
Concord	16,293	29,031	1,092.69	0.2452
Conway	1,213	18,805	655.57	0.1824
Cummington	657	21,157	867.67	0.2078
Dalton	6,797	15,227	803.43	0.2262
Danvers	24,100	20,303	1,447.65	0.2154

Notes: Table 4 continued

City or Town	Population	EQV	Exp ($)	WFTE
Dartmouth	23,966	16,870	647.06	0.2072
Dedham	25,298	19,804	836.51	0.2265
Deerfield	4,517	20,795	543.28	0.2020
Dennis	12,360	47,087	808.28	0.1870
Dighton	5,352	18,296	692.98	0.2709
Douglas	3,730	14,686	691.43	0.2643
Dover	4,703	44,333	1,116.15	0.2493
Dracut	21,249	12,057	653.35	0.2569
Dudley	8,717	13,112	612.66	0.2194
Dunstable	1,671	20,347	967.93	0.3962
Duxbury	11,807	22,741	1,094.01	0.2933
East Bridgewater	9,945	12,559	820.05	0.2896
East Brookfield	1,955	13,555	632.74	0.2690
East Longmeadow	12,905	18,582	830.76	0.2293
Eastham	3,472	60,023	985.05	0.2127
Easthampton	15,580	11,374	610.25	0.1966
Easton	16,623	14,823	712.66	0.2608
Edgartown	2,204	123,094	1,439.14	0.1800
Egremont	1,311	31,732	634.19	0.2156
Erving	1,326	61,003	1,649.93	0.1739
Essex	2,998	22,158	810.48	0.2014
Everett	37,195	23,874	977.83	0.1867
Fairhaven	15,759	12,260	666.40	0.2212
Fall River	92,574	6,394	758.31	0.2013
Falmouth	23,640	34,966	900.39	0.2365
Fitchburg	39,580	9,467	771.23	0.1769
Florida	730	44,616	1,239.51	0.3033
Foxborough	14,148	16,766	871.02	0.2761
Framingham	65,113	17,631	889.56	0.2128
Franklin	18,217	12,626	842.53	0.2769
Freetown	7,058	18,362	696.81	0.2742
Gardner	17,900	10,737	700.87	0.1943
Gay Head	220	103,227	1,371.69	0.1395
Georgetown	5,687	16,388	827.47	0.3148
Gill	1,259	16,481	811.12	0.2376
Gloucester	27,768	20,055	901.38	0.2139
Goshen	651	27,143	780.12	0.2684
Gosnold	63	154,651	2,195.87	0.1635
Grafton	11,238	12,903	669.19	0.2357
Granby	5,380	12,100	714.35	0.2642

Notes: Table 4 continued

City or Town	Population	EQV	Exp ($)	WFTE
Granville	1,204	22,782	707.81	0.2325
Great Barrington	7,405	17,542	746.10	0.2116
Greenfield	18,436	12,790	784.01	0.1960
Groton	6,154	19,841	786.17	0.2367
Groveland	5,040	15,802	892.45	0.2841
Hadley	4,125	27,055	709.36	0.1846
Halifax	5,513	13,120	613.48	0.2468
Hamilton	6,960	21,106	654.84	0.2307
Hampden	4,745	14,485	766.74	0.2762
Hancock	643	28,165	662.73	0.2351
Hanover	11,358	18,463	951.81	0.3179
Hanson	8,617	12,649	813.06	0.3229
Hardwick	2,272	9,696	707.04	0.2198
Harvard	12,170	8,907	301.92	0.0979
Harwich	8,971	40,363	920.07	0.2180
Hatfield	3,045	16,493	718.98	0.2030
Haverhill	46,865	10,025	1,014.01	0.2332
Hawley	280	19,286	805.16	0.2293
Heath	482	31,535	889.86	0.2429
Hingham	20,339	21,869	895.24	0.2445
Hinsdale	1,707	16,251	698.25	0.2185
Holbrook	11,140	12,738	846.08	0.2787
Holden	13,336	16,512	746.31	0.2376
Holland	1,589	22,442	817.28	0.2836
Holliston	12,622	17,969	901.27	0.2982
Holyoke	44,678	8,588	725.04	0.2107
Hopedale	3,905	15,198	803.20	0.2338
Hopkinton	7,114	21,127	772.38	0.2553
Hubbardston	1,797	15,314	852.33	0.2928
Hudson	16,408	13,091	785.57	0.2619
Hull	9,714	12,930	1,424.64	0.2962
Huntington	1,804	14,279	865.15	0.3091
Ipswich	11,158	17,387	847.13	0.2188
Kingston	7,362	16,979	790.29	0.2368
Lakeville	5,931	15,896	686.09	0.2487
Lancaster	6,334	12,624	610.04	0.2030
Lanesborough	3,131	15,050	752.94	0.2272
Lawrence	63,175	8,160	728.16	0.2269
Lee	6,247	14,016	750.74	0.2289
Leicester	9,446	10,544	580.25	0.2481

Notes: Table 4 continued

City or Town	Population	EQV	Exp ($)	WFTE
Lenox	6,523	17,231	686.03	0.1875
Leominster	34,508	11,931	654.77	0.2070
Leverett	1,471	17,009	581.37	0.2079
Lexington	29,479	30,785	1,101.71	0.2392
Leyden	498	24,839	774.75	0.2325
Lincoln	7,098	30,389	821.07	0.1207
Littleton	6,970	20,201	824.97	0.2518
Longmeadow	16,301	20,968	978.88	0.2558
Lowell	92,418	8,239	676.23	0.2120
Ludlow	18,150	13,471	675.64	0.2173
Lunenburg	8,405	14,539	767.66	0.2866
Lynn	78,471	9,256	958.23	0.2224
Lynnfield	11,267	26,050	816.56	0.2546
Malden	53,386	9,819	746.53	0.1911
Manchester	5,424	33,831	986.12	0.2310
Mansfield	13,453	17,305	779.57	0.2931
Marblehead	20,126	29,062	1,026.46	0.2007
Marion	3,932	33,800	920.66	0.2289
Marlborough	30,617	15,044	812.26	0.2287
Marshfield	20,916	16,934	877.89	0.2779
Mashpee	3,700	55,730	1,068.26	0.1958
Mattapoisett	5,597	20,976	818.94	0.2524
Maynard	9,590	17,716	877.28	0.2275
Medfield	10,220	18,767	892.03	0.2655
Medford	58,076	14,336	741.56	0.1742
Medway	8,447	17,095	1,004.90	0.3270
Melrose	30,055	14,171	820.84	0.2181
Mendon	3,108	18,063	698.54	0.2479
Merrimac	4,451	11,144	775.15	0.2665
Methuen	36,701	13,640	725.44	0.2249
Middleborough	16,404	12,625	717.77	0.2724
Middlefield	385	25,790	766.76	0.1974
Middleton	4,135	21,640	1,341.97	0.2859
Milford	23,390	13,647	753.25	0.2379
Millbury	11,808	10,205	723.37	0.2448
Millis	6,908	16,807	823.52	0.2678
Millville	1,693	9,492	676.74	0.2846
Milton	25,860	17,251	746.23	0.1557
Monroe	179	31,397	1,435.72	0.2793
Monson	7,315	11,398	725.16	0.2293

Notes: Table 4 continued

City or Town	Population	EQV	Exp ($)	WFTE
Montague	8,011	16,502	1,088.12	0.2222
Monterey	818	38,545	755.38	0.1980
Montgomery	637	19,152	876.63	0.3245
Mount Washington	93	86,065	1,495.19	0.1613
Nahant	3,947	22,865	783.04	0.1617
Nantucket	5,087	122,155	1,565.02	0.1517
Natick	29,461	19,351	962.87	0.2296
Needham	27,901	27,006	1,214.48	0.2194
New Ashford	159	51,987	686.26	0.1346
New Bedford	98,478	7,535	751.01	0.2245
New Braintree	671	15,604	795.94	0.2593
New Marlborough	1,160	41,250	629.89	0.2041
New Salem	688	16,468	812.61	0.2529
Newbury	4,529	20,722	701.23	0.2611
Newburyport	15,900	13,604	785.76	0.2529
Newton	83,622	23,654	1,058.49	0.1698
Norfolk	6,363	14,840	774.29	0.2683
North Adams	18,063	8,171	695.09	0.2217
North Andover	20,129	19,996	639.24	0.2171
North Attleborou	21,095	13,050	653.39	0.2375
North Brookfield	4,150	10,988	707.83	0.2741
North Reading	11,455	19,005	856.47	0.2626
Northampton	29,286	12,415	693.21	0.1836
Northborough	10,568	18,263	825.12	0.2754
Northbridge	12,246	10,542	575.48	0.2387
Northfield	2,386	20,930	777.57	0.2176
Norton	12,690	12,041	740.47	0.2536
Norwell	9,182	20,377	1,042.75	0.2803
Norwood	29,711	17,835	1,214.23	0.2312
Oak Bluffs	1,984	59,526	1,409.28	0.1854
Oakham	994	17,948	825.23	0.2414
Orange	6,844	8,248	618.85	0.2416
Orleans	5,306	56,672	1,028.61	0.1681
Otis	963	49,107	858.48	0.2467
Oxford	11,680	10,548	688.63	0.2746
Palmer	11,389	12,020	650.02	0.2329
Paxton	3,762	18,607	664.94	0.2253
Peabody	45,976	15,145	940.16	0.2309
Pelham	1,112	17,968	765.60	0.2121
Pembroke	13,487	16,735	812.26	0.2845

Notes: Table 4 continued

City or Town	Population	EQV	Exp ($)	WFTE
Pepperell	8,061	14,167	822.54	0.2651
Peru	633	21,722	572.83	0.2422
Petersham	1,024	24,326	875.87	0.2807
Phillipston	953	19,570	817.24	0.3134
Pittsfield	51,974	12,381	837.95	0.2198
Plainfield	425	20,184	1,005.67	0.2421
Plainville	5,857	17,142	774.57	0.2565
Plymouth	35,913	27,283	866.68	0.2428
Plympton	1,974	19,650	758.82	0.2585
Princeton	2,425	19,357	758.61	0.2570
Provincetown	3,536	36,340	1,470.25	0.1673
Quincy	84,743	13,559	1,272.63	0.1775
Randolph	28,218	13,541	847.90	0.2591
Raynham	9,085	14,706	762.40	0.2868
Reading	22,678	17,788	896.11	0.2440
Rehoboth	7,570	17,768	746.34	0.3021
Revere	42,423	10,831	811.64	0.2108
Richmond	1,659	24,177	641.45	0.2192
Rochester	3,205	19,261	657.01	0.2731
Rockland	15,695	10,634	819.35	0.2415
Rockport	6,345	33,712	844.56	0.1793
Rowe	336	392,560	3,202.04	0.2220
Rowley	3,867	16,126	780.38	0.2632
Royalston	955	16,262	841.08	0.2368
Russell	1,570	17,599	765.31	0.2715
Rutland	4,334	12,224	592.49	0.2317
Salem	38,220	15,780	1,152.60	0.1738
Salisbury	5,973	19,973	847.12	0.2825
Sandisfield	720	33,458	763.84	0.1844
Sandwich	8,727	46,625	1,059.36	0.2373
Saugus	24,746	19,037	808.16	0.2368
Savoy	644	18,913	669.27	0.2610
Scituate	17,317	18,929	997.76	0.2598
Seekonk	12,269	20,776	698.80	0.2644
Sharon	13,601	19,285	947.07	0.2696
Sheffield	2,743	26,187	634.57	0.2418
Shelburne	2,002	13,227	724.47	0.2333
Sherborn	4,049	33,984	1,147.68	0.2685
Shirley	5,124	8,134	465.80	0.1852
Shrewsbury	22,674	16,565	685.19	0.2000

Notes: Table 4 continued

City or Town	Population	EQV	Exp ($)	WFTE
Shutesbury	1,049	22,574	691.23	0.1981
Somerset	18,813	30,325	909.23	0.2483
Somerville	77,372	8,454	728.53	0.1640
South Hadley	16,399	12,001	588.53	0.1899
Southampton	4,137	15,371	615.49	0.2543
Southborough	6,193	27,079	1,095.84	0.2725
Southbridge	16,665	9,871	559.81	0.2252
Southwick	7,382	14,413	681.22	0.2533
Spencer	10,774	9,718	580.41	0.2594
Springfield	152,319	8,633	849.58	0.2188
Sterling	5,440	18,132	757.83	0.2623
Stockbridge	2,328	33,484	903.16	0.1991
Stoneham	21,424	15,921	783.10	0.2087
Stoughton	26,710	14,680	729.67	0.2710
Stow	5,144	23,328	891.89	0.3229
Sturbridge	5,976	19,294	858.33	0.2718
Sudbury	14,027	27,468	1,081.61	0.3061
Sunderland	2,929	14,442	380.61	0.1022
Sutton	5,855	16,806	637.78	0.2768
Swampscott	13,837	20,814	982.34	0.1933
Swansea	15,461	14,656	611.39	0.2646
Taunton	45,001	9,760	691.63	0.2123
Templeton	6,070	10,705	646.03	0.2441
Tewksbury	24,635	14,987	782.10	0.2933
Tisbury	2,972	45,121	1,003.12	0.1925
Tolland	235	111,830	1,427.23	0.2749
Topsfield	5,709	25,398	882.49	0.3248
Townsend	7,201	12,337	733.97	0.2573
Truro	1,486	87,618	1,225.02	0.2176
Tyngsborough	5,683	14,936	699.77	0.2726
Tyringham	344	47,442	710.78	0.1119
Upton	3,886	15,008	754.64	0.2498
Uxbridge	8,374	12,778	644.70	0.2180
Wakefield	24,895	16,827	878.89	0.2107
Wales	1,177	13,772	829.97	0.3018
Walpole	18,859	17,647	942.72	0.2545
Waltham	58,200	17,938	868.65	0.1783
Ware	8,953	10,239	555.33	0.2025
Wareham	18,457	16,146	727.08	0.2590
Warren	3,777	10,527	684.05	0.2477

Notes: Table 4 continued

City or Town	Population	EQV	Exp ($)	WFTE
Warwick	603	23,997	836.48	0.1721
Washington	587	18,910	770.77	0.2101
Watertown	34,384	17,537	881.34	0.1740
Wayland	12,170	28,406	1,170.83	0.2523
Webster	14,480	10,228	666.97	0.2056
Wellesley	27,209	29,501	1,049.00	0.1767
Wellfleet	2,209	77,637	1,254.24	0.2011
Wendell	694	18,256	879.79	0.2611
Wenham	3,897	20,570	681.28	0.1824
West Boylston	6,204	16,344	738.93	0.2024
West Bridgewater	6,359	16,009	857.09	0.3028
West Brookfield	3,026	14,359	714.55	0.2388
West Newbury	2,861	19,416	905.50	0.2721
West Springfield	27,042	16,552	732.08	0.1842
West Stockbridge	1,280	22,969	663.86	0.2137
West Tisbury	1,010	88,228	1,171.50	0.1834
Westborough	13,619	21,316	864.44	0.2472
Westfield	36,465	11,729	623.20	0.1983
Westford	13,434	16,131	798.81	0.2961
Westhampton	1,137	21,416	744.63	0.2566
Westminster	5,139	21,522	653.84	0.2684
Weston	11,169	40,675	1,260.02	0.2101
Westport	13,763	18,775	625.25	0.2165
Westwood	13,212	29,004	1,085.98	0.2590
Weymouth	55,601	13,156	803.09	0.2331
Whately	1,341	21,126	562.24	0.1827
Whitman	13,534	11,829	788.59	0.2953
Wilbraham	12,053	17,888	904.80	0.2635
Williamsburg	2,237	14,283	712.09	0.2285
Williamstown	8,741	14,529	674.73	0.1592
Wilmington	17,471	21,573	1,015.53	0.3072
Winchendon	7,019	9,765	775.99	0.3021
Winchester	20,701	24,260	1,043.60	0.2439
Windsor	598	27,676	817.83	0.1978
Winthrop	19,294	10,682	654.41	0.1893
Woburn	36,626	18,492	832.90	0.2168
Worcester	161,799	8,832	1,060.06	0.1992
Worthington	932	22,597	735.70	0.2276
Wrentham	7,580	15,567	819.54	0.2254
Yarmouth	18,449	37,119	832.51	0.1852

Notes: Table 4 continued

C True BASIC on a Macintosh Computer

C.1   The Desktop and the Mouse

This appendix contains a brief introduction to running True BASIC on a Macintosh computer. It is designed to get you up and running True BASIC with a minimum of fuss. The Macintosh computer has a user-friendly user interface; however, there are still a few things to learn.

The screen on a Macintosh is usually called the *desktop*—a good name because it describes how you use the screen. You can arrange the information on the screen similarly to the way in which you can arrange information on a real desktop. For example, you might take a file out of a file cabinet and spread its contents out on the desktop. Instead of file cabinets, the Macintosh has a disk drive (or possibly several disk drives). One can take a file out of disk drive and spread its contents out on the desktop. On a real desktop, one often has several files open. The Macintosh can also have several files open. On a real desktop, one file can be opened on top of another and obscure the lower folder. The same can be done with the Macintosh desktop. A careful worker can place several different files on different parts of a desktop so that he or she can see them all at once. The same is true about the Macintosh desktop. The desktop is more than a name for the Macintosh screen; it is a powerful metaphor describing how one uses the screen.

One of the most important ways that you interact with the Macintosh is by figuratively pointing to things on the desktop. This is accomplished by means of a *mouse*. As you move the mouse around on the real desktop, you will see a cursor moving around on the Macintosh desktop. Try it.

C.2   Menus

The Macintosh is more than just hardware. Every computer relies on supervisory software that organizes the way in which other software operates. This software is sometimes called the *operating system*. Much of the power of the Macintosh comes from its operating system. Before the Macintosh most personal computers had operating systems that were like restaurants that expected users to arrive with their own menus—

and not just any menu but a menu that listed all the information about
the food that happened to be available at that particular restaurant.
The restaurant often served very good food, but unless you knew the
menu you could not order the food. The Macintosh was the first widely
available personal computer that provided its users with menus. At the
very top of the desktop you will see in the lefthand corner a tiny apple
and to the right of the apple a series of words like "File" and "Edit."
These are the names of the menus. To see what is on a particular menu,
you first point to the name of the menu by moving the mouse until the
cursor is on the name of the menu. Then press the mouse button. You
will see a list of items appear indicating the choices that one can make
from that particular menu. Try it. Move the cursor to each menu name
in turn; then press the mouse button and examine the list of choices in
that menu. After you've read the list, release the button and move on
to the next menu.

C.3   Finding and Starting True BASIC

In order to use True BASIC you must find it. Depending on your system, True BASIC may be on a hard disk permanently attached to the
computer or on a diskette that you must insert into the Macintosh disk
drive. Your teacher will probably tell you where True BASIC is.

If you're lucky, the system may be set up so you will see the True
BASIC "icon" on the desktop. If you don't see the True BASIC icon,
first make sure that any necessary diskette is in the disk drive. You
will see on the desktop several different icons. Each icon represents
something, and it looks like the kind of thing it represents. For example,
a diskette is represented by an icon that looks like a diskette. A folder
full of files is represented by an icon that looks like a file folder.

To open a file folder to see the files inside, you first point to the
folder by moving the cursor on top of the folder, and then you press
and release the mouse button twice in rapid succession. This is called
double clicking. It is a bit of an art, and you may have to try it several
times before getting the hang of it. If you double-click too slowly or too
quickly, nothing will happen. When you double-click correctly, the file
will open and its contents will be displayed in a window. The same is

true about a diskette icon or the hard disk icon. You can look inside and examine the contents by pointing and double-clicking.

After you've examined the contents you have the option of "closing" the window. Each window has a title bar with the window's title in the middle. At the far left is a *close box*. You close a window by putting the cursor in the close box and and clicking (pressing and releasing) the mouse button.

Your instructor may have told you where True BASIC is. If so, follow his or her instructions. If not, you can probably find it. Look for an icon with a likely sounding name and open it. Browse around, opening and closing diskettes or the hard disk or various folders to find True BASIC.

Once you've located True BASIC, put the cursor on top of the True BASIC icon and double-click. You will see the True BASIC menus across the top of the desktop. The menus have names like "File," "Edit," and "Run." The rest of the desktop will be filled by one large window with the title "Untitled." You will write your first program in this window.

C.4   Typing a Program

Typing a program is very simple: just start typing. As you type on the keyboard, what you type will appear in the "Untitled" window. You will notice two cursors on the screen. The blinking cursor indicates the position where the next character typed on the keyboard will appear automatically—immediately following the last keystroke entered. The second cursor, or *mouse-cursor*, is connected to the mouse. With the mouse cursor, you can indicate where to enter a character anywhere on the screen.

You may make some mistakes typing. The Macintosh provides several ways of correcting mistakes. If you discover a mistake just a few keystrokes after you've typed it, the easiest way to correct it is by using the delete key. Each time you press the delete key, one character will be erased, and the cursor will move back one space. After you've deleted your error, type what you really intended to type.

If you don't spot your typing mistake immediately, you can use the mouse to position the mouse cursor immediately to the right of the error. Press the mouse button. The blinking cursor will now appear at the point indicated by the mouse cursor. Now you can use the delete key to erase your error and then type what you intended. Notice that as you type, the new typing is automatically inserted into the material already in the window. It is much easier to correct errors on a Macintosh than on a typewriter for this reason. If you leave out a few letters or a few words on a typewriter, you may need to retype everything simply because there isn't room to make the correction. The Macintosh automatically makes room for new material.

If you need to erase a lot of material, you can select the material to be deleted by using another mouse technique, called "dragging." First, place the mouse cursor immediately to the left of the first character that you want to eliminate. Now press the mouse button and hold it down. While holding the mouse button down, move the mouse cursor to the point immediately to the right of the last character that you want to delete. As you do this, the material you want to delete will be displayed in white on black. This technique is called *dragging*. It is often used to select a block of material on the screen. To erase the entire block, press the delete key. If you made a mistake while dragging and selected the wrong block of material, you can deselect it simply by clicking the mouse button anyplace.

Now you're ready to create your first program. Type:

```
PRINT "Hello, world."
END
```

C.5   Running a Program

The next step is to run the program. You will be opening the Run menu and choosing the menu item Run. This is the general procedure for choosing a menu item.

1. Look in the menu by pointing to the menu name and pressing and holding the mouse button down.

2. Slide the cursor down the list of menu items *holding the button down*. As you reach each item, that item will be displayed in white on black.

3. Choose an item by releasing the mouse button while that item is displayed in white on black.

If you change your mind at any time, you can close the menu without making a choice by moving the cursor back up to the menu name and then releasing the mouse button.

If your program worked correctly, a new window appeared and obscured the "Untitled" window. Then "Hello, world." appeared at the top of this window. Admire the output of your first program. To return to the "Untitled" window, point the cursor anyplace inside the "output" window and click.

There are, unfortunately, many possible mistakes that you might have made but mistakes are easy to correct on the Macintosh. We will look at two mistakes to illustrate the kinds of things that might go wrong and how you might fix them. Our first mistake involves a typing error. Delete the correct program and type in the following program:

```
PRIMT "Hello, world."
END
```

Notice the typographical error—"PRIMT" instead of "PRINT." True BASIC doesn't know how to "PRIMT." Neither do we. An error of this kind is easy for True BASIC to catch. Run this program. Notice at the bottom of the "Untitled" window that the message "Illegal statement" appears. This is True BASIC's way of telling you that it doesn't understand what you've asked it to do. The cursor will be blinking next to the offending statement. This is True BASIC's way of helping you locate the error. To the left of the "Illegal statement" message is a box. Put the cursor in this box and click to acknowledge the message. Now you can correct the mistake as described earlier and then run the corrected program. Errors like this one are fairly easy to find. True BASIC knows something is wrong when it sees something that doesn't make sense, and it gives you an appropriate message.

The next error is more subtle. Erase the last program and type in the following program:

```
PRINT "Hello, word."
END
```

Run this program. It appears to work just fine. The program makes perfect sense as a program. However, it doesn't do what you want it to do. It types the words "Hello, word." instead of the words "Hello, world." True BASIC has no way of reading your mind. It doesn't know

what you want the program to do. Part of the art of programming—
an important part of the art of programming—is checking the results
produced by the program to be sure that you have not made an error of
this sort.

C.6   Stopping a Program

Most programs stop automatically when they are done, but there are
some exceptions. Some programs ask the computer to do too many
things. The computer might need days or even years to finish. Other
programs contain errors that would cause them to run forever. For
example, the program

```
LET i = 1
DO WHILE (i < 10)
   PRINT "Joe"
LOOP
END
```

will run forever printing "Joe" over and over and over. You can interrupt
any program and make it stop immediately by selecting the item Stop
in the Run menu.

C.7   Saving Programs

Now let's suppose that you've written a program and want to save it.
The file menu has items for saving or retrieving a program. Go up to
the file menu, open it, and look inside. You will see a number of items
in this menu. We will discuss four of these items:

1. Save As: This is the choice that will enable you to save a program
   for the first time. Select this item. A dialog box will appear. Think
   of this dialog box as a waiter who has come to take your order. You
   have various options. One option is to forget the whole thing and
   ask the waiter to leave. To do this, put the cursor in the cancel box
   and click. You can make the waiter reappear by choosing the Save As
   option from the File menu again. Macintosh waiters are enormously
   patient and efficient. They will appear immediately at the touch of a
   mouse button and will leave quietly if the customer changes his or her

mind. When you save your program, it will become a file along with many other files. You need to give it a name and to remember that name so that you can later retrieve the file. You should see the words "Save your program as" just above a box. Inside the box is a blinking cursor. Type the name of your file in this box. If you make a typing mistake, you can correct it in the usual way. Now you should tell True BASIC where to put your file. You have many options. Your teacher will tell you where to keep your files and how to use this dialog box to instruct True BASIC where this file should be saved. Finally, save your file by putting the cursor in the save box and clicking the mouse button.

2. Save: This item is used when you are working on a file that was saved earlier, some changes have been made, and you would like to replace the old version by the updated version. This item will save the new version and in the process erase the old version. There is no dialog since True BASIC already knows the name of the file and where it is kept.

3. New: This item is used if you've been working with a program and now want to start working on a new program with a clean window. Selecting this item will clear the window and give you a new "Untitled" window. When you do this, you will lose all the information in the old window. Because of this, True BASIC will display a dialog box asking whether you want to save the contents of the old window.

4. Open: This item allows you to make use of a file that you or someone else saved earlier. Selecting this item causes True BASIC to display a dialog box asking you the name of the desired file and where it is located. Your instructor will give you additional instructions about where to keep your files and how to respond to this dialog box.

C.8   Arranging the Desktop

You can arrange the Macintosh desktop in the way that is most convenient for your work. True BASIC uses two windows. Normally only one window is visible at a time, and it takes up the entire screen; however, you can rearrange the desktop in another manner. Each window can be made as large or as small as you like. In the lower right corner of each window you will see two small boxes. The smaller of these two partially obscures the larger. These two boxes are called the *size* boxes. The two boxes symbolize the different possible sizes for the window. To change the size of a window, put the cursor in the size boxes, press the mouse button, and while holding the mouse button down move the cursor. As you move the cursor, you will see an outline of the window change size. When the outline is the size that you want, release the mouse button. Try this several times, experimenting with different sizes.

You can also move a window around on the desktop. To move a window, place the cursor anyplace within the title bar at the top of the window, depress the mouse button, and while holding the mouse button down move the cursor around. As the cursor moves, you will see an outline of the window move around. When this outline is where you want the window located, release the mouse button.

Finally, the output window can be made to appear or disappear. To make the output window appear, select the item "Output" from the "Windows" menu. To make the output window disappear, select the item "Close Output" from the windows menu.

Often a window is too small to hold all the information one would ideally like it to hold. For example, a True BASIC program is frequently much too big to fit in a window. Think of a window as a "window" that allows one to look into a file. The window is often too small to see the whole file at once. At the right side of each window you will see one arrow (pointing up) at the top and another arrow (pointing down) at the bottom. If you position the cursor on either of these arrows and press the mouse button, the window will slide up or down, or scroll, allowing you to see a different part of the file. There is also a box at the right side of the window between the two arrows. By dragging this box up or down, you can see different parts of the file.

C.9   Ending a Session

When you're done with True BASIC, select the item Quit from the File menu. If you are using your own diskette for your programs, eject the diskette from the disk drive by dragging the icon for the diskette to the trash bin at the lower right corner of the screen.

C.10   A Final Word

I have touched only briefly on a few of the features of the Macintosh and True BASIC. Although I have covered enough so that you should be able to use True BASIC on a Macintosh, the more that you know, the more you will be able to do. It would be very worthwhile to buy and read a book about True BASIC and the Macintosh. The books published by True BASIC, Inc. are particularly good.

D   True BASIC on an IBM or Compatible PC

D.1   Finding and Starting True BASIC

Depending on your system, True BASIC may be on a hard disk permanently attached to the computer or on a diskette you must insert into the disk drive. Your instructor will tell you how to start True BASIC. He or she will probably give you a diskette that has True BASIC, some data files, and room for you to store your own programs.

When you have successfully started True BASIC, the computer screen will be divided into two parts or two *windows*. The top window is called the editing window. This is where you will write your program. The bottom window is called the history window. Output from your program will appear here. You will also use the history window to give True BASIC various commands. You can move back and forth between the two windows by using the F1 and F2 keys (at the far left of the keyboard). The F1 key moves the cursor into the editing window. The F2 key moves the cursor into the history window. Try these keys and watch the cursor move back and forth between the two windows. Leave it in the history window for the next paragraph.

When True BASIC starts, the editing window has room for 17 lines, and the history window has room for 7 lines. You can change the sizes of the two windows by typing a command like

```
SPLIT 10
```

which will divide the screen so that the editing window will have 9 lines and the history window will have 15 lines. The number following `SPLIT` is one more than the number of lines to be displayed in the editing window. Because `SPLIT 10` is a command that True BASIC will execute immediately, the cursor must be in the history window when this command is typed.

D.2   Typing a Program

Typing a program is very simple. Make sure the cursor is in the editing window and start typing. As you type on the keyboard, what you enter will appear in the editing window. The blinking cursor indicates the position where the next character typed on the keyboard will appear. You may make some mistakes typing. The computer provides several ways of correcting mistakes. If you discover a mistake just a few keystrokes after you've typed it, the easiest way to correct it is by using the delete or backspace key. This key is marked by an arrow pointing to the left and is usually located close to the upper righthand corner of the keyboard. Each time you press the delete key, one character will be erased and the cursor will move back one space. After you've deleted your error, type what you intended.

If you don't spot your typing mistake immediately, you can use the four cursor keys to position the cursor at the right end of the error. This is a group of four keys located at the right end of the keyboard. Each of the four keys is marked by an arrow indicating the direction in which that key moves the cursor. After you have moved the cursor to the right of the error, you can use the delete key to erase your error and then type what you intended to type. Notice that as you type, the new typing is automatically inserted into the material already in the window. It is much easier to correct errors on a computer than on a typewriter for this reason. If you leave out a few letters or a few words on a typewriter, you may need to retype everything because there isn't room to make the correction. The computer automatically makes room for new material.

Now you're ready to create your first program. Type:

```
PRINT "Hello, world."
END
```

D.3   Running a Program

The next step is to run the program. Press the F2 key to move the cursor into the history window. Now type the word RUN. If your program worked correctly, the words "Hello, world." appeared in the history window. Admire the output of your first program.

There are, unfortunately, many possible mistakes that you might have made, but mistakes are easy to correct on the computer. We will look at two mistakes to illustrate the kinds of things that might go wrong and how you might fix them. The first mistake is a typing error. Change your program to

```
PRIMT "Hello, world."
END
```

Notice there is a typographical error here: the word "PRIMT" instead of "PRINT." True BASIC doesn't know how to "PRIMT." Neither do we. An error of this kind is easy for True BASIC to catch. Run this program. True BASIC will print the message "Illegal statement." This is True BASIC's way of telling you that it doesn't understand what you've asked it to do. The cursor will be blinking on the offending statement. This is True BASIC's way of helping you locate the error. Now you can correct the mistake as described earlier and then run the corrected program. Errors like this one are fairly easy to find. True BASIC knows something is wrong when it sees something that doesn't make sense and it gives you an appropriate message.

The next error is more subtle. Erase the last program and type in the following program:

```
PRINT "Hello, word."
END
```

Run this program. It appears to work just fine. The program makes perfect sense as a program. However, it doesn't do what you want it to do. It types the words "Hello, word." instead of "Hello, world." True BASIC has no way of reading your mind. It doesn't know what you want the program to do. Part of the art of programming—an important part—is checking the results produced by the program to be sure that you have not made an error of this sort.

D.4   Stopping a Program

Most programs stop automatically when they are done, but there are some exceptions. Some programs ask the computer to do too many things. The computer might need days or even years to finish. Other programs contain errors that would cause them to run forever. For example, the program

```
LET i = 1
DO WHILE (i < 10)
   PRINT "Joe"
LOOP
END
```

will run forever printing "Joe" over and over and over. You can interrupt any program and make it stop immediately by holding down the Ctrl key and pressing the key marked Scroll Lock.

D.5   Saving Programs

Now let's suppose that you've written a program and want to save it. True BASIC has commands that will let you save a program and that will let you retrieve a previously saved program. The command

```
SAVE World
```

will save the program in the editing window under the name World. If True BASIC responds to this command with a message "File already exists," then someone has already saved a program with the same name on this disk. If you do not want to lose that older program, then you should save your current program with a different name. If you want to replace the old program with the current program then use the command

```
REPLACE World
```

Note that both **SAVE** and **REPLACE** are commands and must be typed into the history window. You can retrieve an old program with a command like

```
OLD World
```

If you want to start fresh with a clean editing window, type the command

```
NEW
```

If the latest version of the current program has not been saved, True BASIC will ask you

```
Do you want to save this file?
```

You should respond y (yes) or n (no).

D.6   Ending a Session

When you're done with True BASIC, type the command "BYE". After True BASIC is closed (you will see a line like "A>" on the screen), remove your diskette.

D.7   A Final Word

I have touched only briefly on a few of the features of the computer and True BASIC. Although I have covered enough so that you should be able to use True BASIC on an IBM or compatible PC, the more that you know, the more you will be able to do. It would be very worthwhile to buy and read a book about True BASIC and IBM or compatible computers. The books published by True BASIC, Inc. are particularly good.

E Answers to Selected Exercises

Chapter 1

Exercise 1.2.8 $3,885.09

Exercise 1.2.9 $3,779.14

Exercise 1.2.10 $4,081.47

Exercise 1.2.12 $51,874.85

Exercise 1.2.13 $74,144.43

Exercise 1.2.14 $22,269.58

Exercise 1.2.17 $12,984.22

Exercise 1.3.21 $418,289

Exercise 1.3.28 $73,571

Exercise 1.4.32 $(5/11, 26/11)$

Exercise 1.5.34 $2,800

Exercise 1.5.38 $106,666.67

Exercise 1.5.40 $120,000

Exercise 1.5.41 $180,000

Chapter 2

Exercise 2.1.1 $3/8$

Exercise 2.1.2 $1/4$

Exercise 2.1.3 $1/4$

Exercise 2.1.4 $1/8$

Exercise 2.1.5 0.3456

Exercise 2.1.9 Independent

Exercise 2.1.10 Independent

Exercise 2.1.11 Dependent

Exercise 2.1.12 Independent

Exercise 2.1.13 Independent

Exercise 2.3.21

Number	Number of Spins		
of Grays	1	2	3
0	0.6	0.36	0.216
1	0.4	0.48	0.432
2		0.16	0.288
3			0.064

Exercise 2.3.23 $(1-p)^n$

Exercise 2.3.25 p^n

Exercise 2.5.33 With a confidence of 93%.

Exercise 2.6.38 With a confidence of 82%.

Exercise 2.6.39 With a confidence of 96%.

Chapter 3

Exercise 3.1.1 1.363636

Exercise 3.1.5 1.58443

Exercise 3.1.6 1.64629

Exercise 3.1.8 Before the rise the equilibrium price is 5.7222. After the rise it is 5.8333. Thus 0.1111 of the 0.20 price rise is passed along to the consumers. Before the price rise 5,422 Byties are baked and sold. After the price rise 5,333 Byteis are baked and sold. Thus, ·the job market for Byties bakers has dropped by about 1.6%. When the price rises to $0.70 the equilibrium price is 5.9444 and the number of Byties baked and sold is 5,244. Thus business has dropped by an additional 1.7%.

Exercise 3.2.11

Day Number	Price
0	.3000
1	.4900
2	.6230
3	.7161
4	.7813
5	.8269
6	.8588
7	.8812
8	.8968
9	.9078
10	.9154

Exercise 3.2.16

Day Number	Price
0	1.2000
1	0.4000
2	2.0000
3	-1.2000
4	5.2000
5	-7.6000
6	18.0000
7	-33.2000
8	69.1999
9	-135.5990
10	273.9990

Exercise 3.2.18   1.00
Exercise 3.2.19

Day Number	Price
0	.5000
1	.8750
2	.9688
3	.9922
4	.9980
5	.9995
6	.9999
7	1.0000
8	1.0000
9	1.0000
10	1.0000

Exercise 3.2.24   If $k \leq 1/2500$, then the price wil go toward the equlibrium price without overshooting. If $1/2500 < k < 2/2500$, then the price will overshoot but will still tend toward the equilibrium price. If $2/2500 < k$, then the price will overshoot and fluctuate wildly around the equilibrium price and eventually crash by becoming negative.

Exercise 3.3.25

Day Number	Price
0	.8667
1	.8667
2	.8667
3	.8667
4	.8667
5	.8667
6	.9467
7	.9787
8	.9915
9	.9966
10	.9986

Exercise 3.4.31 For $q = 0.0$ the modified demand is 400. For $q = -0.5$ the modified demand is 440. For $q = 0.5$ the modified demand is 360.

Exercise 3.4.33 1.0220

Exercise 3.5.44 Using the maximin criterion one should not buy a lottery ticket. Using the maximax criterion one should buy a ticket. Using the maximum expected payoff criterion one should not buy a ticket.

Exercise 3.7.46 For Player A, any value of p gives the best possible maximum payoff—$0.50.

Exercise 3.7.47 Player A will win on the average $0.08 per game. As long as one of the two players plays the maximin strategy the results will be the same.

Exercise 3.7.48 For Player B, $q = 1$ gives the best possible maximum payoff—$0.90.

Chapter 4

Exercise 4.1.3 The light ray will bounce off the mirror at $x = 100$.

Exercise 4.1.5 $x = 2.1544$ and $y = 2.1544$.

Exercise 4.1.7 $(8.5, 8.5)$.

Exercise 4.2.9 The light ray will bounce off the mirror at $x = 1$.

Exercise 4.2.10 $(2, -1)$.

Exercise 4.2.11 $(2, -1)$.

Exercise 4.3.15 The light ray will bounce off the mirror at $y = 0.8241$.

Exercise 4.3.16 The light ray will bounce off the mirror at $y = 0$.

Exercise 4.3.17 The two apparent positions are $(3.42941, 3.18224)$ and $(2.97462, 2.97462)$. The position of the observer does make a difference.

Exercise 4.3.18 The two apparent positions are $(2.97462, 2.97462)$ and $(3.23494, 3.23494)$. The radius of the mirror does make a difference.

Exercise 4.4.24 You would look fatter because a horizontal section of the mirror is concave. You would appear to have normal height because a vertical section of the mirror is flat.

Exercise 4.4.25 The minimum occurs at the point $x = 63.53$.

Exercise 4.5.26

$$S(x) = \frac{\sqrt{625 + x^2}}{30} + \frac{\sqrt{2500 + (100 - x)^2}}{22.5}$$

Exercise 4.5.27 The minimum occurs at the point $x = 53.65$.

Exercise 4.5.28 The apparent position is $(88.9875, -20.041)$.

Chapter 5

Exercise 5.1.1 $17,546

Exercise 5.1.2 $15,389

Exercise 5.2.4 $1,582

Exercise 5.2.7 0.2975

Exercise 5.3.15 $27.27

Exercise 5.3.16

Town	Population	Per Capita EQV	Lottery Formula
Westville	15,000	15,000	16.25
Northville	25,000	10,000	24.37
Southville	50,000	7,000	34.82
Eastville	20,000	12,000	20.31

Exercise 5.5.28

Town	Ideal Allocation	Actual Allocation
Town A	$8,250,000	$702,128
Town B	$3,500,000	$297,872

Exercise 5.6.31 7,185

Exercise 5.6.32 14,097

Exercise 5.6.33 6,912

Exercise 5.7.39 For Brookline the estimated per capita expenditures would be $909.22.

Chapter 6

Exercise 6.1.1

$p(1) = 130$, $p(4) = 285.61$, $p(7) = 627.49$, $p(10) = 1,378.58$.
$p(2) = 169$, $p(5) = 371.29$, $p(8) = 815.73$,
$p(3) = 219.70$, $p(6) = 482.68$, $p(9) = 1,060.45$,

Exercise 6.1.2

$p(1) = 800$, $p(4) = 409.60$, $p(7) = 209.72$, $p(10) = 107.37$.
$p(2) = 640$, $p(5) = 327.68$, $p(8) = 167.77$,
$p(3) = 512$, $p(6) = 262.14$, $p(9) = 134.22$,

Exercise 6.1.3

$p(2) = 810$, $p(5) = 590.49$, $p(8) = 430.47$,
$p(3) = 729$, $p(6) = 531.44$, $p(9) = 387.42$,
$p(4) = 656.10$, $p(7) = 478.30$, $p(1) = 348.68$.

Exercise 6.1.4

$p(4) = 1,012.50$, $p(7) = 1,441.63$, $p(10) = 2,052.63$,
$p(5) = 1,139.06$, $p(8) = 1,621.83$, $p(1) = 711.11$,
$p(6) = 1,281.45$, $p(9) = 1,824.56$, $p(0) = 632.10$.

Exercise 6.2.7   The equilibrium population is 655.17. The first few generations are: $p(1) = 28.71, p(2) = 80.87, p(3) = 215.55$.

Exercise 6.3.21

$$\frac{a-1}{.001a}$$

Exercise 6.3.22 If $a < 1$ then the nonzero equilibrium point is negative, which doesn't make any sense for population models.

Exercise 6.3.23 $a = 1$ is the dividing line.

Exercise 6.5.31   The equilibrium populations are 0 and 454.55.

Exercise 6.6.35   More sensitive to p than to q.

Exercise 6.6.36   More sensitive to q than to p.

Index

The MIT Press, with Peter Denning as general consulting editor, publishes computer science books in the following series:

ACM Doctoral Dissertation Award and Distinguished Dissertation Series

Artificial Intelligence
Patrick Winston, Founding editor
Michael Brady, Daniel Bobrow, and Randall Davis, editors

Charles Babbage Institute Reprint Series for the History of Computing
Martin Campbell-Kelly, editor

Computer Systems
Herb Schwetman, editor

Explorations with Logo
E. Paul Goldenberg, editor

Foundations of Computing
Michael Garey and Albert Meyer, editors

History of Computing
I. Bernard Cohen and William Aspray, editors

Information Systems
Michael Lesk, editor

Logic Programming
Ehud Shapiro, editor; Fernando Pereira, Koichi Furukawa, Jean-Louis Lassez, and David H. D. Warren, Associate editors

The MIT Press Electrical Engineering and Computer Science Series

Research Monographs in Parallel and Distributed Processing
Christopher Jesshope and David Klappholz, editors

Scientific and Engineering Computation
Janusz Kowalik, editor

Technical Communication
Ed Barrett, editor